# A RESTATEMENT OF ECONOMIC LIBERALISM

*Also by Samuel Brittan*

*Also published by Macmillan

# A Restatement of Economic Liberalism

Samuel Brittan

**M**
MACMILLAN
PRESS

First edition (under title of *Capitalism and the Permissive Society*) 1973
Reprinted (with alterations) 1973, 1976
Second edition (under present title) 1988

Published by
THE MACMILLAN PRESS LTD
Houndmills, Basingstoke, Hampshire RG21 2XS
and London
Companies and representatives
throughout the world

Typeset by Wessex Typesetters
(Division of The Eastern Press Ltd)
Frome, Somerset

Printed in Hong Kong

British Library Cataloguing in Publication Data
Brittan, Samuel
A restatement of economic liberalism—
2nd ed.
1. Liberalism   2. Laissez-faire
I. Title   II. Brittan, Samuel, Capitalism
and the permissive society
330.1    HB95
ISBN 0–333–42082–9 (hardcover)
ISBN 0–333–42083–7 (paperback)

To the memory of my father

'If men were actuated by self-interest, which they are not – except in the case of a few saints – the whole human race would co-operate. There would be no more wars, no more armies, no more navies, no more atom bombs . . .

I do not deny that there are better things than selfishness, and that some people achieve these things. I maintain, however, on the one hand that there are few occasions upon which large bodies of men, such as politics is concerned with, can rise above selfishness, while on the other hand, there are a very great many circumstances in which population will fall below selfishness, if selfishness is interpreted as enlightened self-interest.

And among those occasions on which people fall below self-interest are most of the occasions on which they are convinced that they are acting from idealistic motives. Much that passes as idealism is disguised hatred or disguised love of power.'

Bertrand Russell, *Human Society in Ethics and Politics*

# Contents

## LIST OF TABLES AND FIGURES

# Preface to the First Edition

The case for competitive markets, as a superior way of coordinating human activities to decisions arrived at by political means, has been frequently put forward over several centuries and just as frequently disputed. There is nevertheless, a great presentational difficulty in stating this case. It is usually understood to mean something like *laissez-faire*: that governments should not bother with business or commercial activities unless perhaps there are glaring monopolies or cartels. Stated in this form it is plainly wrong, on almost any prevalent set of value judgements. One only has to think of public health regulations or the disadvantages of free and unrestricted parking in a busy street, without going into anything more controversial or subtle, to see that this is so.

Yet, if an attempt is made to make the arguments more convincing and set out the conditions which have to be fulfilled – the necessary background of laws, and of financial and other policies – if market forces are to yield a reasonably satisfactory result, the reader is likely to feel cheated. The simplicity of a simple slogan that we can accept or reject has gone. If the necessary conditions are stated in detail, the result is a series of textbooks (which are far from being in perfect agreement with each other); and the question seems too expert for the normal educated citizen or elected politician. Alternatively, if one tries to simplify and summarise, the result can seem so vague and general that it may seem compatible with almost any policy.

Yet it is highly dangerous to give up the attempt. For there is a connection, however, difficult to state, between economic, personal and political freedom. It is also paradoxical and worrying that so many of the young and the radical, who rightly put great emphasis on personal freedom and who are sceptical of the claims of authority, should be so intolerant of private initiative in the so-called economic sphere.

One of the objects of this book is to persuade the open-minded reader that the *right kind* of market economy can be an instrument of human freedom and a way of satisfying human wants rather than a hollow dogma to quiet businessmen's consciences. The greater part of the space is, however, devoted to the difficulties and problems that have arisen in the various attempts to expound such a 'liberal' economic philosophy – 'liberal' in the sense that it welcomes market forces and the price mechanism as *potential* forces for good. To do this will require venturing well outside the area conventionally regarded as 'economic'.

It is hoped that a few guidelines, which will be neither oversimplified slogans nor impossible technicalities, will emerge. But the main emphasis is on the underlying arguments. There is more chance of arousing the interest of the sceptical reader if he is invited to listen to, and participate in, debates inside the 'liberal' camp, than if he is presented with a fixed doctrine that claims to solve all problems; and arousing interest is half the battle. The main enemy of the economic liberal is not reasoned opposition, but bored hostility, whether that of the businessman or politician who thinks his attitude 'unrealistic', or of the radical student who thinks that 'it isn't where it's at'.

An authoritative study of the whole area would be a full-time labour of many years, involving highly technical studies of areas ranging from academic philosophy to mathematical welfare economics and the empirical analysis of modern business. Even then it is doubtful if any one person could undertake it, or whether if he did, the result would be coherent and convincing. Instead, I have attempted to tackle the subject from a variety of different angles in the hope of shedding a little light. The aim of the following essays is to open up some lines of discussion rather than to formulate watertight theories; but I am immodest enough to hope that those who specialise in more formal or mathematical models, or in the statistical testing of hypotheses, will find in this quarry some material worth further development.

The fairly long Prologue, 'Capitalism and the Permissive Society', which provides the title essay, is a deliberately provocative statement of my main conclusions. It is written with the minimum of qualification and is designed to be comprehensible to people who do not normally look at writings on political economy. For this reason it inevitably depends more than the other essays on personal judgement; and those whose main interest is in analysis may be able to see it in better perspective if they look beforehand at some of the subsequent essays.

The principal arguments are developed in Chapter 1. The first, and by far the longest, of the essays, it is entitled 'A Restatement of

Economic Liberalism'. After stating certain fundamentals, it goes on to examine the traditional arguments for market forces. Although these retain a kernel of validity, if stated with sufficient care, some of the most important considerations lie in a different area: in the excessive and incompatible expectations from political activity now current, not least among those who are most cynical about individual politicians. The title of the second essay 'Jobs, Prices and Trade Unions' is self-explanatory. It is a very summarised treatment of endlessly debated matters relevant to a modern market economy; its aim is not novelty, but to penetrate the mists with which political tactfulness and peripheral technical controversies have obscured the essentials of the subject. The third essay, 'The Economics of the Alternative Society' seeks to raise its sights from the immediate squabble of interest groups and to analyse the role of economic freedom in a less materialistic environment than the present. It attempts to take a little further some of the issues raised by the Prologue, with which it has a natural link, and is the one essay which makes some very modest claim to originality. It is also one of the very few whose opening quotation is not taken from David Hume.

An empirical survey that I have made of the approach of economists, politicians and commentators to policy questions, entitled *Is There An Economic Consensus?*, is being published alongside the present volume; and its results may shed some additional light on the questions discussed here. In both books I have attempted to present the arguments in a form which will still be useful to those who do not share my judgements, and impart a certain amount of information as well as analysis and advocacy.

As already indicated, I have made no attempt to be gratuitously original; the footnote references are accordingly no mere formalities, but indicate a number of distinguished works in which some of the themes touched upon here are more fully developed and elaborated. If there is a difference of emphasis between what is presented here and the principal writers of the 'economic liberal' school, it is that some of the latter have tended to see the main threat to freedom as coming from the 'left', whereas I tend to see both threats and opportunities from many different points of the political compass.

One of the main concerns of this book is to stress the liberal alternative as a valid, and in my view, superior ideal to the collectivist one, and not just to knock the latter. If we are, in

Professor Hayek's words, 'to free the process of spontaneous growth from the obstacles and encumbrances that human folly has erected', our hopes 'must rest on persuading and gaining the support of those who by disposition are "progressives", those who, though they may now be seeking change in the wrong direction, are at least willing to examine critically the existing system and to change it wherever necessary'.[1]

It may strike some readers that the 'liberal utilitarianism' presented in Chapter 1 is such a heavily qualified form of utilitarianism that it is closer to some modern version of the social contract doctrine, such as that recently put forward by Professor John Rawls, than to any recognised form of utilitarianism. Fortunately the question does not have to be resolved at the ultimate philosophical level. The starting-point of any assessment of institutions and policies for the economic liberal is the goals and desires of individual human beings rather than some supposedly superior conception of the public good. This individualistic element is common to both utilitarian and contract doctrines, in contrast to those of a more perfectionist or paternalist kind.

It would have strengthened my case if I could have incorporated Professor Rawls's argument for the 'priority of liberty'. This attempts to 'rule out' any sacrifice of basic liberties in exchange for economic and social gains, however large the latter. My failure to do so reflects, I am afraid, more than the unfortunate fact that Rawls's path-breaking book *A Theory of Justice* appeared after my own manuscript went to press. The arguments he provides for the priority of liberty, while persuasive and appealing (and pointing in a similar direction to some of the more informal reflections in the early part of my own Prologue) do not seem to me entirely conclusive. There still seems no alternative to a political pluralism in which different goals have to be balanced against each other; and, although reasoned discussion of the relative weights to be given to each of these in different situations is possible, there remains an irreducibly subjective element in the choices made.

The most controversial part of the present book may well be found in the final Appendix, an early and almost, undergraduate piece, written before I had acquired even such limited prudential experience of how to guard my flank as I may have since attained.

In that Appendix I draw attention to the 'successive circles of obligation' that people have, which are strongest towards those who are personally closest to them, somewhat less strong to those with whom they have national, racial, religious or cultural affinities, and weakest of all towards the human race in general. I argue that a frank recognition of these facts would be preferable – and lead to more humane results – than the customary proclamation of universal benevolence as the ideal to which all should aspire.

The real difficulty of this concept is not that it is reprehensible, but that it relates to a private code of morality in which the weights will differ from person to person, and is therefore not easy to translate into a set of public rules on which all, or most, can agree. For this purpose some impartial guide such as Rawls's 'veil of ignorance', in which we ask ourselves what criteria we would accept if we did not know what our own particular station in society was to be, is clearly more suitable. But it still leaves open the question of the reference group; that is of the exact society in which we are to imagine ourselves to be ignorant of our station. It is far from obvious that this should be the whole human race. The idea of a weighting system in which we attach smaller, but non-zero, weights to people outside our own country still seems to me a helpful one for traditional types of foreign policy questions. It may even give us some clue in our present confused situation where there is strong and emotional disagreement about the relative degrees of obligation to British subjects, fellow members of the EEC and members of the Commonwealth of varying degrees of 'kinship'. But I can scarcely claim to have scratched the surface of the whole question of 'reference groups' which is one of the most neglected areas of both moral philosophy and of empirical political analysis.

When it comes to the domain and content of economic policy, the position reached in this book is very similar to that of US theorists of the 'public choice' school. This is that the dissection of 'failures' or 'imperfections' in the market place does not automatically set up a presumption in favour of political intervention; nor does it provide an easy guide to the form that such intervention, when it is desirable, should take. For the political as well as the market process is subject to 'failures' and 'imperfections' in satisfying and reconciling the desires of citizens; and it is illegitimate to argue that people who are guided by self-interest (however defined) in their role as producers or consumers, will act totally differently when they shift from the economic to the political arena. (This point is made very well by Professor James Buchanan in his introduction to *Theory of Public Choice*, ed. J. M. Buchanan and R. D. Tollison.)

The fact that, in the course of my own observations as an economic journalist, I arrived at conclusions remarkably similar to those which had been worked out on a deductive basis by scholars on the other side of the Atlantic, may have more than a personal interest. For too long economists have based their policy prescriptions on the assumption of a benevolent (and sometimes even omniscient) despot. The pressures, constraints and incentives affecting politicians, civil servants and their advisers, should be subjected to the same analytical scrutiny as are those affecting business firms, trade unionists and consumers. If this were done, public debate on economic topics might well take on a much less crudely interventionist form than it does at present.

If it were the custom to dedicate books to one's contemporaries, this one would undoubtedly be dedicated to Nigel Lawson and Peter Jay. I have discussed the central problems of this book with the former over a long period and with the latter over what is also now a number of years. Many of the ideas discussed in the following pages are either developments of points first made by one or other of these friends, or attempts to cope with criticisms that they have made. As it is mainly a certain fastidiousness of standards which has prevented them from going into print first on some of the central logical and philosophical problems raised, the least I can do is to record my gratitude to them for many enjoyable discussions.

I must add a special word of thanks to Professor John Williamson, who commented on the first draft of Chapters 1 and 3, and nobly helped me to straighten out the logic of certain arguments even when he did not share some of the underlying judgements. William Keegan, David Watt and my brother Leon Brittan commented on the draft Prologue, and Andrew Best was an invaluable counsellor on general problems of construction.

A great many other friends and colleagues have discussed with me directly or indirectly the material. Although it would not be feasible to list all their names, I can at least record my gratitude in general terms. They are responsible for my opinions only to the extent that they failed to argue me out of them.

Although he was not involved in this book, I cannot omit from these acknowledgements a special reference to Professor Peter Bauer. It was he who first introduced me to economic studies in Cambridge and brought home to me at an early stage that there was no alternative to making up my own mind on key issues. More recently he encouraged me to persist in thinking through certain themes which now feature in Chapter 1.

Last, but far from least, I must thank Mrs Anne Shotts, who not only typed but deciphered the bulk of the manuscript and whose devoted efforts made publication possible.

Finally I must thank George Allen & Unwin Ltd and Simon & Schuster Inc. for permission to use the extract from *Human Society in Ethics and Politics* by Bertrand Russell.

*May 1972*        SAMUEL BRITTAN

# Preface to the 1987–8 Edition

Economic systems are usually discussed from the point of prosperity and efficiency. This book, originally published in 1973 under the title *Capitalism and the Permissive Society*, put the emphasis on their relation to personal freedom.

At the time I was not alone. The first three post-war decades saw a small minority stream of books with titles such as *Capitalism and Freedom* or the *Constitution of Liberty*, which asserted that there was a strong link between free market capitalism and freedom in a wider sense. My aim in my own book was to examine these contentions in more detail and try to distinguish between the kinds of state activity which posed a threat to a free society and those which did not.

Since 1973 a strange paradox has arisen. The case for the market is now far more widely accepted politically; and it is less of a lonely, although it is still a minority, voice in intellectual circles. Yet that case is now almost always put forward in terms of prosperity, efficiency, or 'accepting hard realities'. The discussion about the bearing of different forms of economic organisation on freedom has all but disappeared.

For this reason, apart from more personal ones, I was delighted by the publisher's invitation to bring out a new edition of my own book. I have left the main text unchanged apart from minor corrections. An essay such as this is a product of a particular time and mood. Nothing would date it more than a frenetic attempt to bring it up to date.

The role of the substantial postscript I have added is different. It is to give a rundown of developments since the original publication. Although it covers some intellectual issues, much of it is inevitably concerned with recent history and detailed policy matters; and I apologise to the reader for not having seen a way to make it shorter. It is not self-contained, and is intended merely to supplement the original text.

By contrast the main theme outlined in the original text cannot date. It is a case for free competitive markets, which dwells on political implications rather than economic technicalities, and which is based on the connection with freedom. It is thus distinct from, and in many ways opposed to, 'neoconservatism', 'the moral majority' or certain interpretations of 'Victorian values' (which are themselves discussed in the Prologue).

The title of the book has been changed from *Capitalism and the Permissive Society*, which is the title of the Prologue, to *A Restatement of Economic Liberalism*, which is the title of the first, and longest, chapter of the book. The new title may give a better idea of the subject; but nothing has been withdrawn or changed. I use 'liberalism' in the old-fashioned English sense explained on pp. 35–7, which is not a synonym for vague general enlightenment, nor the property of any political party, but represents a set of priorities with which it is possible for people of goodwill to disagree vehemently.

In two later books, *The Economic Consequences of Democracy*,[1] and *The Role and Limits of Government*,[2] I have gone into detail on the obstacles in the way of market liberalism. These later books may thus appear more pessimistic. But to me they are complementary. No explanation of difficulties and obstacles is worth while without a prior statement of the goal which they obstruct, and that is provided here.

Readers interested in special aspects might like to know that I have taken the discussion of utilitarianism, and its relation to liberalism, further in *Role and Limits*. This last book also contains a more extended treatment of macroeconomic policy, both domestic and international. *Economic Consequences* contains some reflections on the politics of economics and the economics of politics.

As for the present volume, any reader who has seen the first edition will notice that the later chapters in that edition, which illustrated the main theme by more ephemeral topical applications, have been removed, in part to make room for the postscript.

\*     \*     \*

Looking back on the old text a decade and a half later, some passages still seem fresh and vivid, while others seem more laboured. But echoing the words written by Edward Elgar at the end of his setting of Cardinal Newman's *The Dream of Gerontius*, I would still say: 'This is the best of me'.

I would not, of course, compare my own efforts with a great

work written in a different medium and under the influence of a very different faith. The similarity is that I doubt if I ever shall be able to write anything that surpasses the original text of this book, or even equal to it, modest though the claims I make for it.

*June 1987*                                      SAMUEL BRITTAN

# Prologue: Capitalism and the Permissive Society

'To declaim against present times, and magnify the virtue of remote ancestors, is a propensity almost inherent in human nature . . .'

David Hume, 'Of Refinements in the Arts'

The values of competitive capitalism have a great deal in common with contemporary attitudes, and in particular with contemporary radical attitudes. Above all they share a similar stress on allowing people to do, to the maximum feasible extent, what they feel inclined to do rather than conform to the wishes of authority, custom or convention. Under a competitive system, the businessman will make money by catering for whatever it is that people wish to do – by providing pop records, or nude shows, or candyfloss. He will not make anything by providing what the establishment thinks is good for them. An individual citizen is free to maximise his income by using his abilities (and his capital if he has any) to cater for public tastes. But he does not have to. He can go for the easiest or most congenial job, or the one with the most leisure; or, like most of us he can find some compromise between these alternatives. In any case his life-style is his own. He can concentrate on personal pleasure, social service at home, the relief of poverty abroad, or any combination of these and numerous other activities.

*Competitive* capitalism is far from being the sole or dominating force of our society and Galbraith is right to force this on our attention. But to the extent that it prevails, competitive capitalism is the biggest single force acting on the side of what it is fashionable to call 'permissiveness', but what was once known as personal liberty. Business enterprise can, of course, thrive and prosper alongside a great deal of 'moral' prohibitions and prescriptions, whether enforced by law or public opinion. But the profit motive will always be kicking against such restraints and seeking to widen the range of what is permissible – whether it is a nineteenth-century publisher launching an attack on orthodox religion or a

1

twentieth-century theatrical or film producer challenging conventional concepts of decency and decorum. The profit motive will act both to stretch the existing law and as a force for its liberalisation.

As against these advantages it is often alleged that competitive capitalism is based on the false values of the 'consumer society'. Critics of this sort often forget that the great virtue of the consumer society is that no one is forced to consume. There may be middle class, or middle age pressures in that direction (and plenty of 'trendy' pressures of other sorts among the young); but social pressures are not the same as edicts enforced by the police, and the rise of the 'counter-culture' has itself set up pressures of an opposite kind, and the range of effective choice has been extended. To the extent that the competitive element prevails, a citizen can be equally indifferent to right-wing attacks on the self-indulgence of modern youth and to the traditional left-wing demand that all economic activity be channelled into some higher national purpose. The ethos of the market economy can be summed up in the vernacular as 'doing your own thing'. A capitalist market economy is not, of course, an equal society. But it is a powerful agent for disrupting existing class barriers and official hierarchies. Indeed, commercial societies are notorious, among those who dislike this aspect, for bringing new people and families to the fore and undermining traditional status barriers.

The expression 'competitive capitalism' is used here in its broadest possible meaning. It does not exclude the existence of a substantial public sector; nor does it prevent the state from carrying out a great many functions which are required if the market is to transmit people's preferences effectively – and this includes a great many measures in the anti-pollution field. But the emphasis is on the profit motive, consumer choice and competition. The conditions required for these activities to lead to tolerable results will be discussed in greater detail in later essays. The aim of this introductory chapter is to state the issue in its simplest terms; and rather than take refuge in terms such as 'mixed economy' or 'social market economy', I shall stick to the more provocative term 'competitive capitalism'. I would add, however, that 'competitive capitalism' is not a partisan slogan. When it comes to the test of practical application, it has at least as many opponents among Conservatives as among Labour supporters, and among businessmen as among trade unionists.

## THE HISTORICAL CONTEXT

The reasons why people hold certain beliefs have no bearing on their validity; to suppose otherwise would be to fall into the same intellectual trap as the worst Marxist or Freudian camp followers (it is not a trap that Marx, and above all Freud would have been guilty of themselves). Examination of the roots of widely held views can, all the same, be useful in explaining why people persist in holding them, despite rational arguments to the contrary, and why the latter fail to make a sufficient impression.

In the discussion that follows I shall begin with a reference to the historical background, go on to the features of the contemporary behaviour of businessmen and others in authority, which seem to confirm the worst suspicions of their critics, and then describe some of the other causes of the rise of anti-capitalist sentiment. With these matters out of the way, the path will be clear for a discussion of the New Left critique of capitalism and of the prospects of dealing with evils such as poverty and 'alienation' under alternative systems. This may seem a reversal of the logical order; but the treatment adopted may be more illuminating for the non-specialist reader who wants to put the economic arguments into a broader context.

Modern ideals of personal freedom, and the accompanying political, economic and legal beliefs, emerged from the religious writers of the seventeenth century and the political and economic philosophers of the eighteenth and nineteenth centuries. Yet, during the period when these ideals formed part of the public philosophy of the country, they were both less important to human welfare and more hedged around with stultifying qualifications than they are today when their credentials are so widely challenged. The period of English history when the capitalist ideal of freedom was most widely acknowledged was the mid-nineteenth century – the age of Peel and Gladstone. Yet, in many ways and for many people, it must have been a very unattractive time in which to live; and economic liberals would do well to acknowledge this fact.

The point most frequently made is, of course, that although living standards were rapidly improving, the mass of people were too poor to enjoy their freedom. This stricture needs to be more carefully stated than it often is. Freedom is not the same as absence of poverty; and to say that a labourer in the 1870s, or an

Egyptian peasant today is 'not really free' is a confusion of thought. If freedom is defined so that the absence of poverty is a necessary condition of its existence, two different values become confused, distinctions which exist in real life are obliterated, and language is impoverished. It is better to stick to the negative concept of freedom, but say that where the majority of the people hardly earn enough to cover their bare physical requirements, freedom may be less important as a goal than an increase of wealth.

The above, however, is well-trodden ground. What is less often pointed out is the limited number of people to whom even the legal freedoms of the nineteenth century applied. Personal liberty was effectively limited to male heads of households over 21. Women and children had as few rights as the subjects of the Eastern despots so much condemned in the Liberal literature of the period; and the same applied to anyone who had once volunteered for the Army or Navy. If freedom is defined as the absence of coercion, there was precious little for a schoolboy or soldier of the period, both of whom were also victims of the passion for flagellation which was (and to some extent still is) the real English sickness. Even for adult heads of households, freedom was carefully circumscribed. There was freedom to start up a business enterprise, freedom to emigrate and freedom to move money over frontiers (all freedoms which we despise at our peril). But in view of the very great powers still in the hands of local JPs, and the ferocious maximum penalties on the statute book, there was far more discretionary power of one individual over another than nostalgic admirers of the Victorian era would admit.

Apart from this, the prohibitions in the law and custom of the land were numerous and oppressive. Whether E. M. Forster's novel *Maurice* is good or bad as a work of literature, one can only recoil with horror at the revelations of the weight of the legal and the social penalties – and above all the burden of guilt – imposed on those whose impulses were not in keeping with the official sexual mores. Among those with 'normal' tastes promiscuity abounded, and was tolerated provided that it was not publicly admitted and the pretences were maintained.

The important point, however, is that both the political and economic philosophy and the capitalist practices of a century ago set in motion a train of events and ideas which eventually undermined the status-ridden conventional society of the time and brought into being the more tolerant England of today. Indeed, the basic arguments for the so-called 'permissive' morality were developed by thinkers in the nineteenth-century liberal tradition from John Stuart Mill onwards (one has only to think of his lifelong campaign against the subjection of women – the genuine article before which 'Women's Lib' groups pall). Many of the classical ideas of nineteenth-century liberalism did not come on the statute book until the 1960s. The battle is still far from won, as can be seen from the sentences still passed on 'obscene publications' or the hysterical and vindictive attitude adopted by so many authority figures towards the problem of drugs.

Growing prosperity and leisure have meanwhile increased the importance and desirability of individual freedom for the mass of the population. The paradox is that just when personal liberty is beginning to govern the life-style of a generation, the economic system which makes it possible has become intensely antipathetic to a great many of that generation's most articulate members. The old opposition to competitive capitalism from the puritan Left that instinctively felt (even when it denied this) that the Fabian state *did* know better, has been succeeded – just when it seemed about to fade away – by fresh opposition from the 'New Left',*

* Like most such expressions, 'New Left' is used by different people in different ways. The term is sometimes used for those radicals who glorify violence, support movements such as Black Power and identify with the 'Third World' as the main hope of revolution now that the Western proletariat has failed them. The prophets or 'modern masters' of such goals are analysed in a highly critical survey entitled *The New Left* edited by Maurice Cranston (Bodley Head, 1970), which deals with figures such as Che Guevara, the latter-day Sartre, Marcuse, Fanon and Laing.

The term 'New Left' is used in this and subsequent essays in a wider sense for the much larger body of people who are against the 'system' which they believe to be capitalist, but have lost the faith of the Old Left in state socialism, and insist on the individual's right to his own life-style. Their positive ideas for reform are varied and often vague, ranging from a watered-down version of the slogans of the 'modern masters' to the very different ideas of pacifism, universal love, mysticism and 'dropping out from society' and schemes for workers' control, 'participation' and opposition to technological advance. To call this very diverse group of people 'hippies' would give a misleading impression of the life-styles of many of those involved. The term that best describes the highest common factor among their beliefs is probably that of 'The Alternative Society', but this is too cumbersome as a shorthand descriptive term; and in both this and in subsequent essays the term New Left is used instead – but always in the very wide sense explained.

which is rightly suspicious of all authority, has no lingering affection for Joseph Stalin (and is Marxist only because that seems a far-out thing to be), but which identifies 'capitalism' with 'the system' and, in its headier movements, has brought back semi-serious talks of 'the revolution'. (To take 'the revolution' seriously is acceptable at many expense account lunches. It is equally 'trendy' to discuss it semi-facetiously; the one thing that is out-and-out 'square' is to be seriously opposed to it.)

## REASONS FOR SUSPICION

Among the middle classes and the establishment generally, adherence to competitive capitalism is, even where it exists, largely a matter of lip-service. Most middle-class voters, who are not business leaders hardly ever mention competitive capitalism, or any of its synonyms, except as dirty words. 'Less government' is a popular cry, not to promote freedom of any sort, but because those who utter it believe that it would lead to a transfer of income from other classes to themselves. The favourite subjects of older middle class conversation are in a different area altogether – capital punishment, abortion or sympathy with South Africa. These are the landmines that aspirant Conservative candidates, or those who manage the annual conference of the Party, have to avoid.

If one looks at the attitudes of leading figures of industry, commerce and finance, their support for capitalism is rarely part of any wider libertarian outlook. Such people are not notable for their championship of libertarian causes outside the economic field. Prominent businessmen have the views that one would very much expect on 'permissiveness', the indiscipline of modern youth, drugs, the prosecution of obscene publications, and so on.

Even in their own professional sphere, the devotion of many in the business community to the competitive aspects of capitalism is usually conspicuous by its absence. While they may proclaim the virtues of competition in the abstract, their own industry is very often a special case qualifying for protective restriction, subsidy or regulation; and the organised leaders of business are often in the forefront of the drive for government intervention, provided that their own financial interests do not appear to suffer (and sometimes even when they do, so great is the failure of nerve).

To come down to a slightly more technical level: the minority among the intellectual classes who bother to read the standard defences of capitalism by writers such as Friedman or Hayek, soon find that the contemporary business leader not merely has seldom heard of the key points emphasised by them such as the rule of impersonal law, consumer sovereignty and the separation of politics from business. On the contrary, his ideal is often that of negotiated deals with government officials on a 'power game basis' for projects for which the consumer would not be willing to pay and which have negative 'spillover' effects. No wonder that capitalism on closer investigation seems no more attractive to our hypothetical inquisitive radical than he had earlier imagined and that thus his New Left views are only further confirmed.

None of this is any cause for surprise and was long ago described by Adam Smith. The typical businessman is, after all, more often an administrator or manager than an entrepreneur. The virtues of capitalism have little to do with the intentions of capitalists; and if there is far more competition in the longer run than the more *simpliste* critics suppose, it is because of the difficulty of keeping out new entrants, products and ideas, rather than because of any lack of desire to do so.

The logic of the system makes the capitalist a two-faced animal. When he faces outward in his business life he is, whether he likes it or not, in a permissive society. However much he spends on advertising, he must in the end persuade people to take his wares; and however much he dislikes the process, he must either influence or serve the public taste; he cannot use the weapon of coercion or the sanctity of tradition. Indeed, much of the business history of the post-war period consists of the replacement of the long-established Anglo-Saxon upper middle class managerial dynasties by immigrants or newcomers of 'non-U' stock, who had no fastidious scruples about catering for the requirements of a more affluent working class.

Yet, although he operates within a libertarian framework in his outside dealings, and he must also have some regard to the preferences of his work force in conditions of high employment, within his organisation the capitalist manager operates by authority and not via commercial forces. Within the wider community the business executive is on the side of authority, he identifies with the governors rather than the governed and expects their support in his difficulties, and he seems to have more in common with unambiguous authority figures such as judges, senior civil servants, generals, or headmasters than with the representatives of permissive culture, whether pop stars or 'trendy left' journalists. Yet, in his own business life, especially if he is a successful innovator, he is engaged in undermining accepted ways and destroying established values and practices.

He is sandwiched between two worlds. He cannot identify himself with radical protest or with anti-authoritarian sentiment of any kind, for he realises that these forces, if unleashed, would sweep away his own position. There was an important exception to this in the heady triumphant phase of the Anti-Corn Law agitation of the 1830s and 40s, when the capitalists had sufficient confidence to rally the masses in a crusade against the established order. But this phase did not last very long; and once their immediate free trading objective had been achieved, the business classes gave Cobden little further support in his dream of world peace through enlightened self-interest. Within ten years of the repeal of the Corn Laws he and Bright lost their seats as a result of their opposition to the Crimean War. The capitalist did not apply the utilitarian calculus he used in his own business decisions to issues of war and peace in which he remained as jingoistic as any other Victorian.

Yet if he cannot thrive as a radical, or 'dove', or apostle of the permissive society, the capitalist – whether entrepreneur or business manager – is unimpressive as a leader in the authoritarian, paternalistic mode. As Schumpeter observed, a bourgeois ruling class completely lacks the glamour of an aristocracy. With neither the trappings of tradition, nor the heroic qualities of the great war leaders or generals, middle class business leaders cannot excite the identification or hero worship which reconcile other people to their wealth and position.

Indeed, the more that other members of the governing classes, such as politicians, civil servants or college heads, model themselves on the successful business manager, the less deference they are likely to attract and the more their authority is likely to be resented. Moreover, the more 'meritocratic' the process of selection, the less the governing classes are differentiated by special accents or special clothes, and the more 'they are just like us' (only luckier, or cleverer or more given to 'swotting'), the more 'they' will be resented. Even the pretence at aristocratic superiority and genteel dowdiness of the governing politicians of the Macmillan–Butler era were more appealing than the habits of their meritocratic successors. The hostility of the latter's opponents is not one whit less, while this is in no way compensated for by a sneaking or deferential respect among the population at large. At most they are tolerated on the strict condition that they bring results.

## THE RISE OF THE WORD MAN

Another characteristic of capitalism is that it tends to nourish in its own midst an anti-capitalistic culture. This was explained many years ago by Joseph Schumpeter in *Capitalism, Socialism and Democracy*, a work largely written before and at the beginning of the Second World War, and which is more up-to-date than most works currently off the press.[1] His basic thesis was that capitalism was killing itself by its own achievements.

Capitalist civilisation is above all rationalist. It is anti-heroic and anti-mystical. The spirit that animates it is the very opposite of 'Theirs not to reason why, theirs but to do or die'. The successful capitalist is forced by circumstances to query the way everything is done and endeavour to try and find a better way. If he relies on a traditional, mystical or ceremonial justification of existing practices, he will be overtaken by someone else and may well sink into oblivion. The breakdown of theological authority, the rise of the scientific spirit and the growth of capitalism were interrelated phenomena. A new ethic arose in the seventeenth century and had grown to fruition by the nineteenth, which blessed empirical and logical enquiry, denigrated the claims of authority and legitimised the profit motive (*inter alia* by removing the mediaeval restraints on usury and the notion of 'just price').

So long as the capitalist and the scientific segments were contained within an essentially aristocratic order, which preserved many traditions, superstitions and entrenched customs and, above all, deferential attitude towards a traditional ruling class – as was the case throughout most of the nineteenth century – capitalism could flourish. But in time the sceptical enquiring attitude was bound to turn on established institutions, and not only on kings or the restricted franchise, but on capitalism itself.

Unfortunately – and here Schumpeter makes no attempt to flatter his probable readers – a refusal to take on trust the customs and institutions of society (which is the negative part of the rational critique) does not itself bring a willingness to accept or understand rational arguments. It requires an intellectual and imaginative effort to understand the allocative function of the price mechanism, to see how a high (relative) price will set in motion forces that will remedy a shortage, how the shift of workers from bankrupt to expanding enterprises can increase prosperity, and eventually benefit even the workers who are transferred. Above all, it takes considerable insight or powers of analysis – and a rare freedom from envy – to see the harmful implications of paying people according to presumed merit rather than market values, or to see the advantages as well as disadvantages of the private ownership of capital and the dangers of simply trying to suppress it. The hostile reaction to some of the features of capitalism just mentioned would be shared not only by collectivists, but by many conventional Tory voters of the middle class, who would simply exhort capitalists not to behave too selfishly, cite instances of bad trade union behaviour and fall back on anti-nationalisation prejudices – in other words, respond with anything but a reasoned defence of capitalism.

Not only does a capitalist civilisation engender a skin-deep rationalism, but growing wealth and the accompanying educational expansion encourage a great expansion in the demand for the spoken and written word and in the supply of those able to produce it. This argument has been elaborated further by F. A. Hayek,[2] who points out that those who gain the public ear consist of two elements: the communicators, who are expert at putting other people's ideas or information across, but are amateurs in the substance; and professional people theorising outside their own field – doctors reforming the political system, engineers putting the economy to right and so on. In both cases they will go for the more plausible rather than the more profound ideas; and failing to understand the logic (or for that matter the real weaknesses) of the capitalist system, they are easily tempted to utter the cheap gibe or go for the state-imposed solution to every problem.

A great deal of press and especially television comment is based on a vague mixture, sometimes watered down, of the Old and New Left. A survey by Jeremy Tunstall shows that 54–59 per cent of specialist journalists writing for Conservative quality and popular publications describe themselves as 'to the left' of their organisations – and 'Conservative' papers are defined to include *The Times* and *Sunday Times*. Only 4–11 per cent describe themselves as 'to the right'. For those working for Labour papers the deviations are much more even, while for the media as a whole, including broadcasting and agencies, there are 44 per cent of left-wing deviationists compared with 12 per cent of right wing ones.[3] For the vast majority of those involved, 'to the left' means *unfortunately*, 'more opposed to the market economy'.

The detailed analysis of specialist categories is even more interesting. There is a strong Conservative bias among fashion and motoring correspondents – just the areas where the attitude to commercial products usually associated with Labour sympathies would be most helpful. On the other hand, a strong Labour bias was evident among trade union correspondents. In view of the harmful effects of union monopolies on employment, personal freedom and prosperity, this is just the area where a left bias is least required.

## THE DILEMMA OF THE ECONOMIC LIBERAL

The economic liberal, who is prepared to justify certain aspects of capitalism, has to face many drawbacks. Unless he is an apologist for business interests, or a party politician, he is bound to be highly critical of the particular forms of capitalism which prevail and of the policies of Conservative and Republican governments. To them he will appear as a far-out radical or, at best, an impractical theorist. Yet, among students and communication media which act as the middle-men for ideas, he will appear as a timid apologist for the 'system'.

A further difficulty is that the type of intellectual professionally qualified to explain the case for capitalism is the economist. Businessmen can usually be relied upon to defend the indefensible aspects of their activities while giving in to their/collectivist opponents on all essentials. Nor is this a criticism; businessmen are paid to operate the system rather than to understand or expound it, and nothing is more pathetic than to see politicians of either party coming cap in hand to industrialists or bankers for advice that the latter are not qualified to give.

Unfortunately, partly as a result of growing specialisation and technicality within the subject, there has been, as Stigler has pointed out,[4] a retrogression in the ability of economists to communicate with other intellectuals. The difficulty is not just that economists are bad popularisers or that their message is unwelcome. It goes much deeper. The real trouble is that economists are no longer sure what it is that they wish to communicate to a wider public. Individual economists feel passionately on particular subjects in opposition to other economists. But they are far less sure of what it is that they can put forward which would both reflect a professional consensus and also convey a relatively simple message to the educated layman.

## THE NEW LEFT ATTACK

So much for the climate of opinion in which capitalism now operates. What, however, are the main objections to competition and the profit motive actually put forward by the new generation of radicals? The New Left critics differ from both their Marxist and their Fabian forerunners in being equally distrustful of market forces and of central planning or bureaucracy in any form. This revival of the more utopian and anarchic strain is a welcome change from the paternalism and emphasis on state power which have for so long characterised socialist movements. Indeed, it ought to make a dialogue between the New Left and the market economists possible in a way it was not possible with either the Webbs or the Stalinist Communists. (Professor Lindbeck cites the case of a pseudonymous writer of the Chicago free market school who, by using a flamboyant style sprinkled with four letter words, at first reading gives the impression of being somewhere on the anarchist wing of the New Left.)

Unfortunately, the fatal flaw in the economic outlook of the New Left is the belief that one does not have to choose between a market and a command economy or between varying mixtures of the two; and that there is a third ethically preferable system which would rely on more spontaneous and less selfish motives. A large part of Assar Lindbeck's *The Political Economy of the New Left*[5] is taken up with a sympathetic but relentless analysis of this fallacy; and I find it strange that Paul Samuelson should give the impression in his polemical foreword that the book will make an impartial or hostile observer take New Left economics more seriously. The opposite effect seems to me far more likely.

Lindbeck conveniently summarises the standard problems of any society which have caused generations of economists to doubt that one can have an economy dispensing with both markets and bureaucratic commands. These are the needs:

(1)  to obtain information about people's preferences;
(2)  to allocate men, machines, land, building and other resources in accordance with these preferences;
(3)  to decide which production techniques to use;
(4)  to create incentives to avoid unnecessarily costly methods, to invest, to develop new technologies and products; and
(5)  (and perhaps most important) to co-ordinate the desires of millions of individuals, firms and households.

This list is provided not by Friedman or Hayek, but by a Swedish Social Democrat whose book is offered to us by Samuelson as an antidote to the former writers. I would only add that four at least of these requirements do not depend on selfishness but on the need for co-ordinating and signalling devices which would still exist even if we could rely more on people's goodwill. Remarks such as Adam Smith's about addressing ourselves not to the 'humanity' but to the 'self-love' of others and Alfred Marshall's about men's motives 'in the ordinary business of life' give a misleading impression. Even if people were actuated by benevolence, they would still need to know what jobs to do and what methods to use to satisfy other people's desires most efficiently, and a coordinating mechanism would be required. At most we could dispense with the fourth item on the list – incentives. Even then the profits or opportunities for high earnings would still be indispensable as *signals*, although any excess wealth gained by following them might eventually be given away to charitable organisations.

Galbraith's influence on the New Left has, as Lindbeck has pointed out, strengthened its temptation to ignore the inconvenient problem of co-ordination. Galbraith fails to explain how the few large firms on which he concentrates – let alone millions of householders and individuals – co-ordinate their activities. He concentrates on planning within firms, and many readers overlook the fact that he has said nothing about relations between firms, except by quasi-mystical references to the 'technostructure'.[6]

Lindbeck also lays to rest the illusion that computers could take over from markets the functions just listed. This belief is more characteristic of the old technocratic Left than of the New Left; but the latter might be inclined to clutch at it as a straw. Complicated messages about preferences, product qualities and information on production processes cannot be coded onto a computer. This is more than a practical impossibility. Even if consumers could immediately translate into computer language their preferences between an indefinitely large set of alternatives made possible by technology, they do not themselves know how they would react to new kinds of goods or changes in quality or innovation in general, for the simple reason that people do not always know how they themselves will react in hypothetical circumstances. Even when it comes to communicating details of production processes it is difficult to envisage how the specifics of 'knowing how' could be put into a computer. Moreover, all this effort, even if successful, would simply reproduce the data already presented by prices, profits and sales figures.

A dominant feature of New Left thinking, again powerfully stimulated by Galbraith, is a denial that the market does allow people to 'do their own thing'. Consumer wants, it is alleged, are artificially fabricated by advertising and other sales techniques. The art of salesmanship has never been regarded as quite respectable. It has, of course, always been disliked by conservative traditionalists and strictures here are no monopoly of the New Left. E. J. Mishan has argued strongly against advertising from the premises of conventional economic theory; and Charles Carter, the Secretary General of the Royal Economic Society and notable university administrator, has outlined a complex scheme excluding from tax-deductable expenses most marketing expenditure, including sales staff and packaging, as well as promotion and advertising, and imposing a prohibitive tax on such expenditure when it exceeds a certain proportion of turnover.[7]

Such writers do not, however, go to the lengths of the New Left and some of its prophets in asserting that firms can create a demand for whatever goods they choose to produce. As Lindbeck has pointed out, the latter is a new form of 'Say's Law' – so much attacked by Keynes for giving too *favourable* an impression of the capitalist system – which asserted that supply created its own demand and which thereby denied the possibility of a depression.

The new form of the law seems to assert that this is true, not merely for the economy as a whole, but for each individual firm or product.

The belief is quite false. Simply because firms do not limit themselves to supplying demands felt by the human race when it left the Garden of Eden, but actively build up a market for their products, this does not mean that they can impose whatever they like on a defenceless public. The British motor industry has not been able to prevent consumers from buying more imported cars; Cunard has been unable to prevent a fall in demand for passenger shipping lines; the Coal Board has been unable to prevent a switch to other fuels; and there are countless other examples.[8] Marketing studies suggest that among products regarded as 'technical successes' only perhaps 10–20 per cent survive market and pre-launching studies, while of those that are launched one-third to one-half are withdrawn as failures within one year.[9]

There are two extreme and equally absurd prevalent models of the role of the consumer. There is, on the one hand, the view that people have innate tastes which firms exist to satisfy. Hardly any reputable economist, however, orthodox, has ever explicitly held this view; but there are incautious statements, particularly in American textbooks, which give credence to this allegation of Galbraith's.[10] At the other extreme is the view to which Galbraith himself comes perilously close, that sees consumers as plastic clay on which the advertisers can impose any shape they like. In fact, salesmanship is part of the process of increasing the range of alternatives of which people are aware. Like many other technological and cultural techniques, it develops desires of which people were not aware before and – the point must be conceded – causes some people to be more dissatisfied with their lot than they otherwise would be. This is part of the price of freedom of communication. Nearly all the products of civilisation – arts, sports and recreations, just as much as running water, telephones or labour-saving gadgets – have been invented and sold to people who were not spontaneously asking for any of them, but were glad to have them when they arrived. It is part of the function of a market economy to suggest new possibilities to people which they are then free to accept or reject. It may be that commercial advertising increases demand for consumer goods relative to 'public goods', leisure or a pleasant environment. But politicians, writers and journalists can and do propagandise in the opposite direction; the activities of the New Left are themselves part of the free market in ideas, and by no means the least successful part of it.

None of this means that the situation in regard to advertising or consumer information is incapable of reform. If advertisers really discovered and used forms of subliminal advertising, which exercised a literally hypnotic effect which people were powerless to resist, the case for legal prohibition of these forms would be strong. On the positive side, much more could be done to encourage the provision of information and views on products from points of view other than the producer's. There is a case for state encouragement and financial support of consumer bodies. It is still too difficult to organise or finance anything analogous to the political 'Opposition' in the commercial sphere.

Another objection to markets, which does not fit very easily with a belief in a 'permissive' morality, but which is sometimes heard from the same camp, is that the exercise of choice itself involves costs and inconvenience which some people do not wish to bear. In many aspects of life an attempt to survey the total range of options would be impractical, because the consumer lacks the knowledge to make it, or irrational, because the benefits are too trivial in relation to the time and effort expended; and there may be advantages in voluntarily delegating the choice to others. Investment and unit trusts spare the investor the bother of selecting his own securities; organisations such as the *AA* and *The Good Food Guide* select hotels and restaurants and group them into convenient grades. Travel agents offer both package and individual tours for people who cannot be bothered to make their own arrangements. There are excellent 'flower clubs' which, for a fixed annual subscription, arrange a weekly delivery of the flowers that happen to give the best value for money at the time of year. This gives access to both expertise and to economies of bulk purchasing which most individuals could not hope to have acting on their own. Every encouragement should be given to such methods of delegating choice; and we can all exercise our own preferences about which purchases to delegate, and to whom.

It is true that we still have to choose between investment trusts, or between advisers on investment trusts, between hotel guides and so on. A resurrected and expanded Consumer Council or similar body could publish lists of organisations fulfilling minimum standards. The appropriateness of the standards and their application to particular instances will always be open to argument and there will be nothing sacrosanct about the lists; but they would, at least, provide reassurance to those instinctively afraid of being cheated by commercial enterprises. In the social service area, no one need be forced to 'shop around' for private education and health services, however much such private provision is encouraged, so long as state services of the present standard or higher continue to exist side by side.

## POVERTY AND EQUALITY

Another common objection to competitive capitalism reflects a renewed outburst of egalitarian sentiment. It is certainly possible to go a long way towards 'levelling up' the conditions of the poorest section of the population under capitalism. A legitimate charge against modern industrial society, which applies to both the 'capitalist' and the Communist countries, is the amount of poverty that continues despite average levels of real income per head which are very high by all past standards. Poverty usually means an income below that required to maintain an adequate standard of living for the family or individual concerned. Although the notion of an adequate standard rises with average income levels, it is not meaningless to speak of a whole society being poor – for example, when the *average* standard of living, however defined, is insufficient to prevent starvation or gross malnutrition. But as society becomes richer, it becomes more and more reasonable to regard the poor as those with less than some given minimum proportion of average post-tax real income (adjusted for family size and other complications). The size of this minimum is necessarily arbitrary. But it is perfectly possible to set up as a goal that no household of average size should have an income of less than, say, a third of the national average. The best available estimate for 1972 is that there are 17 million households with, on average, disposable incomes approaching £2600. The proposed minimum would then be nearly £900 – more for families with several children, less for smaller households. (For comparison, the supplementary benefit rates amounted to nearly £660 for a married couple plus about £100–£150 per child according to age.) This figure will rise in future years both with real income and inflation.* By guaranteeing an income of this kind, there is a limited sense in which the poor need not always be with us. Poverty is partly an absolute and partly a relative phenomenon. A family, which earns a given and small proportion of the national average, is not poor in the same sense when this involves having only one car and having to share a swimming pool as when it involves infants dying of starvation.

In Chapter 3 a suggestion is made for a guaranteed income, to be provided at first in the form of a negative income tax, but eventually to be distributed as a social dividend to all, whether at work or not. It is presented there as a way in which those who did not wish to participate in a consumption-oriented, work-obsessed society could 'opt out' of it, without imposing an unwanted revolution on the rest of the population. The main object of such a scheme would, however, be to provide guarantees against extreme poverty for everyone. Yet we would be wise not to expect too much from it, especially in the early years. As Professor Harry Johnson has pointed out,[11] there are limits to the degree of earnings transfer, whether in guaranteed incomes or other forms that the bulk of the population will tolerate; and there are many poor people who do not share the anti-consumption ethos and who would be glad of the opportunity to earn more than any feasible income guarantee is likely to provide.

The most promising, although most difficult, way of helping such people is to increase their opportunity to acquire the skills that are demanded in the market place. Lack of knowledge of technical trends and opportunities leads children to follow their parents' occupation into what Professor Johnson has called 'perpetual pockets of poverty'. While the provision of 'free' or subsidised information or training would help, the inclination of those who are hostile to market forces is to conserve the population of existing districts and industries by a variety of make-work devices, which hinder the geographical and occupational mobility which would, in the long run, provide the victims of change with their best opportunities.

Many kinds of discrimination make for poverty. Racial

* In 1986 there were an estimated 19 million households with average net disposable incomes of approximately £12 500. An average minimum income of one-third amounted therefore to nearly £4200. The long-term supplementary benefit rate for a married couple from July 1986 was just over £3150 p.a., plus £500 to £750 per child. These figures exclude housing benefit.

discrimination is a less important factor in Britain than in the USA, but there is plenty of discrimination against the old, by compulsory retiring ages, and against the young, by forcing children to stay on at school for longer and longer periods. It is worth noting that the more profit-seeking and less bureaucratic a firm, and the less hamstrung it is by unions or staff associations, the more incentive it will have to provide work for elderly people who may not be worth a normal wage but who may still be able to render some productive service.

In his discussion of the forces which could improve opportunities for the poor, Professor Johnson rightly gives pride of place to the general level of employment. A high demand for labour exercises a perennial effect to 'upgrade labour skills', and to find suitable opportunities for people of impaired mental or physical capacity. The scarcer that labour is in general, the more incentive there is 'to devise square holes in the economic system to accommodate the square pegs available'.

If anyone still believes that the pressure of demand for labour and the overall unemployment percentage can be fixed by the Treasury at any level it chooses by manipulating some financial levers, then the remedy is clear. But if, as becomes more and more obvious each year, the ability of the authorities to do this is limited by union exercise of monopoly power, the implication is rather different.

Apart from their overall economic effects, trade union monopolies – by raising relative wages in a few supposedly skilled or semi-skilled trades, such as the motor industry or printing – reduce the welfare of other workers. Trade unions on both sides of the Atlantic have also raised unemployment by insisting on above market wage rates and/or minimum wage laws for the less skilled occupations. Those particularly hard hit have been the untrained, or less easily employable, who could have found a niche at wages corresponding to their productivity, but have now been pushed out of the labour market and onto relief, to the applause of the bogus humanitarians.

To many critics, however, egalitarianism involves not only a 'levelling up' in the conditions of the poor, but also an elimination of all major disparities of income so that no one is much above some general average. How far it is either possible or desirable to go in this direction will be discussed in some detail in the next essay. It is certainly possible to modify the distribution of income and wealth without destroying a market economy, if appropriate methods of redistribution are used. But there are limits to the process. Despite the achievements of capitalism in breaking down class barriers, any viable capitalist system does involve the existence of individuals many times wealthier than average. The same applies to non-capitalist economies where market forces are allowed a role. This can be seen, for example, in the tendency in some Eastern European countries to pay bonuses out of profits to managers of state undertakings, which has obvious analogies to capitalist practices.

If all material differentials are intolerable, then the only alternative is centralised direction of labour. This is a lesson of Western economic theory and Communist economic practice which will not be refuted by any number of 'demos' or vituperative outbursts. There comes a point at which radicals of all hues have to choose between their commitment to freedom of choice of occupation and life-style, and extreme egalitarianism. With those to whom equality of material reward is the single absolute value to which everything else must be subordinated, no further argument is possible. But I doubt very much if this is the ultimate position of most of today's young radical. If they could understand that the single-minded pursuit of equality would lead to the sacrifice of other valued goals most of them would probably modify their attitude. Too much New Left writing seems to assume that it is *necessarily the case* that the wealth of some individuals is the *cause* of the poverty of others. As Lindbeck has put it, economic activity is seen as a zero-sum game, where what is gained by one person is lost by another. This ties in all too well with the distaste for patient analysis which is one of the less attractive features of 'the movement'.

The New Left has a much better case when it attacks the concentration of power in the hands of what President Eisenhower called the 'military-industrial complex', or the scandalous ability of interest and pressure groups of all kinds to obtain special favours ranging from import controls to tax exemptions, tariffs and subsidies. Although these influences may be specially noticeable in the USA, they are not exactly absent in Britain. Tempting though it may be to quote the stock example of the special tax depletion allowances, production and import quotas for American oil producers, I am not persuaded that the tax privileges for British home owners – which redistribute income from the poor to the better off – are on an altogether higher plane of virtue.

What the radical critics so frequently fail to realise is that many of these abuses are the result of the absence of competitive market pressures, not their presence; and this is, in turn, due in most cases to extensive paternalistic intervention of the kind for so long preached by a dominant section of the Old Left. It is too easy to persuade politicians and officials whose own money is not at stake that journeys to the moon, ever more advanced aircraft, or home-based computer industries, should be subsidised from the public purse. Governments find it notoriously difficult to separate genuine defence needs from the inevitable desire of the military-industrial complex for elaborate, ever more expensive forms of hardware. It is not an accident that the danger of the 'New Industrial State' is greatest in just the area where government involvement with business is at its closest and most specific. Professor Galbraith is so intent on ridiculing market-oriented economists (for the benefit of a mass readership that will accept on trust his account of their views) that he accepts a quite unnecessarily fatalistic attitude to the trends about which he is supposed to be worrying, and dismiss all remedies that do not involve even more frequent and personalised involvement between government and business.[12]

The remedy for these evils is the direction of more competition, more reliance on markets and more reliance on the price mechanism, adjusted to take into account 'social' costs and benefits at present unpriced. It does not lie in the 'suppression' of capitalism and greater concentration of power at the centre. To cite Lindbeck yet again: would Concorde be less likely to have been built if the British and French Governments not only co-operated with the aircraft producers but also entirely owned them (as they partially do already)? The valid elements in the New Left objection to the cult of technology and growth of measurable GNP arise from the intervention of governments to impose on the community more hardware of every sort, whether computers, satellite systems or common-or-garden machinery benefiting from 'investment incentives', than would be provided if firms interested in these areas had to compete unaided for the customer's purse.

'ALIENATION'

One early Marxist concept now back in fashion as a basis for anti-capitalist sentiment is that of 'alienation'. I wish I could think of a less ungainly name for the relation between many workers and their employment but it does refer to a real and undesirable phenomenon. It can be used, not just rhetorically, but to refer to a sense of powerlessness which many people feel within large organisations, a feeling of meaninglessness about the operations performed and of a lack of any intrinsic satisfaction outside the wage packet. The archetypal example is that of the car assembly-line worker who performs identical repeat operations of a nature and at a pace over which he has no control.

Again, however, although the complaint is correct, the diagnosis and remedy offered are frequently wrong. As Edwin G. Dolan has remarked in a penetrating analysis of the concept, published interestingly enough in the Chicago-based *Journal of Political Economy*,[13] alienation arises not so much from the system of property relations – whether capitalism or Soviet-style Communism – as from a particular stage of industrial and technological development involving the combination of an extreme division of labour with the wage system in large impersonal institutions. The individual can, of course, in present-day capitalism choose to avoid jobs with such characteristics, at the expense perhaps of less take-home pay; and the greater the place of competitive forces in the system the greater this choice is likely to be.

Nevertheless, the habit of deference to authority – alternating perhaps with bloody-minded rebellion against it – that grows up when the majority of the population have jobs characterised by the alienation syndrome, affects the whole character of society. The key variables are probably the proportion of the population in paid employment and the nature of the jobs they perform. After sadly quoting figures showing the decline in the proportion of the self-employed, one perceptive author speaks of the dangers that arise 'if society is progressively turned into one great hierarchy of employment'. As many exercises of freedom are of little direct interest to the employed, 'they cannot see the need for them, and they attach little importance to opportunities for action which hardly ever occur in their lives'. If the reader is wondering which neo-Marxist I am quoting, it is F. A. Hayek, in *The Constitution of Liberty*.[14]

Characteristically, but correctly, Hayek believes that these dangers are aggravated by tax and other legislation which discourage the independent businessmen or professionals in the supposed interests of the employed. He emphasises the need to preserve a body of men of independent means and to avoid replacing the present number and variety of employers by public corporations all dependent on the state.

There is, however, more to be said. Just as the extreme division of labour and movement away from self-employment is an expression of one phase of technological development, future technological advance may make possible a movement in the reverse direction. It is already a commonplace that the development of both factory and office automation should reduce drastically the number of routine jobs and increase the demand for jobs involving the discretionary use of varied skills.

Another less obvious aspect of the growth of potential output that advancing technology makes possible is that it will become sensible to work in ways that are, in the technical (although not economic) sense, inefficient. The deservedly famous passage in Marx's *German Ideology* where he speaks of a society in which it is possible for anyone to 'hunt in the morning, fish in the afternoon, rear cattle in the evening, criticise after dinner' was, as he knew, not possible in his own day. But it should be possible to take out some of the fruits of the much higher level of productivity we may expect in the future in the form of a deliberately 'wasteful' and pleasanter pattern of work and/or in shorter hours, rather than in more and more material goods.

There is already an incipient tendency for a rise in the ratio of self-employed. A number of jobs, especially in the building and catering trades are shifting from an employee to a quasi-entrepreneurial basis – a development that is held back by various kinds of government intervention and by the hostility of organised unions. During the period in which the majority are bound to remain paid employees in the strict sense, there are two ways in which their influence over their working environment can be increased. One is 'workers' control' or 'industrial democracy'. The other is freedom of choice of occupation, or voting with one's feet.

The two approaches are not incompatible. By all means let us experiment with every sort of choice for giving people more say in the organisations in which they work – although my own feeling is that what people most want is, in the first place, to be informed in advance so that decisions are not sprung upon them and secondly, to be consulted so that they can express their views before it is too late, rather than to attempt themselves the tasks of management.

Another point, not generally realised, is that to the extent that workers really want to have a say in management, those firms who are responsive will find it easier to attract workers. Thus, if there is a real demand for greater workers' participation (although not for expropriating the owners), this too can be brought about by the market.

If the above remarks seem a little removed from reality, the main reason lies in the part played by the restrictionist activities of the trade unions themselves. Catering for minority tastes in, say, hours of work, or in preference for a more relaxed tempo of work, is a costly business. It can be costly because of the kind of preferences involved, or simply because they are minority tastes and an employer who caters for them will have to do more searching around for staff. These are real costs, which would exist in a non-capitalist society; and an employee who wishes to be treated in this way must expect smaller take-home pay. Unfortunately the insistence of union activists on levelling up all wage differentials between workers of comparable skills would soon discourage any employer who tried to cater for such minority tastes or attitudes. It will also not have escaped attention that the possibilities of shopping around depend on the state of the labour market. They were not worth much in the interwar period and they were of only limited use in the early 1970s in high unemployment areas like Scotland. Here again trade union monopoly activity has, as already noted, a key role in reducing the overall demand for labour that can be maintained without provoking an inflationary explosion.

## STUDENT DISSENT

The remarks made about the advantages of 'voting with one's feet' compared with control from below are particularly relevant to student dissatisfaction. One characteristic of university education is that it is provided at below market-clearing prices. Government grants create an excess of demand over supply for places. Thus, not having to compete for custom, academic institutions are under no market pressures to take into account student preferences. This enables them to run universities to suit their own tastes, whether paternalistic or self-centred.

This inability to vote with his feet – increased by the extreme difficulty of transferring grants from one university to another – makes the student-consumer dependent on a monopoly supplier, a situation guaranteed to create tension and animosity. Although any specific student protest may be misplaced, it is a safe prediction that there will always be some justified grievances arising from the built-in incentives that exist for university administrators and senior staff to suit their own convenience and taste rather than that of students. This explains many of the arrangements for faculty tenure, the priority given to research and publication over teaching, common pay scales linked to seniority rather than ability, minimal student-staff contacts and privileged access of senior staff to the more convenient parking spaces, lifts, common rooms, lavatories and so on. Hence, too, the attempts to enforce arbitrary rules of personal conduct or compulsory residence requirements.

These examples and quotations are taken not from any protest manual but from a paper by Professor Alan Peacock and Anthony Culyer, published by the pro-capitalist Institute of Economic Affairs.[15] It is when they come to remedies that the authors differ from the New Left. The conventional remedy of the latter, 'student participation', is likely to erode the gains from the specialisation of labour among students, teachers and administrators and thus lead to 'dissipation of effort' which 'might be better spent on the main objective: learning and research.' There is also the long term probability that 'student power' will be 'effectively nullified by the complexity of the administrative machine and the expertise of the professionals in its use.' The authors might have also added the danger of disproportionate influence by the professional organiser or 'barrack room lawyer' type of student over colleagues who prefer to spend their time in other ways.

The market alternative proposed by Peacock and Culyer is that 'universities should receive their main financial support through the medium of student choice of university and not directly from the state'. This would involve payments to students to cover fees and living expenses, and ease of transfer of such payments from one institution to another free of the quirks of local education authorities.

The chances of such a use of taxpayers' or ratepayers' money to increase effective student power under the present grant system are almost nil. The only way that students could acquire larger sums to spend at their discretion would be if part or the whole of these sums were in the form of student loans, with repayment obligations related to future earnings. Such a switch from grants to more generous loans would achieve two objects which student radicals claim to have at heart: an increased say in conditions affecting their own life and work, and an egalitarian influence over the general distribution of incomes. For, looking at lifetime, rather than immediate earnings, non-repayable grants from taxpayers to students are a transfer from a lower to an upper income group. It is a sign of the poverty of much progressive thought that the loan idea should be regarded as a reactionary proposal to be opposed at all costs.

The present system provides the worst of all worlds. On the one hand, the grant system is a net transfer to those who can expect to earn more than the average income over their working lives. On the other hand, *during their period at university* students (most of whom do not have the degree of parental support that they did in earlier generations) belong for the time being to the poorest section of their age group. This fact goes a long way to explain a new element in student radicalism.

Students have often tended to be severe critics of the existing order. The novel feature of recent years has been the identification of considerable numbers with the proletarian side in a class war which they have tried to whip up to the best of their ability. This comes out in pathetic attempts to show solidarity with every strike and in participation in militant trade unionism, efforts which often meet a decidedly cynical response from the objects of their affections. Professor Harry Johnson is right to draw a direct link between these attitudes and the large private cost to the student of university education, which he defines as 'the difference between his grant and the earnings he could obtain in commercial employment.' It is not surprising that 'cheeseparing in grants leads the student to identify emotionally with the poorer classes of the community – a great help to sincere protesting'.[16] But the remedy lies not in a losing battle for better grants but in finding new forms of student (and perhaps university) finance.

These problems do not, however, end at university. One result of the great expansion of higher education is that the number of graduates has exceeded the growth in the number of jobs of sufficient status to meet their expectations. The latter is admittedly a highly subjective notion; but many graduates now do jobs for which a degree was formerly neither necessary nor usual. While it remains true that most graduates will belong to the upper quartile of the income distribution, they are no longer the elite group they were in the first post-war decade.

Schumpeter foresaw this problem somewhat prematurely on the basis of the Interwar Depression when he wrote of the graduate failing to find a job worthy of his years of education and spoke of people who were 'literally unemployable' and fodder for the critics of capitalism. It is not, however, necessary to put the point so maliciously. Many of the young people in question have been forced through the examination rat race as a result of an overemphasis on formal education by the more paternalistic forces in society of which they and their employers alike are victims; and the limitations on their initial career prospects are, in part, due to the encouragement given to large corporations and the discouragement of small enterprises and independent professional activity by would-be egalitarian systems of tax.

## CONTEMPORARY RADICALISM

These economic influences, although important, are not the whole story. There are certain ideological and cultural aspects of contemporary radicalism which deserve at least a brief examination. The collectivist movements, about which Schumpeter and Hayek wrote, stretch from Marxism of various sorts to the 1945–50 Labour Government – although the arguments were later extended by Hayek to the conscious pursuit of egalitarian policies in the 'Welfare State' of the 1950s and 1960s. Even Friedman, whose work on the subject is of most recent vintage, directs his fire against schemes for increasing the authority and the role of the US Federal Government.

The latest outbreak of radical fervour, after a period in which ideological conflict was supposed to have died down, is, in many respects, different. The emphasis is on personal freedom and not on the state. The apostles of the 'Alternative Society' do not see salvation through the boards of state corporations; and they do not believe that a mixture of Old Etonians, professional managers, officials, generals and retired trade unionists become agents of radical change by means of the magic word nationalisation. Nor do they set much store by state economic plans; and they are repelled rather than attracted by many aspects of the technocratic dream of transforming society by means of science. All this is a change for the better.

Associated with this is a great stress on personal sensual gratification and on giving free reign to instincts, emotions and feelings. The older socialist movements had their roots in the puritan tradition and were nourished by a moral or aesthetic disapproval of the conspicuous consumption of the rich; and many people who were attracted by socialist theories felt, like Mr Harold Macmillan, that the right wing was much more fun. Today the position is reversed. The leaders in consumption, the film makers, and the leaders of fashion tend to be on the left; and although they may be economically better off under a Tory government, there is little love lost on either side.

Of course reality is far more complex. The puritan tradition lingers on amidst the new hedonism – this is the kindest explanation of the otherwise hypocritical campaign against the Macmillan government at the time of Profumo, in which so many people, from Bow Group sympathisers to *Private Eye*, worked themselves up into such a state of delighted indignation. The early twentieth-century British Labour Movement comprised the beery heartiness of the trade unionist as well as Mrs Webb's sense of sinful indulgence in the occasional cup of tea or coffee after a meal. The establishment, whether Whig or Tory, always contained a respectable aldermanic element as well as the more hedonistic 'society' figures. Moreover, the technocratic passion for quantification and 'hard facts' is, if anything, still a growing force in the professions and among the generation of academics now coming to the fore – and it is still a religion among politicians of the generation of Wilson and Heath and even those slightly younger, although it reflects a set of values that is now passing. Such cultural lags are among the platitudes of history. But nothing at all can be said on social trends if one is not prepared to simplify or generalise; and the contemporary New Left – and even more the less overtly political 'youth culture' – are both hedonistic and suspicious of authority.

The removal of inhibitions and barriers, so evident in the more casual and comfortable style of contemporary clothes, is highly desirable. It is the end road of the libertarian and utilitarian ideals professed by the bewigged philosophers of the eighteenth century and the Victorian political thinkers in their frock coats. The artificiality and conventionalism of the eighteenth century and the repressive respectability of the nineteenth century did produce the tensions and anxieties discussed, for example, by Freud in *Civilisation and Its Discontents* (although Freud carefully refrained from prescription).

Unfortunately, although perhaps inevitably, the emphasis on instinctual gratification has been associated with a revolt against rational thinking – whether of the empirical or the logical type – in favour of 'thinking with the belly'. Bertrand Russell rightly remarked that 'reason is and should be the servant of the emotions'; and it was necessary to dethrone reason from the exaggerated point of esteem in which it was then held. The trouble is that reason has been dismissed even as a servant and many apostles of the 'Alternative Society' are impatient of it in any role. This leads to a total sweeping aside of any but the most superficial and short-term approaches to, say, bad housing conditions or poverty; and it is not a climate in which belief in a market economy – or any other rational approach to policy – is likely to flourish.

Anyone who believes these observations exaggerated should turn to that extremely useful publication, Nicholas Saunders' *Alternative London*.[17] Its second longest chapter is entitled 'Mystical' (coming behind 'Crafts' but in front of 'Drugs' in terms of length). This opens with a lament that the Christian churches have lost the essence of religion, which is 'to let the pure light inside flow out freely rather than ooze out discoloured'. Another analogy is to see oneself 'as God suppressed by being encased by layers of shit'. We read of Meher Baba who promised in 1935 to give his disciples the secret of the world after 35 years. He died after 34, 'yet his following is growing still'.

The present reaction against the artificialities of civilisation in favour of the instinctive, the physical, the sensual and the mystical, has been foreshadowed for a very long time. The immediate predecessors of the present romantic sensualists were, in fact, the New Right that grew up, especially in Continental countries, towards the end of the nineteenth century, and which openly proclaimed 'thinking with the blood'. This New Right may have drawn inspiration from the myth of an uncorrupted past, but it vied with the Marxists in demanding a sweeping overhaul of national life. It was an attempt to escape from the frustrations of urban and industrial life to move to a more emotional and physical plane of existence, usually accompanied by intense nationalist feelings. It can be traced in writers such as Nietzsche, Kipling, d'Annunzio or D. H. Lawrence. It would be absurd to identify these men with the perversion of the gas chambers, even though the Nazi period is a warning of the direction in which these ideas can lead in unscrupulous or unsophisticated hands.

The perennial argument on the connection between Wagner's music dramas and Nazism illustrates the essential point. It is *because* they appeal to basic emotions, instincts or archetypal patterns, that his works have their strange power and fascination – even for those who think that they are responding to the music only and ignoring the Nordic myths. These very deep-seated human drives are capable of producing both the worst and the best in the species – the sublimest love, the greatest heroism, and also the lowest depths of cruelty and lust for death.

We have, of course, moved away from Lawrence and Wagner. The more extreme beliefs and practices of present-day opponents of the 'system' were perhaps foreshadowed by much that went on in the late Roman Empire. The third century writer Plotinus, far and away the leading philosopher of the age, is described by as level-headed a senior historian as Professor Michael Grant, as 'the pioneer of psychedelic experience for the West'.[18] Nevertheless, Plotinus represented a rational extreme, by the standard of age, trying to achieve his ends 'by purely cerebral, intellectual discipline – not by schizophrenia and not by drugs and not by religion.'

More characteristic was the mode of life of the early Christian monks as described by Gibbon. Like many modern hippies, who have rejected private property and the consumer society, 'the candidate who aspired to the virtue of evangelical poverty, abjured at his first entrance into a regular community the idea, and even the name, of all separate or exclusive possession.' Gibbon remarks:

The aspect of a genuine anchoret was horrid and disgusting: every sensation that is offensive to man was thought acceptable to God; and the angelic rule of Tabenne condemned the salutary custom of bathing the limbs in water, and of anointing them with oil. The austere monks slept on the ground, on a hard mat, or a rough blanket; and the same bundles of palm-leaves served them as a seat in the day; and a pillow in the night. . . . Thirty or forty brethren composed a family of separate discipline and diet; and the great monasteries of Egypt consisted of thirty or forty families.

It could almost be a description of a hippy commune. One cannot resist quoting Gibbon's remark about the more 'savage saints' of both sexes who 'contemptuously cast away all superfluous encumbrance of dress' and 'whose naked bodies were covered only by their long hair' (*Decline and Fall*, Chapter 37). Just as Gibbon's description was unfair as a description of many of the monasteries, which 'transmitted by their indefatigable pens' the 'monuments of Greek and Roman literature' through the Dark Ages, and many of whom suffered a natural descent from 'powerful and dangerous virtue' to 'the common vices of humanity', it would be equally unfair as a description of many of those who affect a hippy-type style. But as far as the extremes of both ideal and practice are concerned, the analogy is convincing. *Alternative London* presents us with a rich variety of communes, many far from the metropolis. One of the more notable contains about 20 people – the men young, the women old. Orders are given daily to one member and imposed by her husband, the founder. Nature spirits help them produce their own food, despite the RAF base next door, and everywhere are cards saying 'Expect a miracle'.

Of course there are differences as well as similarities compared with the phenomena about which Gibbon was writing. Above all, the early Christians were ascetics who took a masochistic delight in mortifying the flesh, while their modern descendants make a cult of sex and promiscuity. We must, however, remember that the early Christians were only one of many rival cults which 'withdrew from the world' in the later Roman Empire. There were others who did emphasise promiscuity in the modern style. Moreover when one passes from a mere lifting of conventions and inhibitions into a cult of promiscuity, irrespective of the great variety of human inclinations and nuances of feeling, we are very near to a new sort of asceticism, or puritanism in reverse.

The external environment in which these practices grow up has uncanny resemblances to that of several Western countries in recent years. There was a very heavy level of military expenditure to guard against the external threat, resulting in hitherto unprecedented levels of government expenditure and taxation; the collection of the necessary funds prompted, according to Professor Grant, a tendency towards a levelling-down egalitarianism; and there were attempts to solve the problems by expanding the monetary circulation with periods of runaway inflation and currency collapse.

The late Roman Emperors were also pioneers in prices and incomes policy and state regulation of trade. Guilds and corporations established closed shops for most trades and crafts. The emperor became the greatest landowner and industrialist and this large public sector was run by an important Ministry in Rome. By the time of Diocletian and Constantine most workers 'were under permanent and inherited obligation to remain at their job'.[19] The saving grace of the system was the inefficiency of its law-enforcement. Nevertheless, the controls, taxes and economic policy of the late Roman Empire eventually paved the way not to metaphorical, but to literal serfdom in the strict feudal meaning of the term.


A TURN OF THE TIDE?

Yet, although these parallels are ominous, the comparison with the late Roman Empire shows only one of several roads along which we might travel. There are also more hopeful possibilities. The great advance of technology brings with it an immense range of options which were quite unknown to most societies before the twentieth century. For all the excesses cited on previous pages, the spirit of most of those who 'opt out' is more critical, less submissive to some mystical fate than that of the Manichaeans, neoplatonists or early Christian monks.

The instinctive revolt against a life grimly devoted to work and promotion is soundly based. There is a healthy mean between the superstitious worship of the Gross National Product and a belief in the sanctity of poverty. Behind the clichés about the 'quality of life' and 'the environment' is a well-founded suspicion of false goals which we are free not to follow.

The mistake of too many radicals is (a) to underestimate the forces working against the cosy 'New Industrial State' that many business leaders would admittedly love to establish and (b) to overrate the potentialities and gravely underestimate the risk of political accountability as a check on economic power. But their rejection of all the many arrangements and institutions which are neither responsible to the consumer through the market, nor politically accountable, nor subject to known laws, is sound and admirable.

In time they may come to see that the remedy is neither to indulge in nostalgia for a pre-industrial age, nor to talk about 'the revolution', but to promote an effective market in which all costs and benefits are properly priced and which are regulated by deliberately impersonal processes. More simply and crudely, there is a need to restore the entrepreneurial and even buccaneering element in capitalism at the expense of the managerial one. Then, given a proper framework of law, taxes and subsidies, we shall have no more Concordes or other loss-making home-based technological industries and produce more of the things that people actually want, whether these be leisure, peace and quiet, or a less hectic pattern of living, more consumer goods, or some combination of all of these.

The 'guerrilla capitalist' battling against the monopoly of the Post Office or broadcasting authorities is a small sign of a change in the direction of youthful energy and dissent. There are signs that some of those who 'opt out' are trying their luck at small scale entrepreneurial activities of their own, supplying many services on a personal, flexible basis impossible to the large public and private bureaucracies. Certainly the time is ripe for a realignment in which the more thoughtful members of the New Left and the more radical advocates of competitive free enterprise realise that they have a common interest in opposing the corporate industrial state.

There are built-in forces in modern society providing a ready audience for specious anti-capitalist propaganda which I have repeatedly emphasised in this prologue. But in optimistic moods I am impressed by the limits to human gullibility. There is a chance – how large I cannot predict – that the modern mixed economy will develop in a less materialist direction through the development of the attitudes and of institutions of a free society rather than through coercion from above or below. The revolt of young people against the pattern of their lives being decided by others or by impersonal forces they cannot influence is fundamentally justified. Precisely the same arguments are to be found in the classical defences of free markets, private property and limited government. Until recently technological limitations were such that freedom could be important only in the lives of a fortunate minority. It is now possible for all who are not afraid of it.

# 1  A Restatement of Economic Liberalism

'The chief benefit which results from philosophy . . . proceeds more from its secret insensible influence, than from its immediate application.'

David Hume, *The Sceptic*

## (a)  FUNDAMENTAL JUDGEMENTS

A liberal is someone who attaches special value to personal freedom. He desires to reduce the number of man-made obstacles to the exercise of actual or potential choice.

The concept of 'freedom' involved is what Sir Isaiah Berlin has called 'negative freedom'.[1] A man is said to be free to the extent that no other human being interferes with his activity. Freedom is not the same thing as equality, self-government, prosperity, stability or any other desirable state of affairs.

There is no need to derive all public policy from any one central goal. There is a plurality of goals which most of us, including liberals, seek to satisfy. These goals may sometimes be complimentary, but at other times are competitive with each other.\* A liberal attaches a specially great importance to freedom compared with other goals, but he need not give it total priority and ignore other goals. Absolute freedom is not even a possible objective, as one man's freedom must be limited to the extent that it interferes with the freedom of another, and there may have to be

---

\* There are some who argue that the weight given to particular goals, when there are conflicts between them, is, or should be, derived from some overriding principle such as utility or happiness. But any such overriding principle is likely to be of such a highly generalised and abstract kind that it will have to be broken into a number of sub-goals for even the most theoretical discussion of actual policy. The concept of a trade-off between goals is, in my view, more useful for the issues discussed in this essay irrespective of whether or not one believes that these goals are final ends or that they are derivable, in conjunction with empirical judgements, from some overriding ultimate criterion.

35

a choice between different types of freedom. All that a liberal can hope to do, as Hayek explains in *The Constitution of Liberty*,[2] is to minimise the role of coercion in human affairs. He cannot eliminate it completely.

The term liberalism has become so extended in contemporary discourse that for many people it means nothing more than a vague 'do-goodism'; indeed, in the USA 'liberal' is often a label for those who wish to extend the authority and role of the central government. Unfortunately, there is no good modern term which will convey the emphasis on personal freedom associated with the traditional meaning of liberalism. 'Individualist' conveys misleading associations. 'Libertarian', which has been used in the USA, is too ungainly. There can be no harm in using 'liberal' in its old-fashioned English meaning so long as this is made clear from the start. The important point is that liberalism in this sense represents a set of priorities with which it is possible for men of goodwill to disagree vehemently. It is not a synonym for some vague form of general enlightenment.

Liberalism, so defined, as has frequently been pointed out, is not identical with democracy. It can exist under a variety of political regimes. There can be personal freedom, both of expression and in economic decisions, under a dictatorship. The temptations the other way round are obvious; but the Enlightened Despots of the eighteenth century such as Joseph II of Austria, consciously tried to increase personal freedom, for example, by abolishing serfdom. A democracy on the other hand can – and too often does – insist on a high degree of conformity by its citizens.

The question with which a liberal is concerned is not so much 'Who is to govern?', but rather 'How much government is there to be, and of what kind?' At one extreme is a liberal regime, in which people are given the maximum freedom to make their own decisions. Next on the scale comes an authoritarian regime, which decides what is good for them (or the regime) over a wide area. But even under an authoritarian system people may have considerable choice in their own private and professional lives, provided that they keep quiet on certain topics and avoid clashes with the positive and negative injunctions of the authorities. Further on the scale is a totalitarian regime, which insists on making every aspect of personal life, including as far as possible thoughts and beliefs, conform to an ideological pattern – 'Big Brother is watching you'.

These distinctions are matters of degree. The most libe, society is likely to have certain restraints on personal conduct (for example, on the taking of drugs or on dress in public places) while in practice, even under the most totalitarian regime, a large part of life in peacetime for a large number of people, will consist of working, sleeping, eating, drinking and sex, in forms very little different to what would occur in a freer society.

What is the particular relevance of *economic* liberalism? The most obvious is an emphasis on the importance of freedom in the economic sphere. The bearing of liberalism on such issues as free speech, artistic censorship or non-interference in sexual activities between consenting adults is clear enough. But many of those who stress such matters do not realise that a commitment to freedom and personal choice also involves freedom to spend one's money in the way one chooses and to select one's own occupation; and this in turn has implications for the organisation of production, pay, prices and all other staple items of economic controversy.

One can make the further claim that the development of economic reasoning has provided insights into aspects of liberty, and perhaps even suggestions for extending it in practice, which go well beyond the realm of material goods. This should make political economy of particular interest to any liberal who can overcome any initial revulsion to its mundane subject matter or the minimum of formal reasoning involved.

The main argument does not, however, depend on this speculative and controversial assertion (which will be taken up further on p. 129). We can provisionally regard economic liberalism as a combination of certain basic views about ends with certain characteristic opinions about how these ends can be best achieved, even though the distinction between means and ends is not nearly as clear-cut as is popularly supposed, and the analysis of possible ways of achieving certain goals is bound to lead to further reflection on the nature of the goals themselves.

## Freedom and coercion

It is worth pointing out that a large weight can be attached to freedom on a number of different grounds. The classical exponent of 'negative freedom', John Stuart Mill, devoted the main part of *On Liberty* to a pragmatic defence of freedom as a means of achieving other ends: discovering truth, fostering independence of character, variety of life styles and so on. Hayek's more recent restatement in *The Constitution of Liberty* rests on very similar grounds. Great stress is laid on men's ignorance of the factors on which the achievement of their ends depends and on the danger of the state enforcing one path or blocking others. Hayek's argument is dependent on the case for progress, especially progress in the discovery of new knowledge. He does not say that progress leads to a better or happier state of affairs. Since human wants change in the process he doubts whether the question is a meaningful one. What matters, he believes, is successful or hopeful striving. It is in the 'living in and for the future in which human intelligence proves itself. Progress is movement for movement's sake.'[3]

'Arguments for freedom' are a risky business. The ultimate value, explicitly or implicitly involved, may be less appealing than freedom as an end in itself. It is perfectly possible for someone to value freedom despite, not because of, the 'progress' it is likely to bring. While it is true that zealous striving for new truths, deep and original thought about human values, imaginative and penetrating literature, and all the other goals with which liberals have identified, will certainly suffer in an efficiently regimented society, they may flourish quite well under an inefficient despotism. Czarist Russia is, of course, the obvious example; and one can also cite Habsburg Austria, which was hardly an ideal liberal society. The existence of obstacles, which are not insurmountable, are often an excellent creative spur. But even in the most favourable cases it would be best to argue that there is, as J. W. N. Watkins has put it, 'a happy coincidence' between freedom as a value in itself and these other benefits,[4] and not to identify them.

A good pragmatic argument for freedom is in terms of an implicit bargain. As Milton Friedman has pointed out,[5] if the case for free speech were considered on its merits and a separate vote were taken on whether the advocacy of communism, birth control, atheism, vegetarianism and other controversial views were to be permitted, the result in a great many cases would be 'No'. It is only by grouping all these cases in a bundle that one can hope for widespread support for freedom of expression. This is because the individual voter is likely to give so much weight to his desire for his own free speech on a favourite issue, where he may be in a minority, that he will in return be prepared to concede free speech to others, as the only feasible way of achieving his object. The argument might well apply to a great deal of personal conduct and not just the written or spoken word.

The best way to put the matter is that freedom lies, as Brian Barry has stated, 'at the *confluence* of a number of different considerations'.[6] Some people would regard negative freedom as an end in itself. Others will value it as a means for achieving other ends. In many cases there will be a mixture of considerations. Different considerations may come to the fore in different cases; and very often people will not have analysed their reasons for valuing it. The vital point for the liberal is that importance is attached to free personal choice, not why this is so.

There are innumerable different ways of classifying the constraints on individual action, related to the many meanings of the word 'can', which have given philosophers so many happy hours. Fritz Machlup has selected from them three different types of constraint which are frequently confused in political and economic discussion: (a) 'I am physically or mentally incapable of doing something', (b) 'I have not enough money to do it' and (c) 'I shall be prevented from or punished for doing it.'[7] This last type of constraint is the coercion which believers in freedom try to minimise. Nevertheless, it is not a precise concept; and it is all too easy to think of borderline cases between the three categories. The purest case of coercion would be where a person's hand is taken in a vice-like grip by some powerful human or automaton and physically forced to take action. But between this and the raised eyebrow of an admired friend there is an infinite series of gradations.

How about, for example, the power of an employer over an employee in a period of high unemployment and inadequate dole? The employee is free to depart and starve, just as a man can choose to be shot rather than do something at gun-point. Thus, although it would be highly dangerous to accept a concept of 'positive' freedom, which would be identified with employment, prosperity or any other popular policy aim, the borderline between 'positive' and 'negative' freedom is far from easy to draw. I should myself be inclined to say that there is more freedom, even in the negative sense, in a fully employed than an underemployed economy, everything else being comparable.

Borderline cases, which always exist, are not, however, a reason for obliterating distinctions. In general, coercion implies limitations imposed on a person's actions by his *fellow men*. Those on the 'left' are often inclined to argue that poverty – especially if it reflects remediable defects in social organisation – is a form of coercion. This makes the term so wide as to render it useless. Poverty is one evil and interference with a fellow man's activities another. Hayek, on the other hand, in *The Constitution of Liberty*, is inclined to go to the other extreme and limit the concept of coercion to *discretionary* control of one man's activities by another. He tends to regard hindrances to actions arising from *general* rules, which do not reflect the will of any particular human being, as akin to the hindrances imposed by nature, in being impersonal.

The distinction between the two kinds of restraint is certainly well worth making. A prohibition is felt more keenly if it is due to the arbitrary exercise of power by another human being, in whose power one is, than if it comes from known laws applicable to everyone placed in similar situations. Nevertheless, Hayek is narrowing the concept of coercion too far in limiting it (as Berlin does not) to the *discretionary* use of political power. A general rule made by human beings, and in principle repealable – for example, banning foreign travel for non-business purposes – is clearly coercive in character.

There is indeed a trade-off between severity and arbitrariness. It is well known that a strict regime in institutions such as schools or armies is resented less if it arises from known rules fairly enforced without favouritism than if the same degree of severity arises from unpredictable *ad hoc* actions of teachers or NCOs. On the other hand, it would be worth accepting some degree of unpredictability, capriciousness or even favouritism in an environment that is on average tolerant of a wide range of behaviour, if the only alternative is an extremely repressive system of prohibitions and sanctions imposed with scrupulous fairness on all concerned.

Coercion is best regarded as the presence of man-made restrictions on the range of actions one may undertake – whether these prohibitions come from restrictive laws, or the discretionary exercise of power by one individual over another. But it is not a one dimensional concept; both the severity and the degree of arbitrariness of the restraints imposed are relevant to assessing the degree of coercion to which a person is subject in any particular situation.

If someone insists on saying that a man's inability to fly to Australia, when he cannot afford the fare, reflects coercion –

because the inability is due to man-made rules requiring monetary payments and human institutions which affect the amount of money a person has – then there is no *a priori* way of ruling his definition out of order. Definitions are a matter of convenience. As J. W. N. Watkins has pointed out,[8] there is a scale of restraints from physical limitations, imposed by nature at one extreme, going on to limitations imposed by the state or society such as the size and distribution of incomes (which may themselves reflect physical or technological constraints as well as social institutions), prohibitions and duties laid down by general rules, and ending up at the other extreme with the arbitrary use of force to impose one man's intentions on another. The argument for drawing the boundary so that a prohibition on foreign travel counts as coercion, while inability to travel due to shortage of cash does not, is at bottom subjective. Low income is one sort of evil and prevention by one's fellow men of choosing one's own way of life within one's income, is another. The only argument I can offer to someone who is not conscious of this distinction is that we are more likely to advance both knowledge and policy if we distinguish between different evils and different desirable aims than if we put every kind of limitation on man's activities into one undifferentiated whole.

Coercion can take a positive form – a law or command requiring a person to do something, such as joining the army – or a negative form – such as proscribing certain activities such as the consumption of liquor, drugs or candyfloss. It would be generally agreed that positive coercion is a greater infringement of liberty; for negative coercion does leave open all the courses not officially proscribed. But negative coercion is coercion nonetheless; and, if the number of prescribed courses is sufficiently large or extensive, it can be highly oppressive. Indeed, in the limiting case a person can be forced to carry out a specific course of action by forbidding every feasible alternative (for example, a man without independent means can be forced to join the armed forces by being forbidden to take a civilian job). Thus, the distinction between positive and negative coercion is one of degree, rather than stark opposition.

An interesting unresolved question, among those who share the concept of freedom outlined above, is whether it is related to the range of alternatives or number of choices open to an individual. Granted that there are no coercive laws preventing one travelling where one wishes, does the opening up of new forms of transport, the railways in the nineteenth century, the airlines in the twentieth century or interplanetary travel in the twenty-first, increase personal freedom in the relevant sense? I am inclined to argue with those liberal writers who reply 'No',[9] on the grounds that this would be to confuse freedom with power or physical opportunity.

The negative form of coercion has, nevertheless, a bearing on the definition of the kind of prosperity that it is worth trying to maximise. Freedom should never be identified with prosperity or want-satisfaction of any kind. But someone who attaches importance to personal freedom of choice is likely to say that a person is 'worse off' (not necessarily more unhappy) if his range of choice is deliberately narrowed by some authority claiming to know his own interests better than he does himself. A paternalist or authoritarian might legitimately take a very different view. A moderate paternalist might say that he is saving the consumer from the adverse effects of candyfloss which he will discover for himself if allowed free choice. A more extreme Hegelian might argue that even if the consumption of candyfloss were not subsequently regretted by individuals, some mysterious organism known as the state or society would nonetheless suffer. Such 'philosophical' differences can be reflected in apparently highly technical discussions on, for instance, the way to measure 'real income'. One of the hallmarks of liberalism of particular relevance of economic policy is a reluctance to justify restrictions imposed upon a person for what someone else regards as his own good.

## (b) LIBERAL UTILITARIANISM

How does liberalism relate to utilitarianism? The latter was defined by a whole series of writers, from Epicurus to Bentham and Mill, as the doctrine that 'actions are right in proportion as they tend to promote happiness' or that 'pleasure and freedom from pain are the only things desirable as ends.[10] Defined in this way utilitarianism and liberalism are different social philosophies, which can often conflict, despite Mill's attempt to prove the contrary.

But in the century since Mill, the emphasis in utilitarian doctrine has shifted from the psychological intangibles such as 'happiness' or 'pleasure' to the satisfaction of wants or desires actually exhibited by people in their behaviour. The early twentieth-century English 'welfare economists', who were the intellectual heirs to the utilitarian tradition, reinterpreted it in this way; and this reinterpretation is probably accepted by the majority of practising economists in their analysis of policy problems. If utilitarianism means satisfying the desires that individual people actually have rather than what some authority or mob think would be good for them, there is then much less conflict with liberalism.

The traditional economist's case for a form of market economy has been based on what might be called *liberal utilitarianism*. This is a belief that individual desires should normally be satisfied to the maximum degree possible without interfering with the desires of others. The utilitarianism involved is a highly qualified one. As already mentioned, it seeks to satisfy the people's preferences as shown by their behaviour and not to measure or promote happiness in any direct way. It proceeds on the presumption that the individual should *usually* be regarded *as if* he is the best judge of his own interests. This presumption can be regarded as an inference from a fundamental belief in the importance of individual freedom; or it can be justified pragmatically as Mill and Hayek attempt to do by pointing out that, however badly an individual will make his own choices, anyone else acting on his behalf is likely to make them even worse, and that the resultant increase in governmental power is likely to block many paths to progress and knowledge that might have remained open if people had been left more to their own devices. *Anti-paternalism* is a useful synonym for the doctrine in many contexts.

The economic expression of liberal utilitarianism is sometimes known as *consumer sovereignty*, but this gives too narrow an impression. It is not only the types of goods and services produced, and the relative amount of each that should depend on the expressed preferences of individuals and families. The same should apply, as far as possible, to the choice between extra earnings and extra leisure, between more take-home pay and more congenial working conditions, and between present consumption and investment for future needs. It is not enough for the liberal that some sort of majority judgement should prevail on these questions; he seeks an economic system in which the great variety of individual preferences in these matters can be gratified to the greatest feasible extent rather than one which imposes some sort of average taste to which all have to conform.

Anti-paternalism is a matter of degree. There is no mysterious logical force which compels someone who favours a free choice between domestic and imported cars to commit himself to the general availability of hard drugs on demand. He does not have to be committed to anti-paternalism to the exclusion of all other values, but he believes that the onus is heavily on the paternalist to prove why any particular set of choices should be governed by the decisions of authority. (There is a distinction, emanating from Mill, between those forms of paternalism which are 'a preparation for freedom' and those which are not. This is too schoolmasterly a justification for restriction. But it would be useful if all paternalist measures, whether anti-drug laws or high taxes on tobacco, could be regarded as under permanent scrutiny and the question of their removal or relaxation considered at regular intervals.)

An additional qualification must be added before any doctrines of providing as many opportunities as possible for people to satisfy the wants they happen to have can be described as 'liberal'. The wants that a liberal will seek to satisfy exclude what Brian Barry, writing as a political philosopher, terms 'publicly oriented wants' and which economists call 'interdependence effects'. In plain English, a preference for butter over margarine or extra leisure over work, would be respected by a liberal. But he would not take into his calculations the 'want' felt by many respectable citizens for compulsory haircuts for long-haired youth, or the want of other citizens for compulsory restrictions on the number of villas or foreign trips that the wealthy can have. Wants of this type are disguised forms of coercion which arise from a desire to regulate the way in which other people spend their lives. The liberal form of utilitarianism is thus a heavily circumscribed form of the doctrine.

E. J. Mishan has, in his role as an economic theorist, explicitly suggested that 'interdependence effects', which are a polite way of describing 'resentment or envy of the achievements or possessions of others' should be sharply distinguished from 'external diseconomies such as smoke, noise and pollution.' The latter should emphatically be a matter of public concern; the former may merely 'elicit sympathy and require psychiatry.'[11] Mishan explicitly suggests, in an excellent textbook on project appraisal, that we should exclude 'interdependence effects' from consideration.[12] Mishan justifies his position on the basis of a supposed 'virtual constitution' containing a number of unwritten ethical propositions which are supposed to command widespread assent. Unfortunately, there is little evidence that this liberal desire to exclude prohibitions and deterrents justified by resentment, does command all that much support. Even some economists wax eloquently about 'interdependence effects' and treat them on all fours with other 'externalities' such as the pollution of rivers. Fortunately such economists have found it almost impossible to evaluate such effects in practice, and this is one of many reasons why the bias of the subject is more liberal, in the excellent negative sense, than many practitioners would personally like it to be.

One of the most fiercely debated topics among economic liberals is the role of changes in tastes, whether spontaneous or 'artificially' induced. From a strictly utilitarian point of view even a spontaneous change of tastes may seem a waste. Demand for commodity X is replaced by commodity Y; capital becomes obsolescent and investment which could have been used to raise real income (that is, supply a greater proportion of expressed desires in the first situation) now has to be devoted to replacing X. Therefore total satisfaction, as Mishan argues, is less than it might have been if God had prevented this change from occurring. *A fortiori*, the deliberate diversion of resources to advertising is wasteful, because it brings about changes of taste which might never have taken place, as well as subtracting resources which might have been used to satisfy existing tastes.

The validity of this argument, even on its own grounds, depends on the assumption that the total capacity for satisfaction remains unchanged. It is undeniable that changes in tastes, whether artificial or spontaneous, reduce the *proportion* of desires that can be satisfied. But if the total capacity for satisfaction increases because human imagination has been stimulated, a person may be better off with a smaller proportion of his desires satisfied after the changes than with a larger proportion satisfied in the original situation. On the other hand, if his total capacity for satisfaction declines – say, because he becomes restless and disturbed – then his welfare is reduced even further than Mishan's formal argument suggests.

To argue this way would, however, be to push utilitarian ethics further than they will go and brings us perilously near to suggesting not only an empirical enquiry into the causes of human satisfaction, but state action to enforce its findings. We would then have the paradox of a form of individualistic ethics apparently leading to Huxley's totalitarian *Brave New World*.

It is best to be frank and say that, in such cases, there might be a conflict between utilitarianism and freedom. To be allowed to attempt to change other people's tastes by non-violent means is an aspect of a free society. If this were banned, or regulated, it would be difficult to justify confining the restriction to advertising. Much political activity, virtually all the arts, and a good deal of philosophical speculation are an attempt to change tastes, and involve a diversion of resources from meeting existing tastes. Unchanged consumer tastes is a useful simplifying assumption in dealing with many practical problems, for example, in cost-benefit analysis, where it is reasonable to assume that changes in taste (for example, in noise aversion) are either slow or less important than the other factors involved. But it is not a valid long-term policy goal. *A free non-paternalist society may thus require a state of affairs which at any time is less than optimal from the point of view of meeting individual desires as they exist at any one time.* There is here yet another way in which liberal utilitarianism is a very qualified form of utilitarianism and why it is necessary to distinguish between the pure and the qualified versions. (Further discussion of the ways in which a belief in individual freedom would conflict with conventional utilitarianism will be found in Appendix II to this chapter.)

## The corrected market economy

A number of overlapping, but far from identical, terms have been used to label an economic system characterised by markets, decentralised decisions and a wide range of choices for consumer and producer. They include *the market economy, the price mechanism, competition, the profit motive, capitalism, private enterprise* and *free economy* to name only a few. These differ considerably in the political direction of their sales appeal.

'The market economy' and 'the price mechanism' are, in concept at least, independent of the structure of ownership; and they do not involve a commitment to the capitalist system. Some would argue that competition and even a form of the profit motive could be combined with state- or syndicalist-ownership, as is attempted for example in Yugoslavia. 'Capitalism', of course, indicates the private ownership of the means of production, distribution and exchange; but it will also be used here to describe a mixed economy which has a large capitalist element. 'Private enterprise' is most conveniently regarded as the slogan of those who wish any shift in the frontiers between the state and private sectors to be in favour of the private one. A 'free economy' is a much looser term which perhaps suggests a combination of several of the other elements – a competitive capitalist market economy, making maximum use of the price mechanism.

The 'market economy' is the most fundamental of all the concepts. As a first approximation, it can be said to describe a state of affairs in which those who own the means of production, distribution and exchange, as well as workers and consumers, pursue their own freely chosen ends rather than some supposed national good. The 'price mechanism' refers to an important part of the mechanism by which a market economy (and perhaps also some other types of economy) function and individual decisions are reconciled with each other.

A market economy can consist largely, or even entirely, of state-owned enterprises, provided that those who run them are allowed to respond to consumer demand and do not have to follow some politically determined 'plan'. As managers of such state concerns do not have a personal stake in their success they cannot be left entirely free to pursue their own ends and our provisional definition has to be modified. Some very general instructions such as 'maximise profits' may have to be given; and they may be reinforced by linking managerial remuneration with the results achieved. Managers running private concerns on behalf of shareholders have also to identify themselves artificially with a quest for profits which largely go to others; and similar conflicts of interest may arise. The opposite of a market economy is a *command economy*, in which the decision about what to produce, and how much, depends not on market demand but orders from the centre. The terminology is, interestingly enough, derived from discussion of Communist bloc countries, where elements of a market economy have had to be reintroduced in uneasy combination with the command element.

The basic insight behind the case for the market economy is that *under certain conditions* the self-interest of one human being *can* further the welfare of other human beings. In contrast to much popular belief trade is not a 'zero-sum game' like chess. Both parties to a transaction can benefit. The *profit motive* is a special case of the use of self-interest as a guiding force. The action of workers in seeking the employment with the best available combination of pay, working conditions and leisure is another. As Adam Smith put it long ago, we rely on the self-interest of the baker to provide our daily bread. Moreover, the forces of competition will encourage him to develop new types of bread and cheaper methods of baking, and prevent him from exploiting the consumers by obtaining an above-normal rate of return.

It is well known that the 'invisible hand' will work reasonably well only if certain conditions are fulfilled. There is a fair degree of consensus among economists both about what these conditions are and the kinds of corrective that may be appropriate if they are not fulfilled. A little will have to be said in very summary form about these conditions and the correctives in the next few pages – probably too much for the non-specialist and too little for the expert. (As the main conclusions of this chapter are not dependent on the details that follow, and a summary is provided, the reader with little taste for this sort of thing can safely skip over these pages to the section on Political Freedom starting on p. 74.)

The intricate controversies of 'welfare economics' concern refinements, paradoxes and conundrums within a body of propositions which are common property to most working economists, but are alien to most politicians and educated laymen. The statement of the conditions for a social optimum on liberal utilitarian assumptions fills many textbooks; and there is no point in trying to compress them in this essay. The basic tautology from which the others are derived is in E. J. Mishan's words that 'the social value of the marginal product of each distinguishable factor is the same in all its existing uses'.[13]

It is unfortunate that so much of the high grade intellectual effort has been devoted first to refining *optimum* conditions, which are never likely to be fulfilled, or to establish that nothing can be said in general terms about the principles of policy unless all the optimum conditions are fulfilled – a proposition which is itself a subject of dispute. It would be Luddite to decry the logical and mathematical exercises which lead to such results. But to use them as a blunderbuss to undermine all policy prescriptions by economists is to leave the field open to any charlatan, demagogue, interest group spokesman, or vote-bidder whose standards of argument are infinitely below those of the average working economist at his shakiest.

For all the difficulties that exist at the most rarefied level, there is in fact a body of 'informal welfare economics', which economists use in discussing real world problems. My *Is There an Economic Consensus?* suggests that two competent economists of different political views are likely to be much nearer in their approach to many problems than either would be to an intelligent layman, innocent of economics, who shared his politics. Indeed, there is probably more agreement among economists on the circumstances in which the profit motive does and does not promote the public welfare than on apparently less political and more technical areas.

The success of a market economy will depend a great deal on a monetary and fiscal framework which will minimise the likelihood of either slumps or runaway inflation. The best efforts of the financial authorities can, however, be undermined by union monopoly power, and this topic cannot be omitted from any economic policy agenda. It is here that economists are under the strongest temptation to abandon the liberal element of the liberal utilitarian tradition. The test, however, is not whether they say they are or are not in favour of an 'incomes policy' but what exactly they propose, and how they would deal with the complications and remoter consequences of any such policy.

The main discrepancies between the interest of individual citizens and the working of the profit motive, even in the absence of monopoly elements, arise from what is called under alternative terminologies, 'external economies' or 'dis-economies' (sometimes referred to as 'externalities'), 'spillover effects' or – most evocatively – 'neighbourhood effects'. These arise as the unintended result of some other activity; their effects are indiscriminate and those responsible can neither charge for them if they are beneficial nor be forced to pay for the damage if they are harmful. Chemical products discharged into a river impose harm on a community downstream which do not enter into the profit and loss account of the firm concerned. An extra car coming into London imposes costs on all other cars and on the passenger transport system, for which the driver does not have to pay.

A great many of these discrepancies can be corrected by general measures without either specific intervention or a 'central plan'. Competition can be encouraged by anti-trust laws or freer trading policies. Changes in the law could make firms liable for some of the 'disbenefits' they cause. Discrepancies between private costs and the 'spillover' costs imposed on others can be corrected by taxes and subsidies. For example, a motorist could be discouraged from coming into London by a congestion tax under which he would equate the marginal convenience of his journey with the marginal increase in congestion cost for everyone concerned and not just himself. This allows greater freedom of choice between motorists of different tastes and needs than does prohibition or licensing. Almost by definition the most important of these neighbourhood effects occur in regard to what is nowadays called 'the environment'.

There is also a category of services known as 'public goods', which cannot be sold in the market because they cannot, for technical reasons, be provided in different quantities to different people in accordance with their preference. One obvious example is defence; another is an urban park, which benefits both those who regard the fresh air and view as worth the cost and those who do not. In all such cases a political decision has to be taken. 'Public goods' are like favourable spillovers which convey indiscriminate benefits. The main difference is that their effects are intended rather than accidental.

The range of pure public goods is narrower than is sometimes supposed. Many services which are treated as public goods, such as health, higher education and social security and parts of housing, are provided collectively, either for frankly paternalist reasons, or as a backdoor method of bringing about some desired redistribution of income. However non-paternalist he is, a liberal utilitarian may still not be satisfied with the distribution of income thrown up by the market. His approach here would, however, be to put the emphasis on social benefits in cash, preferably through a negative income tax, rather than, on 'free' services in kind.

Policy disagreements among economists of an anti-paternalist hue are at several different levels. There are some quite important technical disagreements. A hoary chestnut is whether one should subsidise industries with declining *long-run* unit cost curves (of which there are fewer than is commonly imagined). Another is whether the rate of interest thrown up by the market really does measure the community's true preference between present and future consumption, whether because of the lack of a fully developed forward market, or other reasons.* An interesting recent controversy concerns the value of what has been given the unfortunate label 'indicative planning'. This can be given a strictly liberal interpretation, as Professor James Meade has done, in the form of providing producers with informed guesses about the consequences of certain possible developments, *which they are then free to follow or not.*[14] The value of such projections and stipulated relationships is an empircal matter depending on the predictability of the relationships involved and the risks that the project may degenerate under political pressure into either an exercise in wishful thinking or attempted government by interest groups.[15]

The really important disagreements do not in all probability relate to these well-known technical issues, and still less to discrepancies between 'ideal' growth paths in some mathematical models and what actually does happen. Just as it is illegitimate to make out a case for non-intervention on the basis of some idealised version of a market economy, it is equally illegitimate to base arguments for intervention on comparisons between messy, real world markets and some ideal plan which could be introduced by an omniscient government free from interest groups and guided solely by disinterested concern for some non-paternalist conception of the public interest.

Major differences within the liberal utilitarian camp reflect much more different beliefs about where the onus of proof should be placed in deciding when to intervene in practical instances. As Milton Friedman remarks, some 'neighbourhood effects' can be conjured up to justify almost any conceivable act of intervention. Most economists would favour taxes and subsidies (and perhaps a few out-and-out prohibitions), when there are large and obvious spillover effects, and would support cost-benefit studies (hopefully of a more sensitive and civilised kind than some we have seen) when large projects with obvious environmental effects are being considered. But to do beyond this and advocate

---

* The whole 'ecological' controversy about whether the growth of material production should be drastically curtailed to preserve a tolerable planet concerns vast 'neighbourhood effects' posited for some future date. Because these threats are remote in time and the growth of our knowledge of ways of meeting them cannot be predicted, the whole problem is shrouded in enormous uncertainty. The controversies are further compounded, however, by differences of view about how much weight to give to the welfare of generations yet unborn.

discretionary state intervention in every private sector activity involves all of at least the three following empirical judgements: (a) that the unpriced spillover effects are likely to be large in relation to the costs of intervention, (b) that officials will have enough knowledge of cost conditions and individual preferences, now and in the future, to improve on the unaided market outcome, and (c) and most important of all, that the government action will not in practice be largely influenced by local, political and industrial pressures (or prestige considerations) which would lead to a worse result than that of the unaided market.

Another kind of apparent disagreement is largely a matter of presentation. To the extent that there is a consensus on how the market works, it can be summarised for popular purposes in ways which are equally valid, but which have a very different political flavour. One economist can say that the market economy works well given the right environmental policies; another, who holds identical views on actual issues, can emphasise how much intervention is required to correct the evils of uninhibited market forces. (We are still at this stage talking about any market economy and waiving the question whether it has to be capitalist.)

There is indeed an ambiguity about the way the term 'market economy' is used in current political and economic discussion. A liberal writer may put forward a positive case for a market economy to emphasise the paternalist and anti-consumer bias of many interventionist policies, to stress that 'production for profit' *need* not be the evil that is supposed in Labour Party demonology, and that the alternative slogan of 'production for use' is, on the most charitable interpretation, a meaningless one. Nevertheless, someone who talks about a market economy is widely understood to mean *laissez-faire*. To meet this difficulty, the German neo-liberals have coined the term 'social market economy'. But, as Hayek has pointed out, the word 'social' is not only vague and confusing, but risks giving the impression that there are such things as higher purposes over and above the purposes of individuals.[16] It is probably best to avoid misunderstanding and to use the colourless expression, 'corrected market economy', if one wants to emphasise that appropriate policies are being followed to provide a suitable environment in which the market can function, and that discrepancies between private and social costs and benefits are taken into account.

## The price mechanism

The influence of prices on economic behaviour in most, if not all, known societies is a fact of life, in no way dependent on the political philosophy of the person observing this influence. Most popular discussion about prices refers to the rate at which their average level (the cost of living) is rising; and economists struggling with the inflation conundrum are certainly conscious of this problem. They are also, however, at least as interested in another aspect of prices – that of prices of different goods and services relative to each other. Prices are here very broadly defined to include items such as wages, rents, interest rates and, indeed, the charge made for any commodity or service that is sold for money or even barter.

Both the demand for and the supply of goods and services are normally assumed to be related to the incomes of those involved in the transactions and to the prices offered or asked, relative to the prices of other goods and services. The effect of price upon supply can be in either direction. An increase in wages for a large category of workers can lead either to more hours being put in, because work is now more attractive relative to leisure, or less hours being put in, because a smaller number now suffice to provide a given target income. The more narrowly the category of work is defined the more likely is a higher price to lead to more effort. A general increase in agricultural workers' wages, relative to other occupations, could lead to fewer hours being put in per worker. It is also likely to lead to more people wishing to become agricultural labourers (or fewer people leaving the land than otherwise); and this may or may not outweigh the effects on hours per worker – the time scale considered being of relevance here. What one can say with great confidence is that an increase in the price expected to be realised for a particular foodstuff, relative to other foodstuffs and to the general price level, will lead to an increase in output of the commodity in question, even if it means switching agricultural labourers from other activities.

The demand for a product or service is normally expected to be smaller the higher the price, relative to the general price level. This relationship of the demand for a commodity to the price charged is a tautology if a person's (or a country's) money income is constant and a particular price varies. After all, if the price rises high enough, expenditure on an unchanged quantity of the commodity in question will absorb the whole of one's income. Although this tautology is interesting in some situations (for example, in the analysis of a devaluation), much more interesting is the sensitivity of the demand for a particular commodity to a change in its price when there is no change in real income (either because other prices move in a compensatory direction or because there are compensatory increases in money income). This pure 'substitution' effect of differences in relative prices is an empirical phenomenon, which can be observed by watching a housewife in a supermarket. The degree of responsiveness to such relative price changes is a matter for observation rather than armchair reflection.

The above is but the briefest of sketches of relations which are elaborated at considerable length in books on economic principles. The *price mechanism* refers not to just these properties of prices, but the way in which they can be used to bring some form of order and co-ordination into a wide range of human activities. *The expression can refer both to the spontaneous adjustments of the market and to the deliberate manipulation of prices by political authorities to change the working of the market – whether in aid of liberal utilitarian goals or more paternalist ones.*

If we are talking of the major products of an advanced industrial society, and not of a few specialist markets or bazaars, it is mainly in the allocation of resources *in the long run* that the price mechanism has a major role to play. If there is a reasonable degree of competition and entry is free to newcomers, prices will bear a roughly similar ratio to costs, including among costs the going rate of return on capital, in different branches of the economy. Assuming a public policy which charges enterprises for the major 'neighbourhood' or 'spillover' costs which do not appear in their accounts (and if possible rewards them for spillover benefits) and reasonably high overall employment, the resulting price structure will indicate to people the true alternatives that are open to society – how many refrigerators would have to be forgone to produce an additional motor car, the sacrifice in output of consumer goods that would make possible a given addition to the number of coach tours or National Park wardens, or the sacrifice of goods and services of all kinds required to make possible a given addition to leisure and so on. In other words, the structure of relative prices gives some idea of what economists call the 'opportunity cost' of different goods and services.

Over the time horizon in question there is unlikely to be shortage or surplus. For we have been considering a period long enough for production be increased to remedy any shortages and reduced to eliminate surpluses. Thus, the relative price structure not only indicates the costs of different items of foregone alternatives, but also represents the valuation that consumers place on their marginal purchases. In this way the market system will produce, in suitable circumstances, the goods that people happen to want, rather than what some authority – or their fellowmen – think they ought to have, in the light of prices that convey information about the true costs of the various alternatives.

For the system to work in this way there must be, in the long run, freedom to compete on all aspects of the service offered. The business apologist cannot be allowed to get away with saying that, despite the existence of a price ring, there is competition in 'quality' or fierce sales rivalry. The consumer is being deprived of the option of paying a lower price with less service by the collusive action of producers. Competition does not presuppose private ownership, although to introduce it into the state sector may require deliberate policies which will go against the grain of those most actively concerned and may run up against the statutory monopoly status enjoyed by industry-wide nationalised undertakings.

This is a convenient place to dispose of the widespread fallacy that the case for the market economy depends on the existence of something called 'perfect competition'. This whole approach is based on an edifice of misunderstandings. 'Perfect' and 'imperfect', when applied to competition, are not terms of praise or blame. 'Perfect competition' is said to exist when a firm faces a 'perfectly elastic' demand for its product. This means that it is responsible for such a small part of total supply, and the product is so standardised and the element of goodwill so small, that the firm can sell all it likes at the going market price. If it raises its prices even slightly it will lose all its customers; if it lowers them, it would be overwhelmed with far more orders than it could supply.

This state of affairs prevails mainly in some produce and financial markets. But the concept of perfect competition was arrived at, not from an observation of such markets, but from an attempt to set out in mathematical form the theory of a competitive economy. Later writers then observed that under certain very restrictive conditions it would produce an 'optimum' pattern of output, with production of goods corresponding to consumer preferences, and with each firm producing on a scale that gave it the lowest possible long-run production costs. The main conditions required for this to occur include static technology and static consumer preferences, and the exhaustion of all economies of scale at a small size of firm. They also include the absence of both direct and indirect taxes, which distort the choice between income and leisure.[17]

The degree of competition in a dynamic economy cannot be measured by reference to the yardstick of perfect competition. As Schumpeter long ago observed, the industries where progress has been most rapid are often dominated by large-scale firms far removed from perfect competition. The most effective kind of competition is from the 'new commodity', the new technology, the new source of supply, the new type of organisation.' The threat of competition of this kind is a powerful influence on existing firms, particularly in oligopolistic situations such as the oil or car industries. At any one time the existing firms are in a privileged position; but prolonged failure to improve products or introduce low-cost methods, or any attempt at monopoly pricing, would attract newcomers which would threaten their hold. This does not mean that the public authorities should just stand aside. But the features to watch are the freedom of entry of newcomers into the industry, and imports into the country, as well as the laws relating to restrictive practices. Perfect competition is virtually useless as a yardstick here.

It is, of course, wrong to suppose that even in the most favourable cases, the self-adjusting price mechanism provides any sort of *optimum* distribution of resources. The most that can be reasonably claimed is that with the aid of the corrective devices repeatedly emphasised in these pages, the price system provides a rough and ready way of making those who take economic decisions pay attention to people's preferences whether as consumers or workers, savers or investors, gamblers or insurers.

Nor does the departure of the pattern of prices from what would be the optimum in a static world, where we were satisfied with the distribution of incomes, matter all that much from the point of view of either prosperity or freedom – the twin goals of the liberal utilitarian. The key influence on either our prosperity or its rate of growth is not whether the price of a specified coach tour relative to a refrigerator is 11:8 when it ought to be 8:11. (Comparisons of exact cost-price relations are mainly of importance when comparing close substitutes, for example, alternative fuels.) What is important, both for freedom and for want-satisfaction, is that, if an increase in the demand for coach tours makes the activity more profitable, the supply of such tours should be allowed to respond and not be held back because some economic planners regard manufacturing output as more important. The effectiveness of such responses, and the speed with which businessmen adopt the procedures that would pay them best and are already in use in the most advanced firms, has more bearing on the rate of growth than exactly how far from the ideal the existing pattern of prices, costs and profits happens to be. This kind of responsiveness to a given economic environment has been christened 'X-efficiency' – which is another way of saying that economists can tell us little about it.

In the foregoing summary explanation I have been very careful not to suggest that prices are used to eliminate shortages of surpluses in any but a long period sense. Day-to-day rationing by price is nowadays more the exception than the rule. Economic activity can be largely guided by market demand, yet prices may be fairly inflexible for many months at a time. Car firms may allocate popular models by 'waiting lists' rather than by raising prices, and they may reduce production of an unpopular car without experimenting with price changes. Branded products do not change in price daily in response to market conditions. Firms with surplus labour are more likely to cease recruitment or declare redundancies than reduce wages, while those with labour shortages may hope to pick up unemployed labour without bidding against other firms. Thus, in the short run, shortages and surpluses may take the place of price changes as signalling devices.

*Free markets* can be said to exist in those markets where the price of an article is free to vary from day to day, or at least at very frequent intervals, in such a way as to equate supply and demand and clear the market. Examples include the stock market, the second-hand car market, many of the food and raw material exchanges, and the house market. The perfect markets, already mentioned, are a special case of free markets where the product is standardised and no individual seller or buyer is big enough to exert a perceptible influence on the price. At the other extreme is the house market, or the art market, where the items on sale are differentiated and individual buyers and sellers have an all too perceptible influence on the going rate.

Whereas the case for the price mechanism to allocate resources in an adjusted market economy derives in the last analysis from the liberal utilitarian value judgements outlined at the beginning of this essay (plus one or two elementary observations about human behaviour), the case for free markets depends on much more concrete empirical judgements. Those who dislike free markets would claim that the short term responsiveness of demand and/or supply to price changes is small; and that free prices generate large and disturbing fluctuations which are aggravated rather than smothered by speculative activity.

A perennial example of this controversy is that over exchange rates. The case for using the exchange rate mechanism to balance international payments in preference to controls or otherwise unnecessary deflation, is a matter of principle. But the case for freely floating exchange rates, in place of adjustments of official parities, is a matter in the last resort to be judged empirically. Nearly all the serious studies that have been made suggest that the allegations that genuinely floating rates fluctuate widely and are disturbing to trade are central bankers' or businessmen's myths. Most of the alleged instances have either been of fixed rates under pressure, or (as after 15 August 1971) of disturbances due to interference by the authorities with the functioning of the market, combined with the belief that rates would be fixed again after political haggles of uncertain outcome. Where genuinely free rates have moved rapidly, it has been due mainly to highly inflationary domestic policies which would, in any case, have brought about a devaluation.[18]

The trap to avoid in discussing all such questions is to compare the degree of instability of actual free markets with some imagined, ideal smooth path of adjustment. A debating point sometimes made against floating rates is that share prices do not move smoothly, but exhibit pronounced fluctuations around their trend. There are reasons for expecting freely floating exchange rates to fluctuate less than share or commodity prices;[19] but it is worth asking why those who make this point do not advocate either extensive official intervention to smoothen out share fluctuations or the fixing of share prices by financial institutions, to be changed only where there is clear-cut evidence of a 'fundamental' imbalance of supply and demand (as actually happens on some overseas exchanges with lesser securities). Can it be that they are not so confident, after all, that the steplike movements resulting from such arrangements would lead to more stability (however that is defined) than actual stock exchanges with all their faults?

A little reflection suggests, however, that even outside the purely financial sector the absence of free markets is only tolerable, from the point of view of either freedom or efficiency, because of the presence of safety valves. Someone on a waiting list for one car model can switch over to a close substitute, often imported; or he can use the second-hand market. Many consumer goods producers aim to have a modest margin of unused capacity in a normal year so that production can be stepped up fairly quickly. The use of bonuses, overtime offers and all the other apparatus of 'wage drift' to entice new workers is well enough known; if some well meaning 'incomes policy' or TUC–CBI agreement were to stop such payments, we should really know the meaning of economic crisis. The relatively free market in furnished dwellings is, of course badly distorted by rent controls elsewhere; but without this safety valve many people would be unable to find rented accommodation at all. Although the text-books may exaggerate the extent to which prices are set on a continuous market-clearing basis in a modern economy, the existence of a number of markets which do work in this way is not a matter of indifference, and they should be encouraged rather than suppressed.

## Environmental effects

So far the price mechanism has been described as a system of automatic adjustment. But, as already mentioned, it can also be used as a weapon of government policy. It can be used by a liberal utilitarian regime to improve the market economy as an instrument for satisfying individual desires. Taxes or subsidies can be imposed where there are spillover costs or benefits which the unaided market does not take into account. Sometimes it may be possible to internalise costs, which are at present external – for example, by imposing an obligation to pay compensation at market values for various kinds of damage to other people's property or amenity. Even where it is impracticable to change the law in this way, a good cost–benefit study will seek to assess the actual value that people affected place on the environmental losses from a proposed new product – either how much they would pay to stop it or how much they would need in compensation to waive their objections. The two approaches can yield very different results, but either is better than ignoring the environmental damage, or abstract debating on 'environment' versus 'growth' which ignores the technical trade-offs and the preferences of those concerned. The effect of a project on property values can also give a clue and, in default of other methods, survey data, properly interpreted, can be of help.[20]

Indeed, state intervention of all kinds, whether motivated by liberal utilitarian considerations or more paternalist ones, can employ the price mechanism. Special depreciation allowances or investment grants are in fact subsidies to investment – which may be justified as an offset to the deterrent against investment provided by the rest of the tax system. The Selective Employment Tax was a price mechanism technique for discouraging the shift from manufacturing to services. The Regional Employment Premium was designed as a subsidy to reduce the cost of labour to the employers in the high unemployment areas.

Clear examples of the use of the price mechanism out of a paternalist desire to encourage certain activities or discourage other include heavy taxes on drink and tobacco and subsidies for sports grounds. (One motive for such taxes may be revenue-raising, but the revenue-raisers could not get away with such heavy discrimination against particular goods if they could not cloak it as paternalist disapproval of 'social vices'.) The interesting point is that the price mechanism is a relatively *liberal means* of carrying out even *illiberal policies*, by comparison with prohibition and orders. State action will impart a bias against smoking and drinking and in favour of sport, compared with the unimpeded action of market forces; but individual behaviour will still vary according to personal tastes.

An interesting example of the use of the price mechanism as a relatively liberal means of control is the proposal by William Baumol and Wallace Oates for the setting up of certain 'environmental standards', for example, to achieve a given level of purification of a river or to halve the level of sulphur dioxide emission into the atmosphere. The justification for imposing these 'arbitrary' standards might be that here is an area where a measure of paternalism is justified – people affected by the widespread application of DDT might lack the technical knowledge to assess its harmful effects and put too low a monetary value on it; or it might be the simple, pragmatic one advanced by Baumol that we do not know the marginal net valuation that people affected would put on the environmental spillover from various industrial activities, and the best we can do is to make a political guess about what the outcome would be if these adverse spillovers could be properly priced.

The interesting aspect of this proposal, which distinguishes it from similar proposals emanating from physical scientists, is that the required environmental standards would be obtained, not by regulations or prohibitions, but by levying a sufficient tax on all effluents poured into a river, which would vary according to the organic waste load of the effluent, or by a tax on smoke emissions.

Professor Baumol justifies his use of the price mechanism approach on the grounds that it is the least costly method of achieving the required standards. Those firms that can reduce smoke or effluent emission at relatively little cost will bear the bulk of the reductions; those for whom such reductions are very expensive or physically impossible will pay the tax (which may, via its effect on prices, reduce their total output). But the argument could also be put in terms of freedom of choice. Taxes are set at a level which is found sufficient to achieve certain environmental standards; but the individual firm is given the choice how far it should pay the tax and how far it should reduce the quantity of its emissions. Those who cannot bring themselves to attach any value at all to freedom for a firm (even though this is likely to benefit the employees as well as directors) have only to transfer the example to activities performed by individuals – taking cars into city centres, 'over-fishing' in rivers, the use of detergents which create disposal problems, and so on.

*An eagerness to use the price mechanism is probably the most important single feature linking the policy views of economists of otherwise very varying persuasions.* Many of those who are most sceptical of the workings of unimpeded free markets are strong proponents of correctives which work by influencing prices. Devaluation, the 'crawling peg', the Selective Employment Tax, the Regional Employment Premium, and parking meters are all price mechanism devices – in a way in which price *controls*, prohibitions, restrictions and quotas are not. This liberal bias of economists does not reflect any moral virtue, but the fact that their professional competence lies almost entirely in assessing functional relations between supply and demand and prices, income and wealth.

Unfortunately, the allocative functions of the price mechanism have never been understood by the general public, or even the politically conscious section of it. This is due partly to a confusion between the goal of price stability (or minimum inflation), which relates to the general level of *all* prices, and price *relativities* between different goods (or occupations). Understanding has not been helped by the incessant exhortation involved in prices and incomes policies; a genuine difficulty is that the correction of long-overdue price relativities – which in practice often means an increase in the prices of basic services such as fuel or rent – will, when other prices are sticky, not merely lead to a once-for-all rise in the general price level, but may also stimulate a continuous process of cost inflation.

Nevertheless, it is doubtful if the confusion caused by the inflationary issue explains entirely the public hostility to the use of price mechanism and its attachment to the medieval idea of a 'just price'. One obvious objection is the distributional point that a change in relative prices always makes some people worse off relative to others. This is rationalised by saying that the poor usually suffer if prices, instead of administrative allocation or queuing is used as a rationing device – rents or school meals being stock examples.

There are, of course, other ways of offsetting any adverse distributional effect of relative price changes by means of the tax and social security system. Moreover, it is doubtful if the price mechanism would gain much in people's affections even if it were clear that its use would not shift the distribution of income against the poor. One did not notice much enthusiasm for the use of metering devices to price scarce road space in towns. (One of the first such meters entered a room in Ernest Marples' house via a broken window.) It is tempting to be patronising and talk about the low level of economic literacy among voters, but I am afraid that hostility to the price mechanism and belief in the 'just price' reflects a deeper illiberalism which is discussed further in later sections and illustrated by the hypothetical example in Appendix II.

## Freedom or prosperity?

Liberal utilitarianism was described as a policy aimed at satisfying wants, with want-satisfaction defined in such a way as to be not identical with but consistent with, personal freedom. The goal of the 'corrected' market economy can very loosely be regarded as aiming to secure a combination of freedom and prosperity. The two are certainly not the same but are not all that easy to disentangle, because once we cease to be mesmerised by the veil of money, prosperity is an even more difficult concept to unravel than freedom; and the problem is not solved by using more technical sounding terms such as 'aggregate real income' or 'economic welfare'. It is worth asking to what extent different types of infringements of the ideals of the corrected market economy are infringements of freedom and to what extent they are simply holding down the level of prosperity.

Let us start with an example heavily weighted towards the anti-prosperity side, the subsidisation of one fuel so that its price to marginal cost ratio differs very markedly from that of close substitutes and where there are no discrepancies between private and social costs of a type that justify such different pricing policies. Now, there is an element of interference even with negative freedom in this operation. If one believes that coercion is a matter of degree, the consumer is being pushed by government into buying more of one fuel and less of another than he would like. But even if there are numerous examples of these distortions in the economy, the effects on freedom are relatively trivial; and the issues are to be regarded as ones of industrial policy rather than human liberty. In assessing the degree of freedom that exists in the society, we should give them little weight compared with questions such as whether conscription exists, the degree of coercion practised on minors, the extent of civil liberties and the absence or presence of censorship.

But we should pause a moment before dismissing such instances altogether even if our main concern is with freedom rather than industrial efficiency. Freedom of choice of occupation and freedom to spend one's money in one's own way are vital freedoms of the negative kind. A system in which a 'Control of Engagements Order' was enforced (as Diocletian attempted more successfully than the Labour Government of 1947) or where a great many activities, which did not harm other people, were prohibited or restricted by severe rationing, would take us far on the road to serfdom. As Fritz Machlup points out, a dictator who wished to decide what it was good for people to consume and which occupations they should follow, could, in theory, achieve his aims by an extreme manipulation of the price mechanism. He could set very high prices for products of which he disapproved and very low ones for those he liked; he could ordain very low wages for some 'undesirable' activities and high ones for virtuous activities.[21] The resulting heavy losses in some occupations could be offset by subsidies. This would be a less unfree society than one in which individual people were told which jobs to do, an example of our earlier dictum that the price mechanism can be a liberal means even of carrying out illiberal policies. Nevertheless, the society could hardly be regarded as other than a highly regimented one.

At what stage 'perverse' intervention in the market economy becomes a serious threat to freedom is a matter of fine judgement – and of interest to those who could not care less about the GNP or economic growth. Personally I would attach a good deal of value to the fringe free markets, such as that in furnished accommodation or in the phenomenon of wage drift, where market clearing prices are allowed to operate. Their suppression, which a misguided reforming government might attempt at any time, would be a serious narrowing of the range of choice otherwise open to people, compared with which the muddles over energy prices or the road–rail fare structure are of minor importance.

A clear example of misguided interference with the market economy, which is of more importance for freedom than for prosperity, is foreign travel restrictions. An instance of the blindness of the Left to the economic aspects of freedom was the readiness of the Labour Government to impose in 1966 a travel allowance which virtually confined Britons to this country, except for a two weeks' cheese-paring vacation, as a cheap political gesture. Yet one of the severest restrictions it is possible for governments to impose on personal liberty in time of peace, which remained in operation for over three years, was greeted with hardly a word of protest from Labour's intellectual camp-followers, many of whom had ample opportunity of travel for official, business or cultural purposes.

Such restrictions on foreign travel have an adverse effect on prosperity, real incomes and living standards; but this is very much a secondary aspect. It is perfectly possible to imagine a situation where there is a political veto on devaluation, or where the adverse effects on the terms of trade of a successful devaluation are believed to be very great, and in which the imposition of a stringent travel allowance makes possible an expansion in output, income and employment, which for most people more than compensates for the travel curbs; and the total package may not have an adverse impact on the relative position of the poor, but even improve it. Yet a severe diminution of personal liberty remains – just as it would if bribes were paid to people to vote for the censorship of political views, resulting in a majority in favour of the measures – a majority who would, by definition, be 'better off' as, given the choice, they had preferred the bribes to free speech.

Both the point and the limitations of liberal utilitarianism, and its derivative, the 'corrected' market economy, can be illustrated by the perennially topical example of 'lame-duck' industries. The Conservative Government after the 1970 General Election set out the case for not propping up such industries in the most unconvincing and repellent form possible. Whether intentionally or not, Ministers gave the impression that imposing discomforts on those managing or working in unprofitable industries was almost desirable in itself because it would 'wake people up to their responsibilities'. They seemed to take positive pleasure in the fact that life would be 'less cosy' or 'less comfortable' in activities for which state support was to have been withdrawn.

To an economic liberal these unpleasant effects are drawbacks, not advantages. The real argument against supporting loss-making activities, which cannot justify themselves on the basis of demonstrable spillover benefits, is the harm that such support inflicts on the material welfare and on the freedom of consumers. Protective devices for lame-duck industries force the rest of the population to purchase goods from a particular source, and to make sacrifices in their living standards for the sake of privileged producer groups. Moreover, if there is any mobility of labour or facilities for retraining and opportunities for jobs elsewhere, the gains to the protected group will diminish over time. Given that we are all consumers and anyone may find himself a lame duck, it is probable that a mutual understanding to abjure these make-work policies (as exists in Social Democratic Sweden), together with generous financial assistance for those making the readjustment, would be in the best interests of most people including the lame ducks themselves.

Although the above argument puts the emphasis on the loss of potential material welfare, the freedom aspect is not negligible. All taxation is a form of coercion – albeit of the negative kind – in that it prevents an individual spending a portion of his income in his own way. If taxation approached 100 per cent and people had to depend on supplies provided collectively, the degree of coercion would be very great indeed. But a lesser degree of taxation is a necessary evil if we are to enjoy the benefits of 'public goods'. The relationship between taxation and coercion is probably a non-linear one. A large amount of negative freedom can exist in a society where the average person pays 20 per cent of his income. A significant erosion has taken place if this proportion rises to 40 per cent, but we could still be talking about a largely free society. At 60 per cent rates it would not be hysterical to say that people's choices were being largely made for them by the state; and at an 80 per cent rate the society would be a free one only in name.* Subsidies out of taxation for aerospace products, high technology computers or shipyards for which there is no commercial demand are, other things being equal, a restriction on people's freedom to spend their money in their own way; and if it is superimposed on a state of affairs where tax rates tend to be in the 30–40 per cent bracket in any case, it has to be very carefully justified by some countervailing material benefit either to some deserving group or to the population as a whole.

## Compensating the victims

Reference to 'generous financial assistance' to the victims of change does expose an inherent ambiguity in liberal utilitarian philosophy, as soon as we come to ask 'How generous?' The liberal utilitarian aim is to provide as much as possible of what people say that they want in the light of correct information about 'opportunity costs'. But in real world changes some people will lose and others gain. To overcome this difficulty, the concept of a

---

* The percentage should, strictly speaking, be net of cash benefits returned to citizens to spend as they like. For some discussion of actual magnitudes, see my chapter in *Taxation Policy* (Penguin, 1973).

'potential Pareto improvement' has been invented for a change in which the gains *could* be so redistributed so that no one is worse off and some people are better off.

Unfortunately the concept of a potential improvement is very ambiguous. Apart from the numerous scholastic paradoxes that fill the literature, the state of the law can make a very real difference to whether a change appears as a potential Pareto improvement or not. A good example is the construction of a new airport. It is quite possible that the maximum sum that the individuals of the area – if they could be properly mobilised – would be prepared to pay to the airport authority not to go ahead would be insufficient to stop construction on a profit-and-loss calculation. So it would look as if the gains exceed the losses and that the airport represented a potential Pareto improvement. The inhabitants could still be compensated by paying them what they would have been prepared to pay to stop the airport.

Now let us suppose that the airport authority is not entitled to go ahead without the consent of the inhabitants. A very much larger sum might be required; so large that the airport would not be built. It would then look as if the losses exceeded the gains and the airport did not represent a Pareto improvement at all. It is not fanciful to suppose that, even if all the inhabitants could be properly organised and could suppress their sense of outrage at the request, they would be only able and willing to pay, say £20m, to stop an airport being built, while if they themselves had the right of veto even £100m would not be enough to persuade them.[22]

Clearly, the wider the range of legal liability and the greater the number of changes which are allowed to take place only on payment of compensation that the victims consider adequate, the slower will be the pace of material change. The wealthier a society becomes the stronger the case for shifting the onus of compensatory payments on to those who want to make the change. For the harm caused by disturbing people's expectations and patterns of life must loom larger the higher the whole community is above the poverty line and the less urgent the overall growth of output.

There are, nevertheless, difficulties in going the whole hog with Mishan and giving full legal rights to the victims of change. There is the obvious incentive to lie or exaggerate. If I have a veto over the construction of an airport, I would be tempted to ask for far more than the sum of money genuinely required to compensate me for the loss I would suffer. But, even if absolute sincerity could be guaranteed, what would be the situation of an old lady who does not believe in the hereafter, who finds that her life would be shattered either if the airport were built or if she had to move? (Sound insulation would be no use, as she has to sit out in the fresh air.) She might rationally regard the whole of the national income of the UK as insufficient compensation.

Transfer this example to a shipyard threatened with closure. Imagine a worker unwilling or too old to retrain, but whose pride would be hurt by being out of work and who would prefer to continue in his present job at his present wage, even if offered an immensely large capital sum as an alternative. The principle of compensation to victims of change has to be watered down in some common sense way to what the majority of those concerned could be reasonably expected to accept. It is often said half-jocularly by the officials and executives involved that it might be cheaper to pay each man now employed £1000 per annum until retired, or a lump sum of £10 000, than to keep a particular mine, shipyard or aircraft project going. If this is really so, it would surely be better to pay compensation and close down the operation.

With large and obvious changes, such as the closing down of a shipyard or an aircraft firm, there will be strong support for actual rather than potential compensation to the victims of change. It is unfortunate that the likelihood of this demand will depend on the publicity generated and emotional appeal of the issue for the media; and one would prefer to see more systematic machinery which could be of help to many victims of smaller changes which do not achieve the same publicity, but which often cause far greater human hardship. Nevertheless, complete compensation of all victims of change would be of doubtful desirability. An anti-interventionist would always be able to argue that the choice of occupation is itself a gamble, and full compensation would involve subsidising high risk activities. His opponent could reply that the ordinary worker cannot choose but take the gamble that is associated with a choice of job, and therefore be confronted with a non-insurable risk. Complete compensation, even as an ideal solution, should apply only to those below a certain income or wealth level, and should not apply to shareholders who are knowingly engaged in providing 'risk capital'.

But, even qualified in this way, full compensation to all victims of change is never likely to be practicable. Differences in attitudes within the liberal utilitarian camp often depend on how far the economist in question insists that there should be an *actual*, as distinct from a *potential*, 'Pareto improvement'. One reason for the hostility to market forces of some unquestionably anti-paternalist economists arises from a preoccupation with income distribution so extreme that changes caused by market forces will not be accepted without cast-iron guarantees that the less well-off will be invariably and fully compensated for any adverse impact they might conceivably suffer. A more middle-of-the-road, and also more reasonable, position is to support market remedies, except where the adverse distributional implications are large and unambiguous and it is clear that compensation will not be paid. In other cases it would be best to favour measures likely to provide prosperity and freedom of choice, while keeping a watch on the overall distribution of income and urging appropriate fiscal changes if this seems to be moving in an undesired direction. One wonders what the position of the less well off would be if the cast iron guarantee approach had been used to block all the changes of the last 150 years.

## A socialist market economy?

It is time to move on from considering the types of correction a market economy requires to the question, so far left aside, of whether a successful market economy needs to be based on *capitalism*. The converse is certainly untrue: capitalism need not involve a market economy. Not only can a system of private ownership of the means of production be highly competitive, but it can even be a *command economy*. The decisions of individual capitalists can be subject to highly detailed instructions given at the discretion of the country's rulers (as in Nazi Germany) or by some central organisation of the capitalists themselves. Historically, however, capitalism has tended more often than not to be associated with a market economy and there are powerful forces impelling it in that direction.

The opposite of capitalism is, of course, socialism; it will be convenient to define it in the old-fashioned way as state ownership of the means of production, distribution and exchange. (The term 'social democracy' will be used in this essay for concepts of socialism which do not involve an insistence on state ownership.)

There was a lengthy debate among academic economists in the interwar and wartime years on whether it was possible to have a socialist market economy. Echoes of that debate have continued in some of the writings on the economics of public enterprise. The conclusions seem to hang on whether a dynamic or static approach is used.

There is no reason why an economy consisting entirely of state-owned enterprises should not provide a known set of goods according to a known technology with known public taste, and according to the signals provided by the market place. Indeed, it could probably improve upon private enterprises by decreeing that managers must ignore any element of monopoly power and relate prices to marginal costs more closely than is likely in existing capitalist concerns. The problems of 'externalities' and spillover would, however, remain, and would have to be dealt with by some combination of price incentives and deterrents and administrative controls, as in capitalist economies.

Where, however, it is a matter of *discovering* what is the lowest cost method (rather than finding a position on a known cost curve) or of inventing products or services for meeting changes needs and tastes, the matter is wholly different. How is a limited amount of investment funds to be allocated among everybody with a bright idea? Or indeed, who are to be the managers and who the managed? It is no use applying a standard discounting technique to future costs and receipts and allocating funds to projects expecting the highest return. For both the receipts and the costs are precisely what are in dispute between the rival claimants.

If all investment funds went through one insurance company and were lent to firms consisting entirely of salaried managers with no personal stake in their concerns, the same problems would arise in a capitalist society. But, fortunately, this is not yet the case. Not only are the lending decisions made by different institutions, but the existence of personal private capital allows people to try out their own pet ideas, either with their own funds, or by using their assets as security for further loans. Even when it comes to reinvestment by existing firms, each management can try to prove the validity of its own ideas, however unorthodox, about the returns from alternative ventures, knowing that it is accountable to its own shareholders and can be thrown out by a takeover bid. Such individual hunches would be more difficult to justify to a National Investment Board, acting as trustee for all the nation's investment funds.

A socialist market economy is still better from the point of view of consumer satisfaction than a socialist command economy, even though it is probably less imaginative than a capitalist one in developing new techniques, products and services. This explains why the economic reforms designed to bring in the profit motive and relative prices more clearly to meaningful costs have led to improvements in Eastern Europe, but why a generally dowdy impression remains and why there is such a great desire to borrow Western techniques.

The nationalised industries in the West, and above all in the UK, have suffered from their symbolic role in left–right politics. This has led to a campaign of ridicule and denigration on the one side and partisan point-scoring on the other. At the time of writing left-wing politicians and academics are fond of pointing to a large book by R. W. S. Pryke,[23] which claims to have shown that, not only have the UK nationalised concerns performed better than private manufacturing industry, but that this is the direct result of nationalisation. Predictably this provoked a rebuttal by George and Priscilla Polanyi of the Institute of Economic Affairs.[24] The argument was partly on the suitability of output per man hour as an indicator of performance, and on whether Mr Pryke had made adequate allowance for the effects of the very much larger input of new capital per head into the state sector. Also at issue were the effects of the inclusion of the fast growing electricity and airways industries in the state sector. These industries have shown rapid productivity gains relative to manufacturing industry in most countries, irrespective of ownership. It was in the end, difficult to believe that anything had been 'proved' by either side.

The one point that did emerge and that was common to both parties was that there had been a large *relative* improvement in the performance of the state sector between the decades 1948–58 and 1958–68. This was related to two phenomena: (a) the loss of effective monopoly power as other sources of energy and transport emerged to compete with state undertakings, and (b) the adoption of a much more commercial approach to the nationalised industries, in which they were given target rates of return, pressed to relate prices more closely to marginal costs and to use modern techniques of investment appraisal, and, above all, given specific subsidies for any loss-making services that they were expected to run.

Even if one accepts that the nationalised industries are capable of putting up a comparable performance to private business in established industries, this tells us nothing whatsoever about how capital would be allocated between new and untried industries and ventures (and individuals wanting to run them) in a completely state-run economy. It is no accident that this side of the Iron Curtain the industries that tend to be state-run are either old established basic ones, such as the railways, buses or coal, or state-subsidised, prestige technology activities such as aerospace and atomic energy. On the other hand, where change is rapid, but not of a broadly predictable kind, and personal contact with consumers or dispersed local knowledge important – such as the retail trade, travel agencies or the profitable end of electronics – private ownership tends to prevail. In the rare cases where state concerns thrive in such trades, it is under the stimulus of strong competition with privately owned rivals.

In sectors which fall behind the two extremes (notably posts and telecommunications), the performance of state monopolies seems, to put it mildly, undistinguished. Some of the most controversial aspects concern the quality of service given to the customer, which is not easily captured by productivity indices. The personal incentive to try out new ideas and respond flexibly to changing consumer demands is normally less in a state enterprise trying to ape capitalist practice than in the genuine article. Not only is there less to gain from success, but there is less to lose from failure. (Salaried managers in large bureaucratic companies suffer from similar drawbacks, but to a smaller degree). As Patrick Hutber observed in relation to the Post Office Corporation's attempts in 1970–71 to imitate what it thought was correct commercial behaviour,'You don't make a bear into a tiger by painting stripes upon its back.'[25]

The stock example, constantly quoted against such generalisation, is the more adventurous spirit shown by the IRI state-holding group in Italy. This has been achieved by removing many of the political constraints which, in a country like the UK, govern public enterprise. The heads of the Italian organisation are given a degree of power without responsibility, which we should rightly hesitate to let such men have. The situation was made tolerable by the fact that state concerns had, up to the beginning of the 1970s, complete monopoly in very few fields and were usually subject to private competition, especially from imports. Should this situation change, as it shows signs of doing, the character of the Italian state sector would be likely to undergo a corresponding transformation. There have, in fact, been signs in several countries of a new role for public ownership and participation – that of saving from liquidation private concerns such as Rolls-Royce that have failed the test of the market, and which can offer no favourable spillovers to justify their subsidisation. This kind of safety net gave the worst of both capitalist and socialist worlds; yet it was welcomed by the less thinking socialists on the grounds that it extended the state sector and showed that 'private enterprise does not work'.

Meanwhile the improvements in the main British nationalised industries have been threatened by a Conservative Government which has been using them as a political instrument in a way that the more crudely interventionist Labour Ministers in the previous Cabinet would have dearly loved, but had been prevented from doing by the Treasury. Examples included arm-twisting to make the nationalised industries conform to the CBI price restraint pledge of 1971, when, unlike private industry, they had not been allowed to rebuild their profit margins and were remote from fulfilling their financial objectives. This was followed by pressure to invest in unprofitable directions as part of the government's reflationary drive. These and many other weaknesses have been pointed out by Christopher Foster in what is much the most perceptive study of the subject available.[26] Foster seems, however, to regard all these misfortunes as being due to remediable errors of particular governments, and puts forward excellent proposals for clarifying objectives and returning to the previous emphasis on profitability. Yet what shines out from his own account is that their nationalised status put these undertakings into the political area irrespective of what White Papers are written by Whitehall economists; and sooner or later any government is going to manipulate them – not to achieve some subtle adjustment between private and social costs or returns, but for short-run political objectives.

## Political freedom

So far this exposition has concentrated on the connection between the capitalist market economy and economic freedom and welfare. But many of its most forceful advocates have prized it at least as much as a precondition for political freedom. The argument is well known. In a capitalist society means are available to advocate socialism (or pacificism or numerous other heresies). Ideas in the forms of books, newspaper articles, plays, films, as well as in more subtle and less obvious forms are sold on the open market; and *the more the profit motive operates* the less a publisher will be influenced by his personal attitudes to the views expressed.

It would be absurd to suggest that there are no obstacles to be faced, especially for someone who wishes to advocate non-trendy heresies (such as opposition to the Race Relations Act) or a cause which has little demagogic appeal but is also outside the gentleman's agreement of permitted partisan dispute (such as devaluation in 1964–7). Nevertheless, the thing can be done. In a 100 per cent socialist economy, the problem of finding an outlet becomes much more difficult. Heads of state publishing enterprises could be told to publish anything that will sell. But this is a very ambiguous instruction, and the fact that publishers are state employees must have some influence; and it is not open to anyone who disagrees with their verdict to set up on his own or find a private patron. The argument is explained and developed at length in Friedman's *Capitalism and Freedom*.

One of Friedman's most telling examples is of the victims of McCarthyite persecution, who found refuge in the private sector. The relevant point here is that political freedom depends on the existence of a large capitalist sector – a 'socialist market economy' will not do. A syndicalist society might be one better than a purely socialist one – the smaller the units in which 'workers' control' reigns the better from this point of view. But it is all too easy to imagine the syndicates exercising a common censorship. The refusal of the printers in a London evening newspaper to print an 'anti-union' cartoon was an ominous portent, and attempts have been made by members of the NUJ chapels to bar opportunities to 'right wing' journalists.

These political considerations point to the desirability of not only of a 'private sector' with dispersed or institutional shareholders, but of some personal fortunes as well. Indeed, freedom of expression is probably stronger if the egalitarian 'correction' of the market distribution of wealth is not pushed too far. For although many controversial books and plays can be and are financed by publishers with institutional shareholders (who are small savers at one remove), the existence of wealthy patrons willing to go against the corporate philosophy (or artistic fashion) of the day is an important additional safeguard. (It made possible, for example, the launching of *Private Eye*.)

The political argument can, however, easily be pushed too far, or in the wrong direction. It does not rule out the existence of a substantial state sector, nor give much guidance on how large it can safely be; nor does it help on a great many of the issues of economic policy which come up every day in a mixed company. Moreover, it can be persuasively argued that freedom of expression (and choice of types of employment, and many other things, too) will be strengthened if there are not merely a multiplicity of firms within the capitalist sector, but a multiplicity of forms of ownership – large private corporations, state-owned enterprises, one-man firms, producer and consumer co-operatives, and so on. This is particularly so where real or alleged technical factors limit the number of outlets, as in television. While a state broadcasting monopoly would be a monstrosity (one has only to recall how Churchill was prevented from speaking on the BBC before the Second World War), freedom of expression is almost certainly greater as a result of the rivalry between the BBC and the independent channels, than it would be if competition were confined to two or three private networks.

Moreover, the value of either private enterprise, or of a multiplicity of forms of ownership, for free expression depends on competition – not on perfect competition, but on the absence of formal or informal restrictive agreements. Friedman himself points to the Hollywood boycott of 'subversive' writers in the 1950s, which was only possible because of a collusive agreement among film-makers regulating who could be employed.

## Forms of economic liberalism

The question of the role of capitalism and state enterprise has brought to light several different traditions within the liberal utilitarian approach to economics. There is the static emphasis on supplying a given set of goods and services by means of known technology. From this point of view a competitive market economy will bring about an optimum solution, subject to well-known exceptions, which in turn have well-known remedies which can be found in standard texts. If one wishes to emphasise the general rule, one is a 'market economist'; if one wishes to emphasise the exceptions and remedies one can be described as a 'liberal planner' of sorts. The zebra analogy is useful. The ideal can be regarded as a market economy with numerous corrective interventions, or a regulated economy making a great deal of use of prices and market forces.

Another type of approach is more dynamic. It puts the emphasis on the role of market forces in stimulating new tastes and new methods of meeting both old and existing tastes. The danger of this approach is that it can be vulgarised into an abrasive outlook which takes positive delight in 'shaking people up'. This is, however, a distortion. There is nothing in the logic of the dynamic case for a market economy which causes one to regard a quiet sleepy country with a low measured growth of GNP as inferior to a thrusting industrial state. All that is implied is that there must be freedom in both countries to innovate or propagandise. If, in the first country, people are unresponsive to sales appeals (other than quietist or ascetic gospels) and do not take to new technology, then there is no warrant for condemning that country and putting it lower in some absurd league table.

The conclusion needs, however, to be carefully stated. A country may have rising expectations and people may be prepared to change their habits to meet them; but growth may be held down because the country may have the misfortune to have a deficient supply of enterpreneurial talent (due perhaps to the educational system), or that talent may be discourged by misguided taxation policies, or irrational official devotion to an arbitrary exchange rate or to the maintenance of a reserve currency role leading to stop–go demand management policies or for numerous other reasons. This was the element of truth in the 'growthmanship' of the 1960s; but it was hopelessly confused by many of its supporters and its opponents with the illiberal value judgement that amenity should be sacrificed without limit for the sake of industrial production.

On the basis of what has been said so far it is possible to subdivide economic liberals on left–right lines (see Table 1).

*Table* 1 Left- and right-wing economic liberals

| Left-wing economic liberals | Right-wing economic liberals |
| --- | --- |
| Belief in strongly redistributive taxes and benefits | Acceptance of income and property distribution that emerges from the market |
| No special stress on ownership | Strong insistence on private enterprise |
| Sensitivity to differences between private and social costs and great readiness to intervene to eliminate them | Readiness to intervene where large, clear and proven discrepancies between private and social costs, but benefit of doubt to non-interference |
| Onus on those responsible for changes to compensate victims | Change desirable if losers cannot 'bribe' those responsible to desist |

A whole-hog left-wing economic liberal believes in what was earlier termed a corrected market economy, with special emphasis on corrections. He has no special interest in the pattern of ownership, but puts great emphasis on redistribution via taxation and social service payments. This will do almost as well as a description of a certain kind of Social Democrat of which Professor Schiller was an obvious example – although it will not unfortunately quite do as a description of even the 'Gaitskellite' wing of the British Labour Party. The right wing economic liberal, on the other hand, has clear affinities with certain strands of Conservative (although not Tory) thought.

The above remarks apply to those who come down consistently on one or other side of the above table. But there is no necessary relation between left- and right-wing attitudes in the different subdivisions. One can, for instance, be highly sensitive to environmental damage and not in the least willing to give the benefit of the doubt to the uncorrected market, yet be an out-and-out inegalitarian. There is probably, however some modest empirical correlation between left- and right-wing attitudes here as in other areas.

## (c)  A FRESH APPROACH

Enough has been said to demonstrate the many possible conflicts and unresolved issues within the camp of those whom I have termed liberal utilitarians and who espouse the 'corrected market economy'. There is, nevertheless, a very good reason for grouping together the common element in the thinking of many people who almost certainly vote in different ways and have different emotional and group loyalties. The link is the belief that the individual should normally be regarded as the best judge of his own interests.

Liberal utilitarians agree that the profit motive *can* promote the general welfare, however much they may disagree on the likelihood of this happening in particular instances. Those who have pondered the problems of the corrected market economy will also realise that, however many interventions and corrections are necessary, there is no need for politicians, civil servants and their expert advisers to attempt entrepreneurial judgements: there is enough on the government agenda without this unnecessary item. A liberal utilitarian who has thought about economic problems is also likely to be highly suspicious of notions such as the superiority of heavy industry over light, goods over services and exports over imports. He will dislike arbitrary physical targets such as 300 000 or 400 000 homes per annum, although he may occasionally accept them – after much critical scrutiny – as a third or fourth best. He will also feel ill at ease with generalised condemnations of the 'consumer society' as *per se* evil.

Moreover, liberal utilitarianism is the one element in a liberal philosophy that can provide guidance, however fuzzy and uncertain, to an applied economist concerned with specific issues. Hundreds of new problems arise every year – whether a bridge or urban motorways should be built and, if so, where; whether VAT should have been introduced, and so on. If liberal utilitarianism is ruled out or – what comes to the same thing – the possibility of 'welfare economics' is denied *a priori*, as is done by some conservative liberals, then the applied economist will be left either to follow some illiberal form of utilitarianism or to adopt the particular variety of paternalist judgement that he imagines his superiors to have. If, alternatively, the 'expert' is denied status altogether, then we deliberately leave unused human knowledge, both of facts and of logical procedures, in favour of pressure group politics, Ministerial infighting, uninformed hunches and all the rest.

Delightful though this last prospect is to many political writers, these traditional political processes do not satisfy the politicians themselves, and the expert is likely to be summoned back after all. But there is a danger that the expert in question will then be the engineer, or business efficiency pundit, or a fanatic for one kind of process or goal at the expense of all others. At least the economist, even if he is not consciously a liberal utilitarian, is concerned to reconcile the different priorities of different human beings. He should know that the concept of efficiency has little meaning apart from human preferences (this is elaborated in Appendix I); and if he is too bemused by his statistical tool kit to be aware of this, it will emerge when he comes to evaluate his results, and when others in his profession come to criticise them.

Although liberal utilitarianism therefore provides an indispensable ingredient in the economic philosophy of those who place a high value on freedom, it is on its own inadequate. It cannot provide much in the way of a simple guide to the non-technician on how he should approach economic problems, or even to the technician when he needs to make assumptions outside the particular problem on which he is working. A great deal of government intervention can be justified without paternalistic judgements, either on 'second best grounds' or sometimes even on 'first best grounds' (to the extent that this distinction can really be made).

If one sticks to the liberal utilitarian approach, every issue must be examined separately, the non-economist will be inclined to throw his hand in, and there will be no check on the total effects of innumerable policies decided separately. Moreover, as we have seen, there is ample scope for personal judgements about what is important and what makes things tick. On many problems one could say with fair confidence: 'You tell me the expert and I will tell you his conclusions.' Nor could the relevant judgements be 'fed in' by politicians or public opinion. One has to be heavily involved in the subject to know where the judgements come in, or how to frame them. It is essential to examine other approaches of a less technocratic appeal.

## Rules versus discretion

By far the most distinguished recent attempt to restate the principles of liberalism, as applied to economic affairs without resort to the traditional utilitarian calculus, has been that of F. A. Hayek's, *The Constitution of Liberty*. The reception of this book was an intellectual disgrace. Most of the popular reviews, and even some of the 'learned' ones, pilloried it, either by holding out certain policy conclusions for amazed inspection, or by saying that it went against the trend of the times. There were a few eulogies from those who thought it a good stick with which to beat socialists and planners, but much too little serious analysis – perhaps because it cut across too many academic demarcation lines.

The book came out in 1960 on the eve of a decade of 'pragmatism', when, under Kennedy in the US and both Macmillan and Wilson in the UK, general principles were at a discount, and the fashion was for 'common sense' intervention by bodies such as IRC or NEDC, which made a virtue of their freedom from all guiding principles, and when all the emphasis was on face-to-face contracts which deliberately blurred the extent to which government coercion was used. After a decade of this sort of pragmatism, the hostile reviews read very badly, even by the narrow criteria of their authors.

Hayek starts with his reasons for valuing freedom, which he defines as the absence of coercion. There must, of course, be some coercion in any state, if only to prevent one man's freedom from clashing with that of another. The practical question is how to minimise coercion and establish as much freedom as possible.

The best guarantee is in his view, not the market economy as such, but 'the rule of law', of which he believes the former to be a corollary. By the 'rule of law' Hayek does not mean any law which has been constitutionally enacted, but government by general, abstract, impartial rules with the minimum of administrative discretion in their enforcement. In other words, government policy should as much as possible take the form of general rules, laid down in advance. Where intervention is necessary, it should, where possible, take the negative form of prohibitions, forbidding certain courses of conduct, but leaving people free to choose from all the variety of permitted actions. (The distinction is, however, not as clear cut as it may seem, as was explained on p. 41.) Even if positive injunctions are unavoidable, they should be laid down in advance with the minimum of administrative discretion in their application.

There is no hard and fast dividing line between general rules and discretionary power. The most watertight statute needs some judicial interpretation, while the most discretionary acts of Ministers and officials take place against some background of law, convention and precedent. The best practical test is not by any administrative or legal classification, but that of predictability. If, by examining the facts of his own case and the known rules, laws and precedents, the citizen can predict what he will be permitted to do, general rules apply. If a great deal 'hangs in the air' because of uncertainty about how a Minister or official or judge will behave – or if his own bargaining skill is crucial – the regime is one of administrative discretion.

The whole concept of judicial discretion or leaving a great deal open to the 'good sense of the jury' conflicts with Hayek's idea of the rule of law. If the definition of pornography or obscenity (if such offences do have to exist) is wide open and depends entirely on public feeling as interpreted by a particular judge or jury, the whole notion of predictable rules goes on board. It may be that in this, and other areas, the key terms must inevitably be vague and changeable in interpretation; but at least the interpretation should change slowly over time, and there should be a high degree of certainty over whether any particular action will or will not be found permissible.

Of course, if laws tend to produce a net balance of undesirable effects, they should be changed. But it is essential to the whole idea that they cannot be changed at a moment's notice whenever a particular effect displeases some ruler or some temporary majority. The more fundamental the laws, the more difficult they should be to change; and this implies the existence of some constitution, whether written as in the USA, or 'virtual' as we fondly like to imagine exists in this country.

Taken as an analysis of what is normally meant by 'law' in legal and informed lay discourse, Hayek's conception is probably one-sided. In an 'Oxford philosophy' type analysis, *The Concept of Law*,[27] Professor H. L. A. Hart points out that in any large group it is simply not possible to operate by means of particular directions given to each individual, and therefore 'general rules, standards and principles must be the main instrument of social control.' But this similarity to Hayek's position is deceptive; for by resting his case on such widespread features of all societies, Hart clearly has something much broader in mind. He clarifies the issue later on when he states that all systems compromise between two social needs:

> the need for certain rules which can, over great areas of conduct, safely be applied by private individuals to themselves without fresh official guidance or weighing up of social issues, and the need to leave open, for later settlement by an informed official choice, issues which can only be properly appreciated and settled when they arise in a concrete case.

Hayek's concept of 'the rule of law' is basically a judgement that maximum emphasis should be on the first aspect and minimum on the second (although it cannot be eliminated altogether). Hart, on the other hand, rejects even the ideal of a rule whose application to a particular case would always be clear in advance, and never leave open a choice at the point of application. The reason he gives is that 'we are men, not gods'. Ignorance of future acts and the 'relative indeterminacy of aim' of the legislator makes such legal determinacy undesirable as well as impossible. Hayek would use the very same argument to reach the opposite conclusion. Because judges or officials are not gods, they cannot foresee the results of particular acts of discretion, and would do better, he believes, to stick to the rules which embody the collective experience of generations of human beings.

The differences between the two conceptions are brought out very clearly by one of Hart's examples: the case of a body set up to regulate an industry according to very general standards, with discretionary power to fix 'fair rates', perhaps after an inquiry into the facts and arguments. In some cases there would be 'no possibility of treating the questions raised by the various cases as if there were one uniquely correct answer to be found, as distinct from an answer which is a reasonable compromise between many conflicting interests.' Needless to say, all this would be worse than anathema to Hayek; but there is no reason to dispute with Hart that the system of regulation he mentions would be a normal Western legal process. It would, therefore, be better to describe Hayek's doctrine as a preference for *impersonal general rules*; the expression 'rule of law' may disguise the very radical nature of what is a goal or proposal and not a description of what the major legal systems of the West aim to do and to exclude. The expression 'rule of law' will, however, occasionally be used in quotation marks in the following pages for Hayek's concept, when the meaning is clear from the context.

Much more interesting than whether they are a correct interpretation of accepted legal principles is the question: how good a guarantee of freedom are impersonal general rules laid down in advance practice likely to be? A preliminary question is: how 'general' do general rules have to be? It is, of course, necessary to single out categories: traffic laws must deal with motorists, sales taxes have to make traders liable, and so on. But can general rules discriminate between industries and occupations? General rules must be impersonal; but by framing one's definitions carefully, a supposedly general law can pick out for specially severe treatment any group or even a single individual. Clearly some further constraint is required.

Hayek is dissatisfied with Mill's proposal that the law should not interfere with purely self-regarding activities, on the grounds that almost all human activities affect others. But, if we are prepared to widen 'self-regarding' to include the activities of 'mutually consenting adults' but not necessarily to cover 'public flaunting', and are prepared to disregard remote and improbable effects, we do have a worthwhile distinction, even though one that yields clear cut results in too limited a number of areas to answer all relevant questions. (For example, my travelling abroad or buying an Italian coat has all sorts of effects on others, if only through its effects on the foreign exchange market.)

Hayek's own proposal is that a general rule should be acceptable to a majority of both those whom it harms and those whom it benefits. Yet, as J. W. N. Watkins points out, in much the most perceptive criticism of *The Constitution of Liberty* that I have read, this qualification is much too strong, as it gives a veto to any minority group in any circumstances.[28] The question whether a law is, or can be, modified so as to be acceptable to both sides is always worth asking. Compulsory third party insurance might be acceptable on these grounds; apartheid would not be. But we could hardly expect a law against banditry (or plain murder!) to be equally acceptable to the Mafia and the rest of the Sicilian population. Or – to take one of Hayek's own illustrations – while a case can be made against policies such as steeply progressive taxation, the mere opposition of the rich to measures from which they would suffer is hardly a convincing argument against them.

More promising is the suggestion that a rule should be acceptable to someone who has not the slightest idea in advance on which side of the distinction he himself will fall.[29] This will often call for a large imaginative effort; but at least it supplies a criterion of disinterestedness. Yet it still leaves open some relevant questions.

In particular, how much 'disinterested' support does a rule require? If it is a bare majority, people would still be able to impose their tastes on others; and there would be no bar to military or industrial conscription and countless other horrors (except for the preference for negative rules – and that would not prevent Prohibition). If, on the other hand, unanimity is required, any obstinate individual would be given a veto on any decision. Moreover, the hypothesis of ignorance of how one might be affected works only for some questions. With sufficient goodwill and imaginative power a person ought to be able to imagine himself ignorant of how he would be affected by proposed laws on property inheritance. He could not simulate such ignorance if the question were one of stricter laws against fast driving. For he would have to imagine his trade-off between safety and speed if his temperament were different to what it is; and to perform the exercise he would have to imagine himself a different person. Further difficulties will be mentioned when we come to discuss 'optimal inequality'.

Consideration of the various suggestions in the field makes one suspect that the quest for a foolproof definition of 'impersonal general rules' is unlikely to succeed. It is, nevertheless, a recognisable ideal. Indeed, the basic concepts of mathematics and formal logic are far from easy to define, let alone those of political and social studies; but this does not mean they are useless. We know that many of the items of the criminal code are as close to impersonal general rules as we can hope to get; we know that the Star Chamber and the Press Gang are at the other extreme. We know, too, if we are frank, that a piece of legislation which defines an undesirable monopoly or restrictive practice – even if only in *prima facie* terms – comes closer to the ideal than one which leaves everything to the discretion of the Minister and his advisers.

Hayek sometimes seems to imply that the connection between impersonal general rules and personal freedom is a necessary one. This makes the whole argument hang on an interlocking set of definitions and does less than justice to his own case. It is better to argue that the connection is a causal one, that there is, in practice, likely to be more personal freedom if maximum use is made of impersonal general rules with the minimum of administrative discretion. This is a more plausible and fruitful line of approach.

In Hayek's own words, 'it is because the lawgiver does not know the particular cases to which his rules apply, and it is because the judge who applies them has no choice in drawing the conclusions that follow from the existing body of rules and the particular facts of the case, it can be said that "laws not men rule".'[30] If those framing the law do not know to whom it might apply and cannot either curtail it or extend it for the benefit of specific individuals, including themselves, they are much less likely to be of an oppressive kind. But the price we must pay for this benefit is that such general rules 'always be applied irrespective of whether or not the consequences in a particular instance seem desirable'.[31]

A system of general and impersonal rules is hardly a sufficient condition for a free society. For many policies clearly involving a high degree of coercion can be imposed in a bigoted society. Examples extend well beyond the Scottish sabbath conceded by Hayek. A ban on all foreign travel or a £50 travel allowance might be justified by general, impersonal rules, and the exceptions such as business or official travel stated quite impersonally. As we have seen, it is very difficult to narrow down the concept of general rules to avoid such cases.

General rules, laid down in advance, should, nevertheless, be supported as one *influence* in favour of personal freedom, even though they are not by themselves enough. There is no one magic recipe for minimising coercion and we should be foolish to abandon the ideal of impersonal rules simply because it cannot *guarantee* the desired result in all cases.

General impersonal rules can be defended not only as a support for personal freedom, but also from a distrust of the other results of discretionary actions. Less bad results, even from the point of view of those initiating a policy, may come from following some standard procedure than by leaving it to particular individuals to issue arbitrary instructions on the basis of their own hunches, prejudices or bargaining skill. As David Hume, who is one of the main sources of Hayek's thought on this subject, observed:

All general laws are attended with inconveniences when

applied to particular cases; and it requires great penetration and experience both to perceive that these inconveniences are fewer than those which result from full discretionary powers in every magistrate, and also discern what general laws are, upon the whole attended with fewest inconveniences.[32]

In our own day it can be argued that there are 'fewer inconveniences' in laying down in advance a permissible range for the growth of the money supply and the 'full employment' budget deficit than in discretionary variation by the monetary authorities. It is also an argument for floating – or genuinely fixed – exchange rates and against the Bretton Woods system. The results of discretionary fiscal, monetary and exchange rate policies have certainly not been so brilliant that one can dismiss this argument out of hand.[33]

What are the specific applications to the general run of domestic economic policy? The principle of generality does not rule out a vast amount of government intervention. It would not present any bar to outright prohibition of night-work for children, nor (unfortunately) to any bar on the consumption of candyfloss. Virtually all actions by means of the price mechanism, such as regional employment premia, investment grants, taxes and subsidies on commodities, and so on, can be stated in highly general and impersonal form; and the degree of official discretion could be made very limited indeed, if we had a government that really believed in the 'rule of law'. Even a complete ban on fresh industrial development in the Midlands or South-East, with exceptions for small extensions up to a specific size, would be compatible with this ideal. What it would not permit is the practice of granting development permission by government officials examining each case on its merits.

There is nothing in the concept of the 'rule of law' to prevent the state from supplying any services it thinks fit, or even from running industries. Professor Hayek's sole proviso is that the state must not have a monopoly in any of these things. Even that stipulation is a borderline case. For a law such as 'No one except the Electricity Generating Board should generate electricity' only fails to be a general impersonal rule if the Generating Board is regarded as a specific person or persons! (Of course many of Hayek's policy views are derived directly from his dislike of coercion and his economic studies rather than via the 'rule of law', and are none the worse for that.)

General non-discretionary rules are mainly applicable to relations *between* individuals and organisations. Specific instructions and discretionary action must play a large role *within* any organisation, whether it is a private company, an army, a hospital or a Government Department, and even in the state sector as a whole. General rules can have some role within organisations; but the main function of general rules is to regulate the relationship of *different* organisations that have no common structure. There is such a command structure within the state sector, vague, loose, and disturbed by feuding barons though it is. This suggests that if the rule of law is to have any flesh and blood meaning, the size of the state sector must be limited. No magic percentage can be given and the detailed composition of the state sector (for example, whether it constitutes a small part of many industries or the whole of a few) matters as well as the percentage of the economy covered.

Because Hayek as an individual has regarded the main threat to liberty as coming from the Left, and because he first came into popular prominence with the *Road to Serfdom*[34] which warned against the totalitarian implication of much fashionable wartime thinking about 'reconstructing society', his emphasis on the 'rule of law' has been too easily dismissed as an attempt to erect one further obstacle to a reforming government. While it is true that 'discretionary intervention' was regarded as the ark of the Socialist covenant by a few misguided Ministers in the 1964–70 Labour Administration, some of the greatest opposition to proceeding by general rules emanates from the conventional establishment. Conservative Ministers, central bankers, senior officials and business organisations loathe the idea of operating according to fixed criteria laid down in advance. 'Flexibility' and 'not being bound in advance' is the theme song of the British practical man, when given his way.

The City of London is a particularly bad example, where nods, winks and arm-twisting have long been preferred to known rules of behaviour. The Bank of England has traditionally preferred to operate by vague requests backed by vague sanctions, rather than by publishing definite rules. The 'new monetary policy' adopted in 1971, providing for a common reserve rule and the abolition of advances ceilings was a step forward, after a rearguard action lasting many years. But even the new arrangements were hedged around with numerous discretionary exceptions and additions (e.g. to prevent excessive competition with building societies); and the Bank was still determined to make admissions to the privileged state of 'merchant banker' depend on discretionary and undisclosed judgements by the Governor and his advisers on no known criteria, and to regulate mergers and new entry among the wider banking community in a similar spirit. It is an explanation, but not an excuse to say that those concerned have transferred methods and procedures which might be appropriate for a private club to the sphere of public policy.

There are numerous examples of the preferences of Conservative ministers for discretionary intervention rather than fixed rules. They clearly regarded arm-twisting by politicians and officials as a lesser evil than legally enforceable and known restraints – indeed, their main argument against Labour's income policies was that they were 'too rigid'. A spectacular example of the contempt of many right wing governments for known rules, generally enforceable, is the way in which the Nixon Republican Administration went round the world in 1971, forcing countries to accept 'voluntary quotas' whose size was determined by the balance of threats, counter-threats and bribes. A believer in the 'rule of law' may dislike any import restrictions; but if there have to be any, it is better that they should take the form of tariffs, which present the same fixed obstacle to everyone, rather than quotas which inevitably discriminate on an arbitrary basis. If there have to be quotas, it is at least better that they should be statutory and known in advance than take the voluntary form, which depends on the sum product of numerous individual attempts at coercion. Nor is it likely that once a government behaves in this way, it will confine such behaviour to 'foreigners'.

A British example was the CBI voluntary undertaking of July 1971 that 200 of the largest firms would limit their price increases to 5 per cent or less in the coming 12 months and report to the CBI Director-General, Mr Campbell Adamson, if for any reason they found themselves unable to comply. This undertaking was supposed to be a *quid pro quo* in return for the government's reflationary measures – although it is in fact extremely doubtful if the CBI undertaking had much effect on the size of the subsequent fiscal package.

The whole undertaking was, of course, nominally a voluntary one. But it was obvious that considerable moral pressure was being put by the CBI on doubters to sign. Any who did not, risked incurring government displeasure; thus the CBI was transforming itself into an organ of government policy – partly in the hope that the TUC might undergo the same transformation. If this does not turn out to be a system of private law, it will not have been for want of trying on the CBI's and government's part. The CBI's original defence – that the ceiling was its own idea and not the government's – missed the whole point of the criticism. A system of discretionary arm-twisting by a private body goes against the principle of impersonal general rules applicable to all, whoever suggested the idea. Moreover, as was quite predictable at the time, it did not take long for the Conservative Government to adopt the concept as part of its own policy; and within a year the CBI was being pressurised by Ministers to renew the price undertaking, which it had then become much more reluctant to do. Thus do 'practical businessmen' embark like lemmings on their own destruction.

One can see how this situation arose. The first preference of a Conservative Government and of industrialists is for non-intervention. But if this is, or appears to be, impracticable, they tend to think that the next best thing is that 'industry should plan itself.' But so far from being a second best, it is the worst course of all. For organisations like the CBI are subject neither to the discipline of the market place nor to political control; and 'industrial self government' is, in the literal sense, irresponsible. If a price ceiling is necessary in an emergency it should be introduced by an elected government by means of an Act of Parliament, which states the forbidden course of action clearly.

Hayek's view is more extreme. It is that the principle of general rules excludes altogether all control over prices and wages. The issue of wage controls is best postponed until we come in the next chapter to the thorny issue of union monopoly power. For the moment we can discuss the issue in terms of prices. Hayek's basic case is that any attempt by the authorities to fix prices would create shortages. For if the prevailing market price is just sufficient to bring supply and demand into line, then the imposition of a different, and presumably lower, price would increase demand, and reduce supply. The resulting shortages would involve allocations of goods by administrative discretion;

and, even if supplying firms made the allocation, they would in fact be exercising state powers that had been delegated to them. One need not waste time drawing up allocation schemes which might be general and impersonal, and not involve administrative discretion. The rationing of a few basic consumer goods in wartime cannot be compared to continuous allocation of a wide variety of goods at all stages of a peacetime economy; and whatever casuistry one wished to employ, a society in which people and firms were told how much they could have of different commodities would cease to be a free one.

The more important question is the soundness of the economic inference. Does price control inevitably involve allocation? The reader will recall our discussion of different kinds of market on pp. 57–9. Where prices normally vary from day to day in a market-clearing way, Hayek is plainly right. As far as the consumer is concerned, this applies mainly to non-processed foodstuffs, above all fruit and vegetables. Serious price control would rapidly lead to shortages, black market and under-the-counter dealings. It is no accident that this is the area in which recent attempts at price invigilation, whether in the UK in the mid 1960s, or the US in 1971, were largely a charade, designed to maintain support for the system in other sectors.

On the other hand, in a large part of manufacturing industry and services, prices are not adjusted to demand in the short term and variations in demand are met by adjustments in output. Short-term costs tend to be either constant or to fall with the volume of output (given the cost accountant's convention in allocating overheads). In this situation most businesses would probably absorb in their gross profit margins the effects of a moderate degree of price control. This would be all the easier as price controls have come back into fashion in periods when there is considerable surplus capacity, but when governments would otherwise be afraid of expanding demand for fear of stimulating inflation.

Obviously one must look beyond the short term. The hope of governments of all political persuasions is that price controls will be reflected back in lower wage increases, because employers will then stand up more firmly to union claims and / or such claims will themselves become more moderate. But to put it mildly, this passing back is unlikely to be 100 per cent effective, if only because of the monetary and fiscal stimulation which tends to accompany such policies.

In some industries the return on capital is likely to be less than it would otherwise be if the controls are kept on for any length of time and do more than permit what businessmen would in any case want to charge. If this is true on average, the share of investment in the national income will fall and that of consumption rise. The government could try to counteract this by higher personal taxes, combined with lower interest rates; but how successful this would be is doubtful* and the process would be very unpopular politically.

In all probability the controls will work differentially and the squeeze on the rate of return be greater in some industries than in others. These industries are likely to underinvest in relation to the demand for their production. But by this time almost anything might have happened: the price controllers (if they are still there) might find some excuse for changing the rules to adjust price relativities to choke off demand, the gap might be filled by imports, and, if the exchange rate is allowed to move to the equilibrium level, this will lead to a change in the composition of exports and imports of a freakish and inefficient kind. (If the exchange rate is wrong, the results will be still worse.) Another possibility is the Hayekian spectre of allocation – especially likely if the exchange rate is not adjusted appropriately.

The above sketch can provide no more than a few very rough pointers to the consequences of price control in conditions of surplus capacity and cost inflation. But it is enough to show that the bogey of allocation and rationing is too remote and problematical to put price control out of court on 'rule of law' grounds which the plain man can understand. Price control is undesirable in the liberal utilitarian sense that it may promote a use of resources that disregards individual preferences. But it can only be consistently attacked on straightforward 'rule of law' grounds if a great deal of discretionary power is left to administrators or to boards composed of both sides of industries.

A clear-cut published price control formula with the minimum of exceptions is the least open to objection on these grounds,

* Many companies would not regard any feasible reduction in the cost or availability of outside finance as a sufficient substitute for their own reduced cash flow.

because the rules of the game would then be known and firm; and some individuals would not be given discretionary coercive powers over others for more than a short emergency period. The reason why Hayek may be ultimately right is that no such formula would be likely to work for long, and the government concerned would either have to phase out the controls or take a large step towards giving its agents discretionary power over the livelihoods of millions.

## Reward according to 'merit'

The most controversial application of Hayek's concept of the 'rule of law' is that he regards it as inconsistent with an attempt to redistribute income on social justice grounds.

If this part of the discussion is to generate light rather than heat, it is necessary to disentangle two different propositions from this argument. Hayek is against any attempt to make rewards of different people correspond to some supposed consensus on the relative merits of what they are doing. This would, he believes, lead to pernicious results undreamt of by those who talk in this way.

Secondly, he is against any attempt by progressive taxation or other means to pursue equality or even 'less inequality' as a deliberate objective. It is a weakness of Hayek's presentation that he intertwines his arguments against payment according to merit so closely with arguments against the state taking *any* view on the distribution of incomes as to make them seem synonymous. The two propositions are separable and it is possible to accept the first without accepting the second. In fact, the first argument against payment by merit is both more important and more firmly based, even though it flies in the face of most respectable thinking, radical and conservative alike, from Plato onwards. It will be most convenient to deal with it now and come back later to the controversy about equality and distribution.

The biggest menace to liberal values is not so much any brand of egalitarianism, but the contention that relative rewards should depend on a political assessment of how much a particular occupation is worth. The objection is not, of course, to selection or promotion 'on merits', particularly in large organisations, where the implied contrast is with nepotism. The objection is to the contention that rewards of different individuals should depend on some sort of collective judgement of society of what they are worth.

Not all Hayek's arguments on the subject are, however, of equal weight. He argues that payment by merit would be a breach of the 'rule of law' because it involves a discretionary judgement by the state on the merits of particular individuals. In practice, however, such judgements tend to be on the relative merits of different occupations rather than individuals. Majority views revealed by the opinion polls show a hierarchy with nurses at the top and politicians at the bottom. But, as we have seen, there can be general, impersonal predictable laws differentiating between categories in this way and it is very much a borderline issue whether such distinctions are to be regarded as a breach of the 'rule of law' ideal.

Hayek is at his most convincing when he argues in Part I of *The Constitution of Liberty* directly from libertarian principles against reward and merit rather than by the roundabout route of 'the rule of law'. His most persuasive proposition is that 'no man or group of men possess the capacity to determine conclusively the potentialities [i.e. the deserts and opportunities] of other human beings and that we should certainly never trust anyone invariably to exercise such a capacity.'[35]

To assess merit presupposes that a man has acted in accordance with some accepted rule of conduct and that someone else can judge how much effort and pain this has cost him. Often, of course, a highly meritorious attempt may be a complete failure, while a valuable human achievement will be due to luck or favourable circumstances. To decide on merit 'presupposes that we can judge whether people have made such use of their opportunites as they ought to have made, and how much effort of will or self-denial it has cost them and how much their achievement is due to circumstances'. This is impossible in a free society or probably at all. Moreover, only a fanatical ascetic would wish to encourage a maximum of merit in this sense. It is more rational for people 'to achieve a maximum of usefulness at a minimum of pain and sacrifice and therefore a minimum of merit'.

Hayek is also right to insist that in a free society a man's livelihood does not depend on other people's valuation of his merit. It is sufficient that he should be able to perform some work or sell a service for which there is a demand. He concedes that as an organisation grows larger it will become inevitable that ascertainable merit in the eyes of managers (or some conventional seniority structure) should determine rewards. But so long as there is no single organisation with a comprehensive scale of merit, but a multiplicity of competing organisations with different practices (as well as smaller organisations and a self-employed sector), an individual still has a wide degree of freedom of choice.

There is, in fact, a still stronger argument against reward by merit than those already mentioned which should influence even non-liberals who do not attach any special value to personal choice. This is that there simply does not exist in modern Western states a sufficiently wide consensus on the relative merits or deserts of different occupations and groups. However resentful they are about it, people will, in the last resort accept a relatively low position in the pecking order if it is due to the luck of the market, or even the greater success of other groups in their monopolistic activities. They may retaliate by organising monopolistic associations of their own to engage in industrial stoppages; but they will recognise that no ultimate judgement has been pronounced. If, on the other hand, their low position seems to result from a moralistic evaluation of their merits made by their fellow citizens through some political process – whether by the government or by boards appointed for the task – they will stop at nothing to get the judgement withdrawn. No one likes being consigned to the rubbish heap by a body of wise men appointed to express the supposed moral evaluations of society. Some evidence for this contention is provided by the much greater political bitterness surrounding public sector than private sector wage disputes, despite the fact that nationalised industries have been careful to rest their case on industrial or national expediency, and to avoid any moral evaluation of the claims made.

An interesting feature of the argument against reward by merit is that it ought to be entirely acceptable to a strict egalitarian. The incompatibility of the two ideals of equality and reward according to merits comes out very clearly in one of the few coherent statements of the egalitarian case to have appeared in recent years, Douglas Jay's *Socialism and the New Society*.[36] There the author clearly states that no man or woman has a greater 'right to happiness' than any other and the fact that people are born 'with an endless variety of character, intelligence, energy and ability, is morally irrelevant to this assertion.'

An egalitarian could easily find a full-blown system of merit assessment even more distasteful than the present mixture or market and traditional status-determined differentials.

> A society in which it was generally presumed that a high income was proof of merit and a low income lack of it, in which it was universally believed that position and remuneration correspond to merit, in which there was no other road to success than the approval of one's conduct by the majority of one's fellows, would probably be much more unbearable to the unsuccessful ones than one in which it was frankly recognised that there was no necessary connection between merit and success.

This is a quotation from *The Constitution of Liberty*, but it could equally have come from an egalitarian socialist inveighing against the meritocracy and arguing against equality of opportunity as an inadequate ideal.

Hayek argues that payment by merit would mean that market valuations of a man's activities would provide him with no guidance about where to use his talents and what risks to undertake. He would have to be told what to do by someone else: in other words, explicit or implicit direction of labour. Here, however, we must be careful. Direction of labour is a plausible result if the principle is pushed too far. But how far is 'too far', and what exactly happens, will depend on certain policy decisions other than the decision to pay according to merit. If, for example, it was decided that a nurse's merit was greater than her market rate of pay, there would be a surplus of girls seeking to enter the profession, and some who had previously come up to standard would be rejected by a selection procedure, thus increasing the discretionary power of the hospital authorities over the careers of those concerned. The effects on the employment of nurses would, however, probably be less than in other occupations because most nurses are remunerated out of rates and taxes.

In the commercial sector, an increase in relative pay for, say, copper plate workers, would not only increase the number of job applicants but would also reduce employment opportunities. If half the jobs in the country were upgraded on a merit basis and the other half downgraded, there would be an exodus of employees from the high merit occupations, where jobs would be chronically scarce, to the low merit ones, where they would be plentiful but ill-rewarded. The only way of avoiding these paradoxical effects would be for the state to give large and expensive subsidies to the favoured trades and/or put heavy taxes on the least favoured ones, thereby substituting a politically determined pattern of output for that preferred by consumers.

But undesirable although all this is to an economic liberal, and restrictive though it is of freedom of consumer choice, it need not amount to direction of labour. The latter would only be necessary if the state begrudged paying the subsidies and raising the taxes, but was not prepared to accept a redistribution of workers towards the low merit occupations. State action to protect the pay of a particular group that stood high in esteem from adverse market forces – whether engine drivers facing the rundown of the rail system or teachers when there is a glut of graduates – would not take us along the road to serfdom. But an across-the-board system of merit evaluation (for example, paying lavatory attendants more than university professors and dustmen more than stockbrokers) would lead to such an unacceptable allocation of resources (involving, for example, great unemployment among the lavatory attendants) and the necessary subsidies would be so unpopular (and themselves another source of distortion of the choice between work and leisure) that widespread compulsion would be an all too likely result. This aspect of the discussion will be taken further when we come to the equality issue.

The alternative to payment by merit is payment according to the market value of a person's activities – *as modified by whatever fiscal action is taken to alter the distribution of income and wealth* (such action is discussed below, pp. 111 et seq.). We do not need to be starry-eyed about the character of this market value. It will be influenced by the attempts of professional associations and trade unions to restrict supply, as well as by traditional views of proper scales. If the supply of clergymen suitable for promotion to archbishop exceeds the demand, the archepiscopal stipend will not, in the short run, be reduced (although it may be less quickly adjusted to compensate for inflation). In other words, it will be a highly imperfect market system in which rewards will not only depend on the mixture of luck, skill, opportunity and monopoly power characteristic of actual markets, but also on arbitrary traditional relativities, which themselves represent the lagged influences of the market relativities of a generation or two ago.

The economic liberal will want to do all he can to remove disparities and inequalities imposed by artificial barriers to entry.

He should be extremely sceptical of the monopolistic claims made by the medical or legal profession, as of the restrictive practices of the craft unions. To the extent that there are professional skills involved, which the layman is not qualified to judge, it should be sufficient for the state to establish a register of qualified persons, leaving it to the consumer to decide whether to go by this register or to seek unqualified help.

Above all, the liberal should be suspicious of attempts of more and more occupations, whether advertising, management or journalism, to emulate the professions and to set up obstacle courses in the shape of examination requirements or 'on the job training', confining entry to graduates, or similar limitations of entry. To the extent that these new qualifications and courses produce results, employers, or members of the public using the services, will give preference to those holding them. To restrict the activities in question to those so qualified, by law or collective agreement, is a pure exercise of coercion to establish a monopoly position. Yet at the end of the day, even if he is relatively unsuccessful in fighting off these evils, the liberal should still regard a pattern of awards, determined politically by governmental action or demagogic use of the organs of publicity as a cure far worse than the disease.

## The role of politics

The argument for payment according to merit is in fact one example of the widespread belief that society as a whole should take decisions now arrived at by separate organisations or individuals, or by impersonal general forces. This claim is much the most dangerous that the economic liberal (or any other kind of liberal) now has to face. He must meet it by an equally strong counterclaim: that in a free society the domain of political action should be limited.

This is a third principle, of comparable importance to non-paternalistic value judgements and a belief in general, impersonal rules, for the contemporary economic liberal. It is also an extremely controversial one and likely to lose me the support of even some of those who have followed the preceding discussion with some sympathy.

The principle is extremely difficult to state, not least because of the ambiguity of the term political. One can legitimately talk about the politics of a family or a school, or a firm or an opera house. But political action, in the sense that is relevant here, involves the coercive power of government. Even this, however, is a necessary and not a sufficient condition. The traffic police are an instrument of governmental coercion; but, except in the case of scandals or controversial change in safety regulations, their operations are not a political issue. For a matter to become political, there must also be conflict and strong feeling. Where free speech is permitted, the conflict is in the open; elsewhere the conflict is either suppressed, or else artificially stirred up against the 'enemies of the people' who do not go along with official requirements. (An alternative formulation is that such countries have no politics, but this has the disadvantage of creating an unrealistic black and white distinction between free and unfree states.)

Hayek has, for many years and in many different terminologies, been trying to draw a distinction between two different strands of the liberal and utilitarian traditions. He has contrasted 'true' with 'false' individualism, 'generic' with 'particularist' utilitarianism, and 'restricted' with 'extreme' utilitarianism. He has contrasted the liberal tradition springing from Hume with that springing in different ways from both Descartes and Jeremy Bentham, and he has erected a chamber of horrors full of things such as 'constructivist rationalism', 'social engineering' and 'scientism'. He has with equal regularity been answered by British writers who maintain that he has created artificial distinctions and misconstrued the English (or Scottish!) tradition.

For a long time my own instincts were on the anti-Hayek side, especially as his distinctions were too often associated with a defence of traditional English public schools against continental libertarian criticism and a defence of the conformist impression made by many young British university-educated men and their continental contemporaries earlier in the century. This was leaning over too far backwards to explain away the more authoritarian aspects of British life.

Yet there remains an uncomfortable feeling that there is something in Hayek's distinctions. The 'social engineers' or 'particularist' utilitarians maintain, in the spirit of Jeremy Bentham, that institutions 'are to be approved and respected only to the extent that we can show that the particular effects they will produce in any given situation are preferable to the effects another arrangement would produce', and, therefore, 'our reason should never resort to automatic or mechanical devices'. Hayek contrasts this with the view stemming from Hume which accepts just as much the test of utility, but insists that no single human intelligence is capable of inventing appropriate rules and institutions which 'have evolved in the process of growth of society' and which 'embody the experience of many more trials and errors than any individual mind could acquire'.[37]

The role played by traditional rules, habits and customs in Hayek's defence of freedom in *The Constitution of Liberty* is indeed an uneasy one. The submission to rules and conventions, whose significance we do not fully understand, jars with the impulse to freedom. There are such things as illiberal institutions, traditions and rules. Above all, Hayek does not really explain the process by which unsuitable traditions should be discarded, except by vague references to trial and error and the variability of the social pressure against individuals who transgress the rules. Yet without Hume's sceptical caution about the powers of human reason, we open the gates to the social engineering approach to politics and society. A particularist utilitarian can always find some defect or 'externality' in every real world activity to justify intervention on the most impeccably non-paternalist grounds. Yet the total effect of a series of such interventions, each decided separately on a discretionary basis, could be to destroy most of the existing avenues of choice with an end result totally different from what was intended, owing to the inability to foresee remoter or less obvious consequences.

There is a genuine dilemma here. The Benthamite, social engineering streak in liberalism can lead to an unlimited profusion of state activity, as one hectic intervention follows another, and one fashionable mathematical model – whether of the determinants of productivity in 1984 or of the ecological balance in 2000 – succeeds a previous favourite. Yet too great a hesitation to intervene, where existing institutions neither provide personal choice nor material welfare, can lead liberalism to ossify into a Burkean conservatism (as happened with Burke himself). We have already met, in an earlier more technical context, the two strands of right-wing and left-wing economic liberalism, both claiming to start from individual desires and choices, but with radically different approaches to state intervention.

Whatever the weight of inherited lore may decree, there is no sphere of human activity that can be *a priori* and forever ruled out of the political domain. In the Depression of the 1930s, the operation of the whole economic system was a matter of legitimate concern. In a grossly pyramided society where, say, 1 per cent of the families earned 99 per cent of all incomes, 'inequality' would be the number one political problem. If the country became plagued by heroin-addiction, the most extreme liberals might want to waive the anti-paternalist presumption to give priority to a sensibly conducted search for treatment – even in a country which had no tradition of repressive rules on the subject.

The point that the liberal can legitimately make is that, although the focus of political interest is and should be constantly shifting, it should also be limited. There is all the difference in the world between having a number of different spotlights of varying strength gradually shifting in direction, and floodlighting the whole countryside. Some judgements, such as that of the claims of defence on resources, have to be made collectively through the political process. Political judgements on other matters, such as the allocation of resources between present and future needs, or the distribution of income, or the aesthetic properties of new towns, or the amounts to be given to help poorer countries, are in a sense optional, in that we can choose to take them inside or outside the political process. The more judgements of this kind that are made politically, and the greater the detail into which they go, the greater the threat not only to liberty and prosperity, but also to social harmony. Paradoxically, by attempting to go too far by state action to remove all conflict and discomfort, we actually increase social tension to danger point.

One of the more striking results of Anthony Downs's pioneering investigation of *The Economic Theory of Democracy*,[38] was how little incentive the ordinary citizen, or even individual member of a pressure group, has to make a serious study of issues. The probability that his vote or voice will turn the scale is so small that neither Downs nor his critics have been able to find a rational argument for voting other than the general duties of citizenship or as an outlet for strong personal feelings. If this is so of voting, it applies *a fortiori* to a detailed study of policy; and any short cut method, such as taking on trust the views of a party with which one has a clear identification, or going by the general impression rival leaders make on a television screen, will be quite rationally taken to avoid time-consuming study, which – even if it were undertaken – would only be feasible over a very tiny range of the total issues. Even individual MPs often find it more convenient to follow their particular faction of their party on a great many issues on which they neither feel strongly nor regard themselves as particularly competent.

The gist of the matter was expressed by Schumpeter long ago when he said that, for most people, the great political issues were 'sub-hobbies' to which they devoted less attention than bridge.[39] This is not a criticism. It is perfectly rational, given the likely extent of individual influence, to regard political TV programmes as forms of show business, to be watched only if they are entertaining. Schumpeter conceded that voters appear to react rationally to issues involving immediate personal and pecuniary profit to identifiable groups. But even here 'it is only short run rationality that asserts itself effectively'. As we move to more general issues of national and international policy, even this short-run rationality goes. Such issues normally take their place 'with those leisure hour interests that have not attained the rank of hobbies'. This rationality leads to a reduced sense of responsibility. 'We need only compare,' as Schumpeter put it, 'the lawyer's attitude to his brief and the same lawyer's attitude to the statements of political fact presented in his newspaper.' In the one case he has the competence and the stimulus to master the material. In the other, 'he does not apply the canons of criticism he knows so well how to handle' in his own sphere. The basic trouble is the lack of the rationalising influences of personal experience and responsibility. In their own private lives people know that more of one thing means less of something else because of the cash constraint. They know that they can improve trade-offs (for example, between the pleasure of living in the country and the discomfort of a journey to work, by a careful choice of location); but they also know that such improvements are not unlimited and cost effort to find.

The absence of this knowledge in the political sphere explains the frequent tendency of democracies to expect too much from government action. If the rate of economic growth is too low, it is supposed to be the government's duty to raise it, until we come up near the top of the league tables; and moreover, to do so painlessly, without any sacrifice of immediate satisfaction. The belief never dies that if we only had a clever enough Chancellor, with clever enough advisers, he would find some kind of monetary magic for achieving this. To make any other attitude is defeatist, cynical and so on. The impetus towards political consistency is not very strong. It is too easy to favour all worthy objects at the same time: more of the national income for the old and sick, the lower paid, the skilled craftsman and better pay for those doing important professional jobs. The one group which people always think is too well paid are politicians – from whom omniscience and omnipotence are expected.

The difficulty of the subject is that there *are* in fact always ways in which the government could, if it were cleverer or more enlightened, improve all these matters. There are mistakes which have held back the rate of growth; there may well be policies which could improve road safety at minimal cost to motorists. Or to put it more generally, better technical or institutional arrangements can always improve the trade-offs, so that we could get more growth for a given sacrifice of personal consumption, or more road safety from a given sacrifice by motorists. It is never wrong to seek for a 'Pareto improvement'. The mistake of the politically orientated is to exaggerate the possibility of improvement, both in the abstract, and in the light of the forces that actually do influence both the electorate and men in positions of power and influence.

The inadequacy of the incentive to make wise decisions applies not only to voters, but to a lesser extent to public officials, whether Ministers, MPs, civil servants or judges. Good decisions involve considerable private costs in time and effort; and the incentive to invest in this way is reduced because the benefit largely accrues to others and the effect on the individual's own career is very vague and diffused. The gains from investing energy in understanding internal politics and hierarchical roles and from playing the organisation game are often greater and more tangible.[40] Some of the same considerations apply to officials of large commercial organisations, although individual responsibility is slightly easier to pin down because company profits can be allocated among divisions in a way that votes cannot be allocated among ministers, policies or departments. But in any case such diminished incentive does less harm in organisations which are not backed by the coercive powers of government.

Even, however, if voters were highly enlightened and could effectively call their rulers to account, there would still be endemic defects in any known political process. Among the most striking of Downs's results (which he might have made more of) was the lack of protection either of the minority by a bare majority, or the majority by a coalition of minorities with strong views on particular issues. This last point is connected with the concentration of producer interests and the dispersion of consumer ones. The beneficial impact of any one protectionist or restrictionist measure on an individual via his professional or geographical interest is far greater than any loss he may bear along with 50 or 60 million other consumers. Thus he is entirely rational to take a producer's view. Political theorists often make the mistake of assuming that if there is a fair balance of policies or bargains between all producers, all is well. But this is simply untrue, even if we forget people such as pensioners and assume that every consumer is also a producer.

For although he gains far more than he loses from restrictionist measures in his own small sphere, he will often lose out on balance, especially in the long run, from the sum total of restrictive measures encompassing the whole field of economic activity. It might pay him to do a deal whereby he renounces his claim to special producer privileges, provided that every other interest group did the same. Yet it is extremely difficult for such a bargain to be negotiated and enforced in a mass democracy. Without the assurance that it would be enforced across the board with the minimum of exceptions, a producer group would rightly think twice of giving up its protections and privileges. These difficulties are aggravated, although not caused, by the geographical basis of representation in parliamentary bodies.

Just as the workings of the market suffer from certain defects, discussed in earlier sections, so does the political process; it it therefore not enough to make some plausible case for a 'neighbourhood effect' or 'externality' to justify government intervention. The cumulative effect of over-extending the political sector must also be considered. It is this desire to limit the domain of the political that distinguishes the economic liberal from some 'social democrats' who would be willing to go along with a great deal of what was said earlier about anti-paternalism and even about impersonal general rules.

To a liberal the market is not just a device to be manipulated by social engineers in accordance with the latest piece of economic research. It is also a mechanism – imperfect and capable of much improvement – which reduces the number and range of decisions which have to be taken by coercive organs after a struggle for votes, power and influence. *Without some presumption of this kind, the bias in favour of some form of market process cannot be supported on supposed grounds of technical economics, even when allied with non-paternalist value judgements; and liberals would do well to acknowledge this fact.*

The direction of the above argument is bound to be distorted or misunderstood by some people whatever disclaimers I add. But perhaps a few very obvious points should be stressed. For all its many weaknesses, democracy is far and away the best method of changing a government by peaceful means; and it is good that governments should be reminded in the most forceful possible way where the wearer believes the shoe pinches, even though the wearer is not an orthopaedic expert. Democracy will work best, however, if it can resist the temptation to expect too much from political activity and to extend the political sphere indefinitely.

Of course it is possible for people to expect too little as well as too much from governments and to make too few collective judgements, as well as too many. Moreover, even if the general bias is too far in favour of political action, there may remain areas where there is too little. But the inherent bias of a *democracy*, which emerges as the élitist elements fall away, is to expect on balance too much. Political action is likely to be more effective, and government more, not less, efficient if limits are placed on the political sphere. Because ministers and officials are blamed for everything that goes wrong anywhere, their feelings of responsibility for the sphere that is indisputably theirs is diminished. It is an organisational commonplace that people perform better if given reasonably defined and limited (if changing) duties than if they are made to feel vaguely responsible for everything that happens around them.

The attribution of total responsibility to governments blunts the edge, not merely of government, but of reformist agitation. A public issue at the time of writing is conditions in some prisons, especially for those on remand who are sometimes acquitted. The *prima facie* evidence suggests that not only are conditions appalling, but that part of their horror is due not to material deficiencies, but to harsh regulations which could be changed at the stroke of a Home Office pen. Yet information of this kind loses its power to shock and stir to action, when it appears as simply one of many other revelations of bad conditions, which are not the direct responsibility of the government, but for which it is made responsible in populist eyes.

## The concept of 'society'

The danger signal for the unwarranted extension of the political sphere is provided by the word 'society' in conjunction with 'modern society', 'society will not tolerate', 'social needs' and similar phrases and slogans. The concept has an interesting history. It was originally invented by the reactionary, nationalist Right to curb the demands of the liberal utilitarians. Faced with the demand to sweep away outmoded institutions, to do away with the authority of kings and bishops and to leave each individual to pursue his happiness in his own way, the conservative replied that this programme was based on a travesty of human nature, it left out of account all kinds of relations among human beings, feelings of national identity to the point of being willing to sacrifice one's life, habits of reverence and obligation, and countless traditions which had a function not immediately obvious to either a Jeremy Bentham or a Saint-Just.

This argument is neither dead nor easy to resolve. But the idea of 'society' and 'social needs' is only a conservative force if there is general agreement on questions of status and obligation. If people agree on hierarchy, it is not too difficult to maintain it in the face of market forces by limiting entry by some form of rationing. The master tailors could maintain the traditional differentials by insisting on long apprenticeships, limiting the number of newcomers and so on. (Of course market forces have always some influence on relativities in the very long run; our concern here is how social values were made effective for substantial periods.) But whether coercion came from some public body, or was enforced by the various groups themselves, the resulting order was relatively stable. Traces of this attitude, of course, prevailed among the craft unions with their traditional ideas of their just status.

But once the traditional consensus broke down, and human expectations were increased, the concept of society as an organism with its own demands became a recipe for unlimited political intervention and for interminable strife. It required unlimited political intervention because it was no longer a matter of protecting established practices that had grown up over the centuries, but of conscious political interference to impose a new scale of status and remuneration believed to be in line with the 'real' needs and desires of society.

The programme will never work for at least two reasons. The actual members of society have violently conflicting views of what a right and just order would be like. The fact that a majority can agree in opinion polls on rough grading of occupations proves very little. What is important is that people should accept the relative positions assigned by others *for their own groups*. It is also doubtful if one can have an organised society in which those who have most responsibility are heavily downgraded; in practice they will try to make up in 'bad, dirty power' for what they lose in 'good, clean money'.[41]

As important as disagreement on relativities is the blown-up expectation of how much there is available to distribute. Where expectations are high and values diverse, some kind of market economy, however imperfect, is a way of enabling people to live peacefully together. It does not require either knowledge of the size of the cake by each citizen or agreement on its distribution. The progressive apostle of 'society' tries to have it both ways: he wants the costy feeling of security and an agreed order of merit characteristic of the hierarchical society, plus the free-for-all in ideas, the radical questioning of all institutions and the levels of aspiration characteristic of a spontaneous, decentralised mercantile society.

Again, it may be possible to improve the trade-offs. But the total programme is arrogant and authoritarian. Unlike traditional authoritarianism, it is of the busy, interfering variety, seeking fresh reorganisations as one campaign takes over from another; and if it were momentarily fulfilled, fresh dissatisfactions and tensions would immediately arise.

As more and more mutually contradictory 'rights' and 'needs' are invented, the gap between aspiration and reality is likely to grow; and growing frustration can lead to growing violence and disintegration. This in turn will lead to demands for harsher penalties, more power for troops and police, as well as anti-liberal clamp-downs on some of the more harmless activities of the 'alternative society' such as pornography and obscenity. Genuine injustices will then be committed by the forces of law and order, which will further increase the sense of outrage of those on the other side.

To attempt to impose a politically determined set of values on a community leads in the developing countries to third-rate dictatorships, with high-sounding slogans and plenty of prestige projects, and has a retarding effect even on statistically measured growth, let alone on the fulfilment of human needs. In the West the result has more often been an anti-interventionist reaction, involving either the electoral defeat of left-wing governments or their settling down into a revisionist programme of marginal trimming.

Inquests are then held and scapegoats found. It was all the fault of Mr X, or 'the balance of payments', or the 'Treasury', or 'the wrong sort of economists', or 'not enough sociologists' or 'Ministers moving too far from their roots in the movement'. Next time, of course it will be 'different' for 'the Party is moving to the left' (as it always does in opposition). Everything was wrong, of course, except the underlying philosophy itself.

There are two main enemies of the liberal outlook rampant at present. One is the widespread view that, instead of emerging from the dispersed actions of millions of individuals, the shape of society should be determined by political decisions which reflect the values of society. It is a sort of totalitarian populism. This is a complicated enemy to nail, as many decisions must be taken politically, and a great deal of government activity is necessary if the interaction on individual decisions is to produce harmonious results. But although it is difficult to define, it is not difficult to recognise. It comes out when one hears expressions such as 'should be banned' or 'everyone should have to . . .'. In a discussion where one person wants to ban cars from towns and his opponent asserts that people have a right to the benefits of the automobile, both are guilty of it. By contrast, when Dr Mishan in one of his more tolerant moods suggests separate residential areas to suit different preferences, with all manner of arrangements from horse-and-buggies only to Los Angeles type urban motorways, he is at least making a constructive suggestion about a complex problem from a liberal point of view.[42]

A threat from another direction is presented by a body of ideas which has at times been given impressive names such as the Corporate State or the New Industrial State. In essence it amounts to the belief in informal directorship of our affairs by the men who run large organisations. 'Gt. Britain Ltd.' is not a bad caricature and conveys the flavour of people who really know what makes things tick, sorting things out together 'without any

ideological nonsense'. The popular image is provided by the
Power Game series. The everyday strength of this position lies in
the close links of many companies with government departments
which buy or heavily subsidise their products. The ideal of those
who think this way is to build up the authority of bodies such as
the Confederation of British Industry and the Trades Union
Congress, so that they have effective powers over their own
members on whose behalf they can negotiate with each other and
the government. The prophets of this brave new world sometimes
assert that it is desirable, sometimes inevitable, and most often
blur the distinction.

A particular offender here is Galbraith, who never makes it
quite clear whether he regrets the advent of the New Industrial
State, or whether he welcomes it as an improvement on
competitive capitalism. Nor can he of all authors say that he is
simply describing and not evaluating. The ambiguity is, of course,
of great advantage. Radicals can approve his general mockery
of supposedly conventional principles, while the business
establishment can have a sneaking admiration for Galbraith
because of his 'realism'. Was he not the prophet of price and wage
controls canonised by the 1971 Republican Administration in its
New Economic Policy?

The dangers of the New Industrial State and of populist
totalitarianism may seem opposed; and perhaps in the last
analysis they are. But it would be possible for demagogic
politicians to ride both horses at once. It is all too easy to imagine
an *ersatz* populism under which a supposedly left-wing
government would try to make the world safe for high technology
'Big Business', in which 'Britain must be in the lead'. The
representatives of the technostructure might be more than happy
to accept the charade of government-appointed directors, or even
of worker representatives – and have the Minister of Technology
to breakfast – in return for a real insulation from market
disciplines and the negative control of the Treasury.

## A provisional summary

It is time to gather up the threads. What then are the main
guidelines with which a liberal should approach economic policy?
The vague term 'guidelines' has been deliberately used in
preference to 'principles'. No attempt to set out the principles of

economic (or any other) policy as a system of deductive inferences from a set of ethical postulates in combination with a set of empirically established regularities has succeeded, or is likely to. Such attempts, when carried out rigorously, have usually led to results of such generality that they are of little use in forming policy.

On the other hand certain general presumptions can be stated. Three main ones have emerged from the preceding pages:

1. Individuals should be regarded *as if* they are the best judges of their own interests, and policy should be designed to satisfy the desires that individuals happen to have, excluding desires to coerce or downgrade other people. This has been termed *liberal utilitarianism*.
2. Policy should be governed by a preference for *impersonal general rules* with a minimum of discretionary power by publicly appointed officials – or private bodies engaged in backstage pressure – over their fellow men.
3. We should try to *limit the domain of political activity* even though we cannot mark out exact boundary lines in advance.

These three guidelines, bringing together strands from rather different liberal traditions, have been put together in this way, because there is no one golden rule of policy which can be guaranteed to promote a society appealing to those who attach a high value to individual freedom. But together they can provide some rough pointers. The three presumptions just summarised are interrelated, but can on occasion conflict with or qualify each other. The second presumption, in favour of general rules, qualifies the liberal utilitarianism of the first presumption; and the third presumption, against overextending the political area, can make one on occasion less keen on general laws than one would otherwise be.

Allied with these presumptions go certain rule-of-thumb maxims, of a lesser status, but still worth mentioning in a summary. These include: 'Look for any self-adjusting mechanisms, whether natural or contrived, wherever possible; if the mechanisms, you find are unsatisfactory, seek to modify their operation rather than to replace them by directives and prohibitions.' Another is: 'It is safer to rely on people's private interests rather than their professed public goals.' This derives from Adam Smith; but the expression 'private interests' has been deliberately used to show that this is not a gospel of selfishness, but rather of relying more on people's private goals, whether personal indulgence, sainthood, charitable works, the welfare of their friends or an infinite variety of possible motives for action other than their professed public policy goals.

A further useful maxim is: 'Irresponsible bodies exercising power, but subject neither to the disciplines of the market place nor to open, political scrutiny and control, are to be avoided.' This must be used with caution, because it leads to a demand that such bodies be made 'politically accountable'. Accountability of this kind can help to strengthen the element of known general principles in their operation and make them less paternalistic, but it also risks overextending the political area of life. Select Committees on Economic Affairs and Parliamentary scrutiny of public expenditure and revenue projections (which I continue to support) are a second best for returning some of the decisions involved to the individual citizen.[43]

The statement of the above guidelines inevitably abounds in vague expressions such as 'over a wide area', 'wherever possible' and their equivalent, alien to formal logic. But for all their lack of rigour they may, nevertheless help to reduce the chances of producing unintended and undesired results through the cumulation of specific policies, each adopted on their own merits. They may also stimulate imagination in the search for policies of which we might otherwise not have thought, or thought less quickly, and they may help to prevent the field from being pre-empted by anti-liberals. They have also a persuasive function in showing that economic liberalism need not be bogus, circular, unrealistic, inhuman, excessively idealistic or otherwise wrong-headed.

The whole outlook I have tried to summarise is consumer rather than producer oriented. It tends to favour the individual or small man and organisation against the big battalions; and it does favour the pursuit of prosperity, provided that that is what people want, and prosperity is interpreted in a non-mechanistic way to include leisure, amenities, congenial working conditions and all the other aspects of living standards which do show up in GNP figures. It favours the permissive 'do-your-own-thing' aspect of the radicalism of the young, but not its intolerant insistence on reshaping the lives and activities of other people. It seeks a society in which the individual is liberated from oppressive working conditions not so much by participation or workers' control, as by the existence of a large variety of differing institutions, between which the individual is free to choose and between which movement is relatively easy.

## (d)  SPECIAL PROBLEMS

### Equality

There is still some more ground to cover even in a non-comprehensive treatment of the subject. This essay started off by defining a liberal as someone who attaches special importance to individual freedom defined in the negative sense. Where does he stand in relation to someone who attaches a special importance to equality in the material things of life? Earlier on I tried to show that the liberal and the egalitarian *should* have a common interest in fighting the notion of payment according to some political decision on the supposed merits of various individuals and occupations.

What has been left open is the question of how far the two ideals can or should be combined. Can one be an egalitarian liberal or a liberal egalitarian? Hayek, as already mentioned, answers with an uncompromising 'No'; and this has at least the merit of focusing on the difficulties and tensions between the two ideals.

What then are the arguments for regarding equality as incompatible with a free society based on a minimum of coercion? Hayek's main 'rule of law' argument is that an attempt to bring about equality by political means is to single out a body of citizens for discriminatory treatment. This is based on the requirement that a general rule must be acceptable to those adversely affected by it; and if one does not accept the requirement for the reasons previously given, the case for equality cannot be demolished on 'rule of law' grounds. Nor can it be demolished by stressing that the only way to make people equal would be to have laws treating them unequally. Such laws could be of an extremely general abstract and impersonal character, distinguishing between people according to some highly general criteria such as income or wealth. Certainly, the wish of a majority of the population to help the less well off, or achieve any other worthy object, should be taken more seriously if it is prepared to foot the bill itself than if the generosity is exercised at the expense of another group, such as the rich from whom it is fondly hoped that endless resources can be squeezed. But this is not the same as giving the better off classes a veto over the tax and social security system.

Hayek is on somewhat stronger ground when he objects to enforced equality because people would have to be told what to do, and freedom of choice of occupation would be at an end. If a state were ever to go the whole hog and decree complete equality of incomes, Hayek would indeed be right. In that case there would have to be the state compulsion to work a minimum amount of hours with much supervision to prevent slacking. Even then some occupations will be understaffed and others overstaffed, as relative earnings will provide no guide. Therefore the state would have to direct labour. Thus, complete equality of incomes would be incompatible with free choice of occupations, as well as with prosperity and efficiency.

Let us, however, start at the other end. How far can one go from the present state of affairs towards equality without bringing in direction of labour? If a stage-by-stage attempt to diminish inequality takes the form of imposing minimum wages, one of the principal effects will be increased unemployment among those whom the measure is supposed to benefit. So it would be better for the egalitarian case to assume that the effort takes the form of progressive income taxes at the top and negative income taxes, or the equivalent in social benefits, at the bottom.

A full analysis of the implications would be highly complex. But there is a basic distinction to be drawn between people who are, and are not, capable of doing each other's jobs. There is a surprisingly prevalent notion that classical economic theory predicts that the most unpleasant jobs should be the best paid; and that if this is incorrect in practice, levelling upwards presents no problem. Both assertions are wrong. People take unattractive ill-paid jobs, such as that of the street cleaner or sewage worker, because they are not able to do, or eligible for, the more attractive ones. (Whether this inability is innate, or the result of inferior education or family opportunities, is not the issue here – we are dealing with the situation that happens to prevail for whatever reason.)

So long as the minimum income, which a negative income tax or other device seeks to promote, is well below the general level of earnings in such occupations, there need be no serious trouble;

and the scheme should help to deal with poverty due to age, illness, large families and so on. But as the guaranteed minimum income approaches and perhaps even exceeds earnings in occupations which are both low paid and inherently unattractive, the supply of workers concerned will seriously fall off. There are then two possibilities. One is that the guaranteed minimum is unconditional. In that case, wages in the low paid, unpleasant occupations will have to rise. This, however, will both reduce the demand for the services in question and stimulate mechanisation and other devices for saving unskilled labour. Thus the level of unemployment and unused resources will rise.

The second possibility is that the minimum income is guaranteed to an able-bodied adult only if he is either working or honestly seeking work. In that case, something very like direction of labour is involved. Without the guaranteed minimum, the relative wages paid to sewage workers, dustmen, hospital porters and countless other unskilled and unpleasant occupations requiring comparable ability, serve in a very rough and ready way to ensure the right distribution between them. If there were too few sewage workers, their wages could be raised relative to the others. But once the guaranteed minimum is above prevailing wages in all such occupations, relative wages have no power to attract or deter, and compulsion is required.

The moral to be drawn from this oversimplified illustration is that an attempt to level upwards beyond a certain point involves a choice between either compulsion, or tolerating semi-voluntary idleness and wasted resources. The further the levelling up goes, the greater the cost in efficiency and the greater the pressure to use compulsion. There are, in fact, disturbing analogies to this model even in some of the present practices of the social security and employment services.

Similar arguments can also apply in the upper ranges. Let us suppose that business executives earn, on average, more than financial journalists, and that the latter are not suitable for business posts. If highly progressive taxation in the relevant bands reduces to vanishing point the difference in take-home pay between the two occupations, then some business executives might prefer to become financial journalists or take up some third occupation. (Business executives will be able to pass on some of their taxes by obtaining higher pre-tax salaries; but this will be by no means a complete offset, as the demand for their services will be sensitive to their *pre-tax* cost.) It is hardly feasible to compel people to become business executives in the way that the late Roman emperors tried to compel people to take up municipal office. The likely result is a lowering of standards in the field of practical business, and an excess supply of financial journalists. Restrictive practices aside, the net result would be a fall in the pre-tax pay of such journalists and an increase in their number (and perhaps their quality). The final equilibrium is likely to involve their being fewer and lower grade business executives and more and higher grade financial journalists than the community required before the tax distortion began.

Let us now make the alternative assumption that a number of financial journalists could have been business executives, but preferred not to, despite the difference in pay. In these circumstances, it is in fact doubtful if levelling downwards is really sound egalitarianism, because for those at the margin of decision, the net advantages of the two professions, pecuniary and other, are already equal. A tax-induced narrowing of differentials will, if it is nevertheless insisted upon, have the same effect as in the last example and lead to an increase in the number of financial journalists relative to business executives.

Finally, let us suppose that the difference of earnings in two occupations calling for similar talents is not due to choices made at the beginning of a career, but is due to a shift in demand for the services in question. It is not easy, either practically or emotionally, for people who have committed their careers to one occupation or industry to make a sudden change. In the absence of equalising taxation a differential would persist for some time, attracting new recruits and the more flexible younger people into the better paid occupation, until eventually supply and demand came into better balance, and the differential would then tend to decrease. A highly egalitarian tax structure will slow down the readjustment. The market price of the service in greater demand would shoot up much higher, and its expansion to meet public demand would be much slower. There would be a loss of efficiency – and the pattern of output would be different from the conforming to consumer requirements – but it would not involve direction of people to specific jobs.

The moral of the various examples is that *general* egalitarian policies need not involve direction of labour, provided the community is willing to tolerate a loss in the efficiency with which its requirements are met. In the limiting case of complete equality, the loss of efficiency would be so great that direction of labour would almost certainly be used in an attempt to limit this loss.

There is thus a three-way trade-off between freedom, equality and prosperity.* Douglas Jay implicitly recognises this when he defines the economic aim of socialism as 'the minimum of inequality that is workable if human beings are actively to use their talents'.[44] (This is much more satisfactory than his attempt a few pages earlier to equate freedom with equality.) As he also makes the libertarian assumption that there will be no compulsion or direction of labour, his implied operational trade-off is between prosperity and equality.

One major difficulty about this goal is that 'less inequality' is inherently ambiguous. Is it equally important to level down the rich or level up the poor? And, if not, what weighting does one apply? The difficulties can be brought out by the following example (Table 2) of a community of only three people:

*Table* 2 Hypothetical income distribution

| Income of individual | First distribution | Second distribution |
|---|---|---|
| A | 28 | 21 |
| B | 12 | 21 |
| C | 11 | 9 |
| Mean income | 17 | 17 |
| Average dispersion from mean ('degree of inequality') | 7⅓ | 5⅓ |

The first distribution would be generally regarded as very unequal. The fortunate A has well over twice as much as both B and C. The average deviation of all incomes from the mean of 17 is

* This three-way trade-off seems to me the underlying message of Henry Wallich's interesting book *The Cost of Freedom* (Harper, 1960). Professor Wallich argues, as against Hayek, that attempts at 'democratic planning' may lead not to serfdom, but to 'pressures for avoiding readjustments, shoring up losing situations with subsidies' and generally doing things 'the easier rather than the better way' (p. 47).

7⅓. In the second distribution the degree of inequality appears to have diminished. The rich A, who now has only 21, has been reduced to much nearer the mean and the scatter is now much less. The average deviation from the mean is now only 5⅓. Unfortunately, however, the poorest of the individuals, C, is now 2 points poorer. (This example abstracts completely from incentive effects and assumes that the amount to be shared is constant.)

The most frequently used measures of income are a shade more sophisticated, but suffer from the same inherent definitional problems. A good example is the Lorenz curve showing the proportion of total income received by cumulative percentages of recipients, starting from the least well off. This is normally summarised by the 'Gini coefficient' (which depends on the area between the diagonal and the curve). Yet, such a measure fails to distinguish between changes in distribution due to levelling off in the upper reaches (more equality at the top) from those due to gains at the bottom (more equality at the bottom), or shifts on either side of the middle. Even for the purposes of ordinal comparisons between two countries or two periods, the Gini coefficient is ambiguous if the Lorenz curves intersect. A comparison of the 66 possible comparisons between 12 countries at different stages of development by A. B. Atkinson shows that in 50 of the cases they *do* intersect.[45] Indeed, Puerto Rico and Italy (around 1950) emerged with lower Gini coefficients – which were supposed to indicate more equality – than Sweden, Denmark and, the Netherlands; and India had the same coefficient as West Germany. The truth seems to be that equality tends to be greater towards the bottom in poor countries and greater towards the top in more advanced societies.

Professor Atkinson states that some overall 'social welfare function' must be specified before different distributions can be compared. But one would have to be both very sure of one's ideal choice among hypothetical distributions and highly expert at this branch of mathematics before accepting any such measure. It would be much better to reject any single index and base judgements on the total shape of the income distribution. The kind of egalitarian who prefers the second distribution (shown on p. 115) to the first may be legitimately charged with being motivated more by envy of the rich than desire to help the poor.

Another difficulty with the egalitarian goal, modified à la Jay, is that human beings 'actively using their talents' (or using 'reasonably fully' the productive abilities of the community) is not a state of affairs which either exists or does not. There is a continuous range with no sharp cut-off point. The extent to which it is realised depends both on the extent to which human talent is employed, rather than being left voluntarily or involuntarily idle, and the way in which these talents are used.

The proposed goal would have to be stated more specifically. One suggestion would be to attempt to reduce incomes in the upper ranges until the point is reached where any further reduction would ultimately damage the bottom $x$ per cent of householders via its effect on incentives, efficiency and the utilisation of resources. The percentage $x$ would have to be an arbitrary one; it could be of the bottom 10 per cent, 25 per cent, 50 per cent, or 75 per cent depending on the precise interpretation being put on egalitarianism. An alternative aim would be to seek a distribution of income that would *maximise* the average standard of living of that of the bottom 10 per cent, 25 per cent, 50 per cent or 75 per cent. The latter interpretation, although most helpful to the poor or less well off, has modified the egalitarian goal so drastically as to call the label itself into question.

Once an egalitarian can admit pragmatic departures from his ideal on Jay-type lines to secure a more satisfactory use of the community's productive resources, he cannot refuse to admit such departures on the consumption side. Hayek's argument in *The Constitution of Liberty*, that the existence of people of independent means was of value to the rest of the population, was predictably received with much scorn by his critics. Yet it is undoubtedly true that wealthy individuals have pioneered new forms of enjoyment in the arts, in sport and in many other fields which have afterwards become available to the majority. This is true whether one thinks of the Esterhazys patronising Haydn, the Medicis nourishing Michaelangelo, or the Victorian leisured class developing cricket and rugby football. The point is even stronger if we extend the concept of consumption activities to cover new ideas in politics, morals or religion. Most of the great campaigns against slavery, or cruelty to children or animals, or for penal reform, depended on the enthusiasm of a minority with means.

There are, of course, many reverse examples in the modern age of working-class consumption styles aped by the smart set; and in the political or campaigning field it is easier in an affluent society to raise funds by numerous small subscriptions. Even so, it is still very useful to have some people of means to supply the initial impetus to get such campaigns off the ground. It would be an extremely bold man who could confidently say that there was no longer a role for the wealthy either in developing new tastes and patterns of living or in supporting good (and bad) causes. The future will probably see a two-way process, with some tastes and activities spreading upwards from the bottom and others downwards from the top.

Those egalitarians who have recognised an element of validity in the above argument have sometimes urged conscious attempts by public authorities to take over the pioneering role of the rich. But such efforts, of which the Arts Council is the obvious model, desirable though they are, inevitably lack the spontaneity arising from private individuals pursuing their own diverse and sometimes eccentric goals. Many of the most useful spillover activities for their fellows have indeed been unintentional results of activities of playboys and *bon vivants*.

Hayek remarks that if no better method were available, one in a hundred or one in a thousand selected *at random* should be endowed with fortunes with which they could do what they liked.[46] This would be worth doing even if only one in a hundred or one in a thousand of those selected used their opportunities in ways that appeared retrospectively beneficial to others. Some egalitarians, if they could be induced to give the argument a hearing, might settle for this method – and it would certainly be better than not having such fortunes at all. The argument for allowing inheritance, as well as other kinds of luck, to play a role is that certain socially valuable qualities will often be formed only in the course of two or three generations.

The real weakness of Hayek's position, which few, if any, hostile reviewers have spotted, is that it is, even in principle, completely and characteristically non-quantitative. There must come a point of concentration of income and wealth when the spillover benefits of the consumption of the rich would be more than counterbalanced by their impoverishing effect on the rest of the population. To allow 1 per cent of households to account for 5 or 10 per cent of total personal consumption may be a price well worth paying for the sake of these spillover benefits (as well as for the incentive effects for the working members of that 1 per cent on the size of the total cake). But if 1 per cent consumed 99 per cent, the price would be clearly too high. Somewhere in between must be a point of balance. (The position in 1970 was approximately that of 1 per cent consuming 5 per cent).

Strictly speaking, a liberal does not have to go any further. Having made the above stipulations and qualifications in relation to the pursuit of equality, he does not have to express a view on the optimum distribution of income or wealth. His concern is with how far any proposed redistribution affects freedom. He is not concerned with the virtues of equality as a goal, and liberals can and do take different views on the matter.

It is, nevertheless, worth asking whether there is any meaningful goal other than equality, or accepting a distribution that emerges either from the existing market, or from a market in which the anti-competitive elements have been reduced, which will be genuinely impersonal, and not involve political judgements of the merits of individuals or professions. For, in the absence of a third principle, there is a real danger that people will think the two impersonal alternatives too extreme and fall back on the dangerous ideas of reward according to merit, or on the 'specific egalitarianism' which will be discussed below.

The most promising third principle is to be derived from the ideas of Rawls already mentioned:[47] the kind of distribution of income and wealth that people would vote for if they were ignorant of what their own position in the scale was to be. Even apart from the imaginative leap, the principle does raise other difficulties. For the different hypothetical distributions for which people would vote would reveal differences in attitude to risk and uncertainty. Someone with a taste for gambling would be interested in seeing that there were some really big incomes just in case he came out lucky. It is not very satisfactory that a majority should be able to impose its preference on gambling versus insurance on the rest of the population.

Yet it is surely much less unsatisfactory than either the Hayek principle, which would give a veto to the richest of the rich, or the crude democratic formula, which would allow 51 per cent of the population to despoil the other 49 per cent. Indeed, there is a great deal of evidence from poll data and MPs' correspondence that the majority of the population who fall in the middle income ranges are jealous both of those in upper ranges – they dislike surtax cuts – and of those at the bottom end – for they dislike family allowances at least as much. Indeed, the second distribution shown in the table on p. 115 might actually be *preferred* by the electorate. (One must remember that most of the votes are with the 'B's.) But only a blind or bigoted democrat would wish to bless such vindictiveness towards rich and poor alike by the mass of mediocrity in the middle.

The ignorance formula does at least secure disinterestedness, which straightforward voting does not. Moreover, *if* it were operated, I would guess that a large degree of consensus would then emerge. The first thought of most people would surely be to avoid finding themselves in some sort of 'depressed tenth'. They would be interested to level up enough to make sure that there was no badly depressed poverty-stricken tail of the income distribution in which, with bad luck, they might find themselves. At this end, they would be more concerned with insurance than with gambling. They would also dislike so large a concentration at the top that it heavily depressed the median income.

On the other hand, they would not like to flatten out the top of the distributional diamond so much that the median income was reduced for incentive reasons. Most people, I would hazard, would also like the idea of a few really large prizes for the lucky minority, although there would be disagreement on the exact size and distribution of the prize money.*

Enough has been said to emphasise the very large area over which the thoughtful egalitarian and a radically-minded economic liberal can agree. Both could join in an onslaught on artificial barriers to entry imposed by unnecessary apprenticeship or professional qualifications. Both can support generous payments to the poorer members of the community. Professor Milton Friedman, who is a rather extreme economic liberal, has rightly stated that the only limitation on this sort of levelling up assistance is the wealth and generosity of the majority of the electorate.[48] Moreover, a thoughtful egalitarian would surely agree that a good deal (although not all) of existing inequality

---

* Professor Rawls himself appears to identify the maximisation of the long run welfare of the most disadvantaged representative person as the sole criterion of distribution with the one that people would choose in such a position of ignorance. I do not think that the two can be *identified* in this way. The considerations which would enter into choice in such a position are more complex and would probably vary from one person to another. The deliberately vaguer statements made above indicate the degree of special concern for the least well off which might be reasonably expected in this hypothetical position.

reflects the non-pecuniary aspects of different jobs. The Jay formula of 'an equal right to happiness' cannot mean equality of money income for jobs of varying degrees of discomfort, hazard or opportunities for leisure. There are occupations such as opera singing or professional sport, where high rewards are not just 'rents' for scarce abilities, but are to a large extent compensation for the very large risks run by any new entrant into these fields; and a rational egalitarian ought to allow the legitimacy of such discrepancies.

The egalitarian and the liberal could also go a considerable way together on the taxation of inheritance and wealth. Neither should see any virtue in a system of nominally very high estate duties with loopholes that make them a voluntary levy. The introduction of a Gifts Tax, and other reforms would make a lower rate of duty more effective than the present high one. Although such a change might be a second best for an egalitarian to duties which were both high and effective, it would be an improvement for both groups compared with the present system. Liberals can perfectly well support the transformation of estate duty into a legacy duty to promote a wider diffusion of inherited wealth – again, a change that would be inferior from an egalitarian point of view to the abolition of inherited wealth, but an improvement on the present.

A liberal utilitarian would also prefer, during a person's lifetime, to tax capital itself rather than the yield from capital, as the latter kind of tax is a heavy deterrent to risk-taking. This would point to an annual wealth tax in *place* of the present differential against unearned income. (The £250 million yield from the differential could have been replaced in 1970 by a wealth tax of 1 per cent on wealth above £20 000 or just over 2 per cent on wealth above £50 000.) The egalitarian inclination to impose the wealth tax *in addition* to the present differential should, however, be checked by reflection on the possible effects of such double taxation on investment, saving and risk-taking. But, even if an egalitarian refuses to be checked by such considerations, the above examples are sufficient to show that there are many reforms which he and the liberal can both advocate which, even if not ideal, are at least an improvement on the present.

The real parting of the ways comes only with the rate of progression on the upper ranges of taxes on income. This does not mean that all economic liberals must share the opposition of Friedman and Hayek to progressive taxation. The expressed sentiments of these economists convey, in fact, a misleading impression; for their attitudes to benefits imply considerable progression in net rates on the lower ranges. What they really mean is that the rate of progression should taper off at a moderate upper limit of well below 50 per cent. Other economic liberals, while wanting to preserve the opportunity for some to achieve high incomes and even found fortunes, would certainly agree that the tax rates should vary with incomes and not only in the lowest ranges. My own personal preference, for what it is worth, would be a gradual climb which levelled out at a marginal rate of 50–60 per cent. One cannot expect egalitarians to like even this in principle; but before they reject it out of hand, they should consider that high nominal rates are, to a notorious extent, avoided or evaded. More effective, if somewhat lower rates, should be at least a second best from their point of view.

There are, in fact, few subjects more conducive to intellectual self-deception, or even dishonesty, than the taxation of personal incomes. Many economists (not to speak of politicians and other commentators) have protested too much about the disincentive effects of high tax rates in the upper income ranges without admitting that they have other grounds for opposition and would be *disappointed* if the disincentive effect were found to be small. This is an unfortunate aspect of the English utilitarian heritage which, on the one hand, asserted that incomes ought ideally to be equal and then, on the other hand, discovered a thousand and one countervailing reasons why they should not in fact be so.

The valuable part of utilitarianism is not the principle of equal weighting for all; but the idea that governments should concern themselves with the satisfaction of people's desires rather than some 'higher' goal such as national honour or prestige, territorial aggrandisement or the enforcement of a divinely sanctioned code of behaviour. Reasons have been given in the preceding pages for believing that equality of incomes would be positively undesirable even if it had a zero effect on the rate of growth of the measured Gross Domestic Product. If both sides openly acknowledged that they were not primarily motivated by the incentives issue, the latter could be analysed more candidly.

The search for debating points affects at least as badly the egalitarian side of the argument. It is easy to scoff at simplistic tax-cutting propaganda by pointing out that taxes on incomes (whether direct or indirect) have a 'substitution' and an 'income' effect, which point in different directions. The substitution effect increases the attraction of leisure over work (and of undemanding work over demanding but better paid work), the higher the rate of tax. The income effect means that people have to work harder to obtain a given income. The two effects works in opposite directions and a tax cut can either be a stimulant or deterrent to effort. But it is disingenuous to pretend that analysis ends at this point. The substitution effect relates to *marginal* tax rates, the income effect to the *average* rate paid by the taxpayer on his whole income (what the Inland Revenue calls the 'effective' rate).

Up to the end of 1970–1, marginal rates were so high relative to average rates on the larger professional and management earnings that the disincentive effect was the one that prevailed (to the extent that the rates were made effective); and it is no rebuttal to point out that equally high marginal rates were to be found at the bottom end of the scale owing to the operation of a series of unco-ordinated means tests. An egalitarian who accepts the Jay qualification about the minimum inequality required for the effective functioning of the system should not want to return to the pre-1971 situation of marginal rates on earned incomes crossing the 50 per cent threshold at £4000, 75 per cent at £7000, and eventually reaching 91¼ per cent. The argument of the agnostic applies with greatest force to those in the income bands above, but not too far above, the average, who paid in 1970–1 a marginal rate of just over 30 per cent. They carried much less conviction in the surtax range, where tax cuts were regarded as more politically controversial.

The whole question is often discussed as if the main issue were the amount of effort expended in a given job, when the main disincentive effects in all probability arise from the choice of one job rather than another. The deterrent effects on risky activities – whether jobs or investment – is a matter of arithmetic and can be worked out for himself by any sceptical reader if he will compare the value of two streams of earnings with different probability dispersions around the same average, under more and less progressive tax systems. Of course, knowledge would be advanced if someone could design a really good empirical test of the total net effects of very high marginal rates at either end of the social scale. The surveys I have seen which purport to refute the disincentive effects do not come anywhere near doing so; few even bear on the question. In the meanwhile, no one has answered Lord Robbins's question: 'If we could not argue that it made no difference if the marginal rate were 20s. in the pound, why should we speak as if the position is so radically changed when the residue from a pound's worth of earnings is 6d or 1s?'[49]

In some ways the most irritating aspect of this whole controversy is the emphasis of *soi-disant* egalitarians on 'non-pecuniary incentives'. It may be possible to create something out of nothing by inventing titles, decorations and orders which will serve as a substitute for take-home pay – although why this should specially appeal to those who claim to dislike social stratification is hard to understand. In any case, this process cannot be carried too far without these badges becoming heavily devalued. For the most part 'non-pecuniary' incentives are the pleasure of accomplishment (or just of passing the time), congenial working conditions, or the desire for power and importance. The first is besides the point, as one of the main functions of giving higher net pay to some people of comparable abilities than to others, is to attract them into jobs which yield comparatively little in pleasures of this kind. As for congenial working conditions, these are an aspect of real income, and there is no particular reason to subsidise them (and we are talking here about company cars, executive suites and dining rooms at the expense of living standards in a person's free time). What there is of the argument rests heavily on a belief that power over others is a lesser evil than high pay and should be encouraged as a substitute. This reverses Keynes's dictum that 'it is better that a man should tyrannise over his bank balance than over his fellow citizens'; and, as he insisted, the two were sometimes alternatives.[50]

Instead of expending effort on trying to restore confiscatory marginal tax rates on earnings from work and capital, those of us who are concerned with the distribution of income would do better to worry about the possible effects of rising land values in a society where land ownership is very highly concentrated. With rising affluence and population, the growing demand for pure space which cannot be increased by human effort could make land very much scarcer relative to labour and capital than it has been in the past; and land rents could come to absorb a higher proportion of the national income. It will be obvious to the reader that I believe that the problem of distribution, as distinct from poverty, has been vastly exaggerated by British egalitarians; and, in particular, that the gain to the rest of the population from eliminating the excess incomes of, say, the top 5 per cent would be negligible or, more probably, negative. But the situation would be very different if 40, 50, 60 or 70 per cent of incomes accrued to a small minority of owners of pure space, the total of which was in no way affected by their work saving or enterprise.

It is too soon to say whether there is anything in this nightmare. The share of the national income going to landowners is still remarkably small for a crowded island. The spectre of a monstrous increase in the landowners' share of the national income has haunted economics since the time of Ricardo. Yet as late as 1969, the share of personal income before tax from property of all kinds was only 12 per cent; and the greater part of this was due to earnings on capital (including home ownership and pension fund income) or interest payments on the national debt rather than to land rents.[51] But the possibility of a virulent attack of the disease of land shortage is high enough to merit contingency planning – more so than many of the other horrors that alarm the prophets of doom.

*The very worst cure for such a situation would be the control of land rents.* If land were so scarce, it would be particularly important to make the most of it, which could only be done by charging full market rents; and, where land is state-owned, this should take the form of parking charges, road tolls, charges for entry to recreational areas and so on. For private land, the object should be to find some way of combining full market rents with a recovery of some of these rents by the general community of taxpayers. The search for some form of taxing pure land values, such as site value taxation, which would not distort the use of land, should continue. But judging by the discouraging experience of the past, such schemes will not be easy to implement successfully; and in the last resort, even the nationalisation of land, provided that it is vested in many different local authorities and other independent bodies who are encouraged to act on commercial principles and compete with each other, would be a lesser evil to those of below-market rents in the envisaged situation. But a better solution, if only it could be brought into effect, would be to make a reality of the slogan of a property-owning democracy. If ether land itself or the financial investments which represented land at one or two removes were more widely distributed, the perverse effects of high rents would be very much reduced.

## Specific egalitarianism

The kind of egalitarianism so far discussed may be termed 'general' egalitarianism. Despite its popularity in certain academic and Whitehall circles and its links with the puritan tradition, it is not a widely held ideal among the public. 'Specific' egalitarianism is more widespread and is a much more important threat to liberty. (Some general egalitarians are also specific egalitarians, but this need not be the case.)

Specific egalitarianism comes in two forms: a mild levelling up form and a strong levelling down one. The mild form is paternalistic, but not viciously so. It is suggested by slogans such as: 'Everybody has a right to a decent home, at a price he can afford, and decent medical treatment and education, irrespective of means.' It can even be justified as a liberal–paternalist compromise on the following lines: 'By all means let people spend their own incomes in their own way, but we are only prepared to be taxed to help the less well-off if we can be sure that the money goes for food, homes, health or the welfare of children and is not free spending money for beer and cigarettes.' One may not like such feelings, but they are not incompatible with a free society, provided that no one is prevented from spending above the state minimum. Indeed, if some variant of the voucher system is used, there is no need for even the provision of the bare minimum to be a state monopoly. The mild form of 'specific egalitarianism' is a misnomer for policies concerned with minima, but the label has already been struck on such policies in the literature on the subject and it is too late to alter it.

This mild form only becomes a menace to liberty, or to the rational conduct of affairs, when the state explicitly or implicitly takes on a commitment that it cannot or will not fulfil. The most obvious example is housing subsidies and rent controls. If the public authorities were prepared to build enough houses and flats to supply to the full the extra demand created by their policies, more of the nation's resources would go into housing than citizens desire. But this would be the limit of state coercion and once sufficient accommodation was built, the rent controls could be allowed to wither away. A permanent housing shortage and the power of public officials over individual lives arises when a country has the controls and the subsidies without a public housebuilding programme large enough to meet the implicit commitment. The threat to liberty, and the many anomalies and inequities, arise not from the intrinsic nature of the aims, but from the acceptance by the authorities under public pressure of a series of *ad hoc* policies without an attempt to think through their longer term implications – an illustration of the dangers of over-extension of the political sphere already discussed.

The stronger, levelling down form of specific egalitarianism comes in a different category altogether. It is symbolised by deceptively attractive slogans such as: 'Nobody should be able to buy a privileged education for his child or better medical treatment simply because he has more money.' Despite its demagogic appeal, it is a severe use of state coercion to limit freedom of choice; and if any doctrine is the true road to serfdom, it is this strong form of specific egalitarianism. A fixed travel allowance to 'prevent anyone buying a better holiday for himself simply because he has money', would be an example of the attitude in question. Usually, however, arguments for this form of specific egalitarianism tend to concentrate on social services such as health and education. The three arguments one meets most frequently boil down to the following:

1. Use of the same education and health service by the whole population is desirable as a common badge of citizenship which reduces the gulf between different sections of society. (This is sometimes called the 'integrationist' argument.)
2. Expenditure on a superior education by better-off families – or even by ordinary families who value education above the average – gives some children an unfair start over others of equal innate ability, and is thus incompatible with equality of opportunity.
3. The supply of goods and services may be 'inelastic' and will not therefore respond to market incentives. Some form of rationing may be required in such cases if the poor are not to be deprived of access to them.

Of the above arguments, only the third, based on the supposed inelasticity of supply of some services, deserves a hearing by liberals, and it is the one which James Tobin stresses in his defence of specific egalitarianism.[52] The eventual judgement here must, of course, depend on questions of fact as well as of values. If there is some reason why the output of a product cannot respond to increased demand, then the market will cease to perform its normal functions on the supply side (although it can still ration available supplies in line with relative preferences). The key feature of a war situation, in which price control and rationing are introduced, is that there are physical constraints on the supply of food and consumer goods which cannot be easily increased irrespective of profitability.

Such a situation is very exceptional for most products in time of peace. The view that it exists in the medical field (the one most frequently cited) – and hence that 'queue-jumping' is reprehensible – is plausible only if one considers the purely short-term elasticity of supply. There is ample evidence that the number who train as doctors and other medical personnel (and who remain in this country) respond to prospects of pay and employment. Nor is there any reason to doubt that non-NHS hospitals and nursing homes would be built in response to an upsurge in the private market. It is no coincidence that nearly all Western European countries, which do not possess a fully-fledged state health service, devote a larger proportion of the GNP to health than does the UK. The short-run inelasticity of supply of medical services may point to a gradualist policy of encouraging private provision, but only an obsessional pre-occupation with the short term would be a reason for a permanent policy of forbidding or restricting it.

The first two of the arguments listed on page 127 leads towards, not merely an egalitarian, but a uniform, society and embodies a set of value-judgements at the opposite pole from that which sets store by individual choice and variety in life styles. There is no justification for the high moral tone sometimes adopted by those who wish education, medical care, insurance, and, in some cases, housing, to be provided exclusively on a common basis by the state. What is there so elevated about a society in which take-home pay is for food and amusement only, and other essentials are provided communally on a free or subsidised basis, without the individual having taken any responsibility for them?[53]

If top priority is to be given to equality of opportunity, in the sense of preventing one child from acquiring any advantages over any other apart from those resulting from genetic endowments, then, indeed, all discretionary or private expenditure on education must be forbidden; and it must be forbidden even if all parents enjoy the same income. But there are many other types of family activities which give some children advantage over others, including the possession of books, foreign travel, or the provision of a 'good home'. An economic liberal can be enthusiastic about policies for giving more opportunities to those starting at the bottom. But absolute equality of opportunity is a mistaken goal. It points inexorably to Plato's recommendation in *The Republic* (based on an extension of Spartan practices) that children should be taken away from their parents at birth and great care taken to prevent them discovering their identity.[54] As Bertrand Russell remarks, 'Plato possessed the art to dress up illiberal suggestions in such a way that they deceived future ages'.[55] The heritage of this brilliant authoritarian still survives in much would-be 'progressive' contemporary thinking. A modern exemplar is James Tobin who, in the well-argued but fundamentally sinister article just quoted, points to the selective US military draft as an egalitarian ideal, suggests the prohibition of volunteering, and actually toys with the idea of setting soldiers' pay well below effective civilian alternatives to perpetrate the draft. If this is representative of the US progressive establishment, the revolt of the campuses is all too easy to understand.

## The role of economics

If egalitarianism is the most explosive landmine for the economic liberal to negotiate, the relation of his doctrines to economics as an academic discipline is the most elusive. One orthodox view is that there is no relation at all, as economics ought to be a positive science, with findings which can be used to advance any political or ethical ideal according to the taste of the user. This is much too simplistic a distinction. The word 'ought' in the above formulation is itself revealing. It is strange, to say the least, that although all the varieties of economic liberalism rank as political philosophies, professional economists have been largely instrumental in developing them. There are no collectivist or conservative philosophies with which mainstream professional economists have had a similar association. Indeed, it is remarkable how far the endeavours to develop a 'socialist economics' have consisted of attempts to transplant the liberal ideas of the market economy and the price mechanism to an environment of state ownership. The lack of any conservative economic philosophy has long been well known and is a point of pride with some conservatives.

A large number of economists are, of course, virulently opposed to any form of economic liberalism. But they are exhibiting a reaction to a strong tradition within their own profession. Although they may think that they are opposing a pro-capitalist position, a little investigation soon shows that the actual policies of pro-capitalist governments bear very little relation to the doctrines of economic liberalism – indeed, Galbraith has taken a justified delight in explaining how Nixon has violated all its tenets. The anti-liberals in the economic profession are ranged against a whole line of philosophically inclined economists from Adam Smith down to Hayek and Friedman rather than against a political party or a group of capitalists. Empirical evidence can be produced to show that there is much greater support for liberal policy positions in an advanced Western economy among economists than among politicians and commentators, and that economists of differing political beliefs often hold common policy positions which distinguish them from other educated laymen interested in public affairs.

This is a somewhat remarkable position for a would-be neutral science. It is related to a profound ambiguity about the subject matter of economics. According to one tradition it is a science of human behaviour in relation to the material things of life, and therefore sheds light on the factors determining the growth of income and wealth. A different tradition sees it as the science or logic of choice (which of the two is itself controversial). According to the latter tradition, there is no such thing as economic ends. Economics is concerned with the allocation of resources, energy and time among alternatives, and the view of the economist as a philistine concerned to multiply material riches is itself a vulgar misconception.

There are usually deep-seated reasons why subjects do not fit neatly into logical pigeon-holes and the matter will not be resolved by proclaiming dogmatically that one or other concept is the right one. There is an inevitable strain between the two approaches, but they have co-existed (often within the same individual) for nearly a century and neither is likely to give way completely to the other. It is simplest, however, to start with the older view – which also corresponds to the layman's image – that economics is concerned with behaviour in relation to material things, particularly where money can be brought into the picture.

The economist has so far had very little to say on many of the most important determinants of output and living standards, in particular on science and technology and attitudes towards change and innovation. Technological matters are the concern of other specialists, and essays by economists on national attitudes and other psychological intangibles carry no more weight than those of anyone else. The main subject on which they can even aspire to a professional competent is the functioning of markets, and, in particular, the way in which supply and demand relate to prices and incomes. As we have already seen, the price mechanism, even when used for paternalist objectives, is a relatively *liberal means*.

In most individual markets price is the most important variable about which the economist can pronounce. Variations in the level of incomes may be important, but in any particular case, there is little that can be done about them. Whether an economist is investigating the steel industry or the structure of fares, there is little he can do about the incomes of those operating in the market; his contribution is likely to be mainly on pricing policy and the disaggregation of costs and receipts from different activities.

It is only when it comes to the attempted management of demand and output in the economy as a whole that an 'economics without price' has been evolved. Keynesian fiscal policy, of the type practised for most of the postwar period, has attempted to control output entirely via real incomes; indeed, the associated forecasts and policy recommendations have been in 'real terms' and have largely abstracted from any influence of either absolute or relative prices. It is therefore not surprising that economists of the 'national income forecasting' school are less wedded to liberal economic attitudes than their colleagues (but also less keen on detailed intervention, as they pin so much faith on global management). Even in their case, however, the role of price is forcibly brought home via the effect of the exchange rate on the external balance; and the competence of economists again lies in their analysis of front or backdoor exchange rates – which are of course a special kind of price. It does not lie in exhortations to export more, or in whipping up enthusiasm inside industrial committees such as the 'Little Neddies'.

Another kind of economics which minimises markets or prices arises from growth models which make the proportion of the national income invested (especially in manufacturing industry) the key to growth and from this go on to suggest that the forcible reduction of the share of consumption in the national income (aided perhaps by overseas aid) is the key to prosperity. This structure of ideas still has some influence in advanced industrial countries; but it always had too many weaknesses to become the main strand of economic thinking there. Differences in investment ratios were found to be inadequate to account for observed differences in growth rates; in any case, the investment differences seemed at least as likely to be a consequence as a cause of growth. Moreover, the idea of the capital market and the rate of interest as having some relevance to choice between present and future satisfactions never entirely lost hold; and the various distortions in the market allegedly keeping investment too low have been offset in recent thinking by the emphasis on environmental spillover which might make it undesirably high. It is mainly in connection with developing countries and the Third World that economic explanations which play down prices and markets have really captured mainstream thinking.[56]

Indeed, economics, conceived as the study of behaviour affecting material wealth, has remarkably little to say on the effects of different political and economic systems and ideologies. There have been fast growing economies in both the capitalist and the Communist world; and even among Western countries there has been almost no systematic relation between growth rates and degrees of intervention. It may be possible by forced draft methods, involving very undemocratic socialism, to increase a country's statistical growth rate, but the benefit of such methods to real living standards lies always somewhere in the future. No country relying on them has yet been seen to give its citizens a higher level of material prosperity than that prevailing in the US or North-West Europe, even when judged by conventional indices.

The obstinate question arises, however, how we should know if and when this overtaking has happened, and here is where the other concept of economics as the logic or science of choice inescapably obtrudes. Talk of material wealth or money incomes 'at constant prices' cannot hide the fact that that is no unique way of measuring the changes in a bundle of hundreds of different sets of commodities and services, the composition of which is constantly changing. Money values can be used to add apples and pears only because, in a market system, relative prices are supposed to give some idea of individual preferences and choices.

It is theoretically possible to reject consumer sovereignty and use some other basis of valuation; but in that case an alternative set of criteria has to be provided.

## Individuals and nations

Despite some lip service to other concepts, such as the social welfare function, the logic of choice as worked out by economists has been the logic of individual choice. Basic to this logic are the following propositions: (a) when means are limited, a given benefit should be achieved at the lowest cost; (b) if different alternatives cost the same, the one yielding most satisfaction should be chosen; and (c) scarcity of means of one sort or another, if only time, always limit the total of satisfaction to be obtained. The important point about these seeming platitudes is that both the costs and the benefits involved are entirely subjective. Professor Robert Mundell has even written of a composer of piano music maximising 'the effect of a sequence of notes always subject to the budget constraint that the notes he inscribes are on the piano and that the sequence of notes is within the physical capacity of a pianist'.[57]

This last example brings out some worries about the economist's concept of rational choice and optimisation. It can be a language for describing almost all human action, a set of predictive statements about how human beings will act, or a recommendation to act in certain ways. The early utilitarians were robust enough to take the third approach; later generations of economists have hesitated to confront head-on the seemingly irrational in human affairs. But if talk of minimising costs and maximising benefits is mainly a language, then very many apparently irrational actions appear rational after all. Professor Harry Johnson has, for example, argued that although the policies of economic nationalism adopted by new nations cause material loss, they also convey psychical satisfaction on individuals in their countries by 'gratifying the taste for nationalism'. He goes so far as to write that 'the psychic enjoyment that the mass of the population derives from the collective consumption aspects of nationalism suffices to compensate them for the loss of material income imposed on them by nationalist economic policies, so that nationalistic policies arrive at a quite acceptable result from the standpoint of maximising satisfaction'.[58]

Whether or not these remarks are tongue-in-cheek, they do suggest that the pure logic of choice could justify the most apparently absurd behaviour. Costly wars involving much human suffering and little tangible reward can be rationalised by saying that the psychic satisfaction from the thought of a certain disputed area being administered by people of one's own ethnic group outweighs all the miseries involved. Yet the making of this translation is not pointless. For it forces people who make it to be more self-conscious than they would otherwise be and ask: 'How much suffering is worth the gratification of my feelings of national pride? How much less take-home pay is worth my psychic satisfaction in Ruritanian ownership of Ruritanian resources?' It is a reasonable guess that self-consciousness about these issues would lead to policies of a less nationalistic blood-and-soil kind than simple reiteration of Horace's 'Dulce et decorum est pro patria mori'. The point is developed in the Appendix at the end of this book. The economic theory of rational choice is based on 'methodological individualism'. The actions and goals of nations and governments are translated into the goals of the individuals who take the decision. The economic approach is, in this sense, reductionist, and here lies its essential affinity with both utilitarianism and liberalism.

If economics is to be a science with predictive value – even if it is to predict only in qualitative terms certain general results and not specific numbers – it must break out of this circle of tautologies. Costs and benefits have to be identified in such a way that they can be related to something observable, not necessarily monetary behaviour in a market; the pursuit of office and votes, and the cost in time and trouble of voting and the pursuit of information have been treated this way, most notably by Anthony Downs in *The Economic Theory of Democracy*. Having identified such costs and benefits, the exponents of the economic approach base their predictions on the assumption that men will act rationally in the face of them – as acting irrationally now has a meaning.

Opposed to this is what Brian Barry has called the sociological approach in his fascinating study, *Sociologists, Economists and Democracy*.[59] This approach was, in origin, largely a right-wing reaction to the French Revolution; it asserted that men were influenced largely by irrational forces and that there were distinct and relatively unalterable national characteristics. In our own day this has been followed by vociferous denials that men can be regarded as calculating animals. They have images of themselves, their rights and duties which cause them to both fall below and rise above self-interest.

Instead of making either/or choices between the two approaches, we would do well to follow Barry in his judgement that the economic approach works better in some areas than others. It is at its best in the analysis of individual markets, although it applies in a clearer and more straightforward fashion to some markets than in others. It gives us some insight into macroeconomic phenomena such as inflation, unemployment and growth, although the sociological point of view is also relevant here. The economic approach has had least to say on the causes (as distinct from the logic) of wars, revolutions, racial tension and other such major issues – although it may make some contribution even here. The trouble is that although sociologists in principle ought to step into the vacuum, they have not been very forthcoming in refutable propositions deduced from a set of axioms alternative to those of the economists.

Even if successful predictions can be made by making inferences from the behaviour of the rational individual, it does not follow that his action will necessarily lead to desirable results. All that the economist can show is that on the basis of certain values and under certain environmental conditions such a result *may* be produced. A sociological approach in which myth, images and stereotypes predominate does not even raise the question of the consequences of following rational self-interest. Moreover, an economist whose predictive success is so dependent on inferences made from rational individual behaviour would be less than human if he did not tend to side with such an individual against those who wished to subordinate his behaviour to 'higher' or other values.

Those economists whose reputation depends on the behaviour of growth models closely linked with a politically determined rate of capital formulation, or who are primarily experts in handling specialist statistics, have vested interests of a very different type. But the main tradition and practice of Western economic theory is still involved – to the regret of some economists – in a view of society centred around the individual rather than groups or metaphysical entities.

## The real difficulties

The real difficulties of economic liberalism lie, not with the economic, but with the liberal part of the concept. Liberalism, in the sense used in this essay, is an individualist ethic. It puts the emphasis on allowing individuals to follow to the maximum feasible extent their separately chosen ends. It is opposed by the desire, which has often been very powerful, for people to merge their own identities into something greater than themselves – whether a country, a regiment, a workers' movement, a tradition of honour, or the abnegation of self in the service of God, to name only a very few of the 'ideals' to which people have often gladly submitted themselves and their personal demands or impulses. As we have just seen in a different context all these activities can be reconciled with liberal beliefs by manipulating definitions. Brünnhilde can be said to be following a desire for self-immolation; a Jesuit who follows the teachings of Ignatius Loyola can be regarded as freely choosing to become 'as a corpse which has neither intelligence nor will'. There is a standing temptation for liberalism, like other ideologies, to avoid uncomfortable facts by taking refuge in tautologous formulations. But these simply evade the fact that the liberal mood is not one for all seasons or types of men; and when people are in the state described, it is absurd even to bring up the question of any liberalism, let alone the economic variety.

As K. R. Minogue has pointed out in that provoking but provocative study *The Liberal Mind*,[60] death is the worst possible evil to the liberal, because it brings to an end all desires, choice or action. 'On liberal premises it is irrational to die for one's country, unless perhaps the self-sacrifice is interpreted as an attempt to minimise the extinction of similarly desiring selves.' But there are moods in which heroism is justified not through some such rational backdoor, but because human life is regarded as serving some superior cause – the nation, the race or the creed.

There are many other difficulties too. In a society in which people are free to choose their own ends and values to the maximum feasible extent, there will be, in Minogue's words, 'many sources of status – money, birth, place of education, intellectual celebrity, popularity and so on'. Many people would undoubtedly prefer a single status system in which 'everyone can be conveniently assessed at a moment's notice.'[61] Much of the psychological desire for an 'incomes policy' comes from this urge. The difficulty, as well as the undesirability of attempting to go back to a status system in the present age has already been argued (pp. 105–8). But the desire exists and Minogue is right to deny that we can have variety without suffering, although wrong to pour scorn on the utilitarian desire to improve the trade-offs.

He goes, however, much too far in regarding liberalism as 'a solemn check on everything that is spontaneous, wild, enthusiastic, uncaring, or distinterested'. This is to equate liberalism with the spirit of Polonius rather than that of the Ninth Symphony. If Minogue wants to call the rationalistic (rather than rational) approach of Polonius liberalism, there is no point in arguing about labels, especially as historically there have been those who valued political and economic freedom purely as a means to some such grey goal; and they have successors who would seek to increase satisfaction by curbing desires, whether through religious asceticism or a ban on advertising. But the market economy has also been defended by a whole line of writers as an instrument for enabling people to follow varied and diverse goals of their own choosing, however wayward and irrational these may seem to others, with a minimum of collision.

Interestingly enough, of the two strands in economic liberalism identified earlier – the more conservative one with its emphasis on rules and conventions and the importance of the undesigned in human affairs, and the radical one which attempts to assess the specific consequences of each proposed action or policy without hindrance from traditional dogma – it is the former, more conservative one which allows greater scope for spontaneous and unorthodox initiatives. What has been called general utilitarianism fits much more easily with individual spontaneity than the 'particularist' brand. This is the grain of truth for 'the reverence for the traditional' which I found so uncongenial on first reading the *Constitution of Liberty*.

Such irritation has not wholly disappeared; for an emphasis on individual freedom must often lead to a desire to change convention and established practices. But if anarchy is ruled out, the only aternative to rules, conventions and tradition is the examination by authority of the specifics of every action which is outside the narrow category of the purely 'self-regarding'; and this is bound to give an enormous emphasis to the conventional wisdom of the age. The ideal would be to have a liberal set of traditions, conventions, and presumptions, which actually value non-conformity, innovation and eccentricity. Where such traditions do not exist, they cannot be invented overnight. The most one can hope to do is to develop the more liberal elements in our own tradition, and to downgrade the illiberal ones of the Eton and the Brigade of Guards type.

The fundamental difficulty for liberals of all hues is the fact of death, which brings to an end all the choices and actions to which they attach so much importance. The difficulty is very much less for other value systems which place the emphasis on the sinking of individual desires into something nobler or baser – whether the class war or the spirit of the universe – which are believed to continue beyond the life of any particular person. For such reasons some liberals have been tempted to shift the emphasis from the individual to the family. Yet this is no more than a compromise. There is an obvious, genetic and non-mystical reason why people should be able to identify with the welfare and freedom of their children and descendants. Yet each member of a family is an individual personality with thoughts, feelings and goals of his or her own; and a country with considerable freedom for family units inside which the head of the household wields despotic powers, such as Republican Rome or Victorian England, is far from being a free society.

## Conclusions

No philosopher's stone has been unearthed in this essay. If there were one simple slogan for limiting the role of coercion of human affairs, and for minimising the power of man over his fellow men, it would have long ago been found and its application to economic policy already known. All that has been formulated have been a few broad presumptions: that the aim of policy should be to satisfy the wants that people happen to have rather than that they ought to have; that our best chance of securing this is through what I have called the 'corrected market economy'; that the corrections and interventions should as far as possible take the form of general rules with the minimum of administrative discretion; and that we should consciously aim to limit the domain of politics and of decisions made by 'society'. This last presumption is the most difficult of all to state precisely, but, perhaps at the present time, the most important. Even these rough guidelines are not worth much to those who have not thought through their justification, or their application to particular areas.

The danger that any broad doctrine, such as the interpretation of the market economy presented above, will either be ignored as too complex, or misunderstood and vulgarised in political application, is great and obvious. So much so that it is tempting to conclude that the attempt to found policy on principle is likely to do more harm than good and that we are better off with the minimum of doctrinal baggage. Political and economic principles, however simple they appear, are normally a complex mixture of value judgements and empirical generalisations. Nothing is finer to behold than a government acting on the right principles (that is, the ones with which one happens to agree). Nothing is worse than a government persisting in mistaken policies out of an obstinate adherence to bad, or misunderstood, or misapplied, principles. An ideal US administration in the 1960s would have had an approach to foreign policy which would have avoided the Vietnam imbroglio in the first place. But as a second best, a pragmatic or even cynical administration, prepared to disengage when it was running into difficulties was infinitely preferable to one that was prepared to press on in Vietnam regardless of the cost, for the sake of some misguided articles of faith.

The probability that people in high public office will have the time or temperament to reflect on the fundamental principles of policy and their application is a low one. The few leaders who have been strongly committed to general positions of any kind in the face of the temptations and distractions tend for that very reason towards the hair-shirt view of life: the sacrifice of the individual to the glory of the nation, a belief in dying for freedom which puts more emphasis on the dying than on the freedom, a preference for doing things he hard way as if this were itself a virtue, or an interpretation of the market economy that puts the emphasis on the disciplinary and cold shower aspects rather than the permissive and pro-consumer ones.

Nevertheless, the so-called pragmatic approach of taking decisions on their individual merits or 'on the facts' is a logical impossibility. Specific judgements cannot be made in a vacuum but implicitly involve both broad empirical judgements of the effects of different types of situations and policies, and value judgements about the desirability of different types of outcome. Paradoxically, it is just because the principles of evaluation of the political empiricist are likely to be vague, muddled and inconsistent that his decisions are most unlikely to be related in any predictable way to any particular set of facts. The judgements of those who believe in treating each issue on its merits are likely to reflect the fashions of the moment, the influence of pressure groups, the clamour of the media, or the whims of the individuals concerned.

The best way of breaking through these difficulties is to regard political and economic philosophies, not as being aimed at the conversion of some great leader, but at influencing the climate of opinion in which decisions are taken, studies made, and advice evolved. It is conventional to believe that the trend of the times is away from a market economy based on 'the rule of law' and a limited political sphere. The most frequent argument is the inevitability of large units allegedly enforced by technological advance. This generalisation is drawn from a very limited number of industries and ignores many tendencies the other way arising from the proliferation of service activities of all kinds and the technological developments – even in the computer field itself – which may open up whole new areas to the smaller firm or establishment. Above all, the generalisation in question vastly underrates the amount of long run competition that does take place even between large units, especially if they are operating in an international market.

The real threats arise first of all from populist agitation for the government or society to enforce a view on every question and to determine the deserts of every man. Secondly, they arise from the undoubted fact that many people can gain, at least in the short term, by forming interest groups which circumvent the competitive process by restrictive practices or by political or industrial action. Once some people have gone in for group politics of this kind, others would be well advised to follow in self-defence. Indeed, the pattern of output and remuneration may resemble more closely that of a competitive economy if militant activity by some groups is matched by equal militancy by others and if monopolistic activities of sellers are matched by those of buyers. Galbraith's earlier notion of 'countervailing power' is a much more useful one than some of his more popular recent concepts. Unfortunately, one of the main troubles with a balance produced by self-cancelling interest groups is that it can have explosive inflationary potentialities (to be discussed in the next chapter).

A sensible economic liberal will not refuse to compromise. The test of his judgement is to pick the compromise that is second or third best, rather than fourth or fifth best, from the point of view of his beliefs. But before one can begin to compromise one has to have some idea of where one would like to go if the circumstances permit. In the case of interest group politics just discussed, it is worth remarking that interest group deals do much less harm if they are concerned with fixing remuneration than if they are supported by restrictions of entry into the groups concerned.

There may be times when the liberal has to decide where the greatest danger lies. Does it lie in a network of deals among men who run organisations or in populist attempts to enforce arbitrary concepts of social justice? Normally, the liberal will want to insist on the rule of law and oppose discretionary use of state power. But circumstances can be envisaged in which covert understandings between the political, business, trade union and civil service establishments – in the National Economic Development Council or anywhere else – may be the only way of heading off populist agitation, and preserving some areas of life from political interference. Faced with the tyranny of would-be perfect justice, it is well known that the liberal sides with the conservative. He need not apologise for this; but he knows that this alliance is temporary, uneasy and full of strain, and if he is wise, he will refrain from sounding the alarm bells too frequently.

But even in more normal circumstances, the liberal will not achieve anything except in alliances of convenience on specific issues at specific times. He must not hesitate to make use of the middle-class dislike of high taxation where this can help achieve a genuine enlargement in personal choice. Equally he must not hesitate to ally himself with the popular dislike of 'Big Business', or traditionalist dislike of technology, to fight off the New Industrial State. It is only by such shifting alliances – and indeed, often in very doubtful company – that liberalism, whether economic or not, has ever made any headway.

The greatest ally of the liberal is the practical failure of attempts to shape society by centralised political means. Although men have a natural inclination to conform and follow fashions and leaders, they have an equally strong and contradictory tendency to find ways round authority and to devise new ideas and projects which neither the conservatives nor the collectivists expected in their ordered vision. There will always be a new product for which no controlled price exists, a new type of skill which society has not decided how to value. Even the highly dirigiste late Roman Empire and the feudal world of fixed status had all kinds of activities going on, which did not fit the established codes, and which historians have difficulty in fitting into a generalised model. After several centuries in which freedom and independence have been part of the official culture, it will be that much more difficult to suppress them; and in contrast to most conservatives and even many liberals I have taken the view that the so-called 'permissive society' is, despite the hypocrisies of some of its advocates, an extension and a strengthening of the liberal tradition.

Of course, to talk about alliances between people of different outlooks is far too mechanistic. Most people, even among the highly educated, react to specific events with very little firm commitment to generalised political philosophies. A liberal would be wise to accept as the first rule of a successful political process 'Don't force a specification of goals or ends' because agreement on specific policies can often be secured among people with divergent ends.[62] Freedom of speech and worship came about (to the extent that it did), not because people believed this approach deserved a trial, but because they found in mutual tolerance the best chance of being able to express their own belief without having their heads chopped off when their opponents where in the saddle. It is in supporting their own claims that the vegetarians, the Communists (in a capitalist society) or the Seventh Day Adventists became supporters of 'free speech'; and what has started out as a means is in time accepted as an end.

Similarly, if enough people find themselves on the liberal side in particular instances, they may find themselves becoming liberals. If they do, they will not have abolished the problems of the human condition – time, decay, pain, ugliness or death – or brought into existence love, friendship, beauty or exhilaration. These are not matters for political or economic systems. Such systems can make life worse than it need be; and the prevention of avoidable harm is the first priority. At the very best political arrangements can slightly improve the conditions under which human beings face their problems and opportunities. Medical and scientific progress can contribute more; but in the end much will always depend on the accidents of genetic endowment and the pleasant or unpleasant, lucky or unlucky encounters with other human beings from infancy onwards. This is the fundamental liberal message and, for that reason, it will never be very popular but will always be there in the background undermining alike the pretences of the hierarchial conservative state and the ordered collectivist society.

## APPENDIX I: THE NON-LIBERAL CASE FOR CAPITALISM

Some form of capitalist market economy is supported by many businessmen and politicians who are clearly not liberal in the sense of this essay. If asked for their reason they might well say that it promotes efficiency. It is quite irrational to seek to maximise *engineering efficiency* under almost any political or economic system. If the heat–energy conversion ratio of a machine can be raised from 49 to 50 per cent by multiplying the cost tenfold, it would be extremely wasteful to do this except under the most freakish conditions of labour supply and final product demand.

*Economic efficiency* is, however, a subjective criterion. A businessman asked to produce $x$ units of a particular commodity will search around the available production methods and any new ones he can discover until there is no further change he can find which will reduce costs any further. He is 'maximising his efficiency' from the point of view of his own self interest. (The exact efficiency conditions have long been given in books on economic principles, but were rediscovered in more complex mathematical form under such titles as 'operational research'.)

But why should minimum costs for a firm be a sign of efficiency from any wider point of view? The price an employer offers for every marginal unit of labour, raw material and other inputs he buys has to be high enough to cover what that unit could produce in its next best employment, before he can succeed in bidding it away. The price paid by the employer therefore represents the alternatives forgone by society to produce an extra unit of the commodity in question.

But how are these alternatives valued? Let us suppose that the final addition to the labour force has come from a cheese factory and the producer we are discussing manufactures ice-cream. There is no objective way of valuing ice-cream in relation to cheese. It is efficient to pay enough to attract an extra worker from the cheese to the ice-cream factory if the person or body judging efficiency accepts consumers' relative valuation of marginal units of the two commodities. If he does not, and values cheese more highly, it might be inefficient to move this man to the ice-cream factory, even though the shift was the most profitable course of action open to the two manufacturers and the man himself.

Productive efficiency can, however, be given a meaning under paternalist value judgements. Suppose that the government decided that the social value of cheese was much greater than the free market price. It would then subsidise the production of cheese, at so much per unit. The cheese manufacturer would then be able to offer higher wages; and it might not then pay the ice-cream manufacturer to bid away any more labour. Thus, entirely different quantities of output, and perhaps different methods of production, might become more efficient on the basis of a change in the methods of valuation of the two commodities. Alternatively, the government might ban ice-cream production as an undesirable product. This is tantamount to a nil valuation of ice-cream; and in the changed labour market it might then pay the cheese manufacturer to take on more men and expand his output still further.

The notion of efficiency only has a meaning in connection with some pre-announced basis of valuation. If the government distrusts the consumer's judgement and announces neither a tax, nor a subsidy, nor a purchasing price of its own, but simply talks vaguely about the evils of ice cream, then the profit motive will not lead to an efficient allocation of resources even from the government's own point of view.

It should *en passant* be noted that many of the most widely used criteria for assessing the worth of different kinds of output cannot derive from any value judgements held by sane men. One can justify consumer valuation on liberal value judgements; one can justify an infinite price for drugs and a subsidy for milk from a paternalist desire to promote health. But there is no system of ethics which puts a special valuation on the balance of payments, or saving foreign exchange or promoting exports to preserve some arbitrary rate of exchange. Only those besotted with two or three decades of official half-truths could suppose otherwise. At most, on certain narrow, short-term nationalist assumptions, the UK can turn the terms of trade in its favour by exporting more, and importing less, than at a free trade exchange rate. This might justify limited import subsidies (or export taxes) if one is confident about the outcome of the ensuing trade war. It cannot conceivably support the view that exports or import-saving produce some special sort of value incommensurable with home output, and have to be promoted quite irrespective of return.

If we clear away these fallacies, the underlying logic of many Conservative supporters of the market economy (and of some others in the nonconformist tradition), who clearly do not accept an anti-paternalist or permissive society, is that the government should seek to influence the direction of national effort by a whole series of taxes, subsidies and bans; and, on the basis of these corrected valuations, market forces could then be allowed to encourage productive efficiency of those things which it is good for us to have.

The liberal can, however, comfort himself with the knowledge that it is extremely difficult to put capitalism into a straitjacket of this kind. There is always an incentive to look for close substitutes for the banned or heavily taxed product, or to invent entirely new goods and services not envisaged in the rule book of the moral censors. Moreover, differences of view among the establishment will frequently prevent very comprehensive systems of paternalist valuation on the lines suggested in the previous paragraph. The example of the Nazi war economy, cited earlier, is very much an exception and not the rule. The history of capitalism has been one of gradual collapse of the restraining walls of authority and convention, with the profit motive always one jump ahead of the Lord Chancellor and the Archbishops. The process could even be beginning in Japan where, until recently, capitalism worked within a very highly authoritarian and dirigiste general framework.

## APPENDIX II: 'FORCING PEOPLE TO BE FREE'

The object of the following illustration is to shed light on the uneasy relation between liberalism and utilitarianism which has been the major underlying problem of this essay. A liberal cannot divorce himself from utilitarianism; for if one attaches great value to individual preferences and choices, policy should be concerned to satisfy people's expressed wants as far as possible. On the other hand, a liberal can never go the whole hog and wish to satisfy wants which relate to the suppression of other people's activities.

Imagine a small community where incomes are initially equal. (The reader may define this equality in any way he likes – the aim is to rule out distributional problems.) A distinguished pianist arrives for a recital. Market research shows that, at the prices initially fixed, the demand for seats will be five times the supply. Should the price be raised to bring demand and supply into line? There is a vote among ticket applicants, which goes 99 per cent against the price mechanism solution. Should the concert promoter, who has been given a free hand to organise the occasion, but who happens to be a liberal, accept the majority verdict or enforce the price mechanism? To simplify the argument further, assume that all ticket applications arrive on the same day by post, and that the only alternative to the price mechanism is some lottery-type selection process, such as using a pin.

Let us assume that the 1 per cent minority consists of keen music lovers. (This need not be the case. Some of them could have supported a pricing solution on grounds of principle.) If their success on their ticket application is representative of the general average, four out of five of them will be extremely disappointed at not receiving tickets for the concert. In other words 0.8 per cent of the community of ticket applicants will be intensely disappointed. (This very fact will lower the real value of their equal money earnings compared with the 99 per cent who are less keen and the 0.2 per cent of the keen and successful applicants.)

The pure democrat will of course say, 'Use the pin'. The old-fashioned utilitarian will try to compare the present dissatisfaction of the 0.8 per cent with the dissatisfaction of the 99 per cent if the price mechanism were used. The modern 'welfare economist', who is a utilitarian of a different hue, will want to avoid interpersonal comparisons of satisfaction. Let us make things easy for him by assuming that the 1 per cent minority who favoured the price mechanism are, before the lottery is held, willingly given payments by the other 99 per cent of such a size that they feel adequately compensated for their low chance of obtaining a seat. The modern utilitarian would now reject higher prices; for the 99 per cent still feel better off without them, while the 1 per cent are now just as well off.

One out of five of all applicants now have tickets. (This has incidentally introduced a chance inequality into the community of just the kind that causes indignation when it arises from inheritance under capitalism.) The utilitarian economist may now suggest that private sales and purchases of tickets be permitted, as both buyer and seller are better off if this happens. This idea is put to the vote, but so great is the objection to the price mechanism that it too is rejected by 99 per cent; and the 1 per cent of dissenters can be compensated as in the previous case. The utilitarian economist then retires, puzzling over the peculiar welfare function of the community, but conceding that dealings in tickets should not take place. For the ban on dealings in tickets combined with the payments to the 1 per cent has brought about a 'Pareto improvement'. The 1 per cent are no worse off because of the compensation and the 99 per cent are better off, because they prefer to pay out the compensation money than see a second-hand market develop in tickets.

An objection may be lodged against the initial solution of charging higher prices on the grounds of the inconvenience and discomfort of choice. The 99 per cent majority may inherently dislike the introspective effort of working out how much money they are prepared to part with to hear a celebrated pianist and prefer a low conventional price and a lottery. But this objection cannot apply to the second price mechanism method of a free market in sold tickets. For those who dislike the effort of choice need not deal in the market and can accept the result of the lottery.

Misunderstandings of the price mechanism apart, the objection of the 99 per cent to the rationing of the tickets by price by the second method must, in the last analysis, reflect a desire not merely for equality but for uniformity of behaviour, which they will probably describe as 'a sense of belonging to the community'. Their overwhelming desire is that everyone who contemplates going to the recital at all should have an equal one-in-five chance of a seat. The thought of some people indulging their tastes by purchasing a 100 per cent chance, and others indulging their different tastes by retiring from the market, causes resentment and dissatisfaction.

A liberal is, as already explained, only a constrained utilitarian. He ignores dissatisfactions arising from the mere thought of how other people are behaving. This follows from his belief in maximising freedom of action provided it does not interfere with that of other people – as it would certainly not do in the case of a free market in seats. The liberal concert director would therefore use one or other form of the price mechanism without holding a vote on the idea at all.[63]

This example is far from trivial. It brings out, shorn of irrelevancies, the hard core case of those who insist that the state should invariably provide education as well as finance it, and of those who would do everything to discourage a private medical sector. It may also explain the psychology of waiting lists for certain high quality expensive cars and the curious national liking for queues which would otherwise appear as a negative commodity or pure 'disutility'.

# 2 Jobs, Prices and Trade Unions

> 'Money, when increasing, gives encouragement to industry, during the interval between the increase of money and the rise of the prices . . .'
>
> David Hume, 'Of the Balance of Trade'

Few subjects can have been the subject of more analysis, commentary and recommendation than the movement of total output, employment, prices and wages – especially in relation to the British economy. Yet there are two reasons why a summary chapter on these interrelated topics cannot be avoided in any restatement of the case for economic liberalism. The first is that the biggest single reason for distrust of *any form* of market economy is the belief that it cannot prevent an unacceptably high, and perhaps explosive rate of inflation – or can only do so at the cost of a politically and morally intolerable level of unemployment. Secondly, and this is connected with the first point, the consensus, which economists seemed to have reached following the publication in 1936 of Keynes's *General Theory* on the analysis and cure of unemployment in an advanced industrial economy, has crumbled in recent years.

It would be most convenient to my general case if I were able to endorse the orthodox Keynesian view that unemployment can nearly always be reduced by a sufficient injection of purchasing power. For an assurance that total employment can be kept up in this way offers us much the best chance of persuading people to accept the disturbances brought by market forces to particular industries, areas and occupations. Indeed, it would then be tempting to argue for a policy of running the economy at a high 'pressure of demand', even if this involved some inflation and exchange depreciation in order to minimise specific state intervention in particular industries of a make-work kind. This is what one might term the 'liberal expansionist' position, from which my book *The Treasury under the Tories*, published in 1964, was written; and too many commentators – whether or not they endorse the liberal half of that goal – continue to write as if this kind of demand management were still possible.

Unfortunately, the assumptions behind this position were questionable even in the 1960s, and have since become quite implausible; and it is no service to economic liberalism, or any other cause, to erect it on an edifice of wishful thinking. The first of the sections that follow will give my assessment of the influence of demand management upon unemployment, the second will discuss union monopoly power and the third will discuss the attitude an economic liberal should adopt to the endless proliferation of schemes for 'doing something' about incomes. But any one expecting me to propose a new once-for-all cure of my own will be disappointed. If such a mechanistic cure existed it would by now have emerged from the millions of words written on these subjects.

## (a)  DEMAND AND UNEMPLOYMENT

The modern tendency to formulate economic theories in a form where they can be tested by econometric techniques is undoubtedly a step forward. For too long economics and the other social sciences had an excessive bias towards armchair reflection. The impulse to collect numerical data and formulate hypotheses which can be tested with all available mathematical and electronic techniques is therefore to be welcomed, provided it does not lead to an uncritical acceptance of every piece of work with the right fashionable trappings.

Unfortunately, there are signs that this is happening. How many times do we read supposedly factual newspaper stories beginning, 'A computer study has shown . . .' or 'A rigorous mathematical study had demolished the belief that . . .'? A slightly less crude form of this approach is too often prevalent among professional economists themselves.

Claims made for such studies in recent years include the demonstration that incomes policy reduced the increase in prices by 1 per cent per annum, that it had no effect at all and that it actually made inflation worse. We have been told that the level of national income at current prices is linked very closely to the supply of money, and that no relation between the two can be demonstrated.

At the beginning of the 1970s a number of highly qualified economists and 'economically literate' politicians endorsed a much discussed econometric model that 'demonstrated' that with adult unemployment of only 2.1 per cent (seasonally corrected), weekly wage rates would rise by only 3 per cent per annum – all without any kind of interference with normal collective bargaining. This is a rate of increase lower than anything experienced since early 1967; in subsequent years a much higher rate of unemployment did not suffice to prevent wages from rising several times as fast. Yet attempts to demonstrate the implausibility of the model, by references to what was actually happening to wages and prices, were dismissed as journalistic, or literary, or on the grounds that 'This may not be perfect, but it is the only serious piece of work we have so far.'[1]

There are, in real life, a large number of economic magnitudes all reacting on each other, and the relationships between them are themselves changing over time. A great deal depends on how these magnitudes (and, in particular, their rates of change) are measured, the exact way in which suggested relationships are stated, the periods chosen and the tests used. Subjects such as the relationship of the home market to exports, or of unemployment and wages, do not become less controversial because the controversies become more difficult to understand, or because hardware has been used for doing the sums.

All this is very far from being a Luddite plea to abandon econometric techniques. It is a plea for a less breathless and credulous assessment of their results. It is unwise to change one's economic philosophy with dizzying rapidity with each purported new finding. One can go quite a long way with certain long established elementary generalisations, and inferences from them. We shall, of course, feel more confident if they can survive modern statistical testing. But, before taking on board the results of such tests – and, in particular, before accepting numerical values for particular relationships – it is worth waiting until a number of studies employing different techniques point in the same direction and have survived professional criticism.

Any attempt to set out summarily a few fundamental notions on unemployment, monetary and fiscal policy must involve a large element of personal judgement. What follows is based on a combination of observations of policies and performance over many years and an attempt to distil what has emerged from academic investigation and debate. Perhaps only a financial journalist would have the effrontery to undertake such a task. Those whose appetite for arguments about demand management is limited and want to get down to the red meat of unions and incomes control will lose little by going straight on to the section on union monopoly power beginning on p. 162.

A convenient starting point is unemployment in an underdeveloped economy, especially one with a dense and rapidly increasing population. No intellectual puzzle is set by the existence of a large amount of open or concealed unemployment in such a country. There is simply not enough of the capital equipment, entrepreneurial activity and managerial and other skills which would have to exist alongside the pool of unemployed if it is to be put to worthwhile work. There may be some very low wage at which it would pay to offer jobs to all the unemployed, even with existing organisation, capital and techniques; but if that wage is below subsistence or what the jobless can obtain from living with their families and tribes, or on relief, the existence of such a theoretical equilibrium wage is of no practical relevance.

In a modern industrial market economy, by contrast, one would expect the stock of capital equipment to be adjusted to the size of the available labour force, and there to be sufficient resources of enterprise and management to adapt both the organisation of business and its physical capital to market requirements. One would also expect the members of the labour force to make some effort to acquire the skills that happened to be marketable, although employers would also have some incentive to take advantage of the relative cheapness of unskilled labourers. (Numerical or algebraic models can be constructed in which technical progress would have such a labour-saving, capital-using bias that it would be cheaper to use robots than pay a subsistence wage; but I am not attempting a complete taxonomy, and it is highly improbable that this is the present state of affairs.)

Now, even if a modern market economy were functioning extremely well, there would be no reason to expect zero unemployment. There is always transitional unemployment while people who have left one job search around among available job opportunities. Of a total of 923 000 unemployed in Great Britain in December 1971, some 315 000 had been out of work for less than two months and a further 60 000 were temporarily stopped or school leavers (the figures are not seasonally adjusted). A certain number of people who are virtually unemployable appear in the official statistics even when there are many unfilled vacancies; at a minimum estimate, these form 150 000 of the long-term unemployed. There are also some 'false' unemployed, those who either work surreptitiously or are not genuinely seeking employment. The number in this latter category has been estimated by Mr John Wood for this period at about 100 000.[2] While these influences lead to a statistical inflation of the number of unemployed, there are other factors giving the official figures a downward bias. It is well known that a US type sample census, in which people are asked if they would like a job, yields higher figures than the British method of basing statistics on unemployment pay. A British type system is itself sensitive to the degree of pressure imposed on unemployed workers to accept available jobs, while a US type system is sensitive to the exact form in which the questions are posed.

Unemployment, however measured, will vary according to the efficiency of labour exchanges and other employment agencies. It will depend on the pace of change in the skills demanded, the availability of retraining facilities, and the willingness of redundant workers to use them – or to accept lower paid unskilled jobs. The unemployment percentage is also notoriously affected by any geographical imbalance between areas where work is available and those where the unemployed live. One can argue whether workers who are unwilling to move should count as involuntarily unemployed; but, because of the spillover costs in congested areas not paid for by the individual employer or employee, it may be positively undesirable to encourage all the unemployed workers to move to where the jobs are rather than vice versa. Trade union wage bargaining and minimum wage laws can also increase unemployment; and if institutional rigidities or union pressure prevent relative wages from falling in other industries to absorb the surplus labour, the national unemployment average will be that much higher. Opposition to adult retraining by unions, or to new entry into occupations, can have similar effects.

It is not necessarily true that the lower the statistical unemployment rate the better. The Redundancy Payments Act and earnings-related unemployment benefits, which came into operation in December 1965 and October 1966 respectively, caused an increase in recorded unemployment, as the cost to the worker of spending time searching for a suitable new job (or for that matter of 'taking a break') was reduced. These measures were desirable both on humanitarian grounds and because it is inefficient for an unemployed worker to be forced by financial pressure into the first available job rather than search for something that really suits his abilities and tastes. But the result of these measures by the time they had worked themselves into the system by the end of 1968 was, according to one study, to add slightly more than two-fifths to the unemployment percentage than would otherwise have been predicted from a given level of unfilled vacancies. This means that a level of adult unemployed of 2 per cent – or somewhat under 500 000 – would have corresponded to well over 2.8 per cent, or 650 000–700 000 by the early 1970s.[3] The estimated correction is a high one, which admittedly takes into account other structural factors, apart from social security legislation, which may have affected the relationship between unemployment and vacancies since the middle 1960s. A more usual correction to make figures between earlier and later periods comparable is to take a straight ½ per cent off the figures for the early 1970s.

So far the discussion has centred on the 'real' forces affecting unemployment. While they are mostly familiar – and, with the possible exception of union influences, uncontroversial – it is only in the last few years that mainstream economists have begun to stress that they set a floor to the extent that unemployment can be reduced by expansionist monetary or fiscal policies. Ill-conceived financial policies can keep unemployment needlessly above this rate, but they cannot force it permanently below it, *and this is so even if we are prepared to pay a sacrifice in faster inflation to achieve fuller employment*. The relevant unemployment rate has been called by various writers the 'natural', 'warranted' or 'normal rate' of unemployment. The labels are all misleading because the percentage in question reflects use of monopoly power which would be too defeatist to label 'natural'. My own term would be simply the 'minimum' or, more pedantically, the 'minimum sustainable', unemployment level.

If the minimum sustainable level of unemployment is regarded as too high and the authorities try to bring it down further by budget deficits or increasing the money supply, trouble can be confidently expected. Let us, to take purely illustrative figures, assume that the minimum unemployment percentage, according to UK definitions of the early 1970s, is 3½ per cent, but that the government tries, by 'boosting demand' in the Budget and through the banking system, to get this percentage down to 2½ per cent. The initial effects of these measures – assuming no perverse effects on confidence or other mishaps – should be to boost output and employment on orthodox Keynesian lines. Eventually, however, the greater demand for labour will lead to an acceleration in the rise of wages. In these more buoyant demand conditions unions will be more aggressive in their claims and employers will be more ready to concede them, or even offer higher wages themselves to retain labour.

The frequent assertion that the state of the labour market has no effect on the rate of increase of wages borders on the fantastic. The original 'Phillips curve' made no allowance for changing price expectations and assumed that an *x* per cent rate of unemployment would be associated with the same rate of unemployment, whether workers were expecting a 0, 3 or 33 per cent rate of increase of prices. That it should have collapsed by the end of the 1960s in the face of the increase in the rate of inflation was only to be expected. The real surprise is that it continued to perform so well as long as it did. If the relationship between unemployment (or, preferably unfilled vacancies) and wage increases is to be represented even approximately by a Phillips curve, it will have to be a family of curves corresponding to different rates of expected inflation.

To return to our original story, let us assume that the government does succeed in getting unemployment down to 2½ per cent. During the expansionary period, some people previously regarded as unemployable will be given jobs, people not even registered as unemployed will enter the labour forces, more overtime will be on offer, there will be less short time, and all the other effects stressed by the high demand school will be in operation. But, with the labour market now much tighter, hourly earnings will increase faster than before and this will in turn lead to higher prices. So long as 'money illusion' reigns and workers and their representatives take no notice of faster inflation the story need go no further. Lower unemployment will have been purchased at the expense of more rapid inflation; and one could argue the pros and cons of the change.

This is, however, only the first stage. As soon as money illusion begins to go and workers begin to think in real terms, they start insisting on still higher wages to make up for the faster rise in the cost of living. But once they obtain them, prices will rise still faster, which will in turn increase the rate of wage-push and give rise to an ever-accelerating inflation. Thus the long run trade-off is not between unemployment and inflation, but between unemployment and accelerating inflation.

*Nothing that has been said above in any way implies that inflation always tends to accelerate. What I have called the 'minimum unemployment percentage' is that consistent with any constant rate of inflation.* (In the above hypothetical example, the 3½ per cent unemployment rate might well co-exist with a steady 7 per cent rate of inflation.) It is only if unemployment is pushed below this minimum level that inflation will tend to accelerate.

In this example, the authorities are faced with a painful dilemma. They may try to keep unemployment at 2½ per cent by ever greater monetary injections. In that case, they face accelerating inflation and an eventual collapse of the national monetary unit as a basis for business calculations[4] – and with it the end to any benefit to employment from their expansionary policies – not to mention the probable political and social repercussions. If the government wishes merely to reduce the rate of inflation to wherever it was when unemployment was 3½ per cent, unemployment may have to shoot well above 3½ per cent, and the process may take many years. This is because of the great difficulty of reducing inflationary expectations once they have become embedded in the system. Should the government be prepared to settle for a new and higher, but steady rate of inflation, it will still have to allow employment to creep back to 3½ per cent; and even then it will take some time for the rate of inflation to settle down. No wonder that in such a situation ministers will be tempted to break out of the dilemma by direct intervention in the labour and goods markets – with what success and at which price remains to be discussed.

The above view is sometimes known as the *theory of adaptive expectations*, because price expectations are adjusted to past experience. In order to explain clearly the basic long run forces which prevent the authorities from being able to maintain whatever pressure of demand and unemployment percentage they desire, an excessively schematic and mechanistic picture has had to be painted. I have not attempted here an account of the pathology of business or electoral cycles which are heavily influenced by time lags. Unemployment may, for example, be above its minimum level, but wages and prices may still be reacting to the demand pressure of months or even years ago. If one had a rough idea of the minimum feasible unemployment level, it would then be safe to reflate demand and unemployment up to that level without further aggravating inflation.

Moreover, although the demand for labour and the rate of cost-determined price increases have a major influence on wage inflation, they are far from being the only influence. Indeed, the basic assertion of the 'adaptive expectations' hypothesis is that workers are interested in the real value of their take-home pay. If real incomes have been squeezed in the recent past, wage demands will be more aggressive than would otherwise have been expected in the same economic climate. Here is probably one of the main explanations of the 1969–70 explosion. This came at the end of a five year period in which real personal disposable income had risen by a third of its long run average – and in the last year and a half of the period it had virtually ceased to rise at all.

The need for such a brake on living standards came partly, but not entirely, from the need to make a large shift from the home market to exports and import-saving in a short space of time. The legacy of such episodes is a more rapid rate of inflation, which governments will find difficult to subdue except by running the economy for a considerable period at *above* the minimum unemployment level.

In more fortunate circumstances, the domestic trade-offs can be made to look deceptively optimistic owing to the operation of time lags. An attempt to push down the rate of unemployment below its minimum may take some years before it produces an accelerating inflation; and the intervening period could be actually beneficial to price stability. If, for example, a government is starting out with an unemployment percentage above the minimum and is trying to reduce it to below the minimum, there are likely to be very large budgetary handouts. These can be used to cut both direct and indirect taxation, and thereby to reduce both actual and (hopefully) expected inflation, as well as to increase the take-home pay associated with any given money wage income. As the tax reductions are financed from the Budget deficit, there need be no corresponding cut in the provision of government services.

Moreover, because of the exceptional rise of output per man which may accompany the early stages of a boom, employers may be able to absorb some wage increases while still increasing profits. Thus, for a time, a virtuous circle may be at work, with price restraint and tax cuts engendering a de-escalation of wage settlements, which in turn put a brake on further price increases, the whole process being oiled by exceptionally fast productivity increases. This is the germ of truth in the 'at a stroke' theory.

The trouble with such a process – even if it can get going – is that by its nature it is temporary. The tax cuts, above-average productivity gains, increase in overtime opportunities, and so on, are all side-effects of increasing the proportion of productive capacity and available manpower employed. Once unemployment is down to the government's target level, all these bonuses came to an end; there are unlikely to be further tax cuts financed by government borrowing, and productivity growth will settle down to its normal rate. Thus, the forces making for reduced price inflation will have spent themselves. Meanwhile, with the higher demand for labour, wage increases will be gathering momentum, starting off a renewed price acceleration, and Hayek's tiger will be off on its run.[5]

This view of the inflationary process cannot be confuted by showing that wages and salaries account for only about half of the cost of total expenditure on home produced goods and imports. Most other costs tend to move in line with labour costs over a sufficiently long term. If employers seek to maintain gross profit margins, this element too will rise with wages. Import costs will also increase in line with home costs, either because other countries are undergoing similar inflationary experience or because, if they are not, we will probably have to devalue. It is only if there is a favourable movement in the equilibrium terms of trade, due, say, to a decline in primary prices relative to manufactured goods, that we can gain a dampening effect from imports; and even this is likely to be small. (A 6 per cent reduction in import prices will reduce the cost of final output by 1 per cent, and reductions on this scale are likely to be rare events.) Taxes on expenditure will – apart from exceptional periods of demand stimulus – also tend to rise in line with money incomes; and items such as interest rates and property rents are also likely to be influenced in an irregular and jerky way by the general trend of money incomes and prices.

Strictly interpreted, the minimum unemployment hypothesis implies that the Phillips curve is in the long run a vertical line. Expansionist demand management policies thus have a permanent effect only on the level of prices and not on output and employment. But, as David Laidler has pointed out, even if inflation is never perfectly anticipated (or over-anticipated), and there is some slight long run gain to employment from expansionist demand management, the policy dilemma remains largely the same. The important contention is that the long run Phillips curve is much steeper than the short term one (with the rate of increase of money wages measured on the vertical axis). If this is so, the greater part of the effects of a demand boost which takes unemployment much below the 'minimum' is temporary, and the authorities then have to choose between allowing unemployment to rise again and an accelerating rate of inflation.

A further elaboration, which embodies one of the basic earlier Keynesian insights, is that the effects of a departure from the minimum unemployment point or zone are not symmetrical. The Keynes of the 1920s already realised that the economic system was highly resistant to downward changes in the general level of wages; and it was on this basis – without departing from neoclassical monetary theory – that he opposed the 1925 return to the Gold Standard at the pre-1914 parity. To this we must add the further observation that the system is also highly resistant to downward changes in the rate of increase of money wages. If unemployment is reduced for any length of time below the minimum level, then – once the money illusion has burst – the economy will be landed with a much faster underlying rate of inflation which will not be easy to subdue. On the other hand, a comparable *increase* in the unemployment level may have only a modest retarding effect on the rate of inflation; and the economy may have to be run at a very high rate of unemployment for a very long time if inflation is to be reduced by that particular route. Fortunately it is not one that election timetables allow.

Because of this inertia of wages and prices, *sudden and severe attempts to halt the expansion of monetary demand will lead to stagnation of output and unemployment, while the beneficial effects on prices will come through slowly and very much later.* This is the origin of 'inflationary recessions'. The case for *flexible exchanges (for deficit countries) arises basically from the difficulty of making large and rapid downward changes in domestic costs and prices or in their rate of increase*; and this is why attempts to secure an underlying payments deficit by deflation *alone* will lead to otherwise unnecessary unemployment and stagnation.

The basic difficulty about convincing people of the validity of the minimum unemployment hypothesis is that money illusion can remain for an astonishingly long time during a period of moderate and relatively steady inflation, such as that which prevailed up to the middle 1960s. Until then wage bargains, interest rates, equity yields, salary arrangements, and similar phenomena were not adapted to the facts of inflation. Adaptation when it does at last come may be sudden; and for a time people may actually overreact on the basis of excessively pessimistic inflationary expectations, which then prove self-justifying. It is for reasons of this kind that econometric verification of the adaptive expectations hypothesis is so difficult. But it is hard to suppose that there can be much money illusion left now. The more that people learn to live with inflation by indexing pensions, wages, contracts, leases and other arrangements, the less the scope for others to gain at their expense during periods of rising prices; and the less favourable is likely to be even the temporary trade-off between unemployment and inflation, and the more likely that higher monetary demand will lead to higher prices rather than more employment.

The notion of a minimum unemployment level, zone or band, presented here is not the most elegant or easily applicable of concepts. It exists only in the long run – because at any one time we are always overshooting or undershooting it; yet its position can shift quite quickly depending not only on structural changes, but on a whole variety of chance factors, including the personalities of union leaders, currents of shop floor and management psychology, and the attitudes and skills of particular governments. It is like looking for a black cat in a dark room but one which is really there and likely to give one a nasty scratch.

The notion is thus tricky, but meaningful. Even the most extreme believers in the Treasury's ability to control 'real demand' have always conceded that there was some effective floor to the unemployment level they could achieve – whether 1, 1½ or 2 per cent – without either being halted by physical bottlenecks, or the system becoming explosive (even if the government were willing to let the exchange rate go). The implication of what I have been saying is that these very low postwar rates of unemployment were, like the high interwar rates, an aberration due *inter alia* to the persistence of money illusion.

The hypothesis presented here would be falsified if we were able to get back to target figures in the post-war range (adding perhaps ½–1 per cent for the social security changes already discussed), solely by the use of fiscal and monetary policy. Unfortunately, the upward climb in unemployment rates in each successive recession in so many countries in combination with faster rates of inflation, reinforces the view that the relationship between unemployment and inflation is not a stable one, but sensitive to price expectations. The existence of these phenomena in so many different countries seems to rule out an explanation solely in terms of the train of events following from the 1967 devaluation. This was no more than an aggravating factor in the British case, just as the legacy of excess demand in the US in the early stages of the Vietnam War was an aggravating factor on a world scale.

Despite the lack of any precise knowledge of the minimum unemployment rate, a recognition of its existence is of background help to the policymaker. It suggests, for instance, that if the rate of increase of monetary earnings is declining – even though still high – employment can be helped by a demand stimulus, although at some cost to the government's anti-inflationary objectives. If, on the other hand, *the rate of increase of money earnings is still increasing, a demand stimulus will risk an explosive inflation without any more than at most a temporary benefit to employment.* In all cases, the question that must be asked is whether the recent behaviour of earnings reflects current labour market conditions, or is really the lagged effect of earlier and different conditions; and, if the latter, an allowance must be made for the lags by some mixture of econometrics and common sense. *But,* if allowing for lags, *a demand stimulus is seen to involve a serious risk of an acceleration in the rise of money earnings, it is a sign that unemployment is above the minimum sustainable level; and, if the latter is considered excessive, it must be tackled by some means other than overall fiscal or monetary policy.*

I conclude this brief survey of current macroeconomic controversies by noting that, at no point, has it been necessary to discuss the dispute between the apostles of fiscal and monetary policy.[6] Both are means for managing demand or controlling the flow of money expenditure. The basic questions raised by the work of Friedman and the monetarists associated with him turn on (a) whether it would be better to place less reliance on discretionary short term policy and more on long term guidelines in both the fiscal and the monetary field (a question alluded to in the previous chapter), and (b) the contention that demand management by whatever means, cannot by itself achieve a predetermined target rate of unemployment or any other 'real' variable.


## (b) UNION MONOPOLY POWER

The preceding involved, but oversimplified, excursion into the complexities of demand management has been intended to set the stage for the basic question: what do we do if the minimum sustainable rate of unemployment is too high to be tolerable – if it represents, not a misleading statistic, but the coexistence of unsatisfied wants and a large number of workers unable to find jobs at the going rates? There is a strong possibility that this situation has begun to recur in the UK and some other advanced industrial countries.

Any number of reasons could account in principle for high minimum unemployment rates. According to 'the economics of Keynes' (as distinct from 'Keynesian economics'),[7] the price that gets stuck at too high a level to secure full utilisation of resources is the long term rate of interest. This, Keynes believed, tended to be above the rate of return on new investment to be expected in a fully employed economy because of psychological or institutional reasons or because of mistaken central bank policy (Keynes varied in the emphasis he gave to these different factors). As a judgement of the interwar period, Keynes may have been right; and he could be right again. But it is difficult to argue that the rate of interest, which after allowing for inflation has often been negative, has been the price that has been too high in the bulk of the postwar period. Overwhelmingly the most important reason for excessively high minimum unemployment rates in countries such as the UK in the last few years is to be found in the maladjustment of a different price – that of labour; or to put it more plainly, the use by unions of their monopoly power.

Excessively high long term rates of interest were, according to the economics of Keynes, a chronic long term problem. But in a depression another problem appeared: expectations about the yield of new investment were excessively pessimistic. This pessimism might not accord with fundamental long term factors, but would prove self-justifying so long as businessmen acted upon it. In this case, public investment projects or boosts to public or private consumption via a Budget deficit, would be desirable as temporary pump-priming operations to help break the vicious cycle of entrepreneurial expectations.

This second kind of malaise diagnosed by Keynes has not necessarily vanished. In an inflationary recession perverse entrepreneurial expectations and union monopoly power can reinforce each other as causes of unemployment. Indeed the exertion of union monopoly power by means of wage push and a subsequent profit squeeze can, as explained below, help to trigger off pessimistic expectations about the return from new investment, which may be partially justified, but will be certainly overdone as a result of the initial shock. Unfortunately, the difficulty of applying the remedies advocated by Keynes are much greater in this kind of recession, because, apart from the normal timing difficulties, there is the danger of triggering off an inflationary explosion.

It will, however, make for ease of exposition if we put aside these complexities for a moment and examine the effects of union monopoly at the level of individual industry or plant. Just as a price ring or cartel among employers can raise unit prices at the expense of a lower sales volume, a trade union can obtain a higher wage per head in its industry at the expense of a lower volume of employment – in other words, by pushing some workers out of jobs. The effects are the same whether the action is overtly aggressive or is a defensive measure to preserve the relative position of a group of workers whose relative position is threatened by industrial change – the popular justification for the coalminers' successful strike of early 1972.

Movements of relative wages have a function to perform in enabling people to adjust to change. If money wages in a declining industry rise less than elsewhere – and that is all that is in question in the postwar setting – there are two principal effects. First, a brake is exerted on the speed of decline via the effects on the final price of the product (and there may also be some further benefit to employment in that industry through a less capital intensive bias in its own modernisation programme). Secondly, the shift in relativities encourages a voluntary and gradual shift of workers to other industries, mainly through a fall in recruitment and the drifting away of younger workers.

If this shift in relativities is frustrated by union monopoly power – still more if it is reversed – the exit of workers from the declining industry is much longer and quicker, and has a much less voluntary character. The result of this is that there are more workers competing for jobs in other sectors.

It is important to be clear in what sense trade unions affect labour markets by exercising monopoly selling power. Union leaders frequently argue that, if there is to be a 'free-for-all', they are part of the 'all' and should grap what they can. The fallacy of this argument lies in the contrast between what John Nelson-Jones has called the 'individual pursuit of self-interest' and its 'collective pursuit'.[8] The former is compatible with the successful functioning of a market economy; the latter is a form of cheating. Mr Nelson-Jones rightly infers that the theoretical answer would be for workers not to bargain collectively; but he dismisses the idea as 'patently unrealistic', believing that ordinary people will never accept that 'what is desirable in individuals is undesirable in groups'.

It is always dangerous to predict what people may or may not eventually accept, especially as for so long very little attempt was made to explain what was involved. After all, governments do not hesitate to prevent employers indulging in the 'collective pursuit of self interest' by anti-monopoly policy; and the popular belief that wealthy employers have a bargaining advantage over unorganised workers is a deep-seated myth. Employers, however wealthy, do not have the power to screw down the wages of workers so long as they are competing among one another and there is a brisk demand for labour.

There are, of course, local pockets where a 'monopsonistic' employer may have an excessive influence. One of the few genuine cases of inferior bargaining positions is that of schoolchildren. They are unable to escape harsh treatment, petty rules or uncongenial conditions by shopping around between schools. This is so (a) because of the restriction of choice in the state sector, and (b) because any available choice may in any case be made by parents. For these reasons efforts to organise genuine schoolchildren's unions (as distinct from attempts by revolutionaries to exploit children's grievances) deserve more support from liberals than many other trade union activities of which it is more respectable to approve.

Over the bulk of the economy, unions, if they succeed in increasing real wages at all, do so at the expense of other employees or of the general level of employment. Up to the end of the 1960s, at least, empirical US studies suggested that most, if not all, the gains of union labour in the USA were at the expense of non-unionised workers and not at the expense of the earnings of capital. British figures suggest that, in this country, unions did succeed in raising the share of real wages relative to profits, even after allowing for cyclical influences – but at the expense of a lower level of employment, output, investment and growth.

It is often wrongly supposed that the influence of union monopoly power is related to the prevalence of national bargaining. A shift to plant bargaining *can* be helpful both to employment and efficiency if it prevents nationally agreed increases being *automatically* superimposed on whatever emerges from local wage drift and plant bargains. This benefit can, however, be frustrated, if union militants in individual plants force up wages and prevent the employer from offering employment at lower rates to would-be outside recruits. The cry among private employers that power has been transferred to the shop floor, and that agreements with national union representatives are useless, suggests that monopoly power can be very effective at plant level. Of course, like other monopoly power, it is not unlimited. A sufficient degree of induced unemployment, resulting from any sudden and obvious increase in the use of monopoly pressure, may exert a moderating influence even on shop floor unionists. Moreover, a plant monopoly power cannot be exercised beyond the point at which the employer would shut up shop altogether or shift elsewhere. This, in turn, depends partly on the degree of militancy in alternative locations in other districts, regions and countries.

The use of union monopoly power at the level of the individual industry or plant *need not* either raise general unemployment or set in motion a cumulative or explosive inflationary process, but it is, in fact, highly likely to do so. A large increase in redundancies, caused by union wage push in some industries, is likely, in any case, to place a great strain on the organisational and adaptive powers of the sectors expected to receive the discharged workers.

If, on top of this either union activity or institutional rigidities prevent a sufficient fall in *relative* wages in these other sectors, a substantial increase in national unemployment is inevitable, which may well reach politically unacceptable levels. This, in turn, is likely to induce the authorities to attempt to keep up employment by pumping money into the economy, which can only be successful at the cost of an accelerating inflation. This is the 'micro' route by which Hayek derives his leaping tiger.

The above view of the relationship between wages and employment is sometimes disputed on the grounds of the supposed imperviousness of the labour market to the influence of supply and demand. The main evidence cited is a persistence of differences in earnings between workers of comparable skill in the same locality. Now, even if it were true that *workers* were indifferent to wage differentials in their job movements, wage differences and changes would still affect employment, provided that *employers* took them into account. A rise in wages in a particular industry is bound to affect employment, both through its effects on the final demand for the product and on the degree to which labour-saving methods are sought; an employer would have to be indifferent to costs, and risk being put out of business by his competitors, if he took no notice of changes in the price of labour in the production techniques he chose to use. Minimum wages, enforced by legislation, have an effect in pricing people out of jobs similar to union monopoly pressure. They are among the main reasons for high unemployment among black teenagers and unskilled white teenagers in the USA.

But, of course, wage differentials *do* affect the supply as well as the demand side of the labour market. No theorist of any sense has even denied the existence of human inertia, ignorance or attachment to traditional places of work, quite apart from the non-pecuniary advantages stressed by Adam Smith. The view that earnings differentials – except when maintained by monopolies – will vanish belongs to the excessively static view of competition criticised in the previous chapter. The most detailed plant-level investigation so far made, by a team of economists in the Glasgow empirical tradition, in work undertaken for the Department of Employment, suggests that low wage plants suffer from higher quit rates or labour wastage than high wage ones. Low wage plants can maintain their labour force, but it is of a fickle and volatile kind; and it is by more rapid transit through these low wage plants that the worker responds to labour market pressures.[9]

High wage plants are able to maintain stricter hiring standards; but the level of wages they pay is often above what is necessary to obtain the required quality of labour; nor are such high wage policies always associated with recruitment drives. The simplest explanation is that where firms are potentially able to earn above the going rate of return, owing to superior efficiency, good luck in their particular markets or some combination of the two, management has enough discretionary power to share the excess profits between shareholders and its own workers. It should be noted that those who lose from such policies are not merely the firm's shareholders, but potential employees for whom entry into the favoured firm has to be rationed. These factors complicate the workings of labour markets; but they do not make them in the least impervious to supply and demand.

Let us now abstract from the specifics of particuliar industries and glance at the consequences of union monopoly power at a 'macro' level. It is best to start by looking at a cost push, where the combined result of all union pressure is to generate a degree of increase in money wages far above the average increase in output per man. Even if we were prepared to accept a rapid, but steady, inflation as a price worth paying for full employment, accelerating inflation would be impossible to sustain for reasons already mentioned. Sufficient monetary and fiscal restraint would have to be used, in the absence of direct controls, at least to stabilise the rate of growth of money wages. There are three possibilities. The most optimistic is that after a temporary increase in unemployment, the system would settle down with a stable rate of inflation and a tolerable approximation to full employment. The most pessimistic is that the appetite and monopoly of union leaders for wage increases – whether through assertive ambition or simply because of incompatible ideas about relativities – would be such that monetary and fiscal policy would be unable to prevent wage increases from accelerating. If the authorities succeeded in stabilising the growth of total money incomes, it would be at the cost of continuously rising unemployment, with nominal national income growing at a steady rate, but shared among fewer and fewer workers. This, if allowed to go on, would lead to the collapse of the system and its probable replacement by something a good deal nastier.

The most likely result of trying to stabilise the rate of inflation by monetary and fiscal policy is intermediate between the two extremes. That is, it would be possible to stabilise the growth of money incomes, but at the expense of an intolerably high level of unemployment – which would be higher still if the government were actually trying to reduce the rate of wage and price increases. This is yet another way of saying that the effect of union monopoly power is to increase the minimum sustainable rate of unemployment; and governments will oscillate between periods of permitting accelerating inflation and periods of high unemployment, and eventually be drawn to intervene directly in the wage-fixing process.

Why, it may be asked, were we able to combine a roughly stable 3 per cent rate of inflation with full employment during the first two post-war decades? One can either argue that union leaders refrained from exercising their full monopoly power, or that they or others were fooled for a long time by money illusion and accepted wage increases without applying a full inflationary discount. The two factors were of course interconnected. The post-war compromise lasted as long as it did partly because various groups such as those living on fixed incomes, white collar workers, professional groups and the lower paid, either failed to organise or (as in the case of holders of fixed interest paper) allowed themselves to be deceived. Once these other groups began to realise what was happening and organised in self-defence, the situation became explosive. The incompatibility of 'free' trade union bargaining with full employment and any non-explosive behaviour of the price level, far from being a *laissez-faire* doctrine, has been stressed for many years by socialist economists such as Lord Balogh.[10] It is also one of Beckerman's conclusions in his study of the lesson of the 1964–70 Labour Government.[11]

So far the 'macro' part of the argument has been expressed in terms of money wage increases, with the real consequences left deliberately in the background. The mechanism by which union monopoly power affects unemployment has been described in terms of monetary and fiscal policies, undertaken to prevent an inflationary explosion, which in turn leads to high unemployment. The neoclassical economists believed, however, that there was a quite *direct* link between *real wages* and employment even for the economy as a whole. If higher real wages were demanded, fewer people would be employed. Keynes in the *General Theory* accepted entirely the idea of a functional relationship between real wages and employment, but argued that general cuts in *money* wages were an unsuitable or impossible way of achieving this, and the result could be better achieved indirectly by other routes.

Between the 1930s, when these arguments took place, and the late 1960s, the influence of real wages in determining aggregate employment (as distinct from employment in particular industries) appeared to diminish in importance. This was partly because direct costs are constant for many firms over a large range of potential output, and the marginal productivity of labour does not fall as output and employment increases. Indeed, given accounting conventions with regard to the spreading of overheads, some employers can even increase wages in the expansionary phases of the cycle, add to employment, and keep prices more stable than they can in the restrictive phases. Between one cycle and another, the practice of recovering wage increases which were out of line with productivity by increased mark-ups prevented too dramatic a gain in the share of labour at the expense of capital.

If, however, the mark-ups become insufficient and the trade unions do succeed, over a period of years, in increasing real wages at the expense of profits, investment is likely to become more labour-saving than it would otherwise be. Capital accumulation creates job opportunities, while labour saving innovations destroy them. In a smoothly progressing economy, there is a balance between the two. There is enough capital accumulation to employ the labour force at the going real wage rate, which will be rising through the time with technical progress and growing real output.

If the stock of capital tends to rise faster than the available labour supply, real wages will be driven up and capital investment will take a more labour-saving form. This is as it should be. But if real wages are pushed up simply by union monopoly power in the absence of a specially rapid growth of capital, new investment will still be given a labour-saving bias, even though there is no labour shortage to justify such a bias. If this goes on for some years, there may simply not be enough capital of a type adapted to consumer demand to employ the labour force – even if it became suddenly and miraculously possible to boost demand without any danger of an inflationary explosion. The UK would then have arrived at a situation reminiscent of that of many underdeveloped countries, where not even the most extreme Keynesians believe that unemployment can be cured by demand expansion alone. The fall in the share of company trading profits net of stock appreciation, as a share of final output, from a range of 10–12 per cent in the decade up to 1964 to 7 per cent in 1970 does not suggest that we are dealing with a flight of theoretical fancy; and figures of net profits properly adjusted for inflation might reveal an even more dramatic drop. A simple price index correction (which does not allow for depreciation and stock replacement) suggests that real profits fell by a quarter between 1965 and 1970.

This influence of real wages on employment is a long term effect. There can, at times, be a much more immediate connection. During a long period of steady and gradual inflation, employers become used to passing on wage increases in the knowledge that their competitors will do the same. But when there is a sudden acceleration in the rate of wage inflation, as at the end of the 1960s and the early 1970s, this confidence falls off; for with the established pattern broken, no one can be sure exactly what will happen to his competitors' labour costs, let alone how they will react; and human inertia will also make an industrialist much less happy about passing on a 15 per cent wage increase, which has hit him out of the blue, than a 6–8 per cent wage increase which he has been paying with minor variations for decades. Thus, even without an exchange rate constraint, the initial result of a sudden wage explosion is likely to be a rise in the share of wages and a severe profit squeeze, leading in turn to a 'shakeout' of labour and a reluctance to invest in the new capacity. Thus, a wage explosion telescopes within a short period a desirable attack on overmanning which would otherwise be spread over a longer period and therefore be easier to absorb.

There has been far too much equivocation and self-deception by economists in the debate on the relation between inflationary wage demands and unemployment. The Conservative ministers who spoke in the early 1970s of trade unions pricing workers out of jobs were *right*, however inadequate their explanation of the process; while those who tried to deny this, whether in political polemics or by the use of short-run pseudo-Keynesian models were *wrong*. This is, to my mind, as certain as any cause-and-effect relation in this subject can ever hope to be.

It is time for frankness about the social and economic effects of trade unions. The belief dies hard that any progressive and enlightened person should either have instinctive sympathy with union wage demands, or at least refrain from giving comfort to their opponents. Even Conservatives who wish to show that they belong to the up-to-date wing of the Party, go out of their way to avoid 'union-bashing'; the controversial 1971 Industrial Relations Act was itself designed, in the minds of at least some of its authors, to strengthen 'responsible trade unionism'. The idea that trade union bargaining may itself be an anachronism as a method of determining wages, or that it has outlived its usefulness, is regarded as too radical to utter in public (although prominent politicians of all parties say so in private). Because anti-union arguments may have sometimes been associated with the type of person who believes in hanging or flogging and regrets the passing of gun diplomacy, this does not make them wrong. To ask 'In whose company will I be?' may be an inescapable shorthand method of approaching questions one has not the time or interest to investigate for onself; but it can be extremely dangerous as a standard procedure. It would be a moderate assessment to describe the trade unions as agencies for increasing the degree of unemployment and for reducing the real living standards of some of the weakest and most unfortunate sections of the population in a period of rapid but uncertain inflation.

## (c)  CHOOSING AMONG EVILS

Enough has been said here – and has happened in the real world – to show that a 'hands off' policy in relation to trade union monopoly power is neither desirable nor likely. The economic liberal who maintains that all would be well with a stable growth of the money supply and a floating exchange rate (both of which remain in my view desirable) has confused what may be necessary conditions for achieving his ideals with sufficient conditions, which they are certainly not. He should not escape the less congenial task of deciding which kind of labour market policies would be least harmful to his ultimate beliefs.

Whether such measures are called 'incomes policy' or not is largely a verbal quibble. The main objection to the term 'incomes policy' is that it diverts attention from the source of the trouble in union monopoly power, particularly when it masquerades as 'prices and incomes policy'. Moreover, in so far as various governments are criticised for 'not having an incomes policy', it points the finger in the wrong direction. As a matter of usage, many (although not all) of the proponents of 'incomes policy' have in mind more illiberal policies than those who choose some other name for the interventions that they desire.

These semantic issues are a secondary matter. The important distinctions to an economic liberal are in the probable effects of different policies, irrespective of their labels. The best solution would be to treat collective bargaining as a restrictive practice, to be permitted only under certain exceptional conditions, such as the existence of monopsonistic power, or very high local unemployment rates, that give employers a genuine bargaining advantage. These could be 'gateways' under which collective bargaining would be allowed, like the 'gateways' in the Restrictive Practices Act, under which trade associations can apply to be allowed to continue price rings.

Unfortunately, an attempt to outlaw collective wage-fixing is not only unlikely to be tried, but, if it were, the law might prove unenforceable without a greater basis of consent than the suggestion would at present command. One must, therefore, also discuss second best approaches. But it is well to bear in mind what the first best suggestion would be, should the opportunity to move towards it arise. Suggestions should not be suppressed because they appear extreme or politically unrealistic. So did, at one time, most of the current conventional wisdom.

An exhaustive classification of plans for influencing wage determination will not be provided here, but only a few notes on various schemes, that have been, are being, or are likely to be, attempted. By no means all the ideas are mutually exclusive, and some could operate at the same time. The nearest to the abolition of collective bargaining and restoring competitive market forces among those considered even remotely feasible, would be to give a central body reserve powers over all *negotiated* wage settlements. Employers short of labour would still be free to offer what they liked above the negotiated minimum to attract workers; but the government or some other central body would have control over the industry-wide rates to which these market premia would be added. This would be worth trying, but there are two snags. One is that union monopoly power at plant level could still generate explosive inflationary forces (and the drift of power to plant level would, of course, be accelerated). The second is that unless the central body were to impose a permanent nil norm (which it should do but would not), we would be back with the familiar problems of norms and criteria.

The type of official intervention that would interfere least with market forces would be one that did not worry about differentials, but periodically wiped out a given percentage of all wages and salaries. Strictly speaking, the reduction would have to be in the totals and not in the percentage increases. This, if it were possible, would eliminate the forces making for cost-push inflation, while retaining the market (adjusted in the ways explained in the previous chapter) as an instrument of allocation. It is something of this kind that many professional economists and Treasury officials have semi-consciously in mind when they speak of 'incomes policy'.[12]

The trouble with this approach is that knowledge of this paring-off process would affect the wage bargainers themselves. Behind the anti-employer façade, wage negotiations are primarily battles *between different groups of workers* over relativities; and the result at the end of the bargaining year is not one for which the losers would willingly have settled. The knowledge that the total wage bill was to be axed by a uniform percentage would be likely to lead to much bigger claims and more bitter and prolonged industrial strife; and the state or employer would afterwards have the herculean task of reclaiming back earnings. Alternatively, the percentage reduction would have to be applied instantly and would depend on a highly complex formula, which would tend to produce ever greater reductions as time went on with all the incendiary risks of such a situation.

Nevertheless, one proposal, sometimes made in association with the paring-off idea, is worth considering. This is an attempt, whether voluntary or statutory, to synchronise pay settlements so that they come into force on the same day of the year. This could not easily apply to industrial plants where local negotiations are going on all the time. But it might work in some industries, particularly in the public sector. This device could not remove the explosive forces generated by incompatible views on differentials, but it might moderate highly inflationary settlements which were entered into simply as an insurance against others doing better. If, for example, the railwaymen, postmen and electricians were satisfied with their existing differentials, a simple known advance date for the payment of the new rates would provide some guarantee against their being outflanked by each other.

The suggestions so far mentioned might slightly alleviate the unemployment–inflation problem, but little confidence can be placed in their being sufficient to do the whole job. Another approach, which does not preclude anything so far suggested, is to concentrate on resisting inflationary wage claims in the public sector. The semi-monopoly position of public enterprises, and their access to the Treasury as a banker of last resort, can aggravate wage-push inflation. These special factors enable public enterprises to take an inflationary lead which may then be followed by the private sector. The government can certainly assist matters by neither 'leaning on' public enterprises to bring industrial peace, nor providing a bottomless purse to finance the ensuing deficits. It can even attempt to move into reverse and use the public sector as the spearhead in an attempt to produce 'de-escalation' or at least 'non-escalation' in private industry. Apart from standing up to public sector strikes, the government can also help by making only sparing use of official conciliation services and by diplomatic attempts to strengthen the resolve of private employers.

There is a great deal more to be said for such policies than it was fashionable to admit when they were inaugurated by the Heath Government in the early 1970s. But even if 'standing firm' in the public sector were ever to achieve its immediate objects, its long term success would depend on the private sector following the lead given. Otherwise the public sector would, in the end, have to raise wages in line with the private sector if it were to retain its employees and avoid becoming completely demoralised. Moreover, the 'standing firm' policy is extremely vulnerable to the demonstration effect of the occasional spectacular defeat, such as that of the miners' strike in 1972, which any non-omniscient government is bound occasionally to suffer through tactical errors and which can undo overnight many months of patient effort.

Above all, the transformation of every dispute in state-owned industries and services into a political confrontation between the government and the trade union movement is an example of just that kind of overextension of the sphere of the political which was condemned in the last chapter. If every public sector wage claim is a test of overall government policy, it becomes very difficult to give much weight to the special circumstances of the particular industry. This problem would be easier if there were (as may have happened by the time these words are in print) a limited revival of something like the old Prices and Incomes Board for the public sector – provided that this Board did not attempt a pseudo-scientific evaluation of different jobs, but worked on the clues it could obtain from the supply and demand situation in the industry concerned and the movement of comparable earnings in the private sector.

Although this part of the discussion has been conducted for ease of exposition in terms of moderating the rate of wage-push inflation, readers of the earlier parts of the chapter will realise that what is at stake is the reduction of the minimum sustainable level of unemployment consistent with non-explosive inflation. Short of treating collective bargaining as a restrictive practice, the best hope for achieving it is a reduction of the monopoly power of the unions on the ground. The Industrial Relations legislation may make a peripheral contribution by reducing the blacklisting of non-affected employers, or by bringing in the 'silent majority' of union members against the militants. But we should not pin too much hope on what is basically a reform of union rather than an anti-monopoly measure.

One of the most interesting proposals here has been made by a left-wing economic liberal, Professor James Meade.[13] This is that the government should lay down a norm, which would not be binding on either side of industry. If unions staged a strike for a claim above the norm various penalties would apply; for example, supplementary benefits would become the liability of the union or the subsequent debt of the individual worker, accumulated rights of redundancy benefits would be lost, and the union would be liable to a tax on strike benefits. A tribunal would determine whether the sanctions should apply.

Unless there were hosts of recognised exceptional cases, almost any strike would be for something in excess of the probable norm. The Meade proposals amount, on analysis, either to the reintroduction of a complex policy for determining merits of individual claims, or to a series of penalties or withdrawals of privileges when union members engage in organised strikes. The latter types of measure should be examined separately on their own merits. Supplementary benefit to strikers' families should, as a matter of course, be loans to be recovered via subsequent income tax deductions. If this were done it would be impossible to make mud-slinging allegations about 'starving people back to work', but the taxpayer would not finance strikers. Nor is it any more reasonable that the income tax machinery should continue to pay out refunds to strikers immediately, while taxpayers who have left a job for other reasons have to wait much longer. Loss of accumulated redundancy benefits might, on the other hand, be unfair to people pushed unwillingly by their fellow workers into a strike. A tax on strike benefits, however, has much to be said for it, although it would be inflammatory in union circles and it might not be worth jeopardising the rest of the Meade proposals by including them in the total package.

A great many other proposals for intervention in incomes settlement are really suggestions for machinery, either for deciding what particular incomes should be, or for attempting to enforce these decisions. This applies to a whole range of suggestions ranging from the presence of a 'public interest' representative at all major negotiations, to a CBI–TUC compact, a Prices and Incomes Board 'with teeth', or a 'tax on excessive wage increases'. All these proposals assume that there should be an attempt to regulate the process of wage determination and not simply to alter the environment in which they take place. The tax proposal, for example, is simply a piece of machinery for penalising wage increases above a permissible level, which would have to be determined by the whole elaborate apparatus of norms, criteria and exceptions, with all their well known problems, distortions, inequities and opportunities for avoidance.

Nevertheless, because of the difficulties of other approaches, direct intervention in wage-fixing has been tried in most Western countries and is likely to be tried again at some stage in this country – perhaps before the reader has seen these words. Although the existence of rampant union monopoly power gives the economic liberal no reason to favour *laissez-faire* in this field, he should also be aware that the heart of any regulation of incomes is the problem of differentials; and the real danger of intervention is that some central body will try to determine how much one person is worth in some quasi-moral sense compared to another. (The pitfalls of this were explained on pp. 92–7.) The liberal should not deceive himself by saying that such intervention is bound to fail.

It is true that econometric investigations of recent incomes policy have been controversial and inconclusive, and suggest that effects in most countries have been at best modest. But this may reflect partly a lack of ruthlessness on the part of social democracies in carrying them out. It is also true that history is littered with unsuccessful attempts to control wages and/or prices. The Roman Emperor Diocletian issued edicts in AD 301–2 fixing maximum wages and prices, enforced under threat of execution, but this did not prevent a galloping inflation.[14] The Statute of Artificers of 1563, which provided for the regulation of maximum wages by JPs, was no more successful in stemming the Elizabethan inflation. The Roman inflation sprang in fact from currency debasement to pay the Imperial Army, the Elizabethan variety from the influx of precious metals from the New World; and no incomes control can offset an excessive increase in the money supply or in government borrowing financed by the banking system.

One cannot, however, rule out some degree of 'success' for incomes intervention combined with a sufficient control of monetary demand. A determined government can, in all probability, control the growth of 'nominal' (that is, money) income and output by monetary and fiscal policy. The role of intervention in the labour market would then be to ensure that the growth of national income took the form of increases in real output and employment, and was not wasted in inflationary increases in wages and prices and rising unemployment. To put the matter in yet another way: the role of incomes policy is to try to see that a limit on the growth of the money supply and on the Budget deficit, which is sufficient to prevent either a runaway or an undesirably high rate of inflation, is accompanied by a tolerable level of employment. Most of the economists who have explained how wage drift, variations in hours of work, upgrading of workers and many other devices of human ingenuity could defeat incomes control,[15] are implicitly referring to a situation of excess demand in the labour market where, even if unions did not exist, employers would bid for labour and push up earnings at an inflationary, and probably increasing rate. Direct intervention in incomes is only feasible once this sort of excess demand has been eliminated.

Given that such intervention is likely to be attempted, the relevant question is: how does one minimise its harmful potential and maximise any possible benefits? One of the most important distinctions to draw is between emergency policies, such as a temporary freeze or ceiling on permissible wage and price increases, and policies designed for permanent operation.

The various short term wages or wage-price freezes have had

greater apparent effects, while the more profound long term policies, which were supposed to follow them, have run into the sand. This was demonstrated by the Cripps, Lloyd and Wilson freezes in the UK; and Nixon's mistake in 1971 was to have made his freeze as short as three months and to put too much weight on the follow-up. A freeze or ceiling has the important additional advantage that it does not attempt to impose supposedly superior criteria on the wage and price differentials determined by the market, but accepts present differentials and postpones any further adjustment for up to say a year. Clearly, a long-term freeze would ossify the economy, but as a short-term shock measure to be used on rare occasions, not too easily predictable in advance, it has its place in the economic policy armoury.

The main case to be made for a freeze or ceiling is that it will reduce the expected rate of inflation and thus the level of wage increases associated in the short run with any degree of slack in the labour market. If the level of unemployment is at, or above, its minimum sustainable rate, then a temporary freeze or ceiling can reduce the amount and duration of any excess unemployment required to reduce the rate of inflation. If the level of unemployment, at the time of the freeze or later, is below the minimum level, then inflation will eventually start gathering momentum again. But even then time will have been bought. If a freeze or ceiling can reduce the expected rate of inflation from 10 to 3 per cent – admittedly an extremely favourable assumption – it will take some years for the pace of inflation to creep back to 10 per cent and the old problem to re-emerge. Time is worth buying with a problem as intractable as the inflation–unemployment one. The real trouble is that the more frequently a freeze or ceiling is repeated, the less will be the effect on expectations, and the shorter the amount of time it will buy.

The logic of threshold agreements is in some respects similar. If the rise in real incomes that the unions are insisting upon is out of line with the productivity trend, threshold agreements will not help. They can help, however, in specific situations when, for some reason, trade unionists are projecting an unnecessarily high rate of inflation into the future. The classic example was the autumn of 1969 when they were projecting the effects of the recent substantial devaluation, and the indirect tax increases imposed to back it up, into the future. By doing so, their fears became self-justifying. In more normal circumstances, threshold agreements can be of some use as an insurance premium when unions are exerting their monopoly power not aggressively, but out of fear of what others engaged in the inflationary race will do. The key question is whether the amount of moderation that can be purchased by threshold agreements will do more to dampen price increases than the threshold compensation itself will to increase it. The situation will clearly vary from time to time according to the state of the cycle, union moods and other influences.

Thresholds or any form of 'cost of living indexing' having the disadvantage that they create a severe obstacle to a reduction in the normal rate of growth of real incomes which may be forced on a country by a variety of circumstances, such as a fall in the overseas market for its products, a major devaluation, a misfortune such as an overseas war, or a mistake in demand management. If threshold agreements are not then suspended, the country could face an inflationary explosion of post-First World War continental dimensions. The conclusion is that threshold agreements may be useful in certain industries, especially in the public sector, where it is both possible to keep a watch on their terms and the desire for insurance is high; but they must always be revocable in an emergency.

Permanent policies of intervention in wage-fixing have been deliberately left to the end of this chapter. The hope of the economic liberal must be that a combination of labour market policies and *ad hoc* expedients of the kind so far discussed can prevent inflation from becoming explosive at a tolerable level of unemployment. He is afraid that an incomes policy will be deliberately used to enforce a pattern of relativities based on a revival of the mediaeval myth that there is a 'just price' for goods and services, which would enable a group of wise men to say how much a milkman is worth relative to a doctor, or what is a fair price for a loaf of bread. This unfortunately is what most people probably have in mind when they talk of a prices and incomes policy. Yet even Lord Balogh vigorously repudiates the pseudo-scientific claims of job evaluation and admits that would-be scientific attempts to measure the worth of a man's work 'are subjective and politically coloured'.[16] Job evaluation is possible within a particular firm or even industry because of the existence of an outside market to evaluate the basic skills attributed to particular posts. If there is no such market, or it is ignored, there is no way of comparing the value of a carpenter's job with that of a lathe operator, or determining how many points to give skill, as against responsibility, irksomeness and all the other attributes in which jobs vary from each other.

Unfortunately, governments that hanker after an incomes policy are strongly tempted to go in for this wrong sort. Even if they stick to generalised restraint on the incomes side they are under a very strong pressure to attempt to buy union support – almost always unsuccessfully – by a whole series of actions, ranging from price controls in the private sector, pressure on nationalised industries to keep prices artificially low, to dividend control and penal taxes on profits and high incomes, or travel restrictions, which not only tend to ossify the structure of industry and bolster inefficiency, but if pushed too far are inimical to a free society.

Whatever may have to be said for public relations purposes, it is as well to say that, except in the case of short-term freezes or ceilings, intervention is needed primarily for wages and not prices and profits. This is often concealed by Whitehall for tactical purposes, and anti-profit gestures are made for the sake of union goodwill. Union leaders are not so easily deceived; and it might be better to state frankly that profits are a different type of animal from wages. There is abundant statistical evidence, cited above, that there has been, taking one year with another, no profit-push inflation in the UK or in most other Western countries, and that, apart from the effects of changing import prices and indirect taxes, the main statistically identified influence on the general price level is the movement of wages in relation to productivity.

If some guarantee is really required that wage restraint will not lead to an increase in the share of profits in the national income, the way to provide it is by adjusting the level of company taxation in the Budget. Such guarantees were indeed given in Budget speeches and other government statements in the Maudling-Brown era; but they were either not understood or disregarded. If they are to be revived again, some allowance would have to be made for the marked falls in the share of the profits in the decade up to 1970, which needs to be reversed if investment is not to be severely hit and employment is to be maintained at satisfactory levels.

The most difficult choice for an economic liberal is whether it would be worse to have income relativities influenced by some sort of CBI–TUC compact (with or without government involvement) or to have a statutory policy. The exercise of economic power by producer groups insulated from both market and political disciplines is obnoxious in a free society. But the one redeeming feature of arrangements of this kind, is that, so long as they lack statutory sanction, they are likely to have many gaps. There will always be some workers and entrepreneurs who do not 'play the game' and charge the market rate for their services. These chinks in the system will provide some opportunity for innovation and personal initiative which may not be there in a government-enforced system. Moreover, given the existence of union monopoly power, it would be a lesser evil for the rival union monopolies to work out a deal on relativities than to impose a high rate of unemployment or an explosive inflation on the public as a by-product of their power struggles.

Where the liberal should draw the line is at any attempt to convey quasi-governmental power on the CBI or TUC, whether by legislation or by ministerial arm-twisting directed against those who do not comply. If government power is to be permanently involved, statutory control exercised through known rules is the only approach compatible with the 'rule of law'. Whether the government delegates the determination of individual cases to a separate board or boards is a secondary matter. The important point is that the criteria should be as clear as possible and the outcome of particular cases reasonably predictable.

If we do have to face centralised determination of, or official influence on, wages and other incomes, it is important for the liberal not just to withdraw in disgust. His fallback position should be to insist that the relative scarcity of different types of workers should be among the factors taken into account by any wage-fixing authority. There is no need for this to be the only principle; traditional ideas of relativities will inevitably temper the speed with which relativities adjust to supply and demand; and fads, fashions and headline pressures will unavoidably play a part in determining the case law. But some recognition of the importance of scarcity or surplus of the type of labour concerned is necessary if we are not to be forced into a painful choice between poor economic performance (which would make social tensions worse) and ultimate direction of labour on the lines analysed in the last chapter. An open admission of the role of supply and demand could also play a part in creating the public consensus on differentials, the lack of which is both undermining the market system and preventing any alternative from operating. An emphasis on market conditions as *one* of the criteria to be used in determining relative incomes would bring home to people that something less was being attempted than an evaluation of relative moral worth and, that if pop singers continued to be paid more than headmasters, this would be a by-product of satisfying consumer choice with no deeper judgement implied.

# 3 The Economics of the Alternative Society

*'Hör auf zu beben*
*Bereite dich zu leben.'*

'Cease from trembling
Prepare thyself to live.'

From lines added by Mahler to
Klopstock's 'Resurrection Ode'
and used in his Second Symphony

There is little that is new in the indictment by the present generation of radicals and revolutionaries of technology and the 'consumer society'. The Bible abounds in admonitions against the vain pursuit of riches. The nineteenth-century Tories derided the commercialism of their Whig and Liberal opponents; prophets such as Carlyle and Ruskin, as well as socialists of the Tawney school, thundered against the acquisitive society; and T. S. Eliot, writing as a Christian conservative was deeply disturbed by the values of a 'mechanised, commercialised, urbanised way of life.'[1]

Orthodox Labour thinkers, such as Mr Crosland, are understandably sceptical of the new fashion;[2] but it has undoubtedly affected the mood of a great many respectable 'progressives' well outside the New Left; and the increase of consumer spending has come to be regarded as an establishment, conservative goal to be scorned by the enlightened.

In the form now fashionable among progressive egalitarians, the anti-materialist attitude contains a great many contradictions. As Assar Lindbeck has pointed out in his sympathetic but critical study, *The Political Economy of the New Left*,[3] 'If additional consumption is so unimportant, why is *equality* in income and consumption so important?' There is also a fundamental incompatibility between the attack on the consumer society and the almost automatic support among most of the New and Old Left for trade union wage claims.

These contradictions reflect, however, the inconsistencies (to

183

put it no worse) of individuals or groups. It is possible to imagine a
genuine change of values which would cause people to place much
less emphasis on the acquisition of additional material goods and
services. This essay is not concerned to argue whether such a
change would be good or bad, but to examine some of the
economic consequences of such a change, and, in particular,
whether it need involve the suppression of market forces and
private property either by some form of command economy or, at
the other extreme, a more anarchic form of behaviour.


## (a) ALTRUISM

It is possible that the revulsion against the pursuit of ever greater
material wealth, at present characteristic of a few radical students
(and also some upper and middle class traditionalists), is a
portent of wider change. It is always worth examining the
implication of developments at present visible only on a small
scale and still very untypical of the bulk of the population. Let us
then suppose that there were a widespread weakening of the desire
towards additional personal consumption. What would be the
consequences?

Such a shift in outlook could come about in various ways, it is
convenient to start off by assuming that it is part of a new ethical
outlook, rather than a mere change of tastes. Both are of course
involved in the movement towards the 'alternative society'; but
the analysis of an ethical revulsion against selfishness is, in fact,
less complicated than that of a shift of preferences from consumer
goods towards other things. To make any progress at all, it is
necessary to proceed in stages.

What, then, follows from the belief that the search for
maximum individual self-gratification is wrong, and from the
desire to see a new order based on altruism rather than
institutionalised selfishness? General altruism is a concept
capable of several interpretations. The most extreme form is the
advocacy of complete unselfishness and total dedication to the
welfare of others. This would be internally inconsistent if adopted
as a general rule. The paradox of total unselfishness is that it is
only possible to be selfless because some people are concerned
with their own selfish desires or needs. If everybody were only
concerned with the welfare of others, there would be nothing for

altruists to do. A second, slightly less extreme form would be to love one's neighbour as much as – but not more than – oneself. A practitioner of such an ethic, carried to its logical conclusion, would devote his efforts to improving the welfare of the human race, or his fellow countrymen, and would be prepared to forego, for their benefit, any excess of his income above the general run. A third sort of altruistic ethic would allow some modest material objectives, by definition less than the maximum obtainable, but forego any available excess for the sake of others.

Altruism and benevolence, if they are to be any other than individual eccentrics, presuppose a certain measure of self-regard; and novelists and psychologists have always known that those who despise themselves cannot love other people. Thus, we can confine our attention to the second and third varieties – an unwillingness to obtain for oneself more than either the generally available average, or some specified minimum, while there are others who are worse off. Various qualifications and permutations of these codes can be envisaged. An ethical inhibition against maximising one's own standard of living, present when the poorest are suffering from malnutrition may, without any fundamental change of outlook, disappear if poverty comes to mean possessing only one car.

This essay is not concerned with those who are only prepared to make such penal sacrifices if others do so as well. My concern here is with the logical consequence of altruism as an individual ethic. An almost insuperable, initial difficulty is deciding what is the correct reference group. Is an altruist to forego personal riches to raise the standard of living of his fellow countrymen or of the entire human race?

It is difficult to find any convincing argument for limiting altruism to the frontiers of the nation-state – except for a pathological nationalist who has intense feelings of brotherhood for his fellow countrymen, but regards everyone else as a member of a different species. There seems no more reason for restricting benevolent and unselfish behaviour to the inhabitants of the UK than to the inhabitants of Greater London or, the enlarged EEC or members of one's own profession. The conclusion would seem to be that the consistent altruist should want the benefit of any limitation on his own living standard devoted to the poorest inhabitants of the poorest countries.

An altruist who felt that 'development aid' did more harm than good could subscribe to purely charitable relief organisations. Apart from worrying about the forms in which this help should be given, or its long-term effect, the altruist may despair at the smallness of the impact of his efforts, and those of like-minded people, if spread thinly over thousands of millions; and he may prefer to make a discernible impact on living standards nearer home, which he is also in a better position to assess for himself. But once he does this, he is conceding that he does not attach equal to every human being; and he can have no tenable objection to the liberal–individualist ethic which attaches most weight to one's family and friends, somewhat lesser weight to professional colleagues or others with shared interests and outlook, and so in ever widening circles until the boundaries of the whole human race are reached. (The implication of such a realistic weighting are discussed in the Appendix on *Morality and Foreign Policy*, on pp. 316–31).

But however the altruist solves these conundrums, one general observation can be made. This is that there is little reason for him to refrain from maximising his own income. The difference between himself and other citizens, if he is logical, should be in what he does with his gains. Indeed, if anything, he should work beyond the point at which the self-centred citizen decides that the extra reward is not worth the effort, in order to increase the surplus he has available for charitable purposes. A society dominated by dedicated and consistent altruists would, therefore, be a pretty puritanical one, which is one of the reasons why I do not find the prospect attractive. Indeed, there have been resemblances to it among the frugal, hard-working devout rising middle classes during several eras of economic advance. The main difference is that the wealth that was foregone in personal enjoyment was devoted only in small measure to improving the lot of other human beings, but was largely devoted to the 'higher' purposes of religion or further capital accumulation.

The important point, however, is that there is no reason why an altruist should not, with the limits to be mentioned below, play to win. The presumption in favour of buying in the cheapest market and selling in the dearest, and gaining the best return on his talents, applies at least as much to him as to his self-oriented colleagues. A businessman does not serve his fellows, least of all the poorest of them, by selling a product at a minimal profit well below that which the market will bear.

If he were to do so, the most likely result would be a misallocation of scarce resources, which is likely to make the community worse off; and there is no presumption that the poor will escape the effects. Even the apparent direct transfer from his own pocket to others by holding his prices down will be misdirected, as a large part of the gain will inevitably flow to those who are, by altruistic lights, undeserving of his largesse. He would be better advised to behave in a normal commercial manner and use the larger sum then at his disposal for redistribution according to his own philanthropic principles.

The above advice, is of course, only an approximation to the truth, due to the imperfections of economic policy. Although it would be best if the state were to lay down rules of the games and adjust its taxes and subsidies so that the pursuit of self-interest also promoted the general prosperity, we know that a market economy will never, in practice, be managed with ideal wisdom. Firms are not always made to pay for the overspill costs that their waste products or their heavy trucks impose on the community. Workers displaced by technological or other change may not be reabsorbed into other jobs – whether because of mistaken official financial policies, or the monopolistic activities of trade unions. Undesirable changes in the distribution of income, caused, say, by a rise in basic food prices, are best corrected via the tax and social security system; but we cannot always rely on the correction being made.

Thus, the playing of the market game must always be tempered by common sense; and this applies not merely to the declared altruist, but also to the ordinary humane citizen. The absence of a law making me pay full compensation for all the foul products my factory pours into a river, does not give me a moral licence to go on polluting regardless (although I may be under financial pressures to do so). There is no general politico-economic outlook that can excuse inflicting specific harm on others, especially identifiable individual human beings in a weaker position than oneself, without attempt at redress. The takeover king who shows the faithful servant of the old firm the door, without asking what is to become of him, is not a good Manchester liberal but a callous malefactor.

These qualifications do not destroy the general presumption against subordinating the profit motive to some supposedly higher ideal. A businessman, however altruistic, should be very careful before reducing his rate of return for some abstract goal, such as 'lower prices', 'an incomes policy', 'the export drive', or 'the need to invest'. He is not professionally qualified to calculate the remoter consequences of supposedly patriotic deviation from the pursuit of his own interest. Nor, in all probability, are those who provide these exhortations. Moreover, even when it comes to avoiding specific harm to known individuals, an altruistic or humanitarian employer would be better advised to concentrate on such matters as the early spotting of redundancies and making personal efforts to retrain and find other jobs for those displaced, rather than attempt to maintain an inflated work force, or to 'buy British' when the foreign product gives better value. Of course, painful dilemmas cannot always be avoided in this way; but the sensible humanitarian will try to minimise them by intelligent planning of *his own* activities rather than by taking pride in the smallness of his profits.

## (b) A CHANGE OF TASTES

An altruist of the kind described may be very fond of consumer goods and simply think it wrong to have more of them than his less fortunate neighbours. It is, however, useful to extend the analysis from altruism to a more general rejection of the striving for ever increasing amounts of goods and services as a false goal.

It is possible that the existence of a minority of people, who had already undergone such a change in tastes and preferred idleness or social security benefit to the extra material gain available from work, may have had something to do with the much higher unemployment figures in the early 1970s than in previous cyclical peaks. But, in default of worthwhile evidence, I should be surprised if this is more than a part of the explanation. In any case, whatever may have been the motivation of the unemployed, there is not the slightest reason to suppose that the saturation of consumer wants is the reason for the difficulties that have occurred in recent years in maintaining 'effective demand' at levels which have previously been customary. The anti-consumption values under discussion are still shared by a minority. Most people could still find plenty on which to spend extra income.

Tastes and behaviour are not, however, immutable; and it is

worth asking whether a revulsion from any further increase in material consumption – feelings which are at present confined to minority groups – would be compatible with a competitive market economy. However strong the historical connection between the rise of capitalism (or earlier mercantile systems) and materialistic preoccupations, need this connection hold good in the future? This question is best investigated by treating the revulsion from the pursuit of ever more goods and services as a pure change of taste in a society that has already reached an advanced level of technology and is capable of producing a Gross National Product that is, by historical standards, high.

It is, however, necessary to distinguish between two forms of aversion towards the consumer society. There is the purist assertion that additional consumption of any kind is of negligible or negative importance. There is also the lesser contention that it is only additions to private consumption that have a zero or negative utility, but that additional output in the public services – whether health, education, or the use of resources to improve the physical environment – is abundantly justified. As Lindbeck points out, Galbraith in *The Affluent Society* simultaneously embraced both versions of the over-consumption doctrine without distinguishing between them (or noting their incompatibility).

This essay is concerned with a swing of taste against consumption of the first and purer form. The second 'pro-public, anti-private consumption' form of the doctrine would still require a concentration on economic growth and efficiency, but the extra resources would be spent by the state and there would be little increase in post-tax real income. It would therefore represent a much less fundamental change.

The simplest case to envisage is that the majority of the population become satisfied with a lower level of material award, in the form of either private or collective consumption, than they could obtain from the earnings of a working week of the present customary length. The higher the general level of hourly real wages (in other words, the more successful 'the system' has been in the past), the more such people there are likely to be; and the less heroic, or ascetic, they will need to be to sustain such an attitude. Let us at this stage assume that they can fill extra leisure hours to their own satisfaction.

A competitive system based on market forces is surely likely to prove most satisfactory to such non-consumers. For a profit-making businessman is not interested in the private values of his workers. If they wish to work fewer hours for less money, or only one week in four, that is their affair. If irregular and unpredictable working habits impose difficulties in keeping up a smooth flow of production, the rate for the job will be *pro rata* less than for workers willing to work in a more regular way. Indeed, as soon as it becomes apparent that there is a pool of potential workers available, who will be easier to recruit or require to be paid less provided that they can work in amounts, and/or at times, of their own choosing, it will pay businessmen to find methods of adapting their methods to such preferences; and those who do adapt in this way will be able to undercut those who insist too rigidly on traditional working practices.*

The difficulties in the way of the 'alternative' culture come from the monopolistic and anti-capitalist element of our society. This would be readily admitted in the case of restrictive practices by businessmen who agree not to undercut each other with irregular labour. But the greatest obstacles arise from union monopolies, who insist on fixing wages and conditions by collective agreements, which do not easily permit variations to suit minority preferences. It would not take long for the shop stewards to 'call everyone out' if an employer were to be found taking an individual workers at below the regular rate in return for an unusual and costly pattern of working hours or a toleration of absenteeism. (The systems now being introduced experimentally are presumably not very costly – they may even be beneficial – for company efficiency.) The point would be blindingly obvious were it not for the traditional association between being on the left and pro-union sympathies. It is no coincidence that the occupations suggested in that excellent publication *Alternative London*,[4] which range from interviewing for market surveys and selling charter flights, to minicab driving, 'busking', window cleaning and working in bistros, are the least unionised of activities. Nevertheless, if the preference for leisure, or irregular work, over take-home pay became sufficiently widespread, even union negotiators would be forced to give it such attention.

* Since this was drafted, timing systems to enable companies to offer flexible work hours or 'flextime' have been marketed commercially. One of the pioneers was Messerschmidt in Germany; and after *The Financial Times* described the introduction of such a system into Pilkington Laboratories (18 April 1972), it was 'bombarded' with enquiries.

An interesting corroboration of this line of argument is the degree of toleration of those who 'opt out' in different countries. It is greatest in countries with vestigial attachment to competitive capitalism such as the US, the UK or Germany; it is least in the centrally planned Communist societies, and in countries with a tradition of state-regulated capitalism and a dislike of market forces, such as France, the position is midway between the two.

If the distaste for accumulation of goods and services came to be predominant, competition would, of course, change its nature. There might still be a good deal of investment and entrepreneurial action, if consumer desires, although modest, were subject to frequent alterations of taste; the 'gear' that is fashionable might be subject to frequent change, or trips to old coal mines might alternate with visits to Kabul or painting one's home in a novel manner as ways of spending leisure.

The need for such continuing investment would reduce social welfare as conventionally defined by economists. For people would have to sacrifice some leisure, or work a little less irregularly or make do with fewer goods and services, to leave aside a margin for this investment. But it could well be argued that it is only such changes of tastes and fashion that would prevent the envisaged society from becoming utterly stagnant. (The alternative view that the bulk of its members would be fruitfully occupied in spiritual contemplation or in personal relations strains credibility a little too far.) It is a defect of the treatment of changes of tastes by writers on welfare economics that these are seen only as wasteful reductions in the standard of living.

Purely for the sake of analysis, let us, nevertheless, assume that consumer requirements are not merely modest but static, and that there is no population growth. *Provided that the transition from the present pattern to this situation is sufficiently gradual*, there is no reason to predict general bankruptcies, the collapse of capitalism, or that it would be impossible for any other reason to give effect to the new pattern of static tastes and desires.

As the growth of consumer demand declines during the transitional period, we should expect that net investment would eventually drop to zero. The rate of return on capital and the real rate of interest would fall off. The situation would be similar to what Keynes had in mind when he spoke of the euthanasia of the *rentier*. Owing to the fall in the rate of return, the share of interest and profit in the national income could be expected to fall drastically over time. Whatever profits there were would largely be distributed, as there would be no scope for reinvestment. Where, however, as in small businesses, profits were a substitute for managerial salaries, market forces would keep them in existence.

The stock of fixed interest securities (including deadweight national debt) would not yield any more real income (unless prices fell); but their capital value and the wealth of their owners would rise severalfold as interest rates dropped, and this would tend to counteract the other forces reducing the inequality of wealthy. The owners of these securities could work even less than the rest of the community – assuming that they, too, did not desire more material goods. But the effect on the welfare of everyone else would, in these circumstances, be trivial. If 90 per cent of the population worked ten hours a week and 10 per cent with fixed interest securities now had to work an average of only one hour, the loss to the 90 per cent from the existence of this private wealth would be one hour more work per week than would be otherwise necessary. Should even this be regarded as unacceptable, the wealth effect on fixed interest owners could be counteracted by means of a moderate annual capital levy.

Mention of Keynes is very appropriate in this context. For the kind of situation here discussed is one in which there could well be involuntary unemployment, in the sense that, in the absence of appropriate policies, effective demand for goods and services might not be sufficient to employ people even for the limited number of hours for which they were prepared to work. Involuntary unemployment, if it occurred, could be cured in this situation by some combination of monetary expansion and budget deficits.

Nor is there anything that need be incomprehensible to the layman in these remedies. All one has to do is to imagine everyone in our ten hour a week 'non-consuming' society receiving a cash sum through the post. Either he would spend slightly more or (if the static wants hypothesis is taken literally) he would want to work less, or some combination of the two would occur. The demand for labour would rise and the supply would fall off, until there was eventually no more involuntary unemployment.

It is worth listing the advantages of maintaining a monetary economy based on the market even in our hypothetical society where consumer wants are very modest in relation to potential output, and have ceased to grow. Obviously a capitalist or mixed economy would, in such circumstances, be a very different animal from anything we now know. The capital goods sector would be very much smaller, as it would be concerned only with replacement and not with expansion or modernisation. Entrepreneurial or technological ability would command a smaller market price; and parts of business, and perhaps government, would become a routine. The society would, in some ways, resemble the mercantile economy that existed before the Industrial Revolution or the more stagnant economies of the West such as Spain or Ireland until a couple of decades ago – with the all-important difference that there would be no involuntary poverty or unemployment to disfigure it.

It is important to note that, in this type of economy, consumer wants would be static but not satiated. There could be no satiation of wants while labour still had a 'marginal disutility' – in other words, while people still regarded work as something which they would rather not do, or would rather do less of, were it not for the need to earn a living. For if wants were literally satiated, but the last hour of work still carried disutility, it would pay people to reduce their hours of work and their earnings until goods reacquired some utility at the margin. The assumption of static wants implies that people would seek to enjoy the benefits of technological progress entirely in the form of reduced hours of work and not at all in increased take-home pay.

The retention of money payments in this static economy would allow people to choose their own combination of goods and services, which would not be possible if consumption were organised collectively; and, most important, people would be able to retain choice of their own employment. Production would be organised as efficiently as possible – which, in this situation, means that given wants could be supplied with the minimum of work hours. For, if a more efficient method were anywhere available, profits would ensue for a temporary period to anyone who utilised them – although these would eventually be eroded by competition and the system return to its static state.

Above all, no one would be forced to conform to a single life style. People who did not share the prevailing anti-consumption, anti-work ethos could 'opt into' the consumer society without disturbing their neighbours; and there could still be luxury hotels or ocean cruises for those who wanted them and were prepared to work to obtain them. At the other extreme, those who were prepared to sacrifice even more monetary income than the majority – in return for, say, a five hour week or highly irregular work – could do so. Indeed, it will have struck the economist reader that the traditional theoretical arguments that competitive markets (subject to certain well known exceptions and necessary corrective devices) produce a 'social optimum' come into their own in the static condition we have been describing – although the result will not look much like capitalism as we know it.

The New Left would probably claim that a less consumption-orientated society could not hope to come into existence, because capitalism would smother it. A great deal of the case boils down, on examination, to the grossly inflated view of the powers of advertising, discussed in the Prologue. Clearly the business community has a vested interest in maintaining at least some economic growth, but its political power to distort choice in this direction almost invariably springs from *interventionist* economic policies designed to prop up unprofitable enterprises in the name of technology, nationalism or a *simpliste* interpretation of full employment; and a bias in favour of intervention is one of the unfortunate heritages bequeathed by the Old Left to the New. Unfortunately, the extensive and indefensible rigging of the market by political authorities to favour particular interest groups, is not the only reason why the opponents of the 'consumer society' feel that the dice are loaded against them. Indeed, if anything, their bias is in favour of such intervention as a matter of principle. Their real difficulty may be that most people do not as yet share their tastes; and toleration of people with different tasts is not always the hallmark of those who talk most about 'liberation' and 'freedom'.

## (c) A WORK-SCARCE ECONOMY

So far it has been assumed that as a result of a combination of advancing technology and declining appetite for further consumer goods, most people will want to work for a very much smaller number of hours than at present. This is certainly one possible inference from the decline of the work-oriented puritan ethos.

But another development is also possible. This is that people will not be satisfied with more idleness or what are now termed 'leisure pursuits', but will find their main enjoyment in activities at present regarded as work. Labour would then become, as Marx put it, 'not only a means of life, but life's prime want'.[5] This may be because of the delight in creativity for which Marx was hoping or for the status reasons mentioned by modern writers, such as Charles Carter, who emphasise that 'it is degrading to have no work'.[6]

Neither the eighteenth-century aristocrat nor the nineteenth-century gentleman of means found lack of work degrading; and in this, as in so much else, there is an analogy between the attitude of the traditional leisured classes and some of the young radicals of today. But we must take, on board at least, the possibility that these will remain minority attitudes, and that for one reason or another many people will wish to have an occupation of the type now associated with earning a living.

Hitherto, we have assumed that in the non-consumer society of tomorrow, as well as in today's world, the last bit of extra work contributed by most people is something that, other things being equal, they would prefer not to do. It is only contributed because the loss of goods and services through lower earnings would be a still greater evil. Even in the ten-hour work society with static wants considered above, it was assumed that if a sudden technological discovery enabled them to buy the same goods and services with only nine hours' work, most people would be glad to make the exchange.

Now let us imagine a society where most people either enjoy their work very much, or at least regard every hour spent on it as a lesser evil to an equivalent hour of 'leisure'. The jargon term 'marginal disutility of labour', mentioned above, is a useful one for the subjective sacrifice involved under present conditions in any net addition to the amount of work a person does. It is normally assumed that, so far as modern standardised procedures allow, people will work up to the point where the extra earnings from an additional amount of labour are equal to the marginal disutility of labour. To work beyond that point would mean an extra sacrifice greater than the value the person concerned puts on the extra earnings involved. One can assume that trade union negotiators, both nationally and at shop floor, transmit, in however imperfect a form, some sort of average view of the length of a working week at which this point is reached.

There is no reason why the first few hours of work a week should not have a positive utility for many people even in our present society. The more hours a person works, the lower this utility will normally be; but, so long as it is positive, he will wish to extend his working week, as he is also being paid in goods and services which he values. Thus, each additional hour of work increases his welfare. It is only when the descending marginal utility curve enters the negative region that there is something to balance against the additional earnings, which are themselves declining in utility as their quantity increases.

In our imaginary society of the future the marginal utility curve for work would have a similar shape, except that we would be sure that it would start at a positive quantity. The problem concerns what to assume about the marginal utility of the goods and services that money income would buy. We should, for the sake of symmetry, assume that this becomes negative once the satiation of wants has been achieved and extra goods come to be regarded as a harmful nuisance. We need to assume that, at a point in the working week where the marginal utility of work is still positive, the marginal utility of goods and services is already negative. So in this society equilibrium would be reached at a length of working week where the marginal utility of both goods and work balanced out at equal and opposite signs, as at present.

The above comparison can be illustrated by the following very simple table (Table 3):

*Table* 3 Utility of goods and work

|  | Marginal utility in equilibrium of: | |
|  | *Goods and services* | *Work* |
| Present society | + | − |
| 'Work scarce' society | − | + |

At present people exchange work, which (at the margin at least) they would rather not do, for goods of which they would like to have more. In the new society, work would be desired for its own sake and goods would be plentiful. At present, people work up to the point where the declining but positive marginal utility of goods is balanced by the increasing marginal *disutility* of extra work. In the envisaged society they would work up to the point where the marginal *utility* of their work was positive and where the marginal utility of goods was negative by an equal amount. In either 'society the point of balance for any group of workers determines the length of their working week. As we shall see, the 'work-scarce' economy is probably not a feasible proposition; but some interesting results can be obtained by entertaining the hypothesis for a while and following out its implications.

There could still be a market economy in this brave new world, but it would be almost the mirror image of the present one. Wages would be negative and goods would be 'free'. Work would then be the desirable commodity. The labour market would be brought into equilibrium by competition in offers of different kinds of work. Just as at present a fur coat has a price in terms of so many mini-skirts or restaurant meals sacrificed to buy it, in this new world one kind of work would have a price in terms of other kinds of work. There might well, for example, be an oversupply of people wanting to prove meals-on-wheels relative to potential dustmen or hospital cleaners. Business activity would then involve the pricing of one type of work in terms of another, so that one hour of providing meals-on-wheels would exchange for several hours of refuse disposal.

The market in labour would, however, differ in important ways from the present market in consumables. One can buy consumption services in two forms. There can be a single act of consumption, such as purchasing a meal or a coach trip. If a person desires the same form of consumption again, he must make fresh payment. Alternatively he can purchase the right to a continuous flow of services over a time, either by purchasing physical assets such as land that will themselves provide a flow of services, or indirectly by purchasing assets which will yield a money income which can be used to finance such a flow of consumption. The existence of intermediate cases, such as consumer durables, which can be analysed either way according to convenience, does not affect the principle of the distinction.

In our present society the emphasis is on individual acts of consumption rather than on the purchase of long-term or permanent rights to consume in the form of property. Indeed, large numbers of people, not all poor, can and do go through life without any property worth mentioning. Where work is scarce, the emphasis would have to be the other way round. While an individual might purchase, say a week's work as a labourer, or as a restaurant worker, there is the question of how he would pay for it. It would in the first place be in terms of money. But he could only obtain money by selling something; and in our hypothetical world the only thing that would be of value would be the offer of scarce work – in which he would have to have a property right.

The question arises how the property rights to different kinds of work would be allocated in the first place. It would presumably be by firms, local authorities, nationalised concerns and voluntary bodies who at present provide employment. Once ambulance workers become prepared to work for 'nothing', the authorities would have to select drivers on grounds of ability, length of previous service or on the principle of first come, first served.

This would, no doubt, be very arbitrary and would look more like a physical allocation than a pricing system. But eventually there would be a market in rights to do an hour's work of different kinds. The price of one hour's cleaning work might be low in terms of opportunities for providing meals-on-wheels. The right to do one hour a week of the latter might exchange for the right to do, say, twenty hours at a laundry. Equilibrium would be established when it no longer paid anyone at the margin to exchange one kind of work for another; and a new class of entrepreneur would spring up who would, for example, offer those with the right to do ambulance work the opportunity to work longer hours in laundries.

If prices were sufficiently flexible, full employment and consumer sovereignty would be maintained, in the sense that everybody would be able to do some work, although not as much as he liked; and would be able to choose between short hours at the more popular activity and longer hours at the less popular ones. This is the exact parallel to the existence of the opportunity to earn a living under the present system, although not to earn as much as one would like, and the choice between larger quantities of cheaper goods and smaller quantities of expensive ones. Businessmen would be rewarded for their middleman activities by the work they did. Successful entrepreneurs would work much longer hours than the average person; and this would be resented as outrageously unfair by egalitarians. The advantages and disadvantages of the market economy would be remarkably similar to what they are in the present society in which shortages are of goods rather than of work.

There are, of course, some difficulties about the analogy between work at present and goods in a future society. There would be the organisational problem of preventing people from working without paying for the privilege. Without some suitable institutional devices people would carry on working up to the point where the marginal utility of an extra hour's effort became zero; and there could then be no market in the right to perform different types of job. Some arrangements would be required to prevent goods and services from being produced, if their nuisance value far exceeded the pleasure that those providing them obtained from their work. This problem is worth noting, without attempting to lay down a legal and organisational blue-print for a different and distant form of society.

There is another reason too for doubting the feasibility of a situation where goods in general have a zero or negative marginal utility. In the simple model above, it was assumed that goods required only labour for their production. It is reasonable to regard capital equipment as labour at one remove. But the production of commodities also requires land. Even if man-made substitutes were available for all the 'original and indestructible properties of the soil', the production and enjoyment of all goods and services requires space. At least two factors of production will always be required: labour and land. Although astronomical increases in output per unit of labour can be envisaged, land-saving innovations are unlikely to be on anything like the same scale – especially if one bears in mind that the product mix demanded by a rapidly advancing society is land-intensive: homes, gardens, roads, airspace, beaches, mountains, and so on. The population increase compounds what in any case would be a growing demand for space. The demand for space-intensive products is equally characteristic of the culture of the alternative society: open space for pop group rallies, solitude for certain types of 'trips', wilderness for hermits and gurus, and countryside for rural communes.

It is thus, in fact, extremely unlikely that either because of a widespread desire for work to kill boredom, or a cultural shift away from materialism, that *all* commodities will cease to be scarce. There are always likely to be some scarce goods and services: scarce in the sense that some people would like to have more of them than are available, irrespective of the distribution of income and wealth in the country.

## (d) A MORE REALISTIC MODEL

Nevertheless, the analysis of a work-scarce, goods-surplus society has been well worthwhile. For one can readily imagine a mixed situation in which some goods are no longer scarce and some types of work are. Some goods are even now so cheap that people of average income can afford to be indifferent to how much they spend on them. There are already all kinds of work – known as hobbies – which people will pay to do. (Standing for Parliament would thus count for some as a hobby.) While for the most part people pay in money (that is, forgone goods) for their hobbies, this is not entirely so. People pay for one type of hobby in terms of foregone opportunities for pursuing another. Members of the establishment pay for sitting on the marginal committee by not being able to sit on yet another on which they place a slightly lower valuation; and they would forego a great many hours on minor advisory groups for the sake of much fewer hours on a really prestigious Royal Commission. We are already moving towards a situation in which many kinds of work have a positive utility; to the extent that market prices prevail, they will have a cost not merely in commodities foregone, but in terms of other kinds of pleasurable work.

On the goods side, a growing number of commodities can be expected to enter a category, which for want of a better label, I shall call 'non-economic'. My definition of a non-economic commodity is one for which the demand is no longer responsive to *relative* prices. In other words, the person or group of people under consideration, will not shift to substitutes, and will buy the same amount whatever happens to its price *relative to other prices*. Of course, if the price of any commodity rises, this will itself reduce the real value of any given income. To allow for this factor, we should assume that real incomes are constant and that a compensating financial sum is paid in such cases to make them so. This is not, of course, a policy proposal, but simply a way of defining 'other things being equal'.* (We are thus defining a non-economic good as one for which the pure substitution elasticity of demand is zero.) The smaller the proportion of

---

* This is indeed Milton Friedman's interpretation of the ordinary demand curve (see *Essays in Positive Economics*, Chicago, 1953).

income going on a particular commodity, the less important is this definitional complication.

It should be noted that a non-economic good is not the same as the usual definition of a 'free' good. The latter is a commodity that is not in scarce supply – each member of the community can have as much of it as he likes without anyone else having to sacrifice any other desired commodity. An example would be fresh air in an uncontaminated rural area. This would have a zero cost in foregone alternatives. Bread might come into the category of a non-economic good, if demand were invariant to price. But it would not be a free good, as farming, milling and baking would take up scarce resources, which could be used to produce alternative goods which the community has now to do without.

My definition of a non-economic good is, however, very close to the usual definition of a 'necessity'; I suspect, however, that there are few necessities, the demand for which is literally unresponsive to relative prices. It is a reasonable guess – although no more than that – that as a community grows wealthier, more and more goods enter the truly non-economic category. There is, of course, always the question of: non-scarce for whom? A starving man with a few pence in his pocket will take into account relative prices very carefully before he decides what to buy. Indifference to price for a growing number of commodities is only a reasonable guess even for the future, if it is assumed that a minimum level of personal income is maintained by state action, and that this minimum itself increases in line with general prosperity.

The opponents of the price mechanism and the monetary economy have a strong case in relation to such non-economic goods, and *only in relation to them*. For if the quantity sold has no relation to price, then the function of prices in helping to allocate consumers' expenditure in line with their preferences disappears. So equally does the function of prices and profitability in allocating production between alternative activities. The whole business of taking money, with all the distributional, clerical and policing problems is thus a costly waste; and the state might as well purchase, in a block order, the quantities required by the public at a price just sufficient to make it worth the while of the supplying firms, and allow people to take as much as they like 'for free' in any convenient way. In this manner, the role of money and prices can be reduced in all those areas of our lives where they are not worth the bother, while retaining them in all the remaining areas in which they are still a vital instrument for combining freedom with prosperity.

Certain traps have to be avoided if this proposal is not to do more harm than good. First, the identification of non-economic commodities is not nearly as obvious as it may seem. For example, domestic consumer demand for salt may be invariant to price, but not industrial demand. It would be very difficult to have free salt for housewives and restaurants only, while a general supply of free salt could lead to an irrational choice of production process in the chemical and other industries.

*Secondly, and even more important, it is essential that a state distribution system for 'free' products should not be given any sort of monopoly whatever.* For example if bread were free, there might still be all sorts of varieties, not supplied by the state authorities, for which people would still be willing to pay. In addition, the number, location, or opening hours of distribution outlets for free bread may not suit some people. *The only way to ascertain whether there are needs or desires left unsatisfied by the state scheme is to allow people to make a profit by trying to do better. Without this safeguard, the above proposal will only bring comfort to the enemies of personal choice and the friends of enforced uniformity.*

The *assumption* of a minimum income rising with the general level of prosperity was made above simply to help with a matter of definition. But I should now like to make it a definite proposal. What I have in mind is *not* statutory minimum wages, which have caused involuntary unemployment wherever they have been introduced, but social security payments to guarantee a certain cash flow related to family size. These would have to be well below the average or median wage if they were not to be ruled out on 'incentive' grounds. But in an affluent society this could still provide a standard of living far above subsistence. This proposal cuts out the whole argument about 'scroungers and shirkers' by giving up the vain attempt to hunt them down. The potential shirker would be told in effect: 'The community is now rich enough to give you two choices: You can "opt out" if you wish and you will receive an allowance, which will be far from princely and well below the normal wage, but will allow you to live, and will also rise as the nation becomes richer; or you can work and go after much larger material prizes.' (I do not need to be told that such a concept would at present be unpopular with the electorate.)

The feasibility of the scheme depends partly on the empirical question of the size of the loss (arising out of the disincentive effect of a 100 per cent marginal rate of tax) from providing guaranteed subsistence to that portion of the population who have skills of relatively low market value, or who are the most work shy.

At the beginning of 1970 George Polanyi and three co-authors published a scheme for a Minimum Income Guarantee that would make up to the Supplementary Benefit Level all incomes at present below.[7] Of the 3 million British householders that were expected to benefit, some 2.3 million were headed by retired people. The disincentive to extra effort from the 100 per cent marginal rate would thus have applied to some 0.8 million people – mostly workers with large families whose earnings were below the Supplementary Benefits minimum.

The real problem, of course, was whether the unconditional guarantee of such a minimum as a 'right' would be prohibitively costly in terms of the number of people stopping work altogether and settling for this minimum. Policy here has been too long dominated by the spectre of Speenhamland, the late eighteenth-century system under which English magistrates made up to minimum levels the wages of farm labourers. This led to large-scale resort to public assistance in preference to work. The reaction of Parliament was the notorious Poor Law of 1834, which confined relief to people entering 'indoor institutions' on very rigorous conditions.

The counter-argument of Polanyi is that such effects were to be expected at a time when the normal wage was no higher than the subsistence minimum. In 1970, probably no more than 2–3 per cent of the full-time occupied population had incomes below the suggested guarantee. The majority of workers would take a large cut in income if they chose to live on State benefit.

Thus, with present attitudes towards material goods, the cost of a modest income guarantee would be small; and only a limited number of people might take advantage of it. A combination of changing attitudes and the effects of increasing prosperity in raising the level of the guarantee would lead to more people taking advantage of it in the future. But then the very same factors would reduce the burden that the provision of this minimum was felt to impose on those who preferred to work for a living.

In the Polanyi scheme, the minimum income guarantee would be given in the form of a reverse income tax. Poor people who worked would thus not receive the full guaranteed minimum, but only the amount by which their actual earnings fell short of this minimum. While the scheme was at this stage, snooping and inspection would be necessary to check on undeclared earnings.

I would hope, however, that this would be only an intermediate stage and that eventually we would be prosperous enough to pay out the guaranteed minimum as a 'social dividend' irrespective of income from other sources. When that happened the whole invigilatory aspect of social security could come to an end – both the feelings of humiliation at the receiving end and the feelings of being duped on the part of the working taxpayer.

An attempt has been made in the last few pages to outline a compromise between a market economy and the beliefs of the alternative society, which combines the best elements of both and is not just splitting the difference. The aspirations of those who wish to opt out of a work-oriented monetary economy are respected and acknowledged by the option of a modest but rising minimum payment, irrespective of effort. In addition a limited but growing number of standard goods and services will be provided without cash payment. This latter aspect will free even the more conventional of us from petty and irritating financial transactions, where there is a real utility loss in attempting too virtuously to maximise utility. Thus, the market economy can hopefully be gradually divorced from the puritan ethic.

But in return for these changes, the apostles of the alternative society must be prepared to tolerate the activities of the remainder of the community who have aspirations for things which are still scarce – whether fur coats, Georgian houses, or visits to baroque churches – and who wish to continue to take part in a monetary economy. Paradoxically, the faster the general advance of prosperity, the earlier these choices between different life styles will become a reality; and anti-growth propaganda only serves to prolong our present materialist and envious ethic.

There is a great deal to argue about in the above proposals on figures and details. But if the New Left reject the offered compromise, which will allow them to practise the values that they preach, and insist on transforming the whole of society in their image then they are at least as tyrannical opponents of free expression as the Greek colonels and the other dictators against whom they demonstrate. This charge is valid whether the proportion who do not accept their values is 99, 49, 9 or 0.009 per cent of the population. Freedom is not a matter of counting heads. Orthodox opinion may legitimately query my suggestions on grounds of *present* cost; but if it rules out minimum incomes for the work shy, or zero prices for non-economic goods, on grounds of principle irrespective of the level of affluence, then it, too, is motivated by just that moralistic resentment of other people's well-being, which it is so fond of decrying in the egalitarians. A liberal should attach a zero value to the pain arising from intolerance of others' enjoyment, from whatever side of the political spectrum this intolerance comes.

## (e) POSTSCRIPT ON COMMUNES

One expression of the dislike of commercial society is the renewed vogue for communes – which so far from being daring innovations are among the oldest kinds of human groupings.

The characteristics of a pure commune may be regarded as the absence of individual income or property and the consequent absence of money inside the organisation, and the willingness of members to work as agreed by collective decision with no relation between work performed and individual living standards – the collective decisions including how to spend the communal income and distribute goods among members. By adopting this extreme definition one is distinguishing a commune very sharply from a mere co-operative and perhaps highlighting the leading ideas behind the concept.

Now there is no reason why communes cannot exist – as kibbutzim do in Israel – within a normal commercial society, buying in the cheapest market and selling in the dearest, while ordering their own internal affairs on non-commercial principles. If all productive enterprises were organised by communes, the economy might not be as responsive to opportunities as it would be with a more directly capitalist form of ownership; but, if the percentage of communal production corresponded to the percentage of the population with a taste for communal living, there would be no cause for complaint. It would be part of the data with which the market would have to cope; and if consumer demand has by then become fairly static in both quality and quantity, this lack of responsiveness will not matter all that much.\*

How an individual commune should organise its affairs is its own business. The main concern of a liberal is with the availability of outward transport from it. Nevertheless, there are certain points that suggest themselves about the way in which a commune might rationally organise its affairs.

The members of the commune are, we may assume, prepared to work an equal number of labour units. These may be measured in hours; but an hour of regular or strenuous work may be regarded as equivalent to more than an hour of irregular or less taxing work. We can either dodge the problem of how the exact equivalence is determined, or regard it as being based on labour market data from outside the commune. Members will, of course, have different abilities; and some products that the commune could make will bring in more revenue than others. It therefore pays the commune to arrange its working activities so that it cannot gain any more revenue – or achieve the same revenue with a smaller amount of labour – by shifting a marginal labour unit from one activity to another. This means that the least productive additional unit of labour must yield the same in all occupations.

This arrangement is not necessarily, however, the happiest one for the individual members of which the commune is composed. For people may not enjoy most doing the job that makes the greatest contribution to the revenue of the group; and some of them might even be prepared to make sacrifices in other aspects of their personal living standards to do something more congenial. One is tempted to suggest that money payments should be reintroduced, but the suggestion will not be followed up, as it is

---

\* It could, in fact, be even more difficult to preserve full employment by demand management policies in an economy of communes than at present. In a capitalist economy, an increase in total money expenditure should lead, at least for a time, to increased output and employment, even if it also brings in its wake some increase in the price level. In an economy of communes the effect will be entirely felt in the price level. For it will pay the partners of a commune to increase their selling price to maximise the value of net returns per head and not to dilute the gain by enlarging its size. Such considerations also suggest that price fluctuations could be greater in a communal than in a capitalist economy. Full employment policies would have to be long term structural ones designed to encourage the setting up of more communes if unemployment develops. (These problems are discussed in J. E. Meade, 'The Theory of Labour-Managed Firms and of Profit Sharing', *Economic Journal*, March 1972 Supplement.)

out of keeping with the beliefs that brought the people into the communes in the first place.

Short of that, there are other expedients which could still increase individual satisfaction. One method would be to allow people to choose their own jobs initially. The commune administration would then see that there were, say, too many library attendants and not enough bricklayers compared with the optimum distribution, and so on. It could then offer people fewer hours of work if they were to switch to the less favoured jobs, but demand more hours at the attractive jobs. It might be able to juggle with the ratio of required hours of different kinds, until there were a voluntary movement of workers towards the required pattern. Thus, a labour market would have been established in hours of work, instead of money wages.

Such juggling might not, however, be possible if the degree of aversion to certain types of work were too great and no reduction in hours required could produce a sufficient supply of manhours in these activities. In that case another way of establishing a labour market in hours of work might be tried. Workers would be assigned work by the commune administration in relation to their aptitudes, but be allowed to trade jobs with other people. Someone assigned a bricklaying job which he disliked might do 20 hours' work in the library in return for which four library attendants would do 5 hours of bricklaying each. Once a labour market with proper prices was established, there would be no need for this neat divisibility; it could turn out that 5 hours' bricklaying was equivalent to 27 hours in the library. The administration would have to make sure that the hours of work being traded were of a standardised degree of efficiency for each occupation. Despite this complication, a voluntary exchange of this sort would be an improvement on either assigning jobs with no choice, or making everyone do a little of everything.

The standard objection to the suggested 'labour market' is that it would reintroduce 'inequality', as some people would work for longer hours than others. The objection presupposes, however, that there is equality in the first place, despite the fact that some people will have been assigned jobs which they detest and others jobs which they quite enjoy doing. Even if everyone did a little of everything (with great detriment to total wealth) the situation would be subjectively one of extreme inequality. For a pattern composed of a small amount of all activities from lavatory cleaning to fishing, typing and writing pamphlets, would suit some people and be hell for others.

Moreover, the inequality of working hours in our imaginary commune would have none of the features to which egalitarians object in our present society. Everyone would start off from the same basis. There would be no inherited unearned income, or differences in ability to pay for education; and shares would be reshuffled in each generation entirely in accordance with relative tastes.

Nevertheless, if unequal working hours were ideologically objectionable, then the commune would have to choose between what might be a very severe loss of prosperity if people were allowed a complete free choice of jobs and strict regimentation if they were not. There is, in any society, a complex three way trade-off between freedom, prosperity and equality, but which is specially noticeable in a commune. Real-life collectives work by some unformulated compromise between free choice and direction of occupation for their members, with perhaps some unofficial barter between jobs as well.

We must now go one stage further and ask what the position would be if an overwhelming majority of the population wished to live in a communal way. Would it be a good idea to abolish money altogether and run the country as one big commune? The reader will not expect me to welcome this idea, but the interesting question is 'Why'?

Even if consumer desires were modest in relation to potential output, this does not mean that people would be indifferent to what they received. In an economy of individual communes, each of modest size, it might be feasible for a purchasing committee to take note of what members like, see which stocks are most depleted, and order accordingly. But how would individual desires be registered in a commune the size of the whole nation? One might imagine moneyless shops, which acquired fresh goods and services according to the stock position and the individual orders it received. But what mechanism would ensure that the working population organised itself to supply what was required? By a heroic stretch of the imagination one might envisage people looking up in a registry which goods were in short supply, which in surplus, and which occupations were in most demand, and shifting jobs accordingly. But let us suppose that dustcarts, and drawing boards, sewage workers and factory managers were all in excess demand. Who would determine which people should leave the jobs where their services are surplus, to become sewage workers or managers or whatever the case may be? We come up against the problem of allocating manpower, which already exists in the individual communes but on a gigantic scale, and without the possibility of tackling it by the informal compromises that can often be made in a face-to-face society.

It is almost certain that money, money prices and money incomes would creep back again in a disguised form, say as computerised indices of the strength of particular demands and the relative attractions of different occupations. The three-way trade-off between preserving the communal principle, preserving free choice of occupation, and prosperity or efficiency, would appear in a particularly harsh form. It is difficult to escape the conclusion that, even in a society where the desire for communal living was widespread, it would be much better to preserve a monetary economy with free market relations between individual communes, which should be left to develop their internal relationships in their own way.

# Postscript to the 1987–8 Edition: The Never-Ending Quest

'I confess I am not charmed with the idea of life held out by those who think that the normal state of human beings is that of struggling to get on; that the trampling, crushing, elbowing, and treading on each other's heels, which form the existing type of social life, are the most desirable lot of human kind, or anything but the disagreeable symptoms of one of the phases of industrial progress.'

John Stuart Mill
*Principles of Political Economy*

## 1. MOVEMENTS SUPPOSEDLY FAVOURING THE MARKET

The first edition of this book was written in 1971–2 and appeared in 1973. This was a dark time for market liberalism. President Nixon's Republican Administration and Edward Heath's Conservative Government had introduced the severest price and wage controls hitherto seen in peacetime. The leaders of the British Civil Service declared the country 'ungovernable' in the face of aggressive, and sometimes violent, union monopoly. Even more important, the basic civil freedoms were under threat. There were leading politicians who would not support the law if it stood in the way of militant movements claiming to speak for the working class. After the defeat of the Heath Government by the National Union of Mineworkers in 1974, there were times when normal bourgeois liberties such as freedom of speech under the law and the right to modest personal property, could not be taken for granted.

As I write this postscript for the 1987–8 edition, the landscape seems changed out of all recognition. Labour Governments in

New Zealand and Australia have indulged in bonfires of controls. There is a debate on market socialism even in the British Labour Party. The virtues of decentralisation, deregulation and dispersed ownership, not only of personal property but also of the means of production, have become the orthodoxy among governments of all political persuasion; and Communist China is making a few tentative steps in this direction. A Socialist Chancellor of Austria and a Socialist President of France (even before their parties lost their absolute legislative majority) were planning the 'privatisation' of state-owned industry. Opposition parties throughout the West who wanted more economic expansion to reduce unemployment were at pains to emphasise that they would not take risks with inflation, and argued with governments in office mainly over the detailed interpretations of 'sound finance'.

A superficial observer might expect me to feel triumphant. The only sadness to limit the triumph would be that I must now hand on the torch to the new political economists who go much further than I did in condemning income redistribution, the welfare state and any government involvement in the economy.

Alas, I must disdain both the triumph and the invitation to pass the torch to supposedly more advanced thinkers. Of course, I am not surprised that the aspects of market economics now in vogue are mixed together very differently from the recipe I had in mind. That is the inevitable contrast between life and vision. But I am vain enough to suppose that my original recipe still has something to offer and am not willing to abdicate in favour of others who may go further, but also take wrong turnings. Above all I have to explain why a joylessness has crept into current attitudes and policies, which are spiritually so far removed from the kind of liberalism which inspired my original text. What is the difference?

## (a) Some distinctions

All labels are somewhat arbitrary; and people rarely fall into neat categories. Nevertheless, the following classification may be of help:

1. Market liberalism
2. The New Economic Right
3. Neoconservatism

**Market liberalism** is a convenient name for the family of ideas to which this book belongs. It is based on a wider ideal of personal freedom of which the economic aspect is only part. This ideal derives from classical liberalism.[1] 'Classical liberalism' may conjure up a picture of high-minded people in frock-coats. But as the Prologue makes clear, its modern extension covers the revolt of the young in the 1960s in favour of people 'doing their own thing', the enjoyment of alternative lifestyles, including that of hippies, drop-outs and flower children, as well as that of bond dealers in the cities of London or New York.

Market liberalism – or its near synonym 'the social market economy' – is compatible with redistribution of income and wealth and may require government action to ensure that the market transmits people's preferences effectively. Its main plea here is that government corrective action should take the form of known rules rather than discretionary and unprincipled intervention, and that it should make use of price mechanism remedies wherever possible.

Similarly, redistribution should be in cash rather than in specific subsidies or payments in kind. There is a full enough agenda here without the state usurping the entrepreneurial role, engaging in so-called industrial strategies, battling for national businesses, fighting imports, or engaging in all the many other activities which are no part of its legitimate agenda. The classical liberal is cautious of extending the sphere of political action too far, remembering that the state is an organ – although not the only organ – of coercion, and that the political process is subject to its own imperfections and distortions.

**The New Economic Right** has emerged since the late 1970s as a fairly distinctive set of doctrines of a rather different flavour. It goes much further than market liberalism towards *laissez-faire* in its economic teaching, has little place for redistribution, and accepts the pattern of ownership which emerges from effort, luck and inheritance. It is profoundly suspicious of public action to cope with externalities,[2] and places great emphasis on denationalisation and on low government spending. New Right supporters see less need for public action to improve the working of the market, and in the US they have attacked not merely the practice, but the principle, of Anti-Trust. They bear some relation to the 'right-wing economic liberals' in the table on p. 77, but go rather further in their attitudes.

While my emphasis in the discussion of unemployment in this

book has been on pricing-out of work, labour monopoly and collective bargaining, the New Right's emphases are on allegedly excessive social security payments, which discourage job search among the unemployed and effort among the poor generally. New Right members come from many different philosophical stables, and some believe they are reacting pragmatically to the deficiencies of the post-Second World War consensus. They might be called Lockean if more of them had heard of John Locke.

**Neoconservatism** is an American term. But it is useful in describing those who flirt with free market ideas, but are mainly interested in restoring traditional values (Victorian or otherwise), strengthening patriotic and family feelings, pursuing a strong nationalist or anti-Communist foreign policy and reinforcing respect for authority.

There is scope for much conflict among different strands of neoconservatives. In Europe they can be anything from highly nationalistic anti-Americans to fanatical supporters of the USA as the main opponent of Communism. Neoconservatives and market liberals differ strongly on the non-economic roots of their policies, but are at one in placing emphasis upon them, often more so than the New Right. Much though I disagree wth many of their policy themes, their writings at their best do discuss issues relating to the moral prerequisites of a free society and the role of shared values, often ignored by those who rely too exclusively on economic analysis.[3]

The difference between the three schools is clearly illustrated by broadcasting. Neoconservatives are most concerned by issues such as alleged bias, undermining of traditional values, or the excesses of violence and sex on the screen. They might call in market processes as correctives for what they dislike in public broadcasting, but these are a means rather than a process to be valued in itself.

The New Economic Right would leave it to commercial forces to liberate broadcasting, while phasing out the licence fee and regulation. If private enterprise broadcast is entirely advertising-financed, it would not worry.

The liberal market school on the other hand does worry about the fact that competition for advertisers is not the same as competition for audiences. A purely advertising financed system will not be a true market properly reflecting consumer choice, certainly while channels are limited. For such reasons the Peacock

Report[4] concluded that positive policies were required to encourage direct consumer payment, and that the transition from the comfortable duopoly to the brave new world of citizen choice needed active public policies.

Market liberals may well find that they are closer to those *social democrats* who favour a 'social market economy' and base themselves on individualist premises, than they are to the New Right on issues such as property rights, redistribution and externalities, and are closer to them than to the neoconservatives on issues of civil and social liberties. Nevertheless, even the most market-oriented social democrats find it difficult to throw off their collectivist heritage.

Meanwhile market economists of all kinds will be keenly aware that they are still outside the intellectual mainstream, especially in Europe, irrespective of whether they are classical liberals, New Right, or neoconservatives. Their work has not prevented mainstream economists from continuing to unveil ever more unconvincing arguments for state intervention, based on the discrepancy between actual markets and more and more refined mathematical optima, without finding it necessary to ask whether real world politicians will have either the knowledge or the incentive to remedy the deficiencies rather than aggravate matters. The view of markets as a *discovery procedure* in a world where tastes and techniques are changing, and information scarce and expensive, has still to penetrate to many mainstream economists. (That this view is still often described as 'Austrian', as if it were something foreign and exotic, is itself revealing.)

An example of the prevailing atmosphere was an article by a young left-of-centre American Democrat, who worked as a researcher on the 1986 Channel Four television series *The New Enlightenment*,[5] which was devoted to the revival of market economics, but was nearer to what I have called the New Economic Right than to market liberalism. He arrived with 'five buttresses against right wing thought'. These were beliefs in 'central planning, affirmative action, the welfare state, the contemptibility of capitalists and the ideal of equality'. These ideals were subsequently knocked down by five heroes of the programme: Hayek, Sowell, Murray, Gilder and Nozick, and the researcher ended up with his head on the side of the Republicans; he compromised with his heart by settling for the 'conservative wing of the Democratic Party'.[6]

What was sad was that a highly-educated, politically sophisticated, young man knew so little of the fallacies behind central planning (fallacies now increasingly recognised in Communist countries) that Hayek's well-known refutation struck him as a revelation, and that he needed Sowell to make him think twice about affirmative action. As a result he is in danger of sweeping aside the case for at least some kinds of Welfare State and the arguments that still exist for redistribution, although not for equality. Neither general education nor specialist training seems to inoculate people against swinging between unreflective collectivism and full-scale acceptance of the New Economic Right.

Nor is the scene so much happer in the world of policy. While the New Right supporters have been making paper forays against the Welfare State and against market correctives gladly accepted by Adam Smith, they have been losing ground in the traditional home of the market economy: industry, services and trade. Despite privatisation and deregulation, there is still, at the time of writing, a political verto on some overseas purchase of ailing parts of the British motor industry. Quotas have proliferated on 'high tech' and 'low tech' imports alike, whether they come from Japan or the newly-industrialising countries. Tax subsidies to home ownership, rent control, rigid restrictions on land use and pension fund privileges remain; and their harmful effects have been magnified by financial liberalisation, in itself desirable.

## (b) The divorce from liberalism

To an economic liberal, what has gone wrong with the movement to market economics is not that it is too extreme or not extreme enough, but that it has been divorced from a wider commitment to personal freedom (usually called 'licence' by neoconservatives). Unfortunately, it is often just those political leaders who claim to be most against state control of economic life, who are most opposed to freedom of personal and artistic expression. But because the main political outlet for market ideas has been among conservative politicians (even though others also implement them), free market supporters have too often turned a blind eye to the total package.

While in 1972 my main task was to put the case for capitalism to supporters of 'permissiveness' (a derogatory name for freedom), my task now is at least as much to explain to upholders of the market the case for personal freedom, without which their arguments remain unconvincing, as well as to others who view the market with distaste.


## 2. INTELLECTUAL DEVELOPMENTS SINCE THE EARLY 1970s

*A Restatement of Economic Liberalism* is based on a presumption in favour of personal freedom. A presumption is something that needs to be rebutted in any particular case.[7] It does not mean there is always a priority of individual liberty over other goals. A prohibition on discharging dangerous lead or asbestos substances into rivers is a restriction on freedom, which in this case gives way to other goals, whether these are described as public health or general welfare. It is dangerous to say that it gives way to other people's *freedom* to lead healthy lives or *freedom* from poisoning, because such interpretations weaken the meaning of freedom by making it encompass any desirable good, and thus deprive it of its specific characteristics.

In every generation freedom is threatened by those who regard the individual person as inferior to some supposed collective whole. This applies to the conclusions reached at the end of a book, first published in 1984, which has been hailed in *The Times Literary Supplement* as 'maybe the greatest work of substantive philosophy for over a century, namely *Reasons and Persons* by Derek Parfit.[8]

This is largely a work of pure philosophy, which it would be out of place to review in the present context, even were I competent to do so. But there are certain inferences which Parfit draws, designed to reduce the importance of the individual and presumably, therefore, his welfare and freedom. Parfit's most novel contention is that the popular notion of personal identity is profoundly mistaken. He reaches this conclusion through a variety of mental experiments, including 'personal division' and 'teletransportation' of personal experiences to new but entirely similar bodies on Mars.

So far from wishing to pour scorne on such mental experiments, I would say that they are too important to be a reserved area for 'professional philosophers'. The effect of Parfit's conclusion on himself is stated as follows: 'It makes me care less about my own future, and the fact that I shall die. In comparison, I now care more about the lives of others. I welcome these effects'.[9]

An example of Parfit's downgrading of the experience and suffering of individuals who now exist is his comparison between (a) peace, (b) a nuclear war killing 99 per cent of the world's population and (c) a war killing 100 per cent. Parfit thinks that the difference between (c) and (b) is *much* greater than that between (b) and (a). While the sentimental liberal like myself is concerned with the horror of the war in which 99 per cent are killed (after much suffering) Parfit is concerned with the possibilities for the human race that remain because 1 per cent survive.

There are value judgements which we are, without self-contradiction, free not to hold. It is indeed uncertain what it means to be the same person over a long stretch of time, both in science fiction experiments and in reality. If there is any moral in this, it may be that we should look at more experiencing subjects rather than less – myself now, my several future selves, my double on Mars and so on. For some purposes it may be more realistic to regard the man of 85 as a different person from his former self when 15. My own reaction is to suppose that there are more experiencing subjects, with whose experiences and freedom we should be concerned, rather than less. This is just the opposite of putting all experiences together into a single collective utility basket which is one of the aspects of utilitarianism, which is neither helpful nor necessary.

The intellectual battle between the individualist and the collectivist is never won, but it remains important to fight it. In the course of ingenious pieces of reasoning thinkers of collectivist temperament from Plato to Hegel and onwards have attempted to dissolve the individual into some collective whole. I am sure that this cannot be done by a *a priori* reasoning. Collectivities do not think, feel, exult, triumph, or despair, and to plan for their benefit is the wrong sort of high-mindedness.

## (a) Utilitarianism revisited

The case for personal freedom stated in the early part of Chapter 1 was defended in a number of different ways and was said to be at the confluence of a number of different considerations'. The presumption in favour of freedom is a value judgement. But, we can argue fruitfully about value judgements, contrary to what many economists suppose.

The reason is that it cannot be shown in advance whether a particular value judgement is basic or not. Take the statement, 'Men and women should be allowed to dress as they like'. At first this may appear as an ultra-liberal basic judgement. But suppose it turned out that mini-skirts caused cancer in the eye of the beholder. The holder of the initial judgement would probably qualify his commitment to freedom of dress to exclude this case, thereby showing that his initial judgement was not basic after all. While it can sometimes be shown that a particular judgement is not basic, there is no way of establishing that it *is* basic in advance of particular circumstances. Where we have not had to face a concrete choice, we may not know what our basic values are. Thus argument by citing actual or hypothetical cases is always worth while.[10]

My own presumption in favour of freedom was not *derived from* utilitarianism, in the way that John Stuart Mill tried to derive it in his great essay *On Liberty*. What I did say was that the presumption in favour of freedom was *compatible with* a highly-qualified form of modern 'choice utilitarianism' designed to satisfy demands and preferences revealed in people's behaviour.

So many qualifications have, however, to be added to utilitarianism[11] – for example, the exclusion of preferences for interfering with other people's behaviour – before it can be compatible with liberalism, that it is natural to see if there is some other set of ethical principles applicable to public policy, which does not have to be so qualified and which would retain the advantages of utilitarianism without its disadvantages.

The most notable attempts in this direction since my original text was prepared have been Robert Nozick's *Anarchy, State and Utopia*[12] and John Rawls's *A Theory of Justice*.[13] The two books together have been more instrumental than anything else in the rebirth of political philosophy as a living subject.[14]

They are, however, very different, not only in political flavour, but in their intellectual approach. Nozick is the leading exponent of the revival of natural rights whereas Rawls is the leading theorist of contractarianism – the modern form of the hypothetical social contract developed by seventeenth- and eighteenth-century philosophers.*

Both schools would claim to provide solid foundations for giving priority to liberty over other goals. But the warning on the non-conclusiveness of such arguments, given early in Chapter 1, still holds good. The main interest of both Rawls and Nozick is in what they have to say about the *distribution* of basic rights, income and wealth.

I argued in Chapter 1 that economic liberalism is compatible with many different attitudes to the distribution of income and wealth, and concentrated on discussing the kinds of redistribution which are, and are not, compatible with a free society. The conclusion can be summarised in the slogan 'Redistribution, yes; equality, no'.

## (b) Just entitlement

One important distinction is between trying to influence the general shape of the income and wealth distribution, and the arrogant attempt to lay down supposedly just rewards for specific individuals and occupations. A further distinction is between generalised redistribution, which takes the form of cash and property rights, and specific redistribution of 'free' or subsidised services such as public housing. The former is more compatible with freedom, though the latter is more popular with the public.

Clearly, however, market liberalism would be stronger if it could be combined with a theory of just entitlement. The lack of such a theory is particularly important for those in the Lockean tradition of non-interference with property rights now embodied in the New Economic Right. But the rest of us, too, should feel happier if state activity in the area could take a principled form, and there was some entrenchment of the rights of both those who gain and lose from redistribution, instead of everything being dependent on the changing whim of temporary political

* Tracing the historical origins is tricky. Some of the same seventeenth- and eighteen-century philosophers, such as Locke, who formulated the social contract, also espoused natural rights, which the contract was meant to preserve. Modern contractarians concentrate on the logic of the social contract, while the entitlement theorists emphasise the natural rights which people preserve before any such negotiations, and still retain.

majorities or pluralities. The issue is becoming more urgent now when the return to capital has risen relative to the market-clearing return to labour, and when there is a much bigger dispersion of market rewards between one kind of worker and another.

Both Nozick and Rawls attempt to provide theories of just distribution. Their case for both basic personal freedoms, and the structure of property and income entitlements, are derived by them from an overriding concept of a just society.

Nozick makes an important distinction between historical or *process* concepts of justice on the one hand, and *end state concepts* on the other. His own ideal is the former. Like Locke, Nozick claims that holdings are just if they have been justly acquired or justly transferred by gift or free exchange in the market. In Nozick's words:

> We are not in the position of children who have been given some portions of pie . . . There is no central distribution. What each person gets, he gets, from others who give it to him in exchange for something, or as a gift. In a free society, diverse persons control different resources and new holdings arise out of the voluntary exchange and actions of persons . . . The total result is the product of many individual decisions.[15]

But how are the initial holdings acquired, and what determines their justice? On what moral grounds can a reshuffle of entitlements in favour of those with least be denied?

In the last analysis Nozick's own set of just rights are asserted rather than established, and they suffer from all the difficulties of natural rights doctrines. Despite the complexities of *Anarchy, State and Utopia*, there is no argument against compulsory transfers to the poor other than by postulating them to be out of order at the outset.

There are other major problems within Nozick's system. The very existence of property, and the exact rights conferred by ownership of a particular asset or income entitlement, depend on collectively enforced rules which could be different to what they are. The ownership of land or a building site or a factory conveys very different rights in some societies than in others. If these rights were obvious we would not need to train lawyers in the complexities of real property and contract law. Nozick does not outline what these rules should be nor even provide criteria for assessing their justice.

Nor has he given us a theory of just acquisition of property rights in the first place. His main argument to date is taken up with what would follow *if we did have* such a theory of just acquisition.

One consequence is supposed to be the rectification of violations of justice in transfer and acquisition committed by one's ancestors. This aspect is ignored by New Right followers and gleefully emphasised by left-wing commentators. The imagination baulks, however, at the idea of tracing injustices committed by one's forebears (one has eight great grandparents and $2^n$ ancestors of $n$ generations ago) before moving over to complete *laissez-faire*. The nearest equivalent that ever formed part of a legal code was the Old Testament injunction to hold a Jubilee every 50 years in which all land would return to its original owners, debts cancelled, slaves freed and the land left fallow. There is no evidence of a Jubilee ever having been observed.[16]

Lest these remarks be thought unfair, let me cite an admirer.[17] 'He [Nozick] was content to criticize opposing positions and merely to explicate his own view, leaving the grander project of providing a positive grounding for it to a later time'. And again: 'The rights ascribed by Nozick to persons are by his own admission not derived from some more primitive moral or factual foundations', they are 'merely adumbrated'. A more hostile critic[18] describes Nozick's vision as 'Liberty without foundations'.

*Anarchy, State and Utopia* is best regarded as 'work in progress', a pointer towards historical entitlement theories in place of end state ones, and a demolition work on the latter. It is not – and I do not think it is intended to be – a political standard for the New Economic Right, even at the most abstract level.

## (c) The new social contract

The revival of social contract theory is a more promising foundation for a liberal society than the historical entitlement approach. Although Rawls's version is the best known, it is part of a larger family of contractarian doctrines. In place of the historical social contract of seventeenth- and eighteenth-century writers, modern contractarians suggest that the basic rules of society should be inferred from a hypothetical contract which it would be rational for people to accept. Contractarians place less reliance on majority voting than do conventional democratic theorists. In principle, the hypothetical social contract is one that people would unanimously accept, although some departure from unanimity may be necessary to prevent people from concealing their preferences for tactical purposes. Majority voting is simply one procedure which may be laid down at the constitutional stage for second-order post-constitutional decisions.

Rawls's particular social contract is one that would be arrived at under the 'veil of ignorance' (sometimes called the 'original position'), which is a device for ensuring impartiality. The idea is to work out the principles on which free and rational persons concerned to further their own interests would desire their community to be run if they did not know their own social or economic place, the market value of their own talents and many other key features of their real situation.* A wealthy man might like to establish principles which minimise taxes for welfare purposes; a poor man might espouse principles of an opposite kind. If one excludes knowledge of one's own actual position, there is some chance of working out the principles on a disinterested basis. A great advantage of Rawls's social contract approach is that it precludes the potential oppression of the minority, which follows from uninhibited majority voting.

Rawls's method is more acceptable than the particular results he derives from it. Indeed, much of the discussion since the publication of *A Theory of Justice* suggests that Rawls expects too determinate a result from his statement of the initial position. The arrangements which people would support under the veil of ignorance would depend on attitudes to risk and uncertainty, as well as other values and attitudes from which people cannot be divested even in a thought experiment if they are to behave as human beings at all. What one can expect from the veil of ignorance, and contractarianism generally, is a narrowing of differences. For instance, if I do not know whether my views or personal tastes will be popular or unpopular with the majority, I may well want to entrench basic freedoms of speech and action.†

---

* R. M. Hare argues, in *Reading Rawls*, that Rawls's rational contractor under the veil of ignorance is only one of three hypothetical choice devices. The other two are the ideal observer (sometimes called the impartial spectator) and his own universal prescriber. These hypothetical devices could, if set out in certain ways, lead to the same result.

† Rawls refers at times to a 'general' conception of justice in which liberty does not have priority over other goods and which applies before 'a certain level of

'May well want to', because the contractarian device will only only work for some basic attitudes and beliefs. The thought experiment will not convince dedicated Ayatollahs of the virtues of religious liberty. Similarly, I would be likely, under the veil of ignorance, to support arrangements for an economic minimum for all, itself linked to general prosperity, lest I turn out one of the unlucky ones. Again only 'likely', because the contractarian has no argument to knock down the person who is totally dedicated to a gamble on achieving wealth or power and who, if he fails, does not care if he perishes in the gutter.

Those of us who do not expect rigorous proof of moral and political positions will not worry that social contract theories cannot convince a fanatic. They might worry, as many commentators on Rawls have done, that the theory contains no 'justice' as commonly understood.[19] Justice normally means giving each citizen his or her deserts, and these deserts can only be determined within a particular legal and moral tradition.

It is indeed closer to normal usage to describe Rawls's system and other contractarian systems as theories of the 'socially desirable', rather than of justice. But this does not deprive them of their value.

The results which Rawls himself derives from the 'veil of ignorance' are as follows:

1. Equal rights to the most extensive scheme of equal basic liberties compatible with a similar scheme of liberties for all.
2. Social and economic inequalities must:
   (a) work to the benefit of the least advantaged and
   (b) be attached to offices open to all.

Principle 1 has priority over 2, and 2(b) over 2(a).

These principles have been subject to widely-varying interpretations. Rawls has been attacked for being everything from a Gladstonian free market liberal to a ruthless egalitarian – and both extremes of criticism find sustenance. 'Equal liberties' can mean different things according to whether the emphasis is on 'liberties' or on 'equal'. The system is much less collectivist if it is regarded as a guide to basic institutions rather than to current policy.

---

wealth' has been achieved. But nearly all his exposition is in terms of the 'special' conception applying when that level has been achieved and when basic liberties have priority (sections 11, 26, 82).

Rawls himself regards rights and liberties, powers and opportunities, income and wealth, as 'social primary goods'; that is not as independent objectives, but as necessary conditions for the fulfilment of a wide range of human ends.

The 'liberties' postulated in systems such as Rawls's (and emphasised by many less formal theorists of democracy for over a century) consist partly of good old negative freedom best defined in Berlin's words 'I am normally said to be free to the degree to which no man or body of men interferes with my activity'.[20] But they also contain certain 'participatory rights' – the right to vote, to stand for office on the same terms as other citizens, to be consulted on decisions, and, in many formulations, to receive education enabling one to play a full role as a citizen. These rights, however important, have to do with ideals of participatory democracy. They may, and often do, enlarge choice, but it only confuses the issue to associate them with freedom, which is a different value.

One resulting worry is that certain devices such as representative institutions, which are convenient ways of changing governments peacefully and indicating where the shoe pinches for particular societies at a particular time, are given a universal status they do not deserve.

Many political theorists try to overcome these problems by using a category called *autonomy*. Albert Weale, for instance, writes

> This principle of autonomy asserts that all persons are entitled to respect as deliberative and purposive agents capable of formulating their own projects and that as part of this respect there is a governmental obligation to bring into being or preserve the conditions in which autonomy can be practised.[21]

Autonomy seems to have priority over freedom, or perhaps it is a version of 'positive freedom'. I still find freedom, pure and simple, the more basic and less question-begging category.

Should either freedom or autonomy be either maximised or equalised? Weale makes an eloquent case against maximisation, saying that it might in some circumstances involve supporting slavery. But the equalisation of liberty can also lead to pretty miserable results if the insistence on equality means that we all have a very small amount. If I had to give a formula, it would be to apply a modification of Rawls's Principle 2(a) to be suggested below to freedom, as well as to economic resources; the reduction of any person's freedom can be justified only if it improves the freedom of the least free representative person.

Much of the discussion about Rawls, especially among economists has centred on Principle 2(a) – that social and economic inequalities are only justified if they improve the position of the least well off – sometimes known as the 'maximin'. It is at least an improvement on straightforward egalitarianism, as the reader can see by glancing back to Table 2 (p. 115).

Nevertheless, this principle does not necessarily follow from the contractarian starting point of the veil of ignorance. The latter supplies a criterion of disinterestedness and thus helps to narrow disagreements, but cannot eliminate differences of subjective preference or lead to a unique result which all people of good will accept.

It is sometimes said that the most natural system to choose under the veil of ignorance would be utilitarianism! There is some force in this contention, especially for day-to-day decisions. But utilitarianism alone can neither guarantee basic freedoms nor safeguard us against the worst maldistribution of satisfactions. There are, however, attractions in trying to combine a personal rights systems and the principle of utility in a hierarchy. An improved Rawlsian system of personal rights based on contractarian reasoning might be most suitable for the basic constitutional and structural features of a society, and utilitarianism may be a better basis for everyday policy.

For instance, my own desire under the veil of ignorance would be to make sure that everyone had a basic minimum defined, not in absolute terms, but in relation to the wealth of my society. This would be a safeguard in case I drew the unfortunate card and found myself at the bottom of the pack. I would also want to ensure a large area of personal freedom where I could make my own decisions, and to ensure political, social, cultural and economic opportunities which could not be literally 'equal' all round, but would be free of barriers or privilege and irrelevant entry qualifications.

Would I carry redistribution beyond the idea of a basic minimum? As already hinted, I would be tempted to turn round Rawls's Principle 2(a) and say that *redistribution* is only justified if it improves the position of the least well off, instead of saying that *inequalities* are so justified. The inversion shifts the onus of proof where knowledge is imperfect and leaves at least a shadow of the entitlement principle by giving the benefit of the doubt to the income or holdings which people have acquired through their own efforts or from gifts and bequests.

A more far-reaching, yet attractive, modification of Rawls is to say that public policy should aim to maximise average income or welfare subject to a 'floor constraint', i.e. provided there is a minimum below which no one can fall. There is some evidence that this is what people would actually choose under the veil of ignorance. It is, of course, not a single solution, but a family of solutions governed by the choice of floor. But an attempt to narrow and systematise, rather than eliminate, differences of opinion is probably the most that can be expected of a general principle of public policy.[22]

### (d)  A modern Hobbesian

One must, however, go beyond Rawls and his commentators. Even a highly selective reference to the new social contract theory must mention James Buchanan's variant.[23] This is designed to reflect existing power realities rather than feigned ignorance. Buchanan's essential point is that, if the structure of rights is to continue to command adherence, it must respect the actual differences in the power of different individuals. It is, thus, not a moral theory dealing with first-best states of affairs. The basic assertion is that everyone would gain from some constraint on the power of the majority of the moment to do what it likes, including those who, for the moment, belong to that majority. The gains would come from greater security and predictability.

So far from underwriting hereditary wealth, Buchanan argues that, if the structure of property rights is to continue to be respected, it needs to be redefined and renegotiated periodically to reflect the changing balance of power between people and groups. The lack of correspondence between, say, the possessions of the owners of hereditary wealth and what the same individuals could acquire or defend in a state of nature, needs to be remedied by periodic changes in the rules of inheritance and its taxation.

The implicit bargain is (it seems to me) a trade-off in which the affluent agree to a reduction in their property rights (in both their non-human capital and the earnings from their own talents) in return for a limit on state redistribution. The better-off make a sacrifice in previously held wealth in return for more certain enjoyment of the remainder. What would the worse-off gain from such a bargain? In return for a limit on the amount of redistribution that they could obtain via the ballot box, they would be secure of the redistribution they already have.

The Buchanan social contract, which is Hobbesian in inspiration, does not attempt an ideal statement of the extent of personal liberty or the distribution of resources. It is rather a suggestion that even an imperfect set of constitutional rules of the game reflecting the power realities of the time, will be better than absolute democracy, or elective dictatorship.

Buchanan's basic fear is that, if elected governments claim to do exactly what they like, then not only is there no limit to attempted state actions, but there is no possibility of predicting how state action will affect us in the future. This is a step towards the anarchistic jungle, to avoid which we put up with the many pains and restrictions of organised society. When the implicit social contract has broken down, but political competition still prevails, people are likely to feel that governments are simultaneously both oppressive and inadequate.

There is an important subsidiary point. If there are no constraints on state action, individuals have a much stronger incentive to invest resources in political activity and to try to use the state machine to supply them with goods (or contracts) on favoured terms. (The activity is now called 'rent-seeking'.) People work to obtain a government that will favour either council tenants or private home-owners; managers of enterprising firms divert their efforts into keeping on good terms with ministers and officials, sitting on time-wasting committees and keeping *au fait* with the latest governmental fads and fashions; and, at local level, people find it wise to keep in with the authorities who dispose of the more desirable school places or subsidised homes.

## (e) Economics of politics

A continuing intellectual development has been the growth of the 'economics of politics', or, more grandly, public choice theory. Basically this is the application of the theory of competition to the political market to the struggle for votes and power, as well as to the functioning of state bureaucracy. Much thinking on economic policy has been rendered worse than valueless by a sharp contrast between the faults of *real world* markets, and the actions of non-existent and improbable *ideally benevolent and omniscient* governments. Real world markets, with all their faults, have to be compared with real world politicians, civil servants and 'experts'.

Although public choice theory has developed by leaps and bounds, it already existed in the early 1970s; and informal consideration of the economics of politics lay behind the main conclusions of the first edition of this book. The case for economic liberalism stated there owed more to fears about the likely nature and result of state intervention than to any starry-eyed belief in the virtues of unrestrained markets.

Research into the political economy of government (mostly unknown to British economists of the Oxbridge tradition) had already revealed various likely governmental shortcomings. They include the lack of incentive for politicians (let alone voters) to study issues, the absence in the political market place of the budget constraint that makes for limited rationality in personal decisions, and the consequent temptation for the voters to expect far more from government than it can possibly provide. Then there is the structure of incentives within bureaucracies, only remotely connected with voter or even governmental preferences; and the tendency of regulatory agencies to become dominated by those whom they are supposed to regulate. There are also the paradoxes of voting theory which make a majority an ambiguous concept wherever there is more than one alternative, the fact that unlike buyers in a commercial market, voters have to vote for policy bundles, and that the alternative of referenda on individual issues flounders on the public ignorance of the actual trade-offs in any particular issue. There is the prevalence of 'rent-seeking' activity already mentioned. Above all, there is the likelihood both of the oppression of the minority by the majority on some issues and of the oppression of the majority by coalitions of minorities on others.

Interventionists who have looked at the analysis of government or political failure, set against the textbook analysis of market failure, tend to retreat into a professional pragmatism. An example is Dieter Helm,[24] who argues for a case-by-case approach without a theoretical presumption either way. This does not stop him putting all the emphasis in a more popular article on the 'core neoclassical theory of perfect competition . . . as a benchmark' against which he appraises existing imperfect markets.[25]

It is, I think, possible to go further in general terms. There are basically two theoretical models of the relations between individual self-interest and public welfare – 'the invisible hand' and 'prisoner's dilemma'. The former explains how the pursuit of private interest promotes the public good; the latter how it undermines it.

The 'invisible hand' encapsulates the market mechanism – how in Adam Smith's famous example the baker and butcher in pursuing their own private interest supply us with bread and meat, and thereby, promote the public good in a way which was no part of their original intention.

The 'prisoner's dilemma' is less well known. It describes the dilemma facing two prisoners, each of whom has a promise of a lower sentence if he confesses. If both follow narrow private interest they end up worse off than if they had followed a rule 'never confess'.*

The simple parable has numerous applications, many of them clearer than the original parable. If we all drop litter in public places (because it saves us the effort to find a bin and the net increase in litter is imperceptible) then in the end we shall be worse off, even from our selfish point of view, than if we have behaved 'unselfishly'. An individual country may feel more secure if it gains a weapon advantage over its rivals. But if every country arms competitively, the net result can be worse for all participants than an agreement on self-restraint.

Nearly all cases where invisible hand or other self-regulating mechanisms fail can be subsumed under the head of prisoner's dilemma. The great task for political economy, hardly even begun, is to map out the area where the invisible hand applies and the area where prisoner's dilemma does. It is only by so doing that supporters of the market mechanism and 'social planners'

---

* There are two prisoners whom the police do not have the evidence to convict of a major crime which they have both committed, but can convict for a minor offence. If only one confesses to the major crime, he goes free while his partner receives a severe sentence. If they both confess together they both receive sentences, only slightly less severe. If neither confesses, both receive the modest penalty for the minor offence.

Each prisoner left alone will think: 'Whatever my partner does I am better off confessing. If he does not confess, I will go free. Even if he does confess, I will get a slightly less stiff sentence. So why should I not confess?' If both follow this narrow self-interest rule, they both receive a slightly less severe sentence; whereas if each had followed the rule 'never confess', they both would escape with the modest penalty (see A. Rapaport, *Fights, Games and Debates*, Michigan, 1960).

can find a common language and attempt to narrow differences by reason rather than political assertion or an unconvincing pragmatism. A political economist who could carry out this task would truly deserve a Nobel Prize.

But a mere static mapping out of territory is insufficient. Invisible hand mechanisms require less coercion and do not depend on the possession of great knowledge or great disinterestedness by government officials. It is therefore desirable to transform, where possible, prisoner's dilemma situations into invisible hand ones by institutional, legal or moral reform. For instance, traffic, traffic lights and rules about left- or right-hand driving provide a framework in which motorists can pursue self-interest with less danger to their fellows. A convention against leaving litter lets park users follow self-interest in other ways (and another one against noisy radios would reinforce the effect).

Sometimes the best way of introducing invisible hand mechanisms will be the assignment of property rights. Nearly all the adverse 'externalities', which are so often cited as arguments for political intervention, arise from the absence of clearly-defined exclusive property rights, or from the transaction costs of certain kinds of contracts. It is because no one owns the air space, pleasant vistas or the ocean bed that market disciplines do not apply, and exploiters and destroyers can escape without paying a price. Where the community does in some sense own resources such as the national road space, it inflicts harm by not behaving like an owner and instead allowing 'free', and therefore wasteful, use of scarce assets. It is not property rights but their absence that is anti-social. None of this implies, however, that the existing distribution of property rights is justified.

## (f) Morals of markets

Valuable though the economic approach to political and other human behaviour is, it is ultimately subordinate to more fundamental explanations. The economic approach takes as its starting axiom that the individual maximises his utility subject to constraints. This is made true by postulate.

The Chicago School goes further in assuming market equilibrium and stable preferences in addition to maximising behaviour and uses all three postulates relentlessly and unflinchingly. This leaves some room for judging the system by its empirical fruitfulness.

My own judgment is that it conceals the most important aspects of markets, as a discovery procedure, in which preferences as well as products are discovered and developed, as emphasised by the so-called Austrian School.[26] The relevant points here is that in all three versions – mainstream, Chicago and Austrian – economic agents act subject to constraints. In contrast to the 'economic imperialists' who believe that their subject is the master key to all human behaviour from war and peace to religion, marriage and divorce, I believe that these constraints are as important as the maximising hypothesis; the key constraints are often not just those of limited budgets, or even the physical and institutional environment, but beliefs and moral codes.

This is not a pious assertion, but an observation that human conduct is rule-bound, whether the rules are explicit or implicit – a truth attested by the saying: 'There is honour among thieves'. Opinion and moral beliefs are the real clue to behaviour, even though the origin and evolution of these beliefs can be studied by economic analysis, evolutionary biology, or any other method which seems promising.

The essential point, as so often, was put by David Hume:

> The governors have nothing to support but opinion. The Sultan of Egypt or the Emperor of Rome might drive his harmless subjects like brute beasts, against their sentiments and inclination: but he must at least have led his mamelukes or praetorian bands like men by their opinion.[27]

Adam Smith's concept of Natural Liberty, or reliance on the invisible hand, so far from being amoral or cynical, represents a highly-sophisticated moral doctrine. Its essence is that in *some areas and under some conditions*, the use of markets avowedly based on self-interest will prove more beneficial than an overt attempt to achieve the public good directly.

It is best regarded as a *prima facie* rule of conduct within a wider system of morality.[28] It fits for instance into a utilitarian system of morality, which is most suitable for everyday decisions, even if it is ultimately subordinated to contractarian principles.

Contrary to popular superstition, neither utilitarians nor other secular moralists suppose it is possible to dispense with traditional morality and work out afresh the effects of every action on their fellow men and women. We do not have the knowledge to assess the effects of our actions on other human beings, especially those more remotely affected by them. For this, if for no other reason, we need prima-facie rules of conduct such as 'Don't tell lies', 'Do not steal', 'Keep promises', or in the public sphere: 'Observe international treaties'.

The Adam Smith 'Invisible Hand' doctrine is one of the more surprising prima-facie rules to have been suggested. The suggestion is that in matters such as buying and selling, or deciding what and how to produce, we will do others more good if we behave *as if* we are following our self-interest rather than by pursuing more altruistic purposes.

Neither Adam Smith, nor any of his successors, with the unconvincing exception of a few modern American 'anarchocapitalists', believe that the whole of public activity should be left to the market-place. A functioning market presupposes a basis of trust (which is itself a form of social capital), a legal system, and an apparatus of law enforcement. Smith did not believe that police and defence should be left to private armies.

Certain background conditions are necessary for the market to produce, not an optimum, but even reasonably satisfactory results. For instance, there needs to be a way of dealing with the more blatant spillovers or externalities – that is, costs imposed on others which do not appear as financial expenses to those who perpetrate them, or benefits for which no reward is received.

Labour and housing markets have to be free enough to give a displaced worker a chance of early re-employment. There needs to be a social security net to look after the victims of change. At a more technical level, either exchange rates or nominal wages need to be flexible enough so that the balance of payments can take care of itself without patriotic exhortation to expert more or import less.

Advocates of the market economy do not devote enough attention to numerous other unstated provisos. The shooting of one's competitors is not an acceptable way of maximising profits or even minimising losses. Nor is the bribery of legislators. But there are less banal and obvious questions. Is it legitimate to try to monopolise a market in the absence of strong restrictive practices legislation? If there are such laws, should we co-operate actively, or merely conform? If certain markets such as those for labour, are clearly malfunctioning, is an employer who tries, as a deliberate policy objective, to provide more jobs, a social benefactor? Or is he meddling in matters outside his influence, and would society be better off if companies confined themselves to promoting shareholders' financial interests?

Theoretical welfare economics is too exacting in setting up impossibly perfectionist yardsticks, but not exacting enough in its silence about the rules, inhibitions and instinctive reflexes – too numerous and subtle to codify – which are the most important modifications in practice of the pursuit of uninhibited self-interest and which at their best internalise many externalities.

The true case for the market mechanism is that it is a decentralised and non-dictatorial method of conveying information, reacting to change and fostering innovation. The full set of assumptions, side-conditions and constraints required for the pursuit of market gain to yield beneficial results can never be fully written down. In deciding – either as policy makers or individual moral agents – when to follow the maxim of the invisible hand and when to depart from it, we need all the help we can get from the traditions and unformulated rules which embody more knowledge than any individual can hope to have. Yet in the end these traditions will never be enough. For they are often contradictory or ambiguous, and we cannot escape conscious reflection about how to interpret them or decide between them.

## (g) Analogy with free speech

No real-world market economy is likely to be even approximately satisfactory in all the background conditions. What then does the businessman, who wants to be a reasonably good citizen, do?

No system of political economy can absolve him from exercising his own moral judgement. Let me take an analogy from a different sphere emphasised by Peter Jay. Freedom of the press is a good general maxim and part of our basic freedoms: 'Publish and be damn'd!' This serves as a warning that any justification for censorship or self-censorship needs to be examined with a jaundiced eye. The harm involved in a particular kind of censorship of self-censorship is often difficult to see because it is indirect. A large part of it is the precedent established. The immediate gain may be direct and obvious. Therefore the general assumption should be 'Publish and be damn'd!' But this general presumption does not absolve the newspaperman or television reporter from examining carefully the possibility that a particular act of publication could be so damaging to specific human beings – for example, information that would interfere with a hijack rescue – that the general presumption must be overthrown.

A similar story applies to the pursuit of profit maximisation or personal gain in a competitive market economy. The absence of effective legislation should not excuse a chemical company for polluting the air – although the competitive advantage gained by an unscrupulous firm over others suggests that the law should (if defective) be put right soon, so that the public-spirited firms are not forced out of business.

These common-sense qualifications do not destroy the presumption that, by following the profit motive, subject to the written and unwritten rules of society in which he lives, a businessman will also best serve the interests of his fellows.

Nor is there any presumption that the altruist, who has an exceptionally strong concern for the welfare of others, should strive less hard for income and wealth, as explained in Chapter 3. Indeed, he should probably strive harder. The difference between the altruist and the average selfish citizen is surely in what the former does with his gain.

But just as there are some rare occasions when a journalist dealing with great diplomatic, military or financial issues should waive his rules and censor himself, there may just occasionally be a 'clear and present' economic danger, where the businessman should reinterpret the rules of the profit game.

Even when this arises, the modifications can be in different elements. They can be within the margin of discretion in interpreting profit-seeking. They can also be modifications in the background rules and conventions which normally *restrain* the pursuit of profit. For instance, it is possible to disregard conventions about going pay rates, thus *removing an inhibition on profit-making*,[30] while at the same time shifting the emphasis to concepts of profit-seeking likely to result in the employment of more rather than fewer people.*

---

* The catch-all term 'corporate responsibility' is sometimes used to describe any and every departure from narrowly conceived profit maximisation. One should be reluctant to give a generalised 'Yes' or 'No' to the concept. The appropriate

## 3.  POLITICAL DEVELOPMENTS

During most of the 1980s market economics was identified in the public mind with the policies of President Ronald Reagan in the USA and Prime Minister Margaret Thatcher in Britain. Some market liberals were embarrassed by this identification, others were pleased to have apparent influence at court. I shall make a few remarks about both leaders, as my readers will expect. But I do so with some reluctance, because in the years ahead market liberalism will have to be argued on its own merits, while both the achievements and the shortcomings of these two leaders recede into history.

As I shall be emphasising some of the differences between Thatcherism and Reaganism and true market liberalism, it is necessary to put my criticisms into perspective by glancing first at what has been happening at the other end of the political spectrum, at the risk of a complete change of gear. Without putting emphasis on developments on the Left, the criticism of the New Right will be out of focus.

### (a)  Left-wing fascism

In the Prologue I speak with some sympathy of the radical developments of the 1960s, in particular of some of the ideas of the Youth Revolt embodied in slogans such as 'Make love not war' and the search for a more spontaneous lifestyle, less bound to bourgeois conventions.

If some of the radicals I had in mind have gone on to become independent broadcasters or make their way in the pop record business, this is not a betrayal, but an example of how competitive private enterprise provides a better environment for the anti-establishment than a planned economy, or a trade union state.

Unfortunately, a very different Left has since developed which deserves to be called the Fascist Left. It is marked by a belief in violence – not as a last resort against a dictatorship, but as a normal procedure, and without too much worry about who gets hurt. It is often marked by sympathy for the IRA or Middle East terrorists or regimes such as Colonel Gadaffi's Libya. Under the

---

response should be not so much hostility or enthusiasm as wariness and suspicion.

slogan of anti-racialism its members resort to a reign of terror, and book-burning in the Goebbels's mould, to suppress every deviant thought. They are sometimes called the Hard Left, but they are the spiritual successors of the Mosleyite marchers and the public school thugs who broke up the college rooms of young aesthetes between the wars.

These strictures on the Fascist Left do not depend on a belief that the law should never under any circumstances be broken. The right to resist an unjust law, in a state which provides no constitutional method of proposing and enacting changes, is one of last resort cherished by liberal thinkers at least from the time of John Locke.

Nothing does more to destroy and cheapen this last resort right than the belief of the members the Fascist Left that violence is justified whenever they cannot otherwise persuade enough of their fellow citizens of their views. Other writers have sufficiently discussed the plethora of sub-Marxist tracts which define constitutional democracy as a sham whenver their own views cannot prevail; and in the case of apologists for Red terrorists, justify violence as a way of striking fear into a society which they have not the faintest idea with what to replace.

In Britain there have been terrorist outrages, mostly associated with the IRA, which have received some sneaking sympathy from the Lumpen Left. But the most important example of the Fascist Left in mainland Britain has been in a series of coal strikes, beginning with the one in 1972, when the then Home Secretary, Reginald Maudling, negotiated a police withdrawal from the Saltley Coal Depot in the face of flying pickets led by the young Arthur Scargill.

It was the next coal strike, that of 1974, which brought down the Heath Government and led to the defeatist mood among establishment politicians and civil servants who declared the country ungovernable. Scargill, then still only the Yorkshire miners' leader, made little effort to hide his tactics. In an interview in the subsequent year he said that the Transport and General Workers' Union had 'had a contractual arrangement with the working class and if they didn't honour that contractual arrangement we'd make sure, physically, that they did. For we would have thrown the lorries and everything else into the dyke'.[31] Thus not only was violence legitimate against the class enemy, it was also legitimate against trade unionists who did not share Scargill's view of the matter.

Thus few people were surprised that the 1984–5 miners' strike saw the physical intimidation of miners who wanted to work, of other workers who wanted to drive fuel supplies, and of police who were trying to keep roads open, being brought to new heights. Scargill, by then president of the Miners' Union, had already said: 'Direct action by working people is the only language this Government will listen to. They are not prepared to listen to logical argument. We must show we are no longer prepared to accept decisions in Westminster which destroy the right to work'[32] and 'Every trade unionist has to be determined to defy the law and render it ineffective'.[33]

A vivid description of Scargill's tactics was given by an *Evening Standard* reporter, Colin Adamson, at the Orgreave Coking plant where pickets had tried to prevent coke being transported to the British Steel Corporation plant in Scunthorpe in June 1984. The previous day had been of comparative calm, and pickets and police had played a friendly game of football.

'All that changed' when Scargill returned to the picket line. 'He went into a field adjoining the main road into Orgreave and began shouting orders like a general on a battlefield'. Violence erupted again

> leaving eight more policemen in hospital, two pickets injured and 23 arrested. Large stones and bottles of cotton wool soaked in paint stripper rained down on the police lines. Three officers received facial burns from these missiles and one was said to be in a serious condition.

While Scargill was marshalling his troops he rounded on the reporter and told his men: 'Get bloody *Standard* out of here, lads'. The reporter was badly shaken as miners hurled him 'bodily away and elbowed' him 'repeatedly in the ribs'.[34]

It was the sight of the Labour leader, Neil Kinnock, and Arthur Scargill embracing on the platform that convinced me, as I wrote in *The Financial Times* at the time, not to 'cease from mortal strife to ensure that Labour as now constituted should never again form the government of Britain'. I was disturbed that academics and merchant bankers, whom I had hitherto respected as individuals, had not burned their boats with Labour as a result of the Party's wholehearted public identification with Scargill – whatever may have been said to journalists under the cover of non-attributable 'lobby' briefings.

Too many British people, who shrink from confronting evil, preferred to discuss the strike in terms of energy policy, and the foolishness of supposing that every pit, however high cost, should be kept open. But such matters – and even Scargill's refusal to hold a strike ballot – were secondary to the methods used to conduct the strike. The worst form of evasion and appeasement in the drawing rooms of London was the attempt to dwell on the faults – real or supposed – of Mrs Thatcher, to avoid backing the country's elected leader against Scargill and what he represented.

The attitude of so many intellectuals in the face of the organised cult of brutality was accurately depicted in Julien Benda's *La Trahison des Clercs*, first published in 1928.[35] This is a book more often mentioned than read. It is in fact largely directed against the vulgar excesses of French bourgeois nationalism and the then prevailing literary cult of brutality. But, even in 1928, Benda extended his strictures against the similar attitudes of those who preached to the working class:

> Organise yourselves, become the stronger, seize all power or exert yourself to retain it if you already possess it; laugh at all efforts to bring more charity, more justice or any other 'rot' into your relations with any other class; you have been cheated long enough by that sort of thing.[36]

Benda saw these sentiments as virtually identical to those animating the supporters of Mussolini's Fascism.

Any reader who thinks this is exaggerated should examine Mussolini's contempt for Parliament and approval of force in the streets, both in the early years of Fascism, and earlier on during his socialist period.[37]

It was not thanks to the talking classes, but to the Thatcher Government, that fuel went through to the power stations, imported coal arrived, and normal economic activity went ahead without a three-day week. Maybe another government would have had no choice but to take a stand. But the credit for having done so, belongs to Mrs Thatcher.

The Prime Minister was criticised for treating Arthur Scargill like General Galtieri and talking about 'the enemy within'. The criticism was the wrong way round. General Galtieri was never a threat to civilised life in Britain in the way the militant miners were – and I am not even now sure that it is right to use the past tense.

There is a British chant, common in left-wing demonstrations, 'We shall overcome'. We did overcome – and even the feeblest government official will now hesitate to urge complete appeasement of union physical power. For this, if nothing else, the Thatcher Government deserves to be remembered.

Left-wing fascism did not die with the defeat of the 1984–5 miners' strike. A further manifestation came in the physical attacks on those who dared cross the picket lines in the 1986–7 dispute, to work in Rupert Murdoch's newspapers in Wapping, which were established in a new plant with workers from outside the printing unions.

As I write these words I have in front of me a report about two members of 'Sogat 82', workers at the Battersea depot of John Menzies, the newspaper distributors and agents, who complain of intimidation because they disagreed with a voluntary levy in support of dismissed employees of Murdoch's News International, unless the levy was approved by a vote of members. One worker had his car tyres slashed and other damage inflicted on his car and also received a death threat. His family had been subject to obscene and threatening calls. His colleague had sold his house and moved to a secret south coast address. They both claimed that the campaign was started by a senior member of the union in prison for violence at the Wapping plant.[38] It should, however, be said, that the worst culprits were often not printers themselves, but rent-a-mob militants from outside the industry. It is part of the dialectics of such confrontations that Murdoch should have prepared himself behind heavily-defended positions, and that Wapping had some of the aspects of an armed camp. These aspects – like the police excesses which usually occur in prolonged violent confrontations – so far from being regretted by the militant left, are greeted with delight as a propaganda weapon in the so-called class struggle.

The saddest aspect of left-wing fascism is the way the noble cause of opposition to racialism has been conscripted into service. The current slogan is 'no platform' to so-called racists in the universities or anywhere else where meetings can be smashed. Even a *New Statesman* correspondent, who defends the 'no platform' policy, says he has listened to the word racist being used for Labour Party opponents of black sections; for Roy Hattersley; for a media studies lecturer who refused to interrupt a lecture to discuss politics with a black student; for an economics lecturer who failed an Asian student.

Yet this same writer refers disparagingly to 'all the right-wing claptrap about freedom of speech and academic freedom'.[39] If 'freedom of speech' is right-wing claptrap, then there is no case against government abuses of the Official Secrets Acts or political attempts to stop controversial television programmes. Freedom of expression is indivisible, and neither claptrap nor right-wing. Indeed neither right nor left is notable for supporting it when it gets in the way of other objectives.

### (b) Reaganism and Thatcherism

Nothing of what has been said about left-wing fascism should make the reader starry-eyed about the Reagan and Thatcher governments which were in power in the USA and Britain in most of the 1980s and which collectivists delighted to depict as the incarnation of free market attitudes. The distinction between right-wing authoritarianism and market liberalism, repeatedly emphasised in the main text of this book, written when Ronald Reagan was Governor of California and Margaret Thatcher Secretary of State for Education, still holds good.

Abstracting from some very important national differences, Reaganism and Thatcherism shared some common features, which in combination, I am tempted to call *The New Spartanism*:

1. A hawkish or super-patriotic attitude to foreign and military affairs.
2. An opposition to social permissiveness and a desire to return to 'traditional values'.
3. Hostility to government economic intervention, often partial and inconsistent, but going beyond that of previous Republican or Conservative governments.

The first two features are the opposite of liberalism in the sense of a belief in freedom and emphasis on the individual rather than a group or nation. Thus, someone who supported a market economy for liberal or libertarian reasons had no reason to be a

Thatcherite or a Reaganite, and he would expect these hawkish and authoritarian attitudes to show in the particular mix of economic policies – for example, the areas in which deregulation was pressed and where it was not.[40]

One has, however, to be careful. A conservative who shares all three of the attitudes listed above is not necessarily making a logical mistake. He or she may welcome exposure to market forces, more because of the disciplines they impose than the freedom they provide. He or she may regard the welfare state, permissive morality, and 'inadequate' military spending, or preparedness to fight, as different examples of the excessive self-indulgence that is supposed to be sapping the West. This New Spartanism may sit ill besides the effortless fortunes made by some shareholders who benefit from takeover bids, or the revival of snobbish and expensive upper-class pastimes typified by the 'Sloane Rangers', but it still exists.

All that has to be said here is that the market economy has been justified in this book on liberal, not New Spartan, grounds. Moreover, nearly all the classic defences of markets of capitalism have been, despite different twists by different authors, on primarily liberal grounds. A full New Spartan justification of the market economy has still to be formuated, and if it were ever done the kind of market economy emerging would differ a great deal from the usual model. (A rough sketch is attempted in Appendix I to Chapter 1.)

A full statement of soft-hearted, but not soft-headed liberalism, would have to go beyond general attitudes and meet the New Spartans on their own grounds. It would have to rebut in detail the arguments for the USA becoming involved in the affairs of Vietnam or Nicaragua. It would have to distinguish between the valid and invalid strictures on progressive education. (In a nutshell, the valid part is the desire to encourage rather than to stifle the expression of a child's personality and interests. This liberal aim has been discredited by association with a dogmatic egalitarianism that seeks to deny innate differences familiar to every mother and nurse, and an attempt to use education in an ill-thought attempt to subvert a supposed 'structure of class domination' erroneously identified with capitalism.)

A liberal would have to distinguish carefully between programmes for dealing with AIDS, which treat the disease as a misfortune against which it is necessary to take precautions, and attitudes like those of James Anderton, Chief Constable of Manchester, who said in 1986: 'Homosexuals, prostitutes and promiscuous people are swirling around in a human cesspit of their own making'. In other words, anxieties over AIDS are being used to justify a moralistic crusade against disapproved lifestyles. To his credit, the Health Minister at the time, Tony Newton, said that he would not use that language himself. But nor would he directly repudiate Anderton, despite being given, several opportunities.[41] Mrs Thatcher herself was more clearly sympathetic, as she was to Mrs Mary Whitehouse, the campaigner against supposedly obscene television, films and plays.

As this book merely seeks to put economic policy in a wider context, and not to be a compendium on all the problems of our age, these signposts should be enough. My greatest complaint about the New Economic Right is not against those who accept a hawkish foreign policy or anti-permissive social views. It is against those who are so keen on the non-interventionist economic slogans of Reagan and Thatcher-type governments that they have not even thought about the wider context, and thus not only fail to function as full human beings, but fail to notice the one-sidedness even of the economic programmes of their heroes.

### Attitude studies

Some empirical work has been done in the USA on the structure of political attitudes relevant to this discussion. There are data which suggest that voters do not buy or reject all three aspects of the New Right package, just listed, but discriminate amongst them.

California voters in 1982 supported several constitutional initiatives to cut taxes but also endorsed a nuclear freeze. Similar combinations of attitudes were shown in New England. At a federal level too, several polls in the early to mid-1980s supported both a nuclear freeze and an amendment to balance the Budget.

Two American political scientists, William S. Maddox and Stuart A. Lillie[42] have suggested the following fourfold classification:

| Expansion of personal freedoms | Government intervention in economic affairs | |
| --- | --- | --- |
| | **For** | **Against** |
| **For** | Left-Progressive | Libertarian |
| **Against** | Populist | Conservative |

*Figure 1*  Issue dimensions and ideological change

*Moral conservatives*, who were against the expansion of personal freedom, believed that divorce, cohabitation homosexuality, abortion, and other contemporary phenomena, were evidence of 'moral decay', while *libertarians* believed that they showed 'greater social tolerance'.

In the 1980 and 1984 US elections libertarians (to be found in great numbers among 'yuppies') voted for Reagan in the hope that nothing would come of his conservative social policies.

### Anglo-Saxon attitudes

Exact reproduction of these studies would be difficult in Britain. Religious affiliation is very much less, and there is an absence of the vociferous fundamentalism so striking in the USA. There are no English counties, for instance, where schools are under pressure to teach 'creationism' as an alternative to evolution.

There was, however, a general sense, in the 1980s, that the climate of government was authoritarian and anti-permissive under the Thatcher Government. ('There is not much of the second around' some of my friends said when I told them I was preparing a new edition of *Capitalism and the Permissive Society*.) Most manifestations in domestic policy were of a petty and secretive kind. Two civil servants, Sara Tisdall and Clive Ponting, were prosecuted – the first was sentenced to six months in jail, the second acquitted – under the obsolete and indefensible Official Secrets Act, for what were essentially breaches of discipline, rather than revelations of national security of use to an enemy. Trade-union membership at the 'listening station' GCHQ was suppressed, with no attempt to negotiate a no-strike agreement as an alternative. The GLC and other metropolitan boroughs were abolished because of their political attitudes – in place of a fundamental review of local government powers and finance. In 1986 the Cabinet Secretary, Sir Robert Armstrong, was subjected to humiliating experiences in an Australian court, in an attempt to suppress secret service memoirs, which gave away no national secrets, but showed the security services in a ludicrous light. In 1987 the BBC, as well as the *New Statesman* was raided, in an attempt to track down alleged breaches of the Official Secrets Act. On each of these instances, individually it might just have been possible to drum up a sort of case. But in total they amounted to a heavy tilting of the balance in favour of the executive and against free speech and open government.

Other aspects of petty authoritarianism abounded. Most notorious were the 'short sharp shock' regimes inaugurated for young offenders, some of whose victims committed suicide. This regime was not based on penal research, but was almost admittedly a sop to the more vindictive and vociferous Tory rank and file. Many courts refused to send young offenders for such treatment, and in the end the special centres were abolished and a tougher regime instituted in normal detention centres instead.

But the area in which Thatcherism showed its least attractive characterics was in the first, hawkish or superpatriotic of the items listed on p. 240, namely the war to recapture the Falkland Islands from the Argentine, in 1982, in which at least a thousand people were killed – a quarter of them British – and several times that many 'wounded' (a euphemism for some of the ghastly injuries sustained) for the sake of 1750 islanders, who could have been resettled in luxury for a fraction of the cost of the war.

A classical liberal could have tried to argue that the suffering of the war was a necessary sacrifice to uphold the principle of resistance to aggression, breach of which would mean far more suffering in the future. I have explained elsewhere why I did not find these arguments convincing.[43] But they were not the main reason why the war was supported, or why its successful conclusion was – for all protestations to the contrary – largely responsible for the government's re-election in 1983. Although this is difficult to prove, it is likely that this war shifted the whole style of the Thatcher Administration into a more authoritarian mould for years to come.

These strictures on the Falklands War do not make any case for the Labour Party. One of the crucial events in precipitating the war was the belligerent speech of the Labour Leader Michael Foot, at the notorious special Saturday session of Parliament after the Argentine invasion. This speech both made it more difficult for the government *not* to invade the Falklands, and provided some assurance that the Labour Party would not be well placed to oppose such a venture. These were echoes of 1956, when Mr Hugh Gaitskell initially reacted very belligerently to Nasser's seizure of the Suez Canal, although he went on courageously to oppose the Suez expedition, with much less equivocation than his successor at the time of the Falklands.

*Political choice*

Left-Wing Fascism and Conservative authoritarianism made a sort of negative case for the Alliance in the late 1980s – more so for David Owen's Social Democrats than for David Steel's Liberals, who were too obsessed with Mrs Thatcher to denounce Scargill in the way that Owen did. But anyone reading this book will not need my advice on how to vote, nor a reminder that parties who have not held office always find it easier to appear with clean hands. Nor – despite Owen's brave words about the social market economy – did the Alliance parties find it easy to avoid splitting the difference between the Conservative and Labour parties on economic policy or avoid espousing a watered-down collectivism. It will be of more assistance to the reader to make a few summary remarks about the Conservative economic record than to discuss the hypothetical policy of parties in opposition at the time of writing.

## 4. THE CONSERVATIVE RECORD

### (a) Government spending

Both Thatcher and Reagan Administrations, and even more their cheer leaders on the New Economic Right, set great store on curbing public spending, and left-wing newspapers dutifully responded with headlines about 'cuts'. But, of course, there were no cuts overall.

In the eight years up to 1986–7, UK total public spending on programmes increased by 14 per cent after allowing for inflation. The more comprehensive total of general spending, which includes debt interest, had risen by over 16 per cent.

Of the 14 main sectors shown in the official White Papers, only two, trade and industry, and housing, had actually experienced real cuts. The reduction in 'trade and industry' reflected a welcome reduction in subsidies in aerospace, shipbuilding and steel. But even more was accounted for by a plunge in the borrowing by the nationalised industries, part of which represented higher charges to the consumer which were required to fulfil official target rates of return. The fall in housing expenditure (gross of capital receipts from the sale of council houses) did partly reflect smaller local authority building programmes. The saving here was, however, offset by the growing cost of mortgage interest relief, which amounted to a revenue loss of £4.5bn in 1987–8.

Thus if the Thatcher Government ever hoped to cut total public spending, that aim was soon abandoned. Its first serious objective was to stabilise public expenditure in real terms. But even that proved impossible to achieve and the aim shifted to keeping the growth of government expenditure below that of the national income so that the public spending proportion could fall as national income grew. That aim, too, may be difficult to achieve. The ratio of general government expenditure, excluding privatisation receipts, to GDP rose substantially in the first four Thatcher years and then gradually declined. But by 1986–7, the public spending ratio was still estimated at 44 to 45 per cent compared with 43.3 per cent in 1978–9, the last Callaghan year (see Table 4). The US under Reagan has had an even more disillusioning experience with the public spending ratio rising in most years after 1980.

Public spending has in fact been under very great pressure in all countries irrespective of the political colour of governments. In the major seven Organization for Economic Co-operation and Development (OECD) members[44] combined, the public spending ratio rose by 8 percentage points in the decade 1965–75 to 34 per cent,[45] by which time there was general agreement to call a halt, again irrespective of politics – but with incomplete success. Nine years later the OECD ratio had risen another 5 or 6 percentage points to nearly 40 per cent.

There are numerous upward pressures on public spending. The first is that because measured productivity increases are difficult both to achieve and to measure in the public sector, prices rise faster than the private sector. (This is known as the Relative Price Effect, RPE.) For example, of the 7.6 percentage points by which the general government share of UK GDP rose in the 20 years up to 1984, only 2.8 percentage points represented higher measured

*Table* 4  Public expenditure trends (excluding privatisation proceeds)

| | *(£ billion)* | | |
| | General government expenditure[1] | | |
| | Cash | Real terms[2] | Per cent of GDP |
|---|---|---|---|
| 1978–79 | 74.6 | 140.7 | 43¼ |
| 1979–80 | 90.0 | 145.3 | 43½ |
| 1980–81 | 108.7 | 147.9 | 46 |
| 1981–82 | 120.6 | 149.4 | 46½ |
| 1982–83 | 133.1 | 153.7 | 47 |
| 1983–84 | 141.4 | 156.3 | 46¼ |
| 1984–85 | 152.1 | 161.3 | 46¼ |
| 1985–86 | 161.3 | 161.3 | 44¾ |
| 1986–87 | 169.2 | 164.5 | 44½ |
| 1987–88 | 178.7 | 167.5 | 44 |
| 1988–89 | 184.6 | 167.2 | 42¾ |
| 1989–90 | 192.8 | 169.6 | 42¼ |

1. Estimated outturn for 1986–7; plans for 1987–8 onwards.
2. Cash figures adjusted to 1985–6 price levels by excluding the effect of general inflation as measured by the GDP deflator at market prices.
*Source* Autumn statement, HM Treasury, November 1986.

volumes. The remainder represent a differential increase in the apparent cost of public sector activities.[46]

There was a deeper problem too. The post-war policies had been based on the assumption of a limited, finite requirement for health services; education, pensions, social security and the like. In the 1960s and 1970s increasing dissatisfaction was expressed with the level of such services, the need for which cannot be measure in the objective way that Beveridge had hoped. The result was a polarisation of attitudes: one school advocated far more state spending and another a much greater role for private provision. The attempt at a compromise or middle way between the two schools inevitably brought unsatisfactory results, with complaints of inadequate provision side by side with complaints about government overspending.

The Thatcher government did not reduce the range of its responsibilities for social security, health or any of the large spending areas. The result was that it had to be as tight-fisted as possible simply to stay where it was. Thus the defenders of the Welfare State saw meaness and cheeseparing all round, while the Radical Right felt that it had been betrayed by the continuing rise in public spending and the pressures for still more.

An instance is the social security budget which rose by almost 40 per cent in the first eight Thatcher years. This was due not only to the large rise in unemployment. Equally important factors were the increase in the number of retirement pensioners, increased requirements for housing and family benefit to supplement low incomes, and greater take-up benefit rights.

The Department of Health and Social Security (DHSS) expected these influences to come to an end; and there were official projections of a plateau in social security spending in subsequent years. But I doubt whether any government will be able to continue to link benefit levels only with inflation, while real earnings of those at work continue to rise fairly rapidly. A true brake on social security spending would require much more selectivity both in child benefits, and eventually in retirement benefits, than governments find politically expedient.

Another instance is that Health Service expenditure is boosted by 0.7 per cent per annum, simply by the changing age composition of the population, and by another 0.5 per cent (on DHSS estimates) by the cost of medical advance. This makes 1.2 per cent without taking into account the RPE effect.

The Thatcher Government's spending bill was also swollen in the first few years by pledges to increase military and police spending, and on 'law and order'. Even if expenditure here flattens out there will be plenty of pressures on other programmes to take up the slack.

The Thatcher Government, like others before it, did undertake a number of initiatives to improve efficiency in the public sector to get more 'bangs per buck'. But possibilities here are limited (a) by the nature of some public sector activities; (b) by forces made known in the economic analysis of bureaucracy and pressure groups; and (c) by the natural, and even justifiable, tendency for costs savings – for example, in the running of hospitals – to be fed back into a higher level of basic provision.

Unlike the New Economic Right, I have always regarded the public spending ratio as a highly unreliable guide to the degree of harmful collectivism in an economy – that is, of the extent to which the organs of state take decisions which would be better left to individuals in the market.[47] Some transfer items which appear as public expenditure, such as state pensions, or child benefits, are cash payments to individuals to spend as they like. Other policies which harm the market system far more do not appear as public expenditure at all. For instance, quotas on textiles, or so-called voluntary understandings with the Japanese on a wide variety of products, restrict the right of the individual to spend his own income in his own way, as well as being price-raising. But they do not cost the Chancellor a penny.

The outstanding example of such 'fiscal illusion' is agriculture, where the true costs in terms of high food prices and the diversion of resources away from their most efficient uses (and into unsightly prairie wheat farms, which inflict negative spillovers of their own), are far higher than the cost of the budgetary transfers to Brussels of which British Governments made such an issue. Closed shops, minimum wage laws, and union monopoly are all other examples of collectivism which do not show in the public spending ratio. Nor even do penal 'taxes on the rich' which have a negative revenue yield and therefore finance no public spending whatever.

The existence of controls, distortions and burdens, which fall on people in their capacity as citizens or consumers rather than taxpayers does not, of course, justify lax control of public spending. Tight control is obviously needed as part of the day-to-day work of government. There are so many vested interests inside and outside the public sector pressing for more funds, and so many pressure groups claiming taxpayers' funds, that controlling public spending is like rolling a stone uphill. Without incessant vigilance by a mean and negative Finance Ministry or Treasury – punctuated by occasional sterling crises or visits from the IMF – public spending would soon exceed the willingness of taxpayers to finance it.

The practical moral of the failure of both the Reagan and Thatcher attempts to cut the public spending ratio is the futility of trying to roll back expenditure without fundamental changes in the agenda of government. Governments have the duty to stand up to monopolistic public sector unions, despite the sentimental and unthinking support these sometimes command. But to try to hold back the volume of expenditure on the health and educational services, without reducing the tasks imposed upon them, or to limit social security outgoings while paying non-means-tested state pension and child benefits, is asking for trouble.

If a government rules out radical changes in public sector obligations, as President Reagan did over US social security, and Mrs Thatcher over the Health Service, one is left with tighter Treasury scrutiny of a basically unchanged range of activities. Actions that the media call 'cuts' are then necessary merely to put a brake on the rate of increase of the public spending bill, which still rises too quickly for those who treat it as an index of excessive government.

## (b) Privatisation and deregulation

The most unexpected of the Thatcher Government's political successes was the promotion of 'privatisation'. Its principal meaning is simply denationalisation. But it also sometimes covers the franchising of, or tendering for, services supplied to the public sector, such as municipal refuse collection and hospital cleaning. Deregulation, although basically an issue of its own, has become involved in the privatisation debate, because of doubts about whether it has gone far enough to make the newly-privatised concerns genuinely competitive.

Although 'privatisation' was regarded as an ungainly word, only used because government publicists could not think of a better one, it acquired favourable overtones. For it appeared to the public to be something different from merely reversing Labour's nationalisation, as previous Conservative Governments had tried in slight degree to do. Operationally, the big difference was that unlike previous attempts, it left a large number of shares in the hands of small investors.

Privatisation was not originally intended to the centre-piece of Thatcherite economics. It hardly featured in the 1979 election manifesto, and was not a major issue in 1983. It came to prominence partly as an ideological substitute for the more basic goal of reducing the role of public spending. Selling state assets proved surprisingly easy while cutting spending proved more difficult than expected.

Privatisation also received a more practical impetus from the sheer difficulty of devising criteria for regulating the nationalised industries. The most traumatic single event was the failure to devise a 'Buzby bond' which would enable British Telecom to borrow on the private market. The inference drawn from these protracted controversies was that an arm's length relationship with nationalised industries was impracticable; and that if they really wanted to escape Treasury control the private sector was the best place for them.

About two-fifths of state-owned industries had been privatised by the end of the second Thatcher Government; and there was suggestion of a further large tranche if there were a third term. The revenue raised by the sale of state assets, which was running at less than £½bn per annum in the 1979–83 Parliament, rose to £2.7bn in 1985–6 and was planned to average nearly £5bn per annum in each of the four years 1986–90, if the Conservatives were returned for a third term.

Nevertheless, revenue-raising was a very subsidiary motivation. Harold Macmillan's remark about 'selling off the family silver' was in character, but wide of the mark. For assets sold by the government were not lost to the nation. At a public finance level, the sale of assets was a way of financing the Budget deficit, alternative to the sale of gilt-edged securities. The Treasury was well aware that the proceeds from asset sales were not available to finance public spending or tax cuts. The effects of asset sales were taken into account in determining the target for public borrowing. The moderate relaxation of fiscal policy in the middle of the 1980s was a quite deliberate move to offset high interest rates and to cushion falling oil revenues. Indeed, the inclusion of asset sales in the 'Public Sector Borrowing Requirement' (PSBR) made that relaxation more difficult by exciting suspicion, and the Chancellor had to publish spending and PSBR figures exclusive of asset sales to calm the financial markets, a matter which overseas governments, wishing to copy the British, did not fully appreciate.

British mainstream economists have tended to judge privatisation by its effects on the allocative and productive efficiency of the enterprises concerned. In the introduction to a useful series of readings on the subject[48] the editors remark that:

1. The performance of all firms is improved by competition.
2. Where competition prevails private firms are likely to do better because of a superior structure of management incentives.

More competition has been introduced in the first giant

corporation to be sold, British Telecom, where Mercury was permitted to enter as an alternative trunk supplier, and BT trunk call charges have been reduced as a precautionary move. But liberalisation was far less than would have been possible technically. The second giant, British Gas, was privatised with its monopoly privileges largely intact, thanks to the support that its chairman received from the Energy Secretary, Peter Walker – a notable Heathite, miscalled a 'liberal Tory' by political writers insensitive to the nuances of language.

The cases where the superiority of private performance has been most clearly established, such as airlines, ferries and hovercraft, and gas and electricity showrooms, have been ones where it has been possible to compare private and public enterprises in competition with each other.[49] Deregulation of express coaches reduced prices and improved provision, even before privatisation of the National Bus Company.

Some notable successes have not been in privatisation as such, but in putting to competitive tender services such as refuse collection or school and hospital cleaning and catering. But predictably, there have been problems of maintaining product quality in the absence of competitive choice by the final consumer. Often the public authority's own in-house services have reduced costs and outbid outside tenderers.

Conventional appraisals of privatisation leave out of account two further aspects, which are quite as important as the direct efficiency effects. The first, which the government trumpeted from the housetops, was to spread share ownership. The second, about which it kept a discreet silence, was to reduce union influence.

One aspect of encouraging small shareholders to acquire privatisation shares was that the proceeds were not maximised. As the majority of the population were still not owners of such shares, the process did involve a regressive transfer from the mass of the population to the relatively better off. I discuss below how a major opportunity was thrown away.

The union power aspect may ultimately be the most important. The state sector – public services as well as state industry – is nearly 100 per cent unionised, compared with well under 50 per cent in the private sector. A long view is needed here. No great change is to be expected in unionisation or in collective bargaining in very large organisations like Telecom or Gas immediately they become private. But privatisation does give scope for the gradual erosion of union influence, starting probably in the smaller and peripheral enterprises, out of the spotlight of publicity. Simply taking issues out of the political arena is a much underrated weapon on the side of common sense and market-based settlements.

There are also ways of introducing competition into what appear to be natural monopolies. For instance, the rail tracks could remain a public monopoly, while competing train operating companies could hire track space. (Some 40 per cent of rail freight is already carried in privately-owned wagons.) Nor is there any reason why electricity generating stations should not compete to supply a national grid. London's airports could compete with each other under separate ownership. British Gas could have operated as a common carrier distributor, charging a transmission rental to concerns selling gas to customers. Contrary to common belief, the postal letter service is not a natural monopoly; and the removal of restraints on competition, irrespective of whether the Post Office is privatised, could be combined with continuing subsidies for rural services if desired.[50]

One kind of competition to supply a service is known as franchising and has been used in relatively new sectors such as North Sea exploration, television spectrum and cable television. But public authorities have been reluctant to surrender discretionary powers by introducing a competitive auction as advocated, for instance, for ITV franchises by the Peacock Report.

In view of the limited extent to which such ideas were adopted, and the perverse influence of nationalised industry management on the terms of privatisation, the editors of *Privatisation and Regulation* remark: 'Denationalisating an enterprise into an uncompetitive environment is likely to be positively harmful'. This is a misjudgement. Not only does it ignore the intractable problems of government relations with the nationalised industries. It ignores the fact that such activity and interest as there has been in deregulation, franchising and contracting out, and prospects for more in future, are largely an outcrop of the privatisation debate. Privatisation has stirred up many corners of the British economy – less effectively than truly radical policies such as unilateral free trade would have done, but more effectively than anything else that was on the political agenda of the late 1980s.

## (c) Limited role of market forces

Apart from privatisation and trade union reform (to be discussed below), there was only a limited amount of radical action to open up the economy to market forces. The abolition of exchange controls in 1979, right at the beginning of the Thatcher Government, was much more important than generally realised, not only for economic efficiency but also for political freedom. There was some action against professional monopolies – for instance, against the artificial segregation of jobbers and brokers at the Stock Exchange and against minimum commissions. The artificial barriers preventing financial institutions, such as building societies and banks, from competing for each others' business were removed. There was limited liberalisation of professional monopolies, for instance spectacles and conveyancing. The other restrictive practices of the law are untouched (and had a powerful defender in Lord Hailsham). In addition, there was a painfully slow 'nitty-gritty' attempt to reduce barriers faced by small businesses.

But outside the financial area progress was very limited. There was nothing comparable to the removal of restraints to competition among the airlines in the US – largely initiated by Senator Edward Kennedy under the Carter Administration – or the court break-up of the AT and T telephone monopoly. Some free market critics of the Thatcher Government concentrate on its cautious and conservative attitude to the state's role in health, education and social security, already discussed. But there are genuine problems about extending market forces in this area; and policy caution here would have been easier to accept if there had been a more radical application of market forces to the main stream of business and industry, which has been their traditional home and where the case for applying them is clear cut.

Policy towards monopolies and restrictive practices (as distinct from mergers and takeovers) was pretty moribund. It can readily be accepted that the most effective competition policy is free trade. But this excuse is not available. For international trade was precisely the area where the Thatcher Government policies were most anti-market. In common with its EEC partners it was engaged in trying to protect, by so-called voluntary quotas, an increasing number of threatened industries, no longer just textiles, steel and cars, but a widening range of electronics and other goods as well. As in other countries, the obsession with buying home products has actively held back the high technology industries the government was supposedly promoting. Instead of a frontal attack on farm protection, at home as well as in the EEC, energies were too long diverted into the narrow issue of the UK Budget Rebate.

At home the Thatcher Government turned away from fundamental reform on issues ranging from rent decontrol to tax reform, support of the motor industry, occupational pensions and minimum wages. Sometimes the Prime Minister was overruled in Cabinet or Cabinet Committees, but at other times she was herself the main enemy of change, as in the case of fiscal subsidies for owner-occupiers.

Too many of her radical urges were wasted on peripheral issues such as the abolition of the elected authority responsible for Greater London and attempts to eliminate local taxes on house values, known as rates, despite the fact that houses are already over-subsidised and undertaxed compared to other assets. (The replacement of rates by a 'community charge' would be likely to raise house prices in the South East by at least 12 per cent and perhaps a great deal more (See *Rates Abolition*, Centre for Economic Policy Research, 1987).) No one seems to have been able to convince Mrs Thatcher that all these subsidies and privileges do not in the end benefit the young suburban couple of Tory fantasy, but spill over into high land prices and interest rates. The combination was too often one of strident rhetoric and timid or irrelevant action.

One source of the problem was the misuse by the Thatcher Government of its post-Falklands popularity. Instead of formulating a coherent programme for its second term to cope with the problems of unemployment, social security and public spending, which it had failed to resolve in its first term, the Thatcher Government rushed into an election in 1983, a year too early. Mrs Thatcher and her advisers suppressed all discussion of these difficult issues – a Central Policy Review Staff paper on public spending in 1982 suffered the equivalent of a public burning – and the Government won a second term without any programme. A few extra seats were temporarily gained, which were occupied by nervous MPs for whom realism meant more handouts. We had the image of severity and the reality of appeasement of interest groups from the Lord's Day Observance Society to the motor industry lobby.

Similar mistakes were made in 1987, when the Thatcher Government again rushed into an election one year before its second term had elapsed. The length and complication of the 1987 Conservative manifesto were not a sign of radicalism, but a substitute for it. The tortuous proposals for schools, housing, local government and urban development were an attempt to find administrative substitutes for genuine market solutions (such as phased rent decontrol of new tenancies or a secondary market in existing ones) from which the Conservative leadership continued to shrink.

Appeasement of interest groups is a normal failing of parliamentary or presidential democracies. The Thatcher Government did not perform here either very much better or very much worse than previous British Governments or the governments of other Western countries, although no doubt the mix of interests it supported was slightly different.


## 5.   COPING WITH INTEREST GROUPS

### (a)  Businessmen's economics

A general climate inimical to market forces in just those areas where they do most good, still persists in most countries irrespective of the political colour of government. The existence of this climate highlights a widespread and misleading confusion between market liberalism and what may be usefully called 'businessmen's economics'. (The latter is virtually identical with what David Henderson calls 'Do It Yourself Economics'.)[51] Because both market liberals and many businessmen are opposed to collectivism and recognise the profitability test, an identity of interest is often mistakenly supposed. This misconception is reinforced by the fact that free market think-tanks are largely funded from business sources.

Such misunderstandings give rise to frustration and disappointment on both sides. Many instances were cited in the Prologue of the difference between market liberalism and characteristic business demands. Since that was written, most of my professional disputes in my day-to-day work as an economic journalist have been with businessmen, who have no more conception than the average socialist politician of a self-regulating economic order co-ordinated by markets and prices, and whose idea of free enterprise policies is that the government should back national enterprises with financial support, special favours and deterrents to foreigners. One of the most sophisticated business leaders began a lunchtime conversation by asking what I had against British industry. This was based on the fact that I favoured a neutral policy towards different sectors rather than special government favours for manufacturers at the expense of the rest of the economy.

Here are just a few examples of businessmen's economics from the wealth of instances given by Henderson:

**Manifest destiny.** The idea that a country or group such as the EEC is destined to be a key producer or exporter of products ranging from food to aerospace. One example is from a government official turned businessman, who complains, 'As a nation we have not succeeded in setting up an effective nuclear construction company'.[52]

**Structure snobbery.** This is the view that some sectors of economic activity are inherently superior or inferior. It is exemplified by the following quotation from Alfred Eckes, a former chairman of the US International Trade Commission – unfortunately one of many thousands that could be given:

> I really don't believe myself that this nation is going to become a nation of hamburger stands, Chinese restaurants, laundries, banks and computer operators. I think we have to have some sort of manufacturing sector.

**Mercantilism.** The view that an increase in exports or reduction in imports must be to a country's advantage.

**Unreflecting centralism.** The view that 'we', meaning the government, have to decide everything, from what to do 'when oil runs out' to whether to be self-sufficient in coal or allow imports. Holders of this view assume that 'competition in markets of the world is between states and that only large states can engage in it'.[53]

All the above are primitive fallacies which one does not have to be a *laissez-faire* fanatic to reject. Why, for instance, should the Cabinet determine the size of the nuclear power programme, the choice of reactor, or the structure of the nuclear industry? In the much smaller Swiss electrical power system, the choice of reactor is made by the utilities concerned and two different systems are in successful operation.

Examples of mercantilism are legion including the arm-twisting of motor companies such as Ford, Vauxhall, and especially Nissan, to buy British components. Other examples are the Buy British policy in the public sector of which Thatcherite ministers actually boasted, or the 'Voluntary Export Restriction' forced on Japanese and less developed country exporters of cars, consumer electronics or textiles.

The most frustrating aspect of the whole debate is that businessmen argue that market economists are cynical and myopic, while they are the long-sighted statesmen. Readers who are in doubt about who is right are strongly advised to study Henderson's small and comprehensive book for themselves. But I cannot omit his assessment (based on close study)[54] of the Concorde aircraft and the UK second nuclear programme as 'two of the worst civil investment decisions in the history of mankind, the third being the Soviet counterpart of Concorde' Nor can I omit his reminder that, although import restrictions are often advocated to protect the poorly paid or workers threatened unemployment, in reality many of the restrictions impinge particularly heavily on the least well off. 'I doubt whether the shirts from Bangladesh which HMG has been so concerned to restrict, would have been sold through Harrods'.

It is because of their mercantilist presuppositions that so many businessmen have responded to the unemployment problem, not by seeking to recreate a functioning labour market, but by campaigns such as *Better Made in Britain*. Why not 'Better made in Yorkshire', or 'Better made in Colorado'? 'Buy national' campaigns in different countries lead to no net gain in jobs, but make all of us poorer through a reduction in the gains from trade. Perhaps I differ from most New Right economists in finding these activities far more shocking than the excesses – and there are some – of welfare spending.

Because the mercantilist fallacy is so widespread, it is worth spelling out just why boosting exports or cutting imports will not create the jobs it is supposed to do.

The basic fallacy is to look at the first impact only and to forget that the balance of payments must balance. The extent of the deficit or surplus on current account depends on the net inward or outward movement of overseas investment funds. An export boost or import curb does nothing to change the basic capital flow. So other exports will be crowded out, or imports crowded in, to maintain the same balance on current account; and the initial stimulus to output and jobs will be offset. (Under flexible rates the process may involve an exchange rate appreciation; under fixed rates it may involve a lower rate of inflation relative to overseas competitors.) Crowding out can also occur if import restrictions raise prices and leave domestic consumers with less to spend, or if export subsidies are financed by taxes which also reduce spending power.

If the imports which are restricted are materials or components for other export or import-competing industries, the costs of production of these latter industries will also rise, undermining their competitive power. Last on the list: the countries harmed by export subsidies or import restraint may retaliate. Even if they do not, they will have less to spend on their own imports from the rest of the world.

A sophisticated mercantilist would admit that the current trade balance would be unlikely to change much as a result of intervention. But he would say that the balance might be achieved at a higher level of activity. The benefit from import restraints, he would claim, would be taken out, not in a lower volume of actual imports, but in an increase in the level of output associated with the same level of imports. (This was the contention of Wynne Godley's Cambridge Economic Policy Group, active in the 1970s and early 1980s.)

This amounts to treating import restraints or export subsidies as a Keynesian stimulus to activity, selectively administered. (We can leave aside the subordinate technical question as to whether it would have to be backed by a monetary or fiscal relaxation.) The question then arises: if it is safe to stimulate demand, why not do so directly instead of via the mercantilist backdoor with its adverse impact on prices and efficiency, not to speak of international relations? (It is safe to stimulate demand only if unemployment is above the Non-Accelerating Inflation Rate of Unemployment, known as the NAIRU. This is explained in Chapter 2 above, pp. 150–62, under the heading 'minimum level of unemployment', an earlier and less ungainly name for the same idea.)

Under a floating exchange rate, a stimulus induced by export subsidies might appear less inflationary than a domestic stimulus because depreciation is avoided. But a better alternative is to run a lower rate of inflation than competitor countries before administering a domestic stimulus. If this is difficult, or the stimulus is unsafe itself, it is a sign that the problems lie in the domestic labour market. A mercantilist stance is likely to make labour and product marked rigidities worse rather than better by insulating domestic markets from international competitive pressures.

## (b) Deficiencies of pork barrel politics

Although arguments should always be answered in good faith, it is also necessary to look further at the forces behind them. For mercantilist policies are but one example of the influence of interest groups of all kinds, which are the biggest obstacle to market liberalism. Many political practitioners, and even quite a few political theorists, believe that politics is essentially about accommodating interest groups – farmers, industrialists, trade unionists, consumers, house-buyers and so on – and that political wisdom consists in finding the right compromise between them. The respectable name for this theory is 'political pluralism'; a more graphic name is 'pork barrel politics'.

What is wrong with accommodating interest groups as a general proposition? One real harm is that interest groups usually make their claims, not on their fellow citizens, but via demands on governments. This approach encourages the notion of government as a universal provider that can create something out of nothing: the government as Santa Claus or Good King Wenceslas who could distribute food and wine to the peasant if he chose to do so. Thus government becomes a universal scapegoat since it cannot satisfy simultaneously the incompatible demands of rival groups.

Secondly, even if the myth of government as universal provider of free lunches could be dispelled, and interest groups realised that their demands were on their fellow citizens, unnecessary impoverishment would still result.

Horse trading between interest groups does not produce a healthy compromise. Each party is likely to be given some concession, the cost of which is spread over the whole community, and thus seems only mildly damaging to the individual citizen. One group may be granted a tariff on foreign imports, another protection from the threat of new domestic entrants, a third a delay in the introduction of new methods or deliberate over-manning (called 'work sharing') to keep up employment. One group may receive an injection of public money to finance a wage increase unavailable in the market; another large section will receive rent controls and subsidies, thus leading to permanent housing shortage, and another large group 'mortgage concessions' leading to over-investment in dwellings.

But the harm done by the sum total of these restrictive practices and special deals is very far from mild. Each of us suffers from the concession to the groups to which we do not belong. We would all be better off in the not-so-long-term if we could achieve the only horse-trading worth obtaining, that is, an agreement by every group to relinquish its special privileges on the understanding that other groups did the same.

(It should be stressed that the appointment of spokesmen for wide-ranging groups such as consumers or home-owners makes matters worse rather than better. Such spokesmen are all too inclined to press for policies such as 'price controls' or 'mortgage tax relief', which are in the end detrimental to the welfare of the community and thus to the people they claim to represent.)

Politics has naturally always had a large element of 'pork barrel' and 'feeding trough' about it. This characteristic was especially true in the USA where 'pluralist' (that is, interest-group) political theory and free-market economics developed, side by side, in splendid isolation. The 'pork barrel' does little harm when government activities and aspirations, and popular expectations of their results, are modest. But when government is the dominant force it is today, 'pork barrel politics' makes for a vast politicisation of life.

As the profitability of a firm becomes more heavily dependent on official decisions, resources begin to be diverted from production to lobbying or 'rent seeking' as it is now called in the economic literature. (Rent in the economist's sense is a payment over and above the minimum required to induce a person or company to carry out his function.) One man prospers because his corporation is subsidised at the critical moment, while another goes bankrupt because he fails to persuade officials that his management is enlightened enough. This type of political auctioneering – and the excessive expectations from collective action that it engenders – poses a grave threat to the functioning of the economy, and, for that reason, a threat to individual freedom and popular government as well.

Most genuine reforms normally involve a jolt to some group or other, even if no more than a shock to traditional habits and reactions. The main political reason for economic inefficiency and slow growth in an advanced industrial country is the special privileges claimed and demanded by hordes of special interest groups.

In the housing market, for example, any worthwhile reform would bring (at least initially) higher rents for tenants and higher tax payments for owner-occupiers. Even though most people would gain from the consequent reduction in basic tax rates, from lower house prices and reduced distortions in the housing market, and from the increased mobility of labour and hence increase in jobs, the immediate impact on the mortgage-holder and tenant will attract most attention. It is not surprising that governments run away from such reforms and pledge themselves to maintain tax exemption on mortgage interest and (sometimes) to hold down rents and interest rates on mortgages – actions which, however attractive to people looking for costless gifts, make the real problems worse.

Interest groups have become extremely good at finding high-sounding titles for their special privilege. A subsidy to home-owners, financed by taxes on people who are on average worse off, becomes easier to advocate if it is called a 'policy for housing'. Subsidies for unprofitable industries, or new industrial projects with little prospect of paying their way, are more easily maintained if they can be disguised as 'industrial policies' or 'a strategy for advanced technology'.

Special privileges arise because each particular government favour has a large beneficial effect on one group, while the cost is spread thinly over the population. But in the end the cost of the sum of all the separate privileges mounts, both fiscally and in terms of economic waste. Moreover, the benefits often spill over to groups other than the intended ones. The intended benefit of tax relief for new home-buyers is received instead by owners of existing property who benefit from the resulting high level of house prices. The intended benefits of agricultural support for farmers are eroded by increase in land prices and rents.

*Tax reform*

As the above example shows, the power of interest groups is the main obstacle to tax reform. I have preferred to put the issue directly, rather than treat tax reform as a technocratic way of improving performance, which experts have prepared and politicians or bureaucrats are too blinkered to implement.

There is no way by which 40 or 50 per cent of the national income can be taken away painlessly in taxes and National Insurance contributions. Reshuffling the way in which these sums are paid is hardly the key to releasing human energies. A shift from direct to indirect taxes could actually make it more difficult to control public spending. Income tax has at least the virtue of being visible. The impact of taxes on goods and services is lost in all the many forces determining prices, as the effects of the Common Agricultural Policy are on food prices.

The three areas crying out for attention are: tax rates above 50 per cent at the top, which yield no net revenues and serve chiefly to satisfy envy; similar and higher implicit tax rates at the bottom, which constitute the poverty and unemployment traps; and the mass of special interest privileges in the middle. The envy factor has to be tackled head-on. The poverty and unemployment traps involve choices about redistribution, and they are discussed explicitly below rather than buried in supposedly technical tax reform issues. Similarly, the removal of special privileges in a Comprehensive Income Tax or, alternatively, their generalisation to everyone via an Expenditure Tax, involves finding a strategy for neutralising the opposition of the beneficiaries, and is best discussed in political economy rather than fiscal terms.

## (c) Buying out interest groups

A case-by-case attempt to root out interest group privilege runs into well-known political problems. The key to success is to recognise that a whole host of such privileges – whether the right to a council house at below-market rents, protection of industries from Japanese or l.d.c. competition, or tax exemptions for pension funds or mortgage holders – have become *de facto* property rights.

In the earlier discussion of just entitlements, I was not able to accept that Nozick, or anyone else, had proved that existing property rights, even of a conventional kind were just. But as a matter of *fact* people cling with extraordinary tenacity to a wide range of what they regard as entitlements going well beyond what the law regards as property. The longer these entitlements have existed, the more any attempt to abolish or reduce them seems to disappoint legitimate expectations, just as the confiscation of conventional property rights would do.

Recognition of claims to tax benefits, welfare state entitlements or international trade protection as formal property rights would have one great advantage. Property rights are tradable in the market-place, and the introduction of exchange leads to a great enlargement both in personal opportunity and economic efficiency.

Two groups of trade-off can be envisaged with interest group property rights. There is what I call the Big Trade-off. This recognises that all of us belong to some interest group. If one group of beneficiaries, such as home-buyers, or industries suffering from import competition, is singled out for repeal, there will be a partially justified outcry. But if all groups are attacked simultaneously, there are the makings of a deal. Farmers and industrialists, home-owners and council tenants, pension and life assurance funds all give something, but gain as well.

If all these privileges are removed simultaneously, there is a good chance of the representative citizen gaining in tax cuts or other benefits what he loses in interest group support. More important, the total gain to economic efficiency will be large enough to make a difference to him personally. There is an analogy here with multilateral disarmament. All countries would be better off with a balanced reduction in weapons of death, whereas no one country dare move alone.

There are obvious political risks in a Big Trade-off. Although, in principle, it should be able to attract a large coalition of voters, it would take great skill and luck for a party proposing it not to alienate most of the electorate. This kind of bargain is normally attempted after defeat or destruction in war, after a hyperinflation or depression, or after the tax burden has become unsupportable, or when the country is effectively in the hands of foreign creditors.

These difficulties make it all the more important to take advantage of the smaller trade-offs which become possible once interest group privileges become marketable property rights. These involve underwriting the distributional gains of favoured groups, while introducing the benefits of trade and removing restrictions on freely negotiated contracts.

An example is tenancies held at below market rents, whether because of rent control in the private sector, or because they are council homes. The problem with rent decontrol is that it would only increase the supply of rented housing if it were expected to last. Political unpopularity arises because sudden decontrol does leave existing tenants worse off. A scheme that could overcome opposition would have to avoid the distributional change and yield benefits quickly, and preferably in marketable form.

A plan for doing just this, which I suggested in the late 1970s, was later revised and developed by another author, Martin Ricketts, in 1986.[55] This is that rights to rent-controlled property should be specified exactly and then made tradable. Ricketts suggests that the property rights should generally be for five to ten years, confined to unfurnished accommodation, and to tenants who have been in occupation for a minimum period. For council tenants the occupancy rights could be lifetime ones. Final decontrol would arrive as the leases ran out. But well before that a flourishing market in secondary letting would arise, either directly or through financial intermediaries.

In 1985, some 11 per cent of households were in privately rented homes and 27 per cent in council tenancies – making 38 per cent in all. These householders had effective property rights in the right to occupancy – at below market rents – of their property. But because these rights were not transferable, they were not seen as property rights at all. The suggested change would thus do more to complete the transformation into a nation of property-owning and to deproletarianise council tenants than almost any other measure.

The reason why tradable occupancy rights might amount to a very cheap lunch from a policy viewpoint is that a restriction is removed. A willing existing occupant and a willing secondary tenant agree to an exchange which is to the advantage of both, but was previously not permitted.

Any measure of rent deregulation will, however, have its full effects only if privileges for owner-occupiers are also reduced. What they are needs a little explanation.

A landlord investing in rented property has to pay tax on his income from rents. But if he lives, himself, in identical property, he will not pay any tax on the annual value of the house. There used to be a tax on imputed rentable values, known as Schedule A; but it fell behind realistic market levels and was abolished in a Conservative 'reform' of 1963. There is thus now a strong distortion in favour of owning and against renting.

The argument for phasing out mortgage interest relief is a second-best one put forward in the knowledge that taxes on imputed non-cash income are even more politically unpopular than taxation of mortgage interest.

A minimal reform well within the realm of the politically possible in the late 1980s in the UK was the abolition of mortgage interest relief against the higher rates of tax in return for a cut in these rates themselves. The latter stuck out badly as internationally uncompetitive after the US tax reform of 1986. But so great was Prime Minister Thatcher's attachment to mortgage interest relief as a result of her emotional involvement with house purchasers that the odds were stacked even against this very modest reform while she was in office; and it will be a hard struggle to secure it under her successor.

## 6.   UK PERFORMANCE

It is time to come back more broadly to the Thatcher record. Here is one characteristic verdict. 'The record on inflation, the reform of trade union practices and the march of privatisation are major political achievements . . . The foreign policy successes in Zimbabwe, Hong Kong and Ireland also reflect . . . political skills and courage'. But 'there is a darker side to Thatcherism: the neglect of inner cities, the rundown in public services and the insistence that the worst off members of society, notably the unemployed, should bear all the burdens of change'.

This notably fair-minded assessment by Adam Raphael,[56] a journalist who describes himself as part of 'the postwar welfare consensus' would be accepted by many political observers of all persuasions. If anything, the positive side is too favourable. The record on inflation, although good by British standards, is no better than the international average. The reform of unions is less spectacular than sometimes supposed; and privatisation warrants but one cheer. The darker side, too, also looks different on closer examination.

Spending on the public services has risen in real terms, not fallen; but the many complaints of rundown can hardly be all imagination. The public services may be suffering from the refusal, either to spend a great deal more on them, or to provide much greater incentives for private provision for those who can afford to. Inner cities are suffering from the colossal housing muddle, comparable to the Common Agricultural Policy (CAP), already discussed. But there is also a social element which US experience has shown is unlikely to be tackled by public housing and infrastructure investment alone.

## (a) Poverty and distribution

But how about the burden on the worst off, which can be more nearly be approximated by statistical estimates? Amidst the clamour of the poverty lobby and its opponents, there have been some still small voices, e.g. those of C. M. Morris and I. Preston, who carried out a careful research programme.[57] Their own political outlook is very similar to Raphael's; but their research is a model of statistical scrupulousness. For instance, family units are adjusted for family size and housing expenditure is excluded, in accordance with best practice in this area.

These authors found a clear increase in the degree of income concentration (a less value-laden word than 'inequality'). The top 30 per cent received 53.58 per cent of all incomes before tax in 1968, when Labour was in office. This had increased to 55.58 per cent by 1977, another Labour year. By 1983, during the Thatcher Government, the top 30 per cent were obtaining 60.47 per cent. The figures after tax and benefit show a similar tendency, but much dampened. The top 30 per cent received on this basis 47.94 per cent of all household incomes in 1968, 48.56 per cent in 1977 and 51.01 per cent in 1983.

In parallel with the shift towards those at the top, there was a shift away from those at the bottom. In 1968, the bottom 30 per cent (many of whom are retired or unemployed) received 9.84 per cent of all household incomes before tax and benefit. In 1977 their share was down to 6.87 per cent and in 1983 it reached 3.76 per

*Table* 5    Income shares (per cent)

| Percentiles | 1983 | | 1977 | | 1968 | |
| | Final | Original | Final | Original | Final | Original |
|---|---|---|---|---|---|---|
| 1–10 | 3.12 | 0.00 | 3.21 | 0.00 | 3.50 | 0.31 |
| 11–20 | 4.75 | 0.36 | 5.15 | 1.76 | 5.48 | 3.66 |
| 21–30 | 5.92 | 3.40 | 6.48 | 5.11 | 6.72 | 5.87 |
| 31–40 | 7.01 | 6.14 | 7.52 | 7.16 | 7.63 | 7.24 |
| 41–50 | 8.17 | 8.04 | 8.54 | 8.63 | 8.55 | 8.42 |
| 51–60 | 9.35 | 9.87 | 9.64 | 10.05 | 9.52 | 9.71 |
| 61–70 | 10.67 | 11.73 | 10.91 | 11.70 | 10.67 | 11.21 |
| 71–80 | 12.33 | 14.20 | 12.52 | 13.80 | 12.15 | 13.05 |
| 81–90 | 15.03 | 17.72 | 14.81 | 16.80 | 14.20 | 15.72 |
| 91–100 | 23.65 | 28.55 | 21.23 | 24.98 | 21.59 | 24.81 |

*Source* J. Kay and C. M. Morris, *Fiscal Studies* (November 1986).

cent. After tax and benefits the share of the bottom 30 per cent also declined but by much less. It fell from 15.70 per cent in 1968 and 14.84 per cent in 1977, to 13.79 per cent in 1983 (see Table 5).

Thus, although the shift was in the same direction both before and after tax and benefit, the latter shift was very much less. The implication is that the tax and benefit system was quite an effective redistributive agent during a period of great change. Benefits did not become more generous – in fact the Thatcher Government substituted indexation to inflation for the (more generous) indexation to earnings previously in force. The point is that the proportion of both retired and unemployed people increased, thereby reducing gross incomes at the bottom, but also increasing payments of benefit. A further factor was a much greater take-up as claimants learned their rights to supplementary and other means-tested benefits.

Poverty is, of course, not the same as concentration or inequality. Morris and Preston also estimate poverty in the absolute sense. They follow one widespread convention by defining those living below the Supplementary Benefit (SB) level as being in poverty. They apply it not to the SB level of the year in question, but throughout to that for 1983. This neatly avoids the trap whereby an increase in SB generosity appears to increase poverty, and vice versa. The 1983 levels are adjusted back to earlier years both on the basis of the Retail Prices Index (RPI),

*Table* 6  Poverty measures (per cent)

|      | 'Absolute' poverty line | | 'Relative' poverty line | |
|------|:----------:|:------------------:|:----------:|:------------------:|
|      | Proportion in poverty | Income shortfall per head | Proportion in poverty | Income shortfall per head |
| 1968 | 11.4 | 2.9 | 4.1 | 1.3 |
| 1977 | 11.6 | 3.2 | 7.7 | 2.2 |
| 1983 | 9.9 | 2.5 | 9.9 | 2.5 |

*Source* J. Kay and C. M. Morris, *Fiscal Studies* (November 1986).

which gives figures of 'absolute poverty', and according to average earnings which gives 'relative' poverty. Table 6 shows that absolute poverty had on this particular definition fallen under the Thatcher Government while relative poverty had increased.

The reader may feel that these moderately reassuring figures conflict with the evidence of his eyes. For instance, there appear to be many more down-and-outs of all ages on the streets of London than before, and more 'buskers' (itinerant musicians) in the London Underground. There is clearly far more involved here than social security levels and pay rates. Other problems include the distorted housing market, more movement to the metropolis by those without means of support, drugs and a general aggravation of the problems of urban life.

Without pretending to solve these, one can still ask a question based on the above tables. Was it necessary for the poorest to have slipped in their relative position? Could they have shared in the general prosperity without reducing national income per head? My tentative answer to the last question now would be 'yes' for the 10 per cent or so shown to be in poverty and 'probably yes' for the next 20 per cent. The right way to have made this redistribution would certainly not have been to have kept the confiscatory marginal tax rates of 83 per cent on earned income and 98 per cent on investment income prevailing in 1979 when Labour left office. The increase in tax revenue from the very top since these high rates were cut to 60 per cent confirms that they were counterproductive.

The resources to help the poor and least well off would have had to come from the bulk of citizens who pay tax at around, or only just above, the basic rate of tax. But they need not have involved higher rates of either income tax or taxes on consumer products.

There are untapped sources: potential savings in special interest subsidies on everything ranging from domestic agricultural support (not all required by the CAP) to the phasing out of owner-occupier subsidies, not to mention a vast miscellany of smaller giveaways from the Forestry Programme to the motor industry. There are also many social security benefits, such as child benefits, which largely go to those well above the poverty line – and this is without bringing in highly controversial questions about the need for universal state pensions, which are effectively tax financed, to those with ample resources. Redistribution and incentive alike would be satisfied by a combination of generous, but selective, benefits, a fairly high but non-progressive income tax rate, and some redistribution of capital (to be discussed in the final section). The gainers would be both the 'wealth creators' at the top and the poor at the bottom: the losers, at least at first, the mass of voters in the middle.

## (b) The unemployment explosion

One of the main reasons for the decline in original income shares of the bottom 30 per cent of the population, and the greater burden thereby placed on the benefit system was, of course, the rise in unemployment from the 1.5 to 3 per cent range which had been normal in the Golden Age up to 1973. It rose to 5 to 6 per cent during the Labour Government of the 1970s, and then exploded to over 10 per cent in the first three years of the Thatcher Government. The rise then continued for a while at a slower rate, but unemployment was still nearly 11 per cent on international definitions in the winter of 1986–7.

In terms of actual numbers out of work, the British total shot up from 600 000 in 1973 to over 3 million in 1986–7, on a seasonally adjusted basis, excluding school-leavers. This was despite a number of changes in coverage, classification and registration procedures, which probably only reduced the total by 200 000 or 300 000 but were counterproductive in exciting public suspicion of the veracity of the official figures.

The high level of unemployment has led to a predictable polarisation of attitudes. To collectivists it has been a long delayed confirmation of the inadequacies of the market system. To the New Right it has been a sign that not only union power, and economic regulation, but the welfare state and public spending, have reached unsupportable levels. The polarisation of attitudes has been much less reflected in government behaviour. For left-wing governments are inhibited by international financial markets, and right-wing governments by electoral attachment to welfare spending, from embarking on very radical changes.

*The UK economic record*

The upsurge in unemployment reflected in part a slowdown in growth after 1973, which was a world-wide experience worth a digression. Comparisons between different parts of the world and different periods of history are shown in Tables 7 to 10. Growth rates are shown over cyclically comparable periods between business cycle peaks.

An aide-memoire to a few key events may help in interpreting the tables. The period 1971–3 saw the collapse of the post-war

*Table 7*   UK rates of growth
(% change – annual rates)

|  | Real GDP[1] | Output per person employed[2] | Real personal disp. income |
|---|---|---|---|
| 1955–64 | 2.8 | n.a. | 3.5 |
| 1964–73 | 3.0 | 2.7 | 3.2 |
| 1973–79 | 1.3 | 1.1 | 1.6 |
| 1979–87 | 1.8 | 2.0 | 2.0 |

1. Based on average data
2. Based on output data
n.a.–n.t. available

*Sources* OECD, CSO, Treasury and author estimates.

*Table 8*   International growth rates
(real GDP % change – annual rates)

|  | OECD Europe | USA | Japan |
|---|---|---|---|
| 1964–73 | 4.7 | 3.7 | 8.9 |
| 1973–79 | 2.4 | 2.6 | 3.6 |
| 1979–87 | 1.7 | 2.1 | 3.6 |

*Sources* OECD, CSO, Treasury and author estimates.

*Table* 9    Inflation[1] (average annual rates)
(peak and trough years)

|      | UK   | OECD Europe | Germany | USA  | Japan |
|------|------|-------------|---------|------|-------|
| 1967 | 2.5  | 3.3         | 1.4     | 2.8  | 4.0   |
| 1974 | 16.1 | 13.3        | 7.0     | 11.0 | 24.5  |
| 1975 | 24.2 | 13.2        | 6.0     | 9.1  | 11.8  |
| 1978 | 8.3  | 9.3         | 2.7     | 7.7  | 3.8   |
| 1980 | 18.1 | 14.3        | 5.5     | 13.5 | 8.0   |
| 1986 | 3.4  | 3.8         | −0.2    | 2.0  | 0.4   |

1.  RPI for UK; consumption deflator for other countries.

*Sources* OECD, CSO, Treasury estimates

*Table* 10    Unemployment
(% of total labour force)[1]

|      | UK[2] | EEC  | USA | Japan |
|------|-------|------|-----|-------|
| 1973 | 2.1   | 2.9  | 4.8 | 1.3   |
| 1976 | 4.5   | 5.0  | 7.6 | 2.0   |
| 1977 | 4.8   | 5.4  | 6.9 | 2.0   |
| 1979 | 4.3   | 5.7  | 5.8 | 2.1   |
| 1982 | 9.8   | 9.6  | 9.5 | 2.4   |
| 1986 | 11.5  | 11.0 | 6.9 | 2.8   |

1.  OECD figures, partially standardised.
2.  UK series on 1987 definition. This is comparable with the OECD for 1986.

*Sources* OECD, CSO, Treasury estimates.

Bretton Woods system of semi-fixed exchange rates. In 1971 President Nixon abolished the residual commitment to convert official dollar holdings into gold, and engineered a dollar devaluation at the Smithsonian Agreement. Early in 1973 the Smithsonian Agreement collapsed and the major nations of the world moved to floating exchange rates.

The year 1973 also saw the first explosion in oil prices. In 1979 there was a second, and almost as great an oil price explosion, associated with the desposition of the Shah of Iran; and in May of that year, a Conservative Government under Mrs Thatcher was elected in the UK. In 1979, too, Paul Volcker was appointed chairman of the Federal Reserve Board, with an anti-inflationary mandate, by the Democratic President, Jimmy Carter. Ronald Reagan was elected president of the USA in November 1980. (He was subsequently re-elected for a second and final term due to expire at the end of 1988.) In the second half of 1982 the debt crisis of the developing countries burst on the scene, which continued up to the time of writing to be contained on a case-by-case basis. The dollar soared to a peak in the spring of 1985, and was helped on its way down by the agreement of the Group of Five Finance Ministers at the New York Plaza Hotel in September of that year. In 1986 the oil price collapsed and, although the Organization of Petroleum Exporting Countries (OPEC) oil producers managed a partial restoration of the cartel at the end of that year, the dollar price of oil remained less than half of its peak level of 1981.

There is no escaping the pivotal nature of 1973, which marked the end of the Golden Age of post-war growth and full employment. Growth rates subsequently fell by at least half throughout the industrial world, including Japan (see Tables 7 & 8). The notorious growth gap between Britain and the rest of Europe did look as if it might be disappearing in the 1980s, but only because European growth rates fell even more than British ones. Absolute levels of output and living standards in Britain remained slightly below the Western European average. (If use is made of purchase power, rather than market exchange rates, GDP per head in Germany was 14 per cent higher than in the UK in 1986. In France it was 9 per cent higher. These discrepancies are much smaller than often supposed.

Throughout the world, the creeping inflation of the post-war period gave way to the alarmingly high inflation rates of the 1970s, of which the oil price explosions were as much an effect as a cause (see Table 9). Britain suffered worse inflation than Europe and the USA during this period. But by the late 1980s inflation throughout the world had been reduced to very low – in some countries negligible or even negative – rates. The figures for 1986 give an exaggerated impression because of the once-for-all impact of the sharp fall in oil and commodity prices, but even underlying inflation rates were lower than before the collapse of Bretton

Woods. Despite talk of 'doctrinaire monetarism' in the early years of the Thatcher Adminstration, British inflation rates, both actual and underlying, remained at about the European average, but a good couple of percentage points above those of Germany and Japan.

The great blow that befell the industrial economies, especially those of Europe, was the seemingly inexorable rise in unemployment, both when inflation was rising and when it was falling (see Table 10). (Even in Japan it has been creeping upwards annually, although from low levels.) Only in the USA did high unemployment look like a temporary price to be paid for reducing inflation. In common with Europe, the USA experienced a sharp rise in unemployment in the 1982 recession, itself partly induced by the Fed's tight money policies. But once inflation had subsided, US unemployment recovered, if not to its Golden Age levels, at least to the rates of the mid-1970s. The USA was thus the only country showing the classic signs of a short-term trade-off between inflation and unemployment of an augmented Philips curve kind (see Chapter 2, pp. 150–62).

Some of the smaller European countries, including some Scandinavian ones, Austria and Switzerland, did manage to keep unemployment well below the area average shown in Table 10. This led some economists to conclude, rather rashly, that the key to avoiding stagflation was corporatism – that is, centralised setting of pay by powerful unions and employers organisations, which are then also highly influential in other areas of policy.[58]

There are several weaknesses about this thesis; the most glaring being that other small corporatist countries – namely those of Benelux – were near the top of the European unemployment league. Corporatism in the countries where it has seemed to work has been part of a wider political consensus – in Austria in response to the near Civil War of the 1930s and the post-war struggle to end the Occupation. Even so, Austria was beginning to find the cost of using the state-owned industries for make-work purposes prohibitively expensive, not to speak of other ways in which the country was losing its model status.

None of which is to deny that countries with strongly established traditions of collective bargaining, and with highly-independent unions, such as Britain, appear at a disadvantage in fighting stagflation compared alike to countries such as the USA, with weak unions and more atomistic labour markets, and to Japan with its relatively tame company unions, and to small countries with highly-centralised union movements with which bargains can be struck.

As for growth: if we compare the Thatcher period of 1976–87, with the previous cyclically comparable period of 1973–9, largely under Labour rule, the growth rates are comparable. Inflation came down more in the Thatcher period; but, after an early few years in which inflation first rose and then fell very sharply, the movement came back into line with world-wide developments.

The big difference between the Thatcher and the Heath–Wilson–Callaghan period was that productivity in the conventional sense of output per head rose faster under Thatcher (and future revisions of the statistics are likely to increase this discrepancy), although it did not recover to Golden Age rates of increase. Unfortunately, the improvement in productivity compared with 1973–9 went to waste in a faster rise in unemployment.

In the second half of 1986, British unemployment started to fall gradually, as far as one could make out through the fog of statistical charges and more stringent registration requirements. But even if this fall reflected more than a temporary boom or the once-for-all effects of community and training programmes, there was a very long way to go before unemployment moved out of the 'low millions'. The main case to be made in favour of the Thatcher experiment nearly eight years after it started, in terms of the real economy, was thus still speculative and forward looking – namely, that *if* unemployment continued to fall (other than through taking people off the register or on to emergency programmes) it might provide the foundation for better growth performance in years ahead, despite the rundown of North Sea oil production.

## (c) Steering the nation's finances

The basic changes in the principles of economic management popularity associated with Thatcherism all started several years earlier. The rejection of the belief that governments can spend their way into full employment came under James Callaghan and Denis Healey during the Labour Government and hit the headlines in 1976. The International Monetary Fund (IMF) was the scapegoat, not the cause, of the turnround. Money supply controls, targets for reduced government borrowing, and attempts to stabilise the share of public spending in GNP all date from 1975 or 1976. Indeed the words 'New Realism' were first used by Peter Jay to describe the Callaghan policies when Ambassador in the USA in 1977–9. Many of the sentences and sentiments of the Howe-Lawson Medium Term Financial Strategy were foreshadowed in the Letter to the IMF written in December 1976, by Labour Chancellor Denis Healey – which was written with much more conviction than Healey afterwards chose to admit.[59]

For the Thatcher Government which came to office amidst the collapse of Labour pay policy, and commitments to 'Clegg' pay rises in the public sector, incomes policy was not an option at the beginning. Its subsequent refusal to countenance pay controls (even via the fiscal system) and rely only on exhortation did however mark a break with immediately preceding governments.

There were, of course, other contrasts between the Callaghan and the Thatcher thinking. The outgoing Labour Government adopted 'sound finance' reluctantly, because it could not see any other option, while the Thatcherite element in the Conservative Government did so out of conviction, amounting in the Prime Minister's personal case to moral certitude. A Labour Government would have been subject to some, if not all, the pressures which pushed the party leftwards in Opposition; and would, almost certainly, have tried to loosen the financial reins earlier than its Conservative successor.

Even if a Labour Government had managed to continue the Callaghan–Healey macro-strategy, it would certainly have become much more agitated at an earlier stage about unemployment than its Conservative successors, and would have intervened much more at a micro-level to keep down the jobless figures. The palliatives would have been a mixture of good and bad. More imagination might have been shown in marginal labour subsidies to try to price particular groups into work and to forestall redundancies. On the other hand, the contraction of manpower in certain industries, needed for long-term structural reasons, might have been delayed further, thus aggravating the underlying problems.

To come back to Thatcher: so far from money supply targets being followed more dogmatically under her Government, they were frequently exceeded, revised upwards and redefined. The first major overshoot occurred as early as 1980, the government's first full year. It is silly to make debating points over these overshoots, as the relationship between specific measures of the money supply and nominal national income, which provided the intellectual foundation of monetary targets, collapsed in most countries, and most spectacularly in the USA and Britain. The question of what to put in their place has still to be satisfactorily resolved in any country, although the reader will find in Chapter 2 (pp. 161–2) – written well before 'monetarism' came into vogue – an emphasis on regulating nominal demand (measured by Nominal GDP) rather than on any particular intermediate indicator. If followed, the suggestion would have saved much confusion.

One well-known and generally admitted error at the start of the Thatcher Administration in its 1979 Budget was the gratuitous 4 percentage points' increase superimposed on the Retail Prices Index (RPI) by a leap in the VAT rate from 8 to 15 per cent, to make room for a cut from 33 to 30 per cent in the basic rate of income tax.[60] This came at a time when the second oil price explosion would in any case have been boosting both prices and inflationary expectations, and when the collapse of the Labour Government's pay policies had triggered off a pay explosion.

The main source, however, of almost all the distinctive economic events, both good and bad, of the Thatcher Administration was the sharp rise in the real sterling exchange rate, which occurred right at the beginning in 1979–81. This was neither intended nor desired, but had the result of transforming what was meant to be a gradualist policy of disinflation into a short, sharp shock. At its peak in January 1981, the sterling index was 25 per cent higher than two years before. This nominal appreciation was superimposed on a pay explosion. Increases in earnings which had started to rise in the later 1970s, after the initial success of Labour's pay limits began to evaporate, reached a peak of 20 per cent in 1980. The pay explosion was aggravated by the notorious pay awards to the public sector workers of the Clegg Commission, set up by Callaghan in the 1979 'winter of discontent' and which all the main political parties understandably but – misguidedly – pledged themselves to implement.

Probably even more important, was the widespread belief at the beginning of the Thatcher era that either financial policy would turn 'accommodative' to finance Clegg-size awards throughout the economy, and/or that a pay freeze was imminent. While in other countries, such as Japan, businessmen and workers accepted that wages could not keep pace with prices during the second oil price shock, no such restraint was shown in the UK until union leaders learned by bitter experience and millions of people had been priced out of work. The Medium Term Financial Strategy, designed to affect expectations in the right direction was not even published until the Budget of 1980 when the peak wage round had already been largely negotiated; and in subsequent years it ran into the credibility problem already mentioned, of being stated in terms of inappropriate measures of money, which had to be overridden.[61]

The sharp rise in sterling was largely an international portfolio movement due to confidence in Britain as an oil producer at a time of world-wide worries about oil supplies, reinforced by the effects of the 'Thatcher factor' on confidence in the UK. It was responsible for the rapid fall in inflation, which took the government's critics and even the official forecasters by surprise; and the resulting pressure on profit margins led to a blitz on overmanning and a productivity spurt in industry. But as the exodus from manufacturing was not offset by sufficient extra jobs elsewhere, and the labour force also grew, the pain took the form of high unemployment.

Even within the context of the Thatcher Government's early domestic monetarism, it might have been possible, as some argued at the time, to provide an exchange rate 'override', so that the monetary targets could be set aside if sterling exceeded certain prescribed limits. This would have put a brake on sterling, via a reduction in interest rates, at an earlier stage than actually occurred, and might have been more fruitful than the arcane arguments about broad and narrow money which preceded the policy switch of 1980–81, when fiscal policy was eventually tightened and interest rates reduced, despite the overshoot of Sterling M3.

### Fiscal policy

I have left fiscal policy until last in this account of Thatcherite economic management, because developments there were much less spectacular than either the government's supporters or opponents supposed, and because of my general dissatisfaction with the way fiscal policy is usually analysed.

Among the mainstream economic establishment, fiscal policy is too often considered in isolation from monetary policy. Many economists condemned the early Thatcher Budgets for being perversely restrictive; and it was the Budget of 1981, which raised taxes in recession, that did more than anything else to inspire the famous letter of 364 economists protesting against government economic policy. These economists ought on their own criteria to have applauded the loosening of fiscal policy later in the 1980s but, of course, they did not. Some supporters of the government's original financial strategy on the other hand thought too much in terms of the debt to national income ratio, which does not provide a sufficient basis for decision for demand management purposes.

To my mind fiscal policy can only be sensibly considered along with monetary policy. Together they influence the movement of nominal demand (usually measured by Nominal GDP, that is, the national income in money terms).

*Table* 11   UK general government balance (% of GDP)*

|  | Change in nominal GDP | Change in RPI | Actual balance | Structural balance | Inflation-adjusted structural balance |
|---|---|---|---|---|---|
| 1978 | 15.4 | 8.3 | −4.2 | −3.7 | 0.4 |
| 1979 | 17.6 | 13.3 | −3.3 | −3.3 | 2.5 |
| 1980 | 16.8 | 18.1 | −3.5 | −1.5 | 4.9 |
| 1981 | 10.0 | 11.9 | −2.8 | +0.7 | 5.0 |
| 1982 | 9.3 | 8.7 | −2.3 | +1.3 | 4.6 |
| 1983 | 8.7 | 4.6 | −3.6 | −0.5 | 1.4 |
| 1984 | 7.1 | 5.0 | −3.9 | −1.2 | 0.6 |
| 1985 | 9.3 | 6.1 | −2.6 | −0.8 | 1.3 |
| 1986[1] | 6.5 | 3.4 | −3.0 | −1.5 | 0.0 |
| 1987[1] | 8.0 | 4.3 | −2.9 | −2.2 | −0.3 |

1. Estimate.
* Applies only to last three columns.

*Sources* OECD, National Income Blue Book, Economic Trends.

As Table 11 shows, after the 1980 oil shock, the Thatcher Government, like most other Western governments, followed a non-accommodating policy, and the growth of Nominal GDP was on a declining trend. (This was despite some modest wobbles associated with the effects on the real activity of the 1984 coal strike and its rebound, and the initially unfavourable effect on world growth of the 1986 oil price fall.) To assess the role of fiscal policy I have used OECD figures for the Budget balance which are not affected by privatisation and other distortions. They reflect international conventions showing higher deficit figures than the British Treasury – excluding not only privatisation proceeds but also the surpluses of the remaining nationalised industries.

I have given the 'inflation adjusted structural balance', for the record, as so many macroeconomists are fond of it. But it is a perverse indicator from the point of view of stabilisation policy. A jump in the inflation rate actually improves the Budget balance on this measure, because of its effect in slashing the real value of the government debt; a measure adjusted in this way thus gives all the wrong immediate policy signals.

The other column giving the 'structural balance' is simply adjusted for the business cycle and is useful for year-to-year changes. But it can be a very misleading indicator over a longer period because of undiagnosed changes in the trend of output or the sustainable level of unemployment. The structural deficit also shows a tightening in the early years and a modest relaxation later.

For making comparisons over a period of years, there is much to be said for taking the unadjusted general government balance, that is, the OECD's measure of the Budget deficit. This had risen to a temporary peak of 5 per cent in 1975, before the Labour Government's agreement with the IMF. By 1979, when the change of government occurred, it was down to 3 to 4 per cent of GDP, where it more or less remained, with a dip during the tight Budget years of 1981–2 and a distortion in both directions before and after the coal strike. Net capital formation was negligible to negative in the government sector. So the deficit was genuine.

As already mentioned, there was a case for a less abrupt fall in the growth of nominal demand than occurred in 1981–2. There is a good deal stronger case against Mrs Thatcher personally for vetoing for so long measures such as full membership of the European Monetary System which might have locked Britain in to a low rate of inflation after the oil and commodity prices fall of 1986. But given the general stance of demand management, the changes in the fiscal-monetary fix are not particularly mysterious or scandalous. The 1981–2 fiscal tightening is best regarded as an offset to a relaxation in monetary policy required to bring down a highly-overvalued exchange rate. Conversely, some loosening in 1985–6 was required to offset the effects of deliberately high interest rates designed to put a brake on the depreciation of sterling at a time of falling oil prices and political uncertainties. The OECD figures probably understate the shift back to fiscal tightness from 1986–87 onwards.

The ratio of the National Debt to GDP remained stable at around 50 per cent since the early 1970s. By then it had fallen very sharply compared not only to the immediate post-war years, but also the interwar period. In contrast to earlier periods, the stability of this ratio in the 1980s owed little to the effect of inflation in devaluing the debt. Thus there seemed little danger of a debt explosion.

*Balance of payments*

The most important structural aspect of budget deficits, is not in my view their effect on debt ratios, but that they represent negative savings. As such they have to be considered in conjunction with private savings and investment trends. They therefore matter much more in a country like the USA, where private savings are low, than in, say, Japan, where they are high. Most European countries come in between.

What are the main effects of an increase in the structural Budget deficit? The traditional view is that they raise interest rates and reduce investment. But with closely-linked international capital markets, the effect is likely to be modified. So long as confidence is maintained, it requires only a small interest rate of differential to attract capital from abroad to plug the gap in domestic savings. (The large interest rate differential against sterling in the middle 1980s reflected not excess Budget deficits, but the market's very reasonable insistence on an insurance premium against the depreciation of sterling.) As the balance of payments must balance, an increase in overseas borrowing must mean an increased current account deficit – or reduced current surplus in the case of a surplus country.

In a nutshell – a Budget deficit large enough to unbalance domestic savings and investment is likely to be met by overseas borrowing and a current payments deficit. Up to a point, which it is extremely difficult to specify in advance, as analysts of the US Budget deficit discovered, the government of the country concerned has a great deal of discretion on whether to be a net overseas borrower or net overseas lender. The decision should depend on the expected duration and purpose of the borrowing. Temporary overseas borrowing by an oil producer to cushion a fall in the oil price makes sense, especially if there had been net overseas investment when the oil price was high. Net long-term borrowing is also sensible for a country developing its resources or building up capital assets, which will create an income to service the debt. But net long-term overseas borrowing to finance government spending makes little sense, although the ability of governments to stay on this path is, as US experience under Reagan shows, greater than the doomsters suppose.

In an advanced industrial country a so-called balance of payments problem is thus a superficial symptom of other failures. There is no balance of payments problem between Texas and California or between Yorkshire and Lancashire. If the US or Britain appears to have such a problem it is due either to deficient domestic savings, amenable to fiscal correction, or to costs and prices out of line with world levels. In the original edition I put great stress on flexible exchange rates as a way of aligning costs and prices to world levels. But subsequent theory and experience alike suggest that depreciation is often likely to be eroded by domestic inflation; and that if pay and prices rise too fast at otherwise reasonable levels of growth and employment, the problem is likely to lie in the labour market, and that exchange rate changes are unlikely to offer a short cut for dealing with it. But my general diagnosis of the balance of payments problems as pseudo or self-created remains.

## 7. THE PROBLEMS OF JOBS AND LOW INCOMES

### (a) Pricing out of work

The excursion just made into monetary, fiscal and balance of payments policy has not unearthed the roots of chronically high unemployment. Why then has the British labour market failed to provide enough jobs to maintain even an approximation to full or high employment? Something has already been said in Chapter 2 about the controversies between the school which blames unemployment on lack of demand, and the view that unemployment results from workers being priced out of jobs. The analysis of that chapter has stood the test of time better than either unreconstructed Keynesianism or technical monetarism.

In principle, either lack of demand or pricing out of work can contribute to unemployment. If there is a collapse in 'demand' – that is, in total spending, or Nominal GDP – one would expect a slump, with people losing their jobs. The most dramatic example was the Great Depression of the 1930s, when the US national income fell by over one-third. Lesser, but still severe, occurred in the USA in the 1982 recession and in Britain in 1980–81, when there was a very sharp reduction in the rate of growth of Nominal GDP, shown in Table 11.

But maintaining an adequate but non-excessive growth of nominal demand is only half, and the less important half, of employment policy.[62] Even if the government and central bank can keep demand within sight of a stable predetermined demand path, there can still be very heavy unemployment if too much of the demand growth is diverted into rising pay and prices, and not enough into output and jobs.

This is indeed what happened in the 1970s and 1980s. Despite occasional under and overshoots, the rate of UK nominal demand growth achieved on average since the trough of the 1980–81 recession would have been amply sufficient to have converted the rise in unemployment into a decline if pay per head had not been rising by 7 to 8 per cent per annum – despite an inflation rate averaging 4 or 5 per cent, and a national productivity increase of 2 per cent.

When it was first suggested that lasting and persistent unemployment was due to excessive pay, and that union collective bargaining tended to destroy jobs, it was treated as a reactionary heresy. But as stagflation and unemployment developed in the 1970s and grew worse in the 1980s, numerous academic studies – which could fill this book several times over – tried to specify in detail the pay jobs relation. Some have concentrated on real pay and some on nominal pay. The most interesting have looked at differentials between age groups, regions and skills, which are not absolutely rigid, but which do not sufficiently reflect changes in relative supply and demand for different workers.

Occam's razor suggests that we focus on the movement of pay and related labour cost *per se*, without prejudging too many issues by putting in front of any the adjectives either 'nominal' or 'real'. The one good point that the opponents of the pricing out theory make is that pay is settled in money terms; and that real wages, in the relevant sense, depend on the profit margin superimposed. In a money economy, pay awards are normally in money terms, which does not mean that people are indifferent to their real value, or will fail to react if their expectations are disappointed.

One interesting intermediate theory is Richard Layard's: he believes that unemployment is caused by union *attempts* to achieve real pay higher than the economic system is capable of delivery. High unemployment is then necessary (although no one may actually will it) to choke off these excessive real pay strivings, which may never in fact be achieved. As Layard has been among the most vocal of critics of the Thatcher approach, and the main force behind the campaigning *Charter for Jobs*, it is worth quoting his diagnosis: 'The fundamental cause of unemployment is wage pressures', which is in turn very much a matter of union strength.[63]

## Europe and the USA

Strong suggestive support for the importance of the pricing-out hypothesis comes from the contrast between the movement of US unemployment and that of Europe. This is even greater than suggested in the tables. Not only was US unemployment in 1987 much smaller at 6 to 7 per cent than the EEC average of 11 per cent. In the words of an OECD study: 'the bulk of USA unemployment was of short duration. In 1985 only 11 per cent of the jobless had been out of work for 12 months or more, compared to 30 to 40 per cent of the large European countries'.[64]

The contrast in unemployment performance was not due to demographic differences. On the contrary, labour force growth was much greater in the USA than in Europe. Indeed, over 30 million jobs were created in the USA in the 1970s and first half of the 1980s. Nor was it due to output differences. Between 1973 and 1985 the average annual growth of real GDP averaged a little over 2 per cent in both the USA and Europe.

The OECD remarks that new jobs have come preponderately from new or small firms. The rapid growth of new firms reflects, among other factors, both the spread of franchising and the relative ease with which individuals can start new businesses in the USA. 'There is a certain built-in competition among states and communities to keep institutional impediments, local taxation and other costs to a minimum, in order to attract investment and employment opportunities'.[65]

But the fundamental difference has been labour costs. The US Council of Economic Advisers' series for real hourly compensation of 'non-supervisory' workers show no net increase between 1968 and 1985 – a rise up to 1978 being cancelled by a fall in subsequent years. During this period real earnings in Europe rose by an annual average of over 2 per cent.

In the first phase of increasing European pay costs in the 1970s, the share of profits and the rate of return both fell. But both of these later recovered as employers responded by substituting capital for labour. The pay increases they awarded were thus at least partly backed by productivity. This productivity was not a natural concommitant of technical progress, but artificially induced by high labour costs and was achieved at the expense of outsiders who were excluded from the labour force. Total GDP, or GDP per head of the whole population, which is a better measure of economic efficiency, did not benefit.

Within the manufacturing sector of the USA, some European-type developments did occur. American unions did succeed in maintaining or increasing their real wages in the 1970s, which led to a sharp rise in the capital to labour ratio, and a sharp decline in manufacturing employment. From 1979–82 onwards, however, unionised workers did make concessions, such as deferring pay increases or accepting pay cuts, and the 'union/non union' pay differential fell sharply.

Pay flexibility in the USA was also helped by the erosion of the real value of the statutory minimum wage which was unchanged in nominal terms for several years after 1981, and fell from 48 per cent of average earnings in the early 1980s to 35 per cent in 1985. In contrast to European countries, the USA was able to accumulate the influx of job seekers from the baby boom by widening the differential between the wages of youth and those of mature adult workers.

The lesser degree of regulation has encouraged US small firms to recruit labour. 'Generally' remarks the OECD, 'employers have the right to hire at will, except where there is a written contract. Larger firms, bound by collective agreement, will frequently contract out to non-union suppliers'.

The clearest quantified evidence is provided for regional pay differentials. States with 'right to work statutes' (that is, exclusion of the closed or union shop) performed much better in manufacturing output and employment. In the old Mid West, where autos, steel and other heavy industry, have found it more difficult to escape union pressures, firms have followed the European model and shed labour. In states with pay below the national average jobs have been gained, and unemployment rates are below average, whether in New England or the South Atlantic Seaboard.

What of the conception – popular among anti-capitalist opinion in Europe and manufacturing protectionists in the USA – that free market growth in the USA was biased towards lower quality service jobs, such as petrol pump attendants, laundry operators or restaurant kitchen staff? The OECD study replies that these perceptions 'seem only to apply to a subset of service industries'. Of the 17.4 million new jobs created in the USA in the decade 1972–82, some 5.4 million were professional and technical, and 3.4 million 'managers, and administrators'. Another 4.2m. were clerical and kindred. Only 3.1m. or well under a fifth of the total increase were in the menial category of general service workers.

But I do not want to pretend that the superior US jobs performance has been costless. The level trend of average real compensation concealed substantial pay cuts that a minority of workers were forced to take. American workers whose services have little market value are forced by the absence of a European-type social service system to accept work at very low wages indeed. The US system is not the best of all worlds.

### Canada and the USA

The most clear-cut evidence that pay pressures have had more to do with the unemployment explosion than have government macroeconomic policies is found in a comparison of US with Canadian experience. The two countries share many common cultural and economic features, enjoy a 3000 mile common frontier, and their business and trade are highly interrelated. Up to mid-1974 the unemployment rate was also very similar in the two countries, never diverging by more than one percentage point, sometimes on one side, sometimes on the other. Yet since then a gap has developed, to Canada's disadvantage, varying between 2 and 5 percentage points.

This occurred despite much more stimulation of demand in

Canada, judged by traditional Keynesian indices. The government deficit in the 1980s rose even faster in Canada than in the USA, but interest rates were little different. The Canadian trade surplus, which dipped in the mid-1970s, climbed in the 1980s to 4 per cent of GNP. The US trade balance by contrast plunged from around zero to a deficit of the same proportion.

The big differences were on the wages side. Real average weekly Canadian wages started to grow faster than American ones in the late 1960s. By the early 1980s the gap exceeded 40 per cent, after which it began to decline very slowly. The Canadian wage boom reflected the boom in natural resources of the 1970s. When this boom subsided, the Canadians were left with a legacy of high real pay. This induced a rapid introduction of labour-saving technology which kept down real unit labour costs, especially when measured in US dollars, but at the cost of a legacy of high unemployment. A combination of union power, minimum wage laws, and more generous social security than in the USA prevented the displaced workers from pricing themselves into jobs in other parts of the Canadian economy.[66]

The causes of the divergence between US and Canadian pay behaviour are not far to seek. Until the mid-1960s the percentage of union workers among the non-agricultural labour force were very similar in the two countries, at around 30 per cent. But from then on the unionisation percentage dramatically diverged. In the USA it started to fall, first gradually, and then steeply, until by 1983 it reached 16 per cent. In Canada, on the other hand, it climbed steeply until the late 1970s, when it reached nearly 40 per cent, since when it has fluctuated with a slight upward tilt. The problem was caused not only by unionisation, but by the threat of it in the non-unionised sectors which made potential employers more reluctant to hire the unemployed at wages that undercut union rates.

Canada derives a larger proportion of its output from regulated or government-owned industries than the USA; and in these industries unionisation tends to be higher, and collective bargaining more rigid. The employers in such industries have no appropriate 'bottom line' for determining appropriate pay scales, and politicians can finance higher pay through increased taxes or increases in regulated prices. British Columbia long had a system of determining forest rents, which left the rent as residual after all other costs,[67] which was virtually an incitement to give into pay demands. (The British ITV levy, which is on profits rather than turnover, has similar effects.)

Opposite developments occurred in the USA thanks to the deregulation of many industries such as airlines, buses, trucking and telecommunications. Some new airlines began without unionised labour; and pay restraint or even pay cuts were observed in most deregulated industries. The authors of the Fraser study believe there were important psychological demonstration effects elsewhere, from highly publicised competitive battles in, for instance, airlines and buses.

There were contributory factors from the social security systems, judging by the replacement ratio. This ratio consists of net income on social security when unemployed, divided by net income when at work. In 1970 the replacement ratio was 40 per cent in both countries. By 1982, the Canadian ratio had risen to nearly 70 per cent while the US ratio had hardly changed. The stringency of administration also eased in Canada relative to the USA. Some two-thirds of the US unemployed are not in practice eligible for unemployment insurance benefits and depend on locally determined relief, which is very different from European or Canadian style social security benefit.

### British union power

Some readers may wonder why I have said so much about the low and declining level of union power in the USA. Has not British union power suffered draconian curbs under Thatcher Governments? Although this is the popular view, the power that has suffered is not mainly monopoly power in the labour market. The three main Acts of 1980, 1982 and 1984 eliminated union immunities against many kinds of secondary, supporting and political action. The remaining immunities became conditional on secret strike ballots; and closed shops had also to be supported by a secret vote. Further changes promised in the event of a third Thatcher Government were in a similar direction, with the notable additions of measures likely to undermine the closed shop.

The greatest successes for this legislation has been the defeat of opposition to modernising working practices and manning levels, for instance in newspapers, coal and steel. Where no effect was visible up to the late 1980s was in union power over pay. The estimated average differential between union and non-union workers, which had been rising sharply in the 1960s and late

1970s, did no more than flatten out after 1979 at the very high level of around 40 per cent, according to estimates by the Centre for Labour Economics.[68]

This is hardly surprising. Increases in pay at the expense of lower recruitment, or even redundancies, among a minority that is offered good terms, benefit the majority of workers. Thus the Thatcher union reforms increased efficiency; but pay benefited at the cost of jobs. Hopes for more jobs in future depend very heavily on the entry of new or less heavily unionised firms, or new entrants from overseas, or self-employment, developments which are bound to take time to make major inroads.

A law really aimed at union monopoly power in the labour market would have either to withdraw basic union immunities as well as ban the closed shop and/or subject collective agreements to the scrutiny of the Monopolies Commission, the Registrar of Fair Trading and the Restrictive Practices Court.[69]

Although UK union membership fell from 53.7 per cent of the labour force in 1979 to 45 per cent in 1985–6, these percentages give an altogether too optimistic impression of the ease with which workers can price themselves into jobs in the non-union sector.

The public services, which account for a quarter of all employment, are almost 100 per cent unionised. Manufacturing, which accounts for another fifth, and where big job losses have occurred, is still highly unionised. Men, whose employment prospects have suffered relative to women, are also more heavily unionised. If men priced out of work in the union sector were to price themselves into work outside that sector, many would have to crowd into relatively limited and unfamiliar occupations, where wages might have to fall to subsistence level or lower.

Towards the end of the second Thatcher Government several ministers began to make speeches attacking centralised collective bargaining, which granted pay awards taking inadequate account of either local supply and demand conditions or regional differences in the cost of labour. National collective bargaining was however most influential, and least likely to be eroded by local arrangements, and the biggest destroyer of jobs in the public sector.

Confirmation that this diagnosis was on the right lines came when it was instantly rejected by many employers and the TUC. But the question for the rest of us is – why did the government wait nearly two parliamentary terms before even tentatively discussing the problem? Why had so little been done to make public sector pay – the whole structure of both professional and regional relativities – more sensitive to market conditions? And why had so much Prime Ministerial time been devoted to second order issues and vendettas?

Continued union power was, however, not the only suggested explanation for the persistent rapid increase in pay in the 1980s. Two other suggestions were (a) that the employers were making the running, and (b) that many of the unemployed would be worse off if they took jobs at market rates of pay.

### Employer behaviour

Although most anecdotal evidence suggested that the employers were indeed making the running, a little caution is required in interpreting it. Some actions which were apparently employer-determined – such as the pursuit of highly-paid, but small, labour forces – may have reflected residual fear of unions or the decision to pre-empt their reappearance. The most ironical possibility of all is that employers offered high wage increases to 'weaken unions', thereby simulating the monopolistic wage settlements that are among the objectionable features of union power in the first place.

But as I have insisted in many other contexts, a simple-minded search for self interest, whether that of unions or corporate management, may not tell the whole story. Both are powerfully reinforced by beliefs and attitudes. Wages are not treated just like any other price. The labour market is the one where the Adam Smith doctrine of Natural Liberty has made least headway and the mediaeval doctrine of the just price has lingered longer. Traditional opposition to large differentials between young and mature workers, or to differentials between high and low unemployment regions, are real obstacles to reducing unemployment. So is the popular hostility to 'undercutting' and the belief that the high wage employer is a good one and the low wage one a bad one, irrespective of employment effects. These inhibitions appear high-minded. But they rationalise the self-interest of the majority of workers already employed over fellow workers without a job. The valid fears lying behind them are best tackled by other methods.

There was indeed one apparently clear-cut reason why employers should have been willing and even eager, in the late

1980s, to raise pay despite low inflation and high rising unemployment. This is the behaviour of profits. Profits recovered from their deep depression at the beginning of the 1980s, and were as high as a proportion of national income, and almost as a return on capital, as during the Golden Age of the 1950s and 1960s.

With profits rising twice as fast as pay in 1981–7, it would have been difficult to have secured downward pressure on pay settlements. Despite warnings about falling international competitiveness, employers *en masse* found for a long time that 7 to 8 per cent pay increases were consistent with rising profits and rising output. Ministerial exhortations to pay less ran up against the fact that employers were well able to afford the pay increases they did in fact grant.

It is a reasonable presumption that, if companies were paying more than they had to pay for workers of a given quality, that they could have increased profits still further by paying lower wages and taking on more workers. But there is no suggestion that the gain would have been very great, especially if their competitors were doing the same thing.

Company heads were, by definition, maximising their utility by their pay behaviour, and included in their utility was not only corporate profitability and the satisfaction of possibly misguided ethical maxims, but such gains as a quiet life and the ability to upgrade the labour force without having to introduce embarrassing pay differentials for workers who differed in aptitudes and attitudes, and to build up a loyal labour force with firm specific skills. Some economics dignified this behaviour by the term 'efficiency wages'.

Ministerial exhortation was in effect telling business executives to concentrate, not on maximising their own personal utility, but on more simple-minded maximising profits, at a time when profits were doing quite well in any case.

## (b)  The insider–outsider conflict

The main text of this book emphasised the importance of the treatment of 'externalities' – costs and benefits of activities which do not appear in the books of those responsible. The main examples were still the textbook ones, such as the polluting chimney stack.

High wages for fewer workers may represent, however, a new

and much more important class of externalities which has arisen in the labour market. It may pay existing workers and employers to settle on relatively high wages which exclude outsiders who have to survive on the dole, the unofficial economy or in low grade jobs.

It may not pay an employer to go to all the trouble of negotiating market-clearing pay rates, when his profits are doing well enough on the basis of normal uniform wage rounds, or he may genuinely need to pay quite high wages to retain his most valued workers; and the cost and controversy of paying individuals, or more closely defined groups, different pay rates reflecting their true market value, may not repay the effort. In some cases this may be because the employer is not trying to maximise his profits, but merely to 'satisfice' – a technical term which means 'get by': The important point is that the wider losses for society – both economic and social – of unemployment are not taken into account.

One policy aimed at the new kind of externality promoted by Martin Weitzman is 'revenue sharing' or 'profit-related' pay systems, on which the profit-related element is not a small add-on, but a major part of normal pay. Left to themselves workers may not be keen on the added risk of such systems, nor employers to find it worthwhile to persuade them. But because of the *externality* involved, it is sound policy to offer a tax incentive – not necessarily temporary – to establish such systems.[70]

*The dual economy*
So far two main explanations for the persistence of high pay rises and high unemployment in the 1980s have been discussed: they are the persistence of more union market power than is generally realised and employer attitudes. But there is a third: that is, that despite very high unemployment, there has been difficulty in recruiting workers of the skills, aptitude and attitudes required for many jobs. This is the explanation many employers gave when they said they had to pay 1980s type wage increases to retain a properly motivated labour force. If asked why they did not recruit any of the unemployed, the answer was rarely clear cut. But it amounted to saying that the unemployed either did not have the right skills or attitudes or lived in the wrong parts of the country.

There was much circumstantial evidence pointing in this direction. Vacancies by the late 1980s were much higher than in some years in the 1970s when male unemployment was less than a third as great. Reported skill shortages also corresponded with those experienced a decade before, when unemployment was much lower.

Another pointer towards the dual economy was that the entire additional rise in unemployment after 1981 was in those without a job for over a year. There was also increased dispersion in pre-tax earnings. The pre-tax real earnings of the bottom tenth of male wage earners rose by only 3.7 per cent over the seven years 1979–86. During this period the middle group received real pre-tax pay increases of 11.7 per cent and the top tenth received an average rise of 22.3 per cent.

The fall in pay relativities at the bottom end, which was still insufficient to price the unemployed into jobs, provides prima facie evidence for a *dual economy*. By this I mean a division between a majority of *insiders* with reasonably well-paid secure jobs or job-prospects, and a large minority of *outsiders* who drifted between ill-paid labour and the dole. Some members of this minority have become demoralised from long-term unemployment. Or they may have been otherwise lacking in the skills, attitudes or geographical locations attractive to business. These distinction help to rationalise the attitude of employers who sided with their existing 'inside' labour forces who preferred high pay to taking on 'outsiders'.

The large hard core of the unemployed could be broken up schematically into:

(i) Those whose earning power ('marginal product' in economic jargon) was so low that it did not pay them to move from social security to a job;

(ii) Those who could not afford to move to the prosperous part of the country because of housing costs.

The existence of the first category was often denied by academic studies which showed that few of the unemployed were, according to the statistics, better off on the dole. The normal device used is the terms of 'replacement ratios', the net income on social security divided by income in employment. According to the Institute of Fiscal Studies, less than 4 per cent of all households, and 8 per cent of households with two children, had in 1985–6 replacement ratios of 90 per cent or more. The average ratios were over 60 per cent; and nearly 70 per cent for families with two children.

But these comparisons were inconclusive. Even if income on social security was only 60 to 70 per cent of net income at work, it did not take much by way of earnings on the side, or do-it-yourself activities, or lost leisure and dislike of regimented working hours, to eliminate the gain from taking a formal job.

The second category of workers deterred from seeking new jobs by the cost of new housing was less controversial. After tax, National Insurance, and child benefit, a sole breadwinner with two children would have taken home a net £165 per week in early 1986. The typical house in the South-East would have cost £44 500. A 90 per cent mortgage on a house of this sort would have cost over £75 per week – or getting on for half his net earnings.

Mortgage interest relief seems to ease the problem, but ultimately aggravates it by driving up land, housing and interest costs. The combined effects of mortgage interest relief, tight control on new building in the South-East on often spurious Green Belt considerations, and rent control much aggravated the problem as already explained.

Policy analysts should shout from the house tops about the perversity of urban policies as bad as those of the Common Agricultural Policy (CAP). At the same time they should realise that deep-seated problems would remain even if political obstacles melted and they had their way. Property and land have always been expensive in capital cities from Imperial Rome onwards. High real estate values are providing signals that low-value-per-acre activities are uneconomic in the nation's economic centres.

The three suggested factors – union market power, employer attitudes, and 'it does not pay to move to work' – may all be in operation. It is, however, unlikely to be just employer attitudes. Theories about 'efficiency wages', that is, the use to employers of a high wage policy to motivate and discipline their labour forces, may explain why pay was slow to respond to slack labour markets in the early 1980s. They can hardly explain the persistence of high pay settlements and high unemployment for so long.

If that were all, more cracks in the wage structure would have developed earlier. Some employers would have risked opposition to taking on larger, low-paid staffs; or overseas-owned firms would have made the plunge. Or the unemployed would themselves have priced themselves into jobs by setting up co-operatives or making use of the many sources of funds now available for new small businesses.

## (c) Market pay without poverty

Market economists often say 'Low pay is better than no pay'. This is right, but does not go far enough into the distributional implications. If pay is lowered (or increased less quickly) to price unemployed into jobs, then – assuming no change in social security levels – those unemployed who step forward voluntarily to fill the vacancies to will gain. But the insiders will lose, relative both to the outsiders and to the owners of capital. (To the extent that the latter are pension fund members they are skewed towards the upper half of the income distribution.)

Nevertheless, as in so many other spheres, an improvement can be made by recognising formally the existence of property rights, in this case the job rights of insiders. The way would then be open for some of the outsiders to take jobs at pay superior to what they can gain on the dole or in the casual economy, but inferior to the pay of the established insiders. They would then gain and the insiders need not lose. (This would be called in the jargon a Pareto improvement.)

The British insistence on the 'rate for the job' makes a two-tier wage system difficult to establish formally. But the trend towards cheaper contract labour is an informal move in that direction. Professor Meade's proposed 'labour-capital partnerships' are intended to combine the benefits of employee ownership and participation with a job-creating effect, by allowing new workers to be hired on terms initially inferior to existing partners.[71] But two-tier pay structures are possible within existing corporate organisations, as some US airlines and other corporations showed when they hired new employees at below the rates for existing workers.

The Weitzman scheme for profit-related pay does in the last analysis work at the level of the individual firm by inducing insiders to sacrifice pay for the sake of outsiders who are hired. There is then the obvious danger that existing workers will seek to influence hire and fire decisions to prevent this from happening. But rather than either throw up our hands in despair or fight a losing battle for absolute managerial authority over hire and fire decisions, it should surely be possible for new recruits *not* to receive the profit-related element in their pay, until they have gone through a laid-down procedure lasting perhaps a few years. The government's legislation on Profit Related Pay specifically explicitly permit such two-tier structures, for tax incentive purposes.

The bigger distributional challenge arises for people who are less badly off on the dole than at work, not because they are lazy or workshy, but because the market value of their pay is less than, or not very different from, the social security minimum.

A sufficient cut in the dole, or a more stringent enforcement of the work-search condition, would undoubtedly force many people to find – or create for themselves – more low-paid jobs, of which the extreme example is selling matches at street corners. Thus the pressures would increase on citizens who already face much less attractive conditions than their fellows. Whomever else such policies helped, it would not be the unemployed.

Thus there are some cures for unemployment – cures only in the sense of reducing the published figures – which are worse than the disease. But if we reject policies for starving the unemployed back to work as we should, is there nothing that could be done to avoid the affront to human dignity and the economic loss from complete lack of declared work by people of low earning capacity? Surely it would still be desirable for people on the dole to be able to earn something extra in a legal way without losing all their social security entitlements, beyond the trivial amounts that can be 'discarded' under present arrangements?

Entitlement to social security for non-retired adults is largely conditional on specific misfortunes, such as unemployment. The system has been described as contingency or 'category' targeting. It is one which has very great difficulties in coping with people who are occasional, casual or part-time workers, or who have very low earnings.

*Unearned income for all*
The most radical way of moving away from the present style of contigency benefits is the basic income guarantee.

The essence of the guarantee is that everyone receives a basic payment from the state. All additional income is subject to tax. The basic payment will of course vary with the number of dependents.

Let us assume that the basic income is £4000 per annum and the tax rate is 50 per cent. Then the break-even point comes when the citizen is earning £8000 per annum in ordinary earnings. On this he pays tax of £4000, which entirely cancels out his initial payment from the state.

Some reformers prefer to start their description with the position of someone earning the break-even level of ordinary earnings, in this instance £8000. If his pay rises to £9000 he pays £500 in tax. If it falls to £7000 he receives a 'negative income tax' payment from the state of £500; and so on for every successive decline in income.

On the other hand, those reformers who start from the maximum sum received by a person with no other source of income, – in this case £4000, usually talk of a 'social dividend'. But as Figure 2 (p. 298) shows, there is formally no difference between the two systems, which is why I have used the term 'basic income guarantee' to cover both. The essential properties of the system are given by the size of the payment to a person with no other income (OG), and the marginal tax rate. Given these properties, it makes no difference whether we want to call it a negative income tax, social dividend, basic income or anything else.[72]

In practice, the different names have, of course, different associations. Advocates of a social dividend usually have in mind a basic payment on which a household, without unusual needs, can just about live; and they are prepared to accept a pretty high tax rate to finance it. Supporters of a negative income tax think more in terms of topping-up low incomes. They are often also prepared to accept a kink in the tax line, with people in receipt of benefit paying a much higher rate – say 70 per cent, which would be called a 'withdrawal rate' – than people above the break-even point. The higher the withdrawal rate, the more that help can be concentrated where it is most needed, but the greater the poverty and unemployment traps – in the sense of specially high tax rates at the bottom end of the income distribution.*

Elements of a negative income tax already exist. The main example is the Family Income Supplement (FIS), to top up the income of poor families, whose head is at work. This has a

---

* The advocates of integrating tax and social security into a negative income tax do not always realise that this is in itself only a desirable administrative simplification. The designers of the integrated system will still have to choose between alternative principles in drawing up the scales of payments.

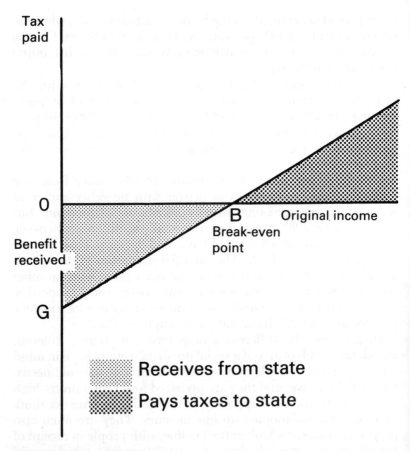

*Figure* 2 Basic income guarantee

withdrawal rate of 50 per cent. It is to be transformed into the Family Credit, which it is hoped, will have a much higher take-up.

A negative income tax or social dividend large enough to replace all contingent benefits including state pensions, and provide everyone in or out of work with at least a minimum subsistence income, would be prohibitively expensive at present. Even if the withdrawal rate were higher than the basic rate – say 70 per cent – the basic tax rate itself would have to be perhaps 50 or 60 per cent to finance the scheme.

Moreover, if there were really to be even a subsistence level benefit for all, without bureaucratic complication, the housing market would have to be reformed. For housing costs are at present so varied, and so unrelated to the standard of accommodation, that they are added on to Supplementary Benefits rather than included in them. (There will also, in any case, always have to be a contingency fund for families with special needs.)

The main reason why any variant of the basic income guarantee would be so expensive is that in order to provide a basic minimum for all and avoid 100 per cent marginal tax rates at the bottom, quite a lot of the benefit would spill over to households well above the minimum into areas of the income distribution where there are a great many households.

Thus the most urgent requirement is to make redistribution and the relief of poverty more cost-effective, that is, to do more with existing taxpayers' contributions. One way would be to pay child benefit only to lower income families, perhaps at a graduated rate. It could also involve means-testing at least part of the basic state pension and facing head-on the fury of the better-off retired who erroneously believe they have paid for their pensions by their contributions. The reward for this exercise of political courage would be a more generous redistribution to the poor, including higher levels of Supplementary Benefit and larger payments to the unemployed or families with children, from a given tax-take.

But what is now utopian need not be utopian for ever. If there is anything in the dream – usually presented as a nightmare – of a vast increase in productivity resulting from the silicon chip, robotics, and other technological advantages, an unconditional basic income for all becomes possible. If the increase in national incomes takes the form of a very large rise in the return of capital, relative to the average return on labour, then such a basic income becomes essential as a way of spreading the new wealth. But even if it is due to an all-round increase in productivity of both labour and capital, it is still highly desirable. The essential condition is that there should be a fairly large gap between national income per head and the basic income. It was the lack of such a gap which destroyed the primitive experiment in guaranteed basic incomes at the beginning of the nineteenth century, known as Speenhamland. It must also be accepted that poverty has an absolute, as well as a relative, component.

The place where a start can be made straight away is to make the Family Credit, now only available to families with children, payable to all. It should also be made more generous relative to other benefits. If this were done, an unemployed person with low earnings capacity could afford to take a low-paid job and have his income topped up, so that he would be still at least a little better off at work than on the dole – which might not be the case today.

Eventually, however, I would hope that a basic payment could be made to everyone as of right. A fully-fledged basic income guarantee would enable people who are content to live at a conventional subsistence scale to do so – on the grounds that a rich society can afford to have some people 'opting out'. Any work done to supplement this minimum would attract tax, initially at a specially high withdrawal rate, but eventually at no more than the basic rate.

Another, perhaps complementary, route to the same goal would be by means of a much more widespread citizen ownership of an equity stake in the nation's capital assets, achieved through the redistribution of corporate shareholdings.

A drawback of the share ownership route is that, as some citizens will dissipate their capital, it will be less effective in relieving poverty, and it will probably require a fresh redistribution of holdings as wealth is passed on from one generation to the next.

Nevertheless, citizen shares are more clearly property rights and less liable to every gust of the political wind than social security payments, even of a negative income tax kind. The link with return from capital is much clearer; and if it were successfully achieved there would be no further grounds for being opposed to profits, or worrying about an increase in their share of the national income.

Moreover, a start could be made on a small scale, for example, by the free distribution of privatisation shares. The citizen ownership principle requires that they be distributed to all adults – or at least allocated on some universal principle – for example, to the retired, or to young people coming of age.

Eventually citizen ownership would require the 'watering' of existing equity holdings. From the beginning ordinary citizens would start to have the advantage of a modest investment income, hitherto confined to a small minority. Eventually, these holdings could be enough to give all households a choice between living on rentier income or topping up that income with earnings from work.

The benefits of a 'modest competence' were enjoyed by the members of the propertied classes of the eighteenth and nineteenth centuries, such as those who figured in Jane Austen's novels. The only thing wrong is that they were available to so few. A modest competence available to all can be regarded as the culmination of popular capitalism or libertarian socialism alike.

These matters are not a digression from unemployment, but central to the problem. Classical economists who rightly argue for market rewards to factors of production usually fail to face the problems of those whose work has a low market value. The challenge for economic and social policy is to find a way of obtaining as much as we can of the benefits of an American-style labour market, without incurring the cost of American-style poverty. The proposal for a basic income – not a minimum wage – for all was made in Chapter 3 on general social market grounds. The case for it is increased manifold by the practical need to find a way of re-establishing a fully functioning labour market with a market-clearing rate of pay, on a humane base which will improve the position of Rawls's 'least advantaged representative person' rather than driving him or her to the wall.

## 8. CHALLENGES TO THE MARKET

### (a) Stagflation

There have been several challenges to market liberalism since the early 1970s. They include the reappearance of mass unemployment, which we hoped to have banished, and a syndrome of financial problem relating to the City of London, international debt and the disappointing behaviour of floating exchange rates.

What these otherwise disparate problems have in common is that they can. be ascribed either to excessive or inadequate observance of market policies according to taste. For instance, the unemployment problem can, as I have shown, be related to the ossification of labour markets. Nevertheless, few market – or any other – economists predicted the unemployment explosion of the 1970s and 1980s. The mainstream British economic establishment, such as the famous 364 economists who wrote to *The Times* in 1981, protesting against the Thatcher policies, were wrong about inflation and wrong about the economy's inability to grow at a reasonable rate without stimulation. But most market economists underestimated the unemployment costs of holding down inflation by monetary means alone until labour markets were reformed: both the immediate cost, and the longer-run effect, known by the unlovely name of 'hysteresis', under which high unemployment, once established, tends to stick, as the long-term jobless becomes less attractive to employers, and industrial capacity becomes adjusted to the existing rather than potential labour force.

What I have tried to show in the preceding section is that the ideas of market liberalism can be developed by new forms of labour contract, redistribution of property rights and income supplementation to avoid both involuntary unemployment and mass poverty. Ideally, the same government would develop both the redistributive and the market-freeing sides, but we may have to be content with a series of lurches by governments of different persuasion, and even this may require a restructuring of British politics.

## (b) Exchange rates

The biggest intellectual, as distinct from practical, setback to market liberalism has been the disappointment of the hopes placed on floating exchange rates, which became general in 1973 – just *before* the first oil price explosion.

Market liberals may believe either that national currencies ought to be left to find their own price against each other, or that money is 'different' to other products and that a single world currency – or at least fixed rates between the main currencies – would be preferable. But as a matter of fact, in the absence of a world political or financial authority, many market liberals did place great expectation on floating rates as a way of depoliticising world trade and removing the mercantilist obsession with the balance of trade.

Nor do I feel it necessary to engage in a *mea culpa*. Floating rates were probably the least bad way by which the world could survive the times of troubles through which the international economy passed after 1973.

The period saw two oil price explosions, followed by an oil price collapse and partial recovery. It saw the emergence of the international debt problem and severe fluctuations in commodity prices. There were two waves of double digit inflation followed by an apparent approach to price stability. There was also a gradual accumulation of barriers to international trade combined with the increasingly obvious idiocy of the Common Agriculture Policy, and labour markets in Europe remained fairly rigid. Yet at the same time there has been an unparalleled liberalisation of financial markets.

The 1980s also saw a growing discrepancy between increasing budget deficits in the United States, which had a low savings ratio, and increasing fiscal austerity in Japan and Germany which had a high savings ratio.

It is doubtful if the world would have weathered these strains, tensions and policy incompatibilities, even as well as it did, without the shock absorber of floating rates. The system has at least the merit of limiting the number of topics requiring international political agreement.

Nevertheless, the combination of national economic policies hardly led to a harmonious development of exchange rates. The dollar doubled against the German mark in the five years up to March 1985. Then, in the subsequent two years it halved and returned to near its starting point.

One did not need to have a view of the right exchange rate pattern to conclude that if the 1980 or 1987 dollar rate was right, then the rate of 1984–5 was absurdly high. The unsustainably high dollar of the middle 1980s had longer-term ill effects, as it put immense corrective pressure on the sectors of the US economy involved in exports or subject to import competition. But as the very high dollar did not last, any adaptations which were made proved to be a mistake. American producers of traded goods had to rebuild market shares after their overseas competitors had entrenched themselves and these competitors were prepared to see their margins squeezed. There was thus a danger of excessive dollar depreciation – that is, overshooting in the opposite direction from the recent past.

The political repercussions were even worse. Protectionist sentiment which was inflamed when the dollar was high, did not die down when the dollar fell. The balance of payments, which was previously mercifully confined to the financial pages of the American press, now occupied the centre of the political stage.

There were parallel effects in the surplus countries. When the dollar appreciated and their own currencies fell, Japan and

Germany were encouraged to become even more dependent on net export surpluses for their growth. When the currency markets turned round, a great burden of adjustment was placed on their economic structure.

Unfortunately it is a big leap from recognition of exchange rate strain to devising an improvement. The fashionable proposal for target exchange rate bands will do more harm than good unless it is accompanied by other domestic measures by the participants.

If we have an exchange rate target and nothing else, it is impossible to say at times when these targets are under strain, whether the onus should be on strong currency countries to loosen their internal policies or on the weak countries to tighten theirs. The world rates of inflation and of demand growth become indeterminate if exchange rates are the only guide.

Many of these problems were tackled automatically under the Gold Standard, which countries temporarily left when real shocks were too great. But we may have to establish man-made substitutes – not necessarily as an improvement, but because no fresh commodity-based standard is yet on the horizon. (The 'Gold Standard' of the American supply siders is not the genuine article, and more like an inflationist's charter.)

If future episodes of over-strong or excessively weak currencies are to be prevented, some consensus will be required about the thrust of demand management in the key countries. The development of Nominal GDP objectives, which I have urged in place of technical monetarism, may need to move the international level.

The average level of world interest rates might, for instance, be revised upwards or downwards if aggregate national income in money terms (combined Nominal GDP) in the participating countries threatened to exceed or fall short of objectives. The distribution of national interest rates around this average would then be adjusted to help the key currencies to stay within their target zones.[73]

There may be some scope for short-term variation in budget balances to stabilise the growth of nominal demand in individual countries. But in a world of fairly stable exchange rates and inflation rates, the long-term thrust of fiscal policy would be directed towards the balance of payments – or, more accurately, to prevent undesired net overseas borrowing or accumulation of overseas assets.

Such policies will involve some move away from national sovereignty – which is a myth in any case – towards joint making of a few decisions of a rather stratospheric kind. The liberal will worry not about the desirability, but the feasibility of the process. The main ground for hope is that the game is a positive sum one. All participants would have benefited from avoiding the currency fluctuations of the 1980s if this could have been done without resort to controls on trade and payments.

## (c) Financial markets

The extreme sensitivity of exchange rates to news or rumours is one aspect of a more general development, namely the unprecedented expansion of the financial sector relative to the rest of the economy and its liberalisation at a pace unmatched anywhere else.

Indeed, most of the controversy at the time of writing concerns not the behaviour of foreign exchange rates, but more populist aspects of the domestic financial markets, such as the increase in competition, the replacement of gentlemen by professionals, a few highly-publicised large salaries and some succulent city scandals. At a slightly more sophisticated level there is concern over mergers and takeovers, that is, that the City takes too 'short-term' a view. There is worry, too, that too much of the brightest commercial talent is being diverted from industry and commerce into the mere swapping of existing assets in the financial markets.

### (i) Enforcing the rules

Part of the hostility to things financial is just the normal human hatred of activities which are not understood – the sort of fear that inspired centuries of anti-Semitism in Europe. If there were no demand for their services from outside the financial sector, members of the financial community could not make a living just by taking in each other's washing. In fact, demand exists for British financial services throughout the world. It would be contrary to the spirit of this book even to cite figures for the financial sector's so-called contribution to the balance of payments. But it is clearly an activity where Britain has a comparative advantage. To clamp down on it would reduce real living standards – and because real wages are so slow to adjust to changed circumstances – jobs as well.

Like any other markets, going right back to medieval fairs, financial markets need rules and bodies to enforce them. The term regulation is unfortunately ambiguous, because it covers both dirigiste measures such as limiting entry in the interests of existing participants, or fixing prices or quantities, which have been a mistake from Diocletian onwards, and the very necessary activity of establishing and enforcing the rules under which competition takes place. Moreover, an economic liberal distrusts a private system of law or self-regulation. The reader will find on pp. 87–8, written a decade and a half before the City of London 1986 deregulatory 'Big Bang', a denunciation of City self-regulation by 'nods, winks and arm-twisting'. The approach then preferred by the City establishment and the Bank of England was a transfer of the procedures of a private club to a sphere where the law of the land ought to apply. The element of mutual cover-up, which might have delayed the experience of notorious scandals, owes more to the relic of the Old Boy ethos and patrician power networks, than it does to the more competitive spirit unleashed by the Big Bang.

## (ii)  The role of secondary markets

If we are to have dispersed ownership, there has to be a secondary market in paper titles to business property and less tangible assets such as government debt. The speed and ease with which such titles can change hands are important, both for efficiency, and the freedom of action of citizens with even the most meagre financial holdings. There is nothing to regret in the disappearance of cartel arrangements such as fixed commissions, or restrictive practices such as the enforced separation of trading from brokerage – akin to the still prevalent distinction between barristers and solicitors and many other arcane procedures and restrictions inside the legal profession.

Nor is it such a bad idea that banks or building societies should have to pay competitive rates of interest on depositors' money, including sums on which cheques can be written. Many of the more esoteric financial instruments have been developed to help business cope with exchange rate uncertainties. Other instruments have opened up lines of credit to businesses or home loan institutions not available before.

Obviously speculative bubbles and overextended or unwise

developments can and do occur. The job of central banks – which now have to act jointly across frontiers – is not to 'know better', but to use their lender of last resort power to ensure that the failure of particular institutions or markets does not spiral into a general contraction of money, credit or spending power, as Bagehot taught long ago.

There is much to be said even for the unpopular activity of takeover battles. A widely-recognised problem of modern organisational theory is that of the 'principal agent'. How does one find incentives for a senior civil servant, health service manager, head of a monopolistic policy utility or managing director of a private sector company to act in the interests of those to whom he is responsible – in the latter case the shareholder – rather than to follow his own goals?

To secure the maximum return on shareholders' assets is an interest, not merely of the shareholders, but of the nation. It is not in the interests of the poor or the unfortunate that assets should be inefficiently or under-utilised. The reformer may legitimately wish to change the distribution of equity ownership, but not – if he is sensible – to hold down the return on capital.

On the other hand, corporate managers left to themselves may well follow objectives such as a quiet life, or profitless growth, or – at the other extreme – safety-first cash mountains. Without the threat that in the last resort an underperforming management will be replaced by a more successful one, a vital incentive to performance is missing.*

We need therefore not so much takeovers' as 'takeover battles'. The Monopolies Commission must always be there as a long-stop to prevent business concentrations which threaten competition, and monopoly and merger law is always capable of improvement. Quite apart from that, those of us who favour decentralisation and are suspicious of big battalions will be happiest when the outcome of a takeover fight is an internal revolution in the threatened company, which is then able to repulse the bidder. But

* In continental Europe, the role of keeping management up to scratch is often played by large banks. But is this closed-door method of decision really preferable? And does not the close connection between banks and corporations provide large concentrations of power at least as objectionable as British or American conglomerates?

unsuccesful takeover bids cannot exercise their galvanising role if there is not at the time a threat of success.*

### (iii) Why the short-term may prevail

Why, however, do the financial markets appear to take such short-term views about economies, currencies, companies and much else? Some of this criticism takes for granted that very-long-term investment with an uncertain payoff is always wiser than taking advantage of immediate opportunities. But high real interest rates, and political and economic policy uncertainties are all relevant here, and wishing will not make them go away. Nor do I have any confidence that politicians or journalistic critics will take a more truly long-term view.

To the extent that financial institutions, nevertheless, do take too short-term a view, a likely reason is that financial institutions are too managerial. Much financial business is now carried on by salaried employees, often young, ambitious and energetic, but who are judged by their performance over, say, a three months period. Stabilising speculation is more likely if many participants are using their own money and can decide for themselves whether to back a longer view. But most of the traders and principals today are employed by pension funds, protected by tax privilege, who are under no pressure to act as profit maximisers, but merely do not want to do conspicuously worse than their peers in any one period.

It was the old-fashioned capitalist, with ample personal resources of his own, who could afford to take the long view. The suntraps of the world are full of prematurely retired, cantankerous characters, who backed their own long-term judgements against the fashions of the moment.

The Thatcher Cabinet lost a golden opportunity of reducing the role of pension funds when it retreated in 1985 from plans for cutting the tax privileges of these funds in the face of interest group lobbies, which ministers could not answer back because of the absurd doctrine of Budget secrecy. Giving in to emotional backbench pressure for preserving every regional enterprise under its existing management will not make up for this mistake.

---

* The first takeover fight I remember was when ICI made a bid for Courtaulds in the 1960s. The bid was unsuccessful; but it did succeed in shaking up the Courtaulds management and led to the emergence of Lord Kearton.

## (iv) One-sided liberalisation

There is a major worry relating to the financial markets. This is the contrast between the liberalisation and greater competitions in these markets, and the continuing restriction and cartel-mindedness of the labour and product markets. Foreign exchange rates and security prices can react instantaneously to new developments, while nominal and real wage rigidities will prevent the price of labour moving to a new equilibrium for many years if not indefinitely. Quota restrictions, whether supposedly voluntary or not, hold up adjustments in trade flows, and these have been increasing while financial markets have been freed. The resulting imbalances distort the international and national economy, and incidentally help to account for high rewards to risk-takers in finance.

There is no way forward through trying to suppress financial markets – partly, but not only partly, because such suppression would drive them underground. Recent tensions emphasise the urgency of rectifying the imbalance by moving to derestrict the product and labour markets. It can hardly be an improvement to introduce artificial rigidities into financial markets so that they become like the labour markets or the old industrial sectors of the old industrial countries.

## 9. ASSESSMENT

### (a) Political

The object of this book, stated in the 'Preface to the First Edition', was to persuade the open-minded reader that the *right kind* of market economy can be an instrument of human freedom and a way of satisfying human wants. The difficulties that have emerged are often the result of not making enough use of market forces, or one-sided use of them, despite all the rhetoric in their favour. Moreover, a great deal of attention is required to provide the right kind of framework – especially the redefinition of property rights and the general rules of the game. Too many free market tracts simply supply reassurance for the believer without attempting to carry forward the argument and analysis.

Although we need to think of how to put together the political coalitions which will advance liberal ideas into practice, this cannot be a substitute for further thought on the precise content and development of the ideas themselves. The most realistic hope is not that one political party will be captured for classical liberalism or the social market economy, but that different aspects will be advanced by different governments and that, on balance, the advances will outweigh the retreats.

Several friends who have seen parts of this Postscript have urged me either to say that Thatcherism (or Reaganism) – despite many shortcomings and backslidings – was a major advance towards liberal market ideas. Others, on the contrary want me to insist that Thatcherism, had nothing in common with any variety of market liberalism from which it needed to be distinguished most sharply to save the reputation of the latter.

To establish either of these positions by cold analysis would require counterfactual reconstructions of how history would have gone under some alternative and specified political regimes in Britain or the USA: a Herculean task which would be unlikely to repay the effort. Alternatively, I would have had to feel either a strong personal commitment to the Thatcher regime or a profound aversion to it, greater than to state authority in general.

In fact, the similarities between developments in America and Britain and in the now less ideological continental countries make me see common forces at work rather than either a monstrous or a messianic creed. In Britain the Thatcher Government did have a notable success in curbing union power, despite the detailed shortcomings, and it did push back the corporatist tide. On the other hand its lack of interest in free trade or economic internationalism, and the anti-market influence it exerted in the all-important housing market, disqualified it from any Cobdenite accolade. Although the whole world was passing through an economic cold spell, more could have been done to protect – not a geographical area such as the so-called North – but the relative shares of the poor and the victims of change. To do so effectively would have involved selective social security policies which, far from being common ground, would have upset the consolidators and the apostles of the Middle Way (that is, the 'Wets') far more than anything that Mrs Thatcher actually did.

The Thatcher economic policies took place against a background of obsessive secrecy, petty authoritarianism and a highly illiberal rhetoric on social and personal issues.

In time Margaret Thatcher will have a qualified biographer, who will explain her remarkable rise and mesmeric influence on political discussion.[74] Meanwhile it would be sad to draw up permanent battle lines on the basis of attitudes to a regime which began in the 1970s rather than on the challenges ahead.

The need to make market policies more far-reaching and radical, yet also more humane, should unify market liberals, however much they differ over Thatcher or Reagan, and also separate them from conventional Conservatives or Socialists or those Alliance leaders who simply want to split the difference between the two main parties, or go back to the 1960s.

## (b)  The road from alienation

The most encouraging developments since the 1973 edition of this book come from outside the narrow sphere of partisan politics. If the reader will refer back to the Prologue, he will see that the market economy I advocated was very far removed from the archetypal assembly line of industrial capitalism. The latter was a transitional phase, necessary before we could reacquire in modern form the virtues of a Jeffersonian democracy of independent householders selling their own wares and beholden neither to the state nor to the large corporations.

The term 'alienation' could, I remarked, be reasonably used to refer to 'a sense of powerlessness which many people feel within large organisations, a feeling of meaninglessness about the operations performed and of a lack of any intrinsic satisfaction outside the wage packet' (p. 72). Many of the civic virtues stressed by socialists and neoconservatives, as well as the taste for freedom cherished by market liberals, threaten to atrophy if society is one great hierarchy of employment. But in contrast to Marx, I attributed alienation not to capitalist property relations, but to a particular stage of technological development.

Since I wrote these words, there have been many developments away from the wages system of the factory or office. These have involved both changes in the nature of work and of the growth of other property rights unrelated to the citizen's particular employment.

One, but the least important, of these changes has been the

revival of individual share ownership, of which the Thatcher Government made so much. Least important because it left about two-thirds of households untouched, and because most of the remainder had trivial amounts of shares, in one or two companies, arising from privatisation. We are still a long way from the state, advocated a few pages back, where the typical citizen has two substantial forms of income: one from work and one from capital ownership, going beyond his home or pension.

A more important move towards Jeffersonian democracy has been the spread of partial or complete workers' ownership of their own enterprises. The first major boost to employee share ownership was provided by the 1978 Finance Act, brought in under the Lib-Lab Pact, and enhanced in subsequent Conservative Finance Acts. A million and a half workers were covered by the late 1980s, including 300 000 who acquired shares in their own enterprises as a result of privatisation.[75] The 1980s also saw the beginning of employee buy-outs, notably in the case of the National Freight Corporation employing 25 000 people, of whom over half were equity holders. On a more modest scale there was a renewal of interest in fully-fledged workers' co-operatives; and the Co-operative Development Agency was established with all party support. In the USA, where employee share ownership has gone further, it is estimated that by the year 2000 there will be more employees in Employee Share Ownership Plans than members of trades unions.[76]

Welcome though these developments are, it would be neither necessary nor desirable for them to extend to all or even most workers. Many people will not want to put too much of their capital at risk in the same enterprise from which they derive their pay, and many others will not want to devote their time to meetings and committees of a management kind. But tastes differ; and where employee shares are provided as a bonus at the expense of other equity holders, the above qualifications will not apply, although holdings can be expected to be correspondingly modest.

A major step towards profit-related pay, in which the profit-related element was not a mere add-on bonus but a substantial and variable part of workers' income would be more important. Although the main justification for fiscal encouragement of such schemes is to make it profitable to create jobs for outsiders, a spillover benefit would be a greater sense of identification with the firm's prosperity and a clearer relation between performance and pay.*

Citizen ownership of capital assets is still in an embryonic phase. By far the most important developments away from the 'alienation' of the large capitalist or state-owned enterprise have been in the organisation of work in a 'small is beautiful' direction.

A specific example I had reason to investigate is the growth of the small-scale independent television producers. I refer here not to the Independent Television franchise holders, who have been granted monopoly rights to advertising financed television in their own regions, but the small-scale producers who did not exist in the 1970s. These now supply a major part of the broadcasting on the Fourth Channel, set up in 1982; after the Peacock Report[77] the Home Office also exerted pressure on the BBC and ITV, to take a proportion of their output from the smaller independents. These producers provided employment away from the big battalions, and were a source of diversity and also of healthy cost comparisons for the BBC and ITV.

Of more fundamental importance, though further away and beset with more difficulties, was the Peacock vision of electronic publishing in which an indefinite number of broadcasters could transmit any programmes they liked within the law of the land to audiences, no longer circumscribed by spectrum scarcity, provided that they could meet their costs from direct consumer payment, advertising, or any other form of support.

Broadcasting is far from an isolated instance. Despite highly publicised mergers in industry and other spheres, the overall trend has been towards small-scale, home-based and self-employment. In the course of the 1980s there was a steady fall in the proportion of hard core full-time regular employees and an expansion of the 'flexible' section of the labour force: self-employed, freelance, temporary workers from agencies, people on short-term contract, home workers, part-time workers and so on. The Department of Employment estimates that in the six years 1981–7, full-time regular employees fell from 70 to 64 per cent of the employed labour force. The long-term fall in self-employment

---

* May employees would put the matter the other way round because they do not realise how far Weitzman-type profit-related pay differs from traditional (and modest) 'profit-sharing'.

came to an end in 1979. In the following six years, the total rose from 7.4 to 10.6 per cent of the employed labour force.

Up-to-date estimates were not available for the most flexible section of all: home-based workers. They amounted in 1981 to just under 30 per cent of the flexible sector. These were in turn divided into those, mainly men, who worked from home as a base and those, mainly women, who were 'working at home'. So far from the popular picture of exploited people working for low wages on tedious, repetitive tasks, they tended to be 'well-educated by national standards and far better qualified than the labour force as a whole'.[78] Two-thirds of the men working at home were doing so out of preference, and emphasised the freedom and flexibility obtained.

A shift to the new or the small is also shown among the hard core employed labour force. A sample study covering 1982–4 indeed showed that all the new jobs created came, on a net calculation, from either new firms or small firms employing less than 20.[79] Larger established firms shed workers on balance. There has also been some growth in 'flexi-time' schemes giving workers choice of how long or when to work.

Clearly part of the trend to self-employment, small enterprises and new enterprises has been a reaction to adversity from people with their backs-to-the-wall facing redundancy and un-employment; it has been encouraged by government schemes such as the Enterprise Allowance and the Business Expansion Scheme, which are open to abuse, especially in the latter case. But they are a more constructive response than reliance on make-work schemes or flooding the economy with money.

This defensive aspect is moreover only one aspect of the move to small-scale operations. An even greater influence is modern information technology, which enables highly-specialised work to be conducted at home and at a distance from fellow workers. The small screen and the microprocessor are reversing the effects of the assembly line, and are doing more to undermine the adversary collective bargaining culture than governments or laws.

## 10. CONCLUSION

Since the 1973 edition the movement of institutions, technology and behaviour has been highly favourable to market liberalism.

The movement of ideas has been much less so. There is more understanding of markets as a form of co-ordination superior to collectivist compulsion. But belief in personal freedom, on which the ultimate justification of the whole approach rests, has taken some knocks, which I hope will prove temporary. People may make many mistakes in the use of freedom, and nature or society may have many unforeseen snags in store. But in the end the dangers from freedom are far, far less than the dangers from heeding those on the left and right who deign to tell their fellow citizens how to live. The arrogance and the absurdities produced by the moral authoritarians and the economic collectivists alike will always provide the supporters of freedom with a chance, so long as they are prepared to take up the challenge.

# Appendix: Morality and Foreign Policy (1957)*

> 'A nation is nothing but a collection of individuals.'
> David Hume, 'Of National Characters'

When we are faced with a political decision, whether it is the determination of the bank rate or the recognition of Communist China, factual knowledge by itself will not tell us how to act. When we have amassed the maximum of technical information about the probable consequences and implications of alternative courses of action, we still have to choose between them. We may make our choice on the basis of the results we desire to bring about, or in relation to some general principle to which we adhere (the two are not necessarily incompatible), or in some other way. But whatever procedure we adopt, no amount of empirical investigation or logical analysis can free us from having to make the value judgement involved in deciding how to act.

It is sometimes asserted that political actions in general, or foreign policy in particular, cannot be judged from a moral standpoint. This is a big departure from common usage, as we would normally suppose, at the very least, that any human act done deliberately, not under duress, and with effects on others (this last requirement may not always be necessary) can logically be judged from a moral standpoint. But even if we decide to use the word 'moral' in such a way that some or all foreign policy decisions either can be, or necessarily are, non-moral in character, this neither frees us from the need to choose nor tells us what choices to make; and nothing follows – one way or the other – from

---

* This essay, hitherto unpublished, was written in the aftermath of the Suez crisis of 1956. Some brief subsequent reflections are to be found in the original Preface at the beginning of this book. If I were writing now, the treatment would in some ways be different, but on the main themes I am unrepentant. Indeed some readers may notice a relationship between the approach to foreign policy in this essay and that to economic policy in Chapter 1.

this linguistic choice with regard to issues such as the role or the desirability of adhering to UN principles.

Nevertheless, statements of the type 'Moral considerations are out of place in foreign policy' are made and in times of stress, such as the Suez crisis, they can become a subject of fierce controversy. People do mean something by remarks of this kind, though there are probably more meanings than speakers, and an examination of two or three possible meanings may be a useful way of introducing some general observations on the conduct of foreign policy.

The assertion 'Moral considerations are out of place in foreign policy' is sometimes meant as a well-justified attack on a certain approach – or rather family of approaches – to international affairs, an approach that is 'moral' only in quotation marks and is better termed moralistic. This approach is easier to indicate than to define.

In its extreme form it involves the view that the political colour of a government may be a sufficient reason for not holding negotiations which would otherwise have been held, and from which one's own side might have benefited; in the present world situation, according to this view bargains based on mutual self-interest should not be made with the Russians or the Chinese because of our disapproval of dealings with totalitarian regimes. And even less extreme exponents of the moralistic approach (who would, of course, resent the label) would regard it as a normal part of the professional duties of a Foreign Secretary to pass judgements on the desirability of the governments and political systems of other countries.

It would be wrong to give the impression that the moralistic approach is confined to right-wing Republicans. Ideological opposition to diplomatic dealings with tyrannies is deeply rooted in a section of the British Left and was evident in the case of Czarist Russia as well as Falangist Spain. Contemporary instances of the moralistic approach are the lectures read out to Western statesmen on their duties and obligations by 'neutralist' conferences in Cairo and Bandung.

The case against the moralistic approach has frequently been made out, and will only be outlined here. What needs to be stressed is that this case does not – or need not – depend on the belief that, in some mysterious sense, foreign policy is a self-contained activity in which our normal ideas of correct behaviour towards other human beings can be ignored. Nor need it rest on any desire to weaken the rules and restraints which governments may aspire to observe in their international dealings.

The first argument for rejecting the moralistic approach is an empirical one. Although this approach may sometimes be rooted in a sincere desire to make the world a pleasanter place, its practical effect has usually been to increase violence and tension. Perhaps the main reason for this is that it tends to deprive diplomacy of its normal function of attempting to ease disputes without recourse to war and of negotiating a settlement when war has broken out. For once a dispute is seen, not as a conflict of interests, but as a struggle between good and evil, then bargaining with the other side is at best an odious expedient, at worst a betrayal of all that is sacred. And a war, once it has broken out, will be pursued until the enemy's system of government has been destroyed. This process was at work in the seventeenth century at the time of the Wars of Religion; in the twentieth century its most disastrous fruits have included the 'War Guilt' clauses of the Versailles Treaty, the doctrine of 'unconditional surrender' and the US refusal to have diplomatic relations with Communist China.

A second argument, which is specially important for those who believe that the above paragraph places too high a value on peace and order compared with other objectives, is that the principles most frequently proclaimed by the 'moralisers' are arrogant and presumptious. The assumption that people in one part of the world are in a position to pronounce on what form of government is suitable to other people in very different circumstances – or to lecture to them on how to behave – is, to say the least, unwise. But, even if we think we know what is best for the inhabitants of other countries, the attempt to impose this knowledge is intolerant. In Mr Kennan's words: 'Let us by all means, conduct ourselves at all times in such a way as to satisfy our own ideas of morality. But let us do this as a matter of obligation to ourselves, and not as a matter of obligation to others.'[1] There is no reason to be tongue-tied about the excesses of Stalin or his successors, but it is not our job to prescribe to the Russians an alternative system of government.

It may sound a little more sophisticated to say that people living under dictatorial regimes should not be forced to adopt a constitutional democratic system, but should at least 'be free to make their own choice of system of government'. It is however often an unsatisfactory way out of the problem. For 'free to choose' is meaningless unless it is laid down how this choice is to be exercised and the usual suggestion is by means of elections or referenda. But unfortunately the habits of behaviour that make this kind of ballot box procedure more than a corrupt farce are the outcome of many years' evolution; they cannot be grafted on to countries that have only known the alternation of tyranny and anarchy. The Middle East is littered with the carcases of legislatures which have been the results of attempts to export the British or French constitution to that part of the world.

Eastern Europe is a special case, where there is clear evidence of opposition to Soviet-type Communism among a large majority of the population and where it would not be unduly moralistic to press for a closer approach to free elections in diplomatic bargaining with the Russians. But it would be moralistic to expect the Russians to agree to this from 'a change of heart' and without any concessions on our part.

A third argument against the moralistic approach is that it is usually put into practice with a hypocritical (although sometimes unconscious) inconsistency, which deprives it of any justification it might otherwise have had. If one is to base one's willingness to negotiate with other governments on judgements of their virtue, the first essential is that consistent standards be applied. Unfortunately, the exponent of ideological politics is usually as selective as he is severe in proclaiming his censure. Aggression becomes vicious when North Korea attacks South Korea but not when Guatamala is attacked by her neighbours. The rigging of elections is inexcusable when undertaken by the Communists in Eastern Europe, but bad form to refer to when carried out by the government of Iraq. The death penalty for carrying arms indicates the new low to which tyranny has sunk in Hungary; in Cyprus it was just an unfortunate necessity.*

---

* The consequences of this approach are illustrated in the following quotation from Prof. Butterfield: 'Many people will no doubt remember the tremendous shock which Hitler's invasion of Norway in 1940 gave to one's moral susceptibilities. A pupil of mine, who had been one of the most authentic of conscientious objectors, and had been exempted from military service, was so appalled by the attack that his whole attitude was shaken and he died not very much later in naval service. I have wondered sometimes what his reaction would have been if he had lived to know that Great Britain had had the prior intention

Quite separate from the attack on the moralistic approach, although too often confused with it, is another and very different meaning of the assertion 'Moral considerations are out of place in foreign policy'. This is that what is right and proper in the case of individuals and their dealings with each other is often not right and proper in the case of states, and vice versa. Indeed this is often said outright. It is a most dangerous assertion; and it is possible to oppose a moralistic outlook without in any way assenting to it.

Insistence on the irrelevance of beliefs about individual conduct to international affairs is, at the very most an expression of one particular set of value judgements with which we are at liberty to disagree. It is particularly insidious, as it is often enunciated as if it were a fact of life which those experienced in international affairs have empirically established and we have therefore to accept; or still worse, it is presented as a conclusion which political thinkers are supposed to have established by *a priori* reasoning, or of which letter writers to certain newspapers have innate knowledge. There are perfectly sound reasons why a naturally humane person may decide on occasion to support a 'tough' foreign policy; he may, for example, believe that in the end less lives will be lost thereby. But it is probable that in many cases people are misled into supporting policies at variance with their own beliefs about right and wrong because they suppose that there is something 'in the nature of' politics or foreign affairs that makes these beliefs irrelevant.

There are, of course, obvious differences between private and international affairs, which it is often important to stress. International affairs concern – though at one remove – large masses of people, rather than a limited number of identifiable individuals. For some purposes it may be helpful to regard relations between states as a special case of the interaction of organised groups, such as companies, churches and trade unions. Indeed, there are striking similarities between some aspects of power politics and the interactions of giant firms under *oligopoly* (that is, rivalry among a small number of concerns in a single market). The business analogy has its deficiencies, but it is closer to the mark than the more frequent comparison of disputes between countries to quarrels among individuals. The treatment

___
of invading Norway – and this even irrespective of the desire to help Finland – and that Hitler, initially unwilling to undertake the adventure, had decided to forestall us.' [Herbert Butterfield, *Christianity, Diplomacy and War* (Epworth Press, 1954), p. 32.]

of nations and their foreign policies in anthropomorphic terms usually leads to confusion, as the issues involved often bear very little analogy to the disputes of private life.

None of these considerations should be allowed to blur the truism that a nation is composed of individuals* and that the 'national interest' is a short-hand way of referring to some of the interests of these individuals – that is to say, the national interest is a function of the interests of individuals.

Nations and national interests are convenient portmanteau terms with which we could not easily dispense (and which will be used liberally in the next section), but as complex entities we are more likely, if we are not careful, to talk of them in a confused and misleading way. When important 'national interests' are at stake, and patriotic emotion is running high, it would facilitate clear thinking to ask 'which interests?'; and, 'who suffers and who gains from an attempt to protect them?' The individuals whose interests are concerned in foreign policy decisions cannot always be named, as they can be in private life. Nonetheless, statements about nations which cannot be related to a series of parallel statements about individuals, not necessarily nameable are nonsense, and dangerous nonsense.

Recognition of these rather obvious points in practice would have far-reaching implications. Take the question of 'armed conflict'. *If* one sincerely believes that it is wrong to kill other human beings except in literal self-defence, or in defence of one's family, then calling the killing a 'war' does not make it justifiable. Most people, who are not complete pacifists, would under pressure make some additional exceptions to the rule against killing. But even they may be misled into condoning killing and being killed through the uncritical use of cliches about 'national interest', 'duty to one's country' and 'military action'. Let us suppose that British troops have intervened on one side in a tribal conflict in South-Eastern Arabia to safeguard certain oil interests. The action is likely to involve the death of British soldiers as well as of additional tribesmen. If someone is asked: 'Are you prepared to support the killing of a certain number of Arabs and send so many British citizens to their deaths to secure for the remaining

---

* Some would include the dead and the unborn among the individuals; I accept this for the sake of completeness, despite the many objections that could be raised.

individuals in Britain whatever benefits they may derive from more secure delivery of a portion of their oil supplies?' and the answer is 'Yes', there is no inconsistency in supporting the action. But if the answer is 'No', and the man has, nevertheless, been in favour of it, he has been inconsistent, and has been misled by the use of abstractions into the support of policies at variance with his own personal beliefs about right and proper human conduct.

It must be admitted that, even if people habitually spoke of foreign policy in individual terms, many extreme nationalist positions could still be logically upheld, although they would be expressed in terms of men's feelings, towards other men of the same nationality and towards foreigners, and in terms of their feelings towards patches of soil, flags, buildings and other symbolic objects. But with the private value judgements at present common in Western countries, assessment in individual terms would bring a new perspective to many issues. Decisions involving loss of prestige – frontier adjustments, evacuation of colonies and the acceptance of arbitrary foreign nationalisations might well take a different turn if the financial costs and human sacrifices of a tough policy were weighed against its actual benefit to individual citizens, the swelling of patriotic breasts included among the benefits.

Acceptance of standard patriotic maxims, such as the duty and honour of fighting for one's country may be – though not necessarily is – the result of a confused and uncritical use of 'country'. If someone believes that the benefits which may result from fighting to the individuals who remain alive are worth the loss of life, the possible grief of his family and the suspension of all the private plans which he and his friends have formed (and he has no scruples about going to war on the particular issue), then he is guilty of no confusion. And he is logically entitled, if he thinks they are important, to include feelings of pride in the extension or preservation of the influence of his government and in the valour of the soldiers of his own nationality among the benefits, for which it is so honourable to fight. But someone who accepts the need to fight for his country, but would not endorse the corresponding propositions about individuals is being inconsistent; and this inconsistency would be avoided, if the issue were not posed in terms of the misleading concepts of 'country', 'honour' and 'vital interests'.

It is quite probable that profound unconscious conflicts and projections are more potent influences behind wars than the perverse use of abstract language. But until we have worked out what would be involved in rational decisions about the employment of military measures and other forms of force, we have no standard by which we can assess the distortions brought about by unconscious conflict, and we have no target for which to aim in any attempt to reduce them or channel them into less harmful forms of expression.

## Codes and rules
Nothing that has been said so far is meant to imply that a Foreign Secretary should consider the interests of all the individuals in the world as of equal importance. It is perfectly reasonable and even desirable for him to make the advancement of the interests of his fellow-countrymen, within the framework of internationally accepted rules, the main objective of his policy, although not with such fanaticism that any interest is pushed regardless of the cost to individuals in other countries.

One of the most important reasons for holding this point of view is a negative one; the alternative to the conscious and open pursuit of national interests turns out in practice to be not a genuinely disinterested and understanding attitude to all mankind, but the moralistic approach. The pursuit of limited and selfish objectives leads to a truce; a more lofty approach to a fight to the finish.

More positively, politicians and diplomats are representatives of people who normally place their own interests above the interests of foreigners. There is no need to discuss in this context the question of how far a democratically appointed minister ought to take advantage of his power and skill to pursue policies, which would not be approved by the majority of the electorate if they were understood. It is clear as a matter of fact that if politicians attempt to move more than a certain distance away from the views of their fellow-nationals, they are likely to be repudiated. Moreover, there is nothing shameful or second-best in a body of individuals, whether a nation or a trade union, attempting to further certain interests which their members have in common. In periods of crisis, enormous harm is done by two opposite kinds of extremists: the so-called idealists, who, in the name of morality, ask the government to abandon any attempt to protect or to advance the interests of the inhabitants of this country, and the so-called realists who favour an international free-for-all uninhibited by the observance of any code of permissible conduct. (This last view is, incidentally, yet another meaning of the proposition 'Moral considerations have no place in foreign policy'.) I suggest as an alternative that good behaviour in international affairs consists not in abandoning the pursuit of national interest but in observing some generally accepted 'rules of the game' in this pursuit. The analogy with business behaviour is again useful here. Company directors are expected to seek high profits; their obligations are limited to what might be called 'fair dealing', a complex amalgam of law, custom and unwritten convention which rule out certain types of business behaviour.

The case for observing an international code rests partly on the disapproval which some of us have for certain instruments of policy, such as unprovoked aggression. But fortunately, it also rests on the belief that, just as it pays a company in the long run, although not in every instance, to observe the business code, so it normally pays a nation to observe the rules applicable to international relations. The dangers that arise if there are no recognised limitations on the type of policy which a country can pursue should need no emphasis today, when there is a risk that some state – especially a small country in an exposed area – might set off a world-wide conflict through miscalculation.

Part of the importance of an international code is simply that it increases the predictable element in the behaviour of states; and greater predictability helps to avert violent and ill-considered actions. It is worth noting in this connection that some of the rules of international good behaviour are, like the rules of the road, highly conventional in character; it does not matter exactly what the rule is, provided that it is kept. The convention confining territorial waters to a three-mile limit from the shore is a case in point.

The view is sometimes put forward that international rules are pious aspirations and that there is nothing to be gained from this country observing them, as other countries do not. This argument usually depends for its appeal on the identification of all international rules with the more ambitious aspirations of the UN Charter. The evolution of any code must be a long and painful process, but over at least a certain portion of the globe some distinctions between legitimate and illegitimate means of achieving objectives are beginning to emerge. The cynic looks at the struggle in Kashmir, but forgets that both India and Pakistan feel under some kind of obligation not to solve the problem by a simple invasion of the relevant territory. He draws attention to the Palestine conflict and the tensions within the Arab world, but forgets that some kind of sanction prevents the major Arab states from settling their differences by simple invasion – and despite the recent Sinai campaign the Palestine conflict has been kept within remarkably narrow bounds considering the bitterness of feeling on both sides.

No one will dispute that these sanctions have been deplorably weak and that they depend to a large extent for their effectiveness on the fear of Great Power intervention; but the argument of the cynic implies that what conventions there are should be thrown to the wind and that the Great Powers should give up trying to enforce them. The existence of an international code is one of the few obstacles to the complete subordination of the interests of weaker countries to those of the Great Powers. If any nation has a selfish interest in fostering it, it is the United Kingdom with its extreme vulnerability to political and economic breaches of faith.

Even in the field of Soviet–Western relations certain unwritten 'Cold War' rules have sprung up, although they are incomplete and badly defined. There are certain parts of the world, which, despite our protestations, we recognise as coming within the Soviet sphere of influence and others where the USSR recognises that her interference will not be tolerated. (This was one of the reasons why the Western Powers did not interfere in Hungary and would have been badly advised to have tried.) These limitations on both sides depend mainly on the knowledge that their disregard may mean an atomic attack; but the point is that the rules, in so far as they exist, lay down how far each side can safely move and the unwritten conventions go far beyond the undertakings of the Atlantic and Warsaw Pacts.

The rules which we should do well to observe in international politics are related to UN principles and the pronouncements of international lawyers, but the relationship is not a direct or a literal one. For the principles and pronouncements are important in this connection only in so far as they provide an approximation to 'rules of the game' which governments endeavour to observe, although often with much backsliding in their actual conduct; or to rules for which force of example may secure a chance of such observance in future.

It is unfortunate that in their campaign against the British intervention in Egypt, Labour and Liberal spokesmen put so much weight on particular UN resolutions or on the probable pronouncement of international law if the issue were ever brought up at The Hague. Politicians excavate for propaganda purposes particular UN resolutions inconvenient to the other side, but no one expects that they will actually cause any country to reverse its policy, and it is no service to international standards of good behaviour to exaggerate the importance of numerical majorities in an Assembly based on the farcical principle of 'one country one vote'.*

The tentative rules which more enlightened statesmen aspire to observe are, in their nature, midway between legal and customary restraints. Laws and resolutions are too rigid a terminology by far to describe the tentative gropings towards an agreed standard of international behaviour. Perhaps it would be most appropriate to regard our aims in this field as the gradual evolution of certain notions about the 'done thing' and 'bad form' in international behaviour.

I have no wish to deny the possibility of exceptional cases, when it may be advisable to disregard the rules. There may be special circumstances where rigid observance is likely to lead to results of extreme undesirability in comparison with turning a blind eye. If we are convinced after long and careful study that a minor military act which is technically aggression would very much reduce the chances of atomic war, it would be perverse to refain out of legalistic scruples. But this is not the type of move which should be undertaken when there is only a gambler's chance of success. *For in gauging the consequences of an individual breach of the international code we must – even from the most narrowly national standpoint – take into account not only its immediate consequences but also its long-term effects in disrupting the still fragile code of international good behaviour.*

*A weighting system*
The recommendations advanced in the previous section go some way, I believe, towards providing usable criteria for foreign policy. But they leave aside some important questions: What do we do if we have qualms about a certain policy in a sphere where

* Although a rigid adherence to the letter of even the UN Charter may sometimes be unwise, there is a much stronger case for obeying UN, *principles* than there is for automatic adherence to the interpretation of them provided by UN *resolutions*.

there are no 'rules of the game' that have gained general acceptance, or when we are wondering whether we ought not to impose restraints on our behaviour additional to those required by the rules? And conversely, just how undesirable do the results of observing the rules have to be before we can contemplate breaking them? And undesirable to whom? And how much long-term weakening of the international code are we prepared to countenance in exchange for a short-term gain? Moreover, if the pursuit of the national interest is to be the main objective of foreign policy, what are to be the other objectives and what place is to be given to them when they conflict with the main one? In the first section it was suggested that the national interest was a function of individual interests. But what is the nature of the functional relationship? Which interests of which individuals are to count, and for how much?

The purpose of this section is to put forward a neo-utilitarian criterion which will not answer these questions but which if accepted, will help the reader to answer them for himself. This criterion could well have been advanced earlier on, but it has been deliberately held back as the main part of my argument can be stated without it.

The criterion can most conveniently be presented in terms of an individual deciding between alternative courses of policy. To abstract from the question of whether a Foreign Secretary should be guided by his own value judgements or those of his countryman, I shall assume for formal purposes that he is voting in a referendum, or in a general election fought on foreign policy issues.

To make his decision he should, according to the suggested criterion, estimate as well as he can the probable consequences of the different alternatives to all the human beings concerned and make his choice on the basis of the effects he would most like to bring about. To do this he must fix his own subjective weights to determine the relative importance of different individuals and interests and the relative importance of short- and long-term consequences.

This criterion involves the value-judgement that it is the effects of an action which govern its desirability. It is therefore opposed to the doctrine that there are certain principles of absolute validity which should be followed irrespective of their effects. (There is however no reason why adherents of the latter view should not

employ the neo-utilitarian criterion in all those cases which do not
come within the scope of their basic principles.)

An immediate objection to this criterion will be that it would
cause enormous confusion if everyone pressed for a foreign policy
to suit his private fancy and that it would undermine that very
predictability which it was earlier stated is so desirable in
international affairs. This is an argument for deciding as much as
possible on some rule-of thumb basis, governed by the highest
common factor of agreement and not bringing up private
principles when they can be avoided; it is also an argument in
favour of following the strategy of the second-best, when the
answer with which the neo-utilitarian criterion provides a
particular person is likely to be acceptable to many of his fellow
citizens. But it is not an argument against the criterion as such.

A more serious criticism is that the criterion is an empty one, as
it is in the determination of the weights that the whole problem
lies. This emptiness is in part deliberate. I am suggesting that in
deciding objectives, as distinct from tactics, a person should make
up his own mind on the basis of his differing attitudes to the
various other individuals in the world. This intensely subjective
element will irritate many people. And there is something
cold-blooded in attempting to give comparative weights to, say,
the lives of British soldiers and foreign civilians, or to the lives of
British soldiers and British civilian economic interests. But this is
done by implication whenever the governor of a dependency
decides on the degree of harshness he should adopt in his
'emergency measures'. The weighting language is indeed an
unattractive one and should be used sparingly; but when the
actual decisions are being made, it is as well to use a language that
brings out as explicitly as possible the value judgements involved
in the various alternative policies.

It is easy to ridicule the weighting concept by asking questions
such as 'How many Egyptian deaths would it be worth having to
get the Canal and unseat Nasser? Would it be worth doing if 100
Egyptians were killed, but not if 101?' It would be absurd to
pretend that we can talk about these weights with any exactness.
But it is a fact of life, which it would be well to recognise, that
many people who would be prepared to see a few hundred
Egyptians killed to secure certain policy objectives would stop
short of killing the whole population of the Nile Valley for them.
To quote Professor Popper, 'The precision of a language depends

just upon the fact that it takes care not to burden its terms with the task of being precise . . . In physical measurements for instance, we always take care to consider the range in which there may be an error; and precision does not consist in trying to reduce this range to nothing, or in pretending that there is no such range, but rather in its explicit recognition.'

The main reason for putting forward this neo-utilitarian criterion is that it does justice to the great diversity in the extent of our feelings of obligations towards different categories of people. Most of us have strong feelings of obligation towards certain relations and close friends, and some feelings towards colleagues, members of the same class or cultural group, and people of our own race, nationality or creed. Different people would place these latter groups in different orders, but the majority would have stronger feelings towards them all than towards the human race in general.

Political conduct, designed to fit these successive circles of feelings of obligation, might appeal to some less exalted than an equal concern for all human beings; but surely it would be preferable to a narrow nationalism which arbitrarily rules out the small but existent sympathies that most people have for their fellow men of different nationalities? How far should we go in sacrificing the standard of living in this country to aid the underdeveloped areas? To what extent should we be inhibited from bolstering up (as distinct from merely dealing with) a pro-British regime that oppresses its own inhabitants? In such problems the use of the weighting concept would bring our foreign policy into line with our own personal outlook and values when not consciously talking politics, and do away with both the spurious altruism and the unnatural harshness which different groups of people are misled into adopting by the abstractions of political discourse.

## A note on Neo-Pacifism

The object of this appendix is to state a particular point of view on the issue of pacifism which fits in with the general approach adopted in this paper, although it does not logically follow from it.

Pacifism, in its extreme form, is part of a complete renunciation of the use of force in human affairs. There is, however, another, and I believe more defensible, form of opposition to war, which might be called neo-pacifism. This holds that neither the defence of national interests, conventionally interpreted, nor even the defence of certain forms of government, is a sufficient ground for the murder and break-up of private lives involved in a major war. This neo-pacifist position has no connection with 'turning the other cheek' and does not necessarily imply that every military action has always been unjustified. It might support a small local war, if that were the only way to stop a more horrible conflict and it might even support a major war if the aim of the other side was, for example, racial extermination. The case for neo-pacifism is particularly strong, in the present East–West conflict. Here people may prefer Communist domination to fighting either because they believe that a Third World War would be even more unpleasant, or because they believe that, whichever side won, free institutions would nevertheless perish in the conflict. But the argument is a general one, which could have been put forward if the atomic bomb had never been invented.

For somebody holding such views, the best tactics would be to act *as if* he were in fact prepared in the last resort to preserve national interests and institutions. The orthodox argument, that unilateral disarmament would be *less* likely to prevent major wars than a policy of possessing sufficient military strength to deter a potential aggressor, is valid for the neo-pacifist. For an unarmed country without alliances is too strong a temptation for other powers and, sooner or later, one of them may start making demands. If the demands are granted for the sake of peace, this is likely to encourage fresh demands. A point will then be reached, where most citizens will be prepared to fight and push aside those leaders who prefer surrender to war. Thus, through a policy of weakness, the country lands itself unprepared into a war which might have been avoided. As a matter of prudence the neo-pacifist, knowing that he is likely to be in a minority, when the crucial test comes, should be the last to support an appeasement policy of the Munich type.

As put forward by a neo-pacifist, the policy of deterrence is undoubtedly one of bluff. For if it came to the test and the deterrent failed, he would meet almost any demands rather than fight. This is not a crucial objection. The starting point of my argument is that many people do not share the neo-pacifist position and would fight rather than surrender; therefore the Soviet leaders would be well advised to assume that the West will defend itself with all available weapons.

But even if this were not the case and all the people likely to make the crucial decisions in the West were converted to neo-pacifism, it would still be worthwhile attempting a deterrent policy. For the Soviet leaders would still not know whether we were bluffing or not (especially if due self-restraint were to be observed in public discussion) and there would be a chance, if only a small one, of avoiding both Communism and a Third World War.

# Notes and References

## PREFACE TO THE FIRST EDITION

1. F. A. Hayek, 'Why I am not a Conservative', *The Constitution of Liberty* (Routledge, 1960) pp. 410–41.

## PREFACE TO THE 1987–8 EDITION

1. Published by Temple Smith, 1977.
2. Published by Temple Smith, 1983; Wildwood House, 1987.

## PROLOGUE: CAPITALISM AND THE PERMISSIVE SOCIETY

1. Joseph Schumpeter, *Capitalism, Socialism and Democracy*, 4th edition (Allen & Unwin, 1954) Chapters 11–14.
2. F. A. Hayek, *Studies in Philosophy, Philosophy, Politics and Economics* (Routledge & Kegan Paul, 1967) Chapter 12.
3. *Journalists at Work* (Constable, 1971).
4. G. J. Stigler, *The Intellectual and the Market Place*, reprinted in *Price Theory* (Penguin Modern Economic Readings, 1971).
5. Assar Lindbeck, *The Political Economy of the New Left* (Harper & Row, 1971).
6. J. K. Galbraith, *The New Industrial State* (Penguin, 1969).
7. C. Carter, *Wealth* (Penguin, 1971) pp. 136 *et seq.*
8. For details of these and many other instances, see *Galbraith and the Planners*, by Professor Frank McFadzean, University of Strathclyde, 1968, and *Economic Fact and Fantasy*, by Professor G. C. Allen, IEA Occasional Paper No. 14, 1969.
9. Lindbeck, *The Political Economy of the New Left*, p. 43.
10. Cited in Galbraith, *Economics, Peace and Laughter* (Deutsch, 1971), p. 72.
11. H. G. Johnson, *The Economic Approach to Social Questions* (Weidenfeld & Nicolson, 1968).
12. For one of many instances, see Galbraith, *The American Left and Some British Comparisons* (Fabian Tract 406, 1971).
13. E. G. Dolan, 'Alienation, Freedom and Economic Organisation', *Journal of Political Economy*, September 1971.
14. Hayek, *The Constitution of Liberty*, p. 119.
15. A. Peacock and A. Culyer, *Economic Aspects of Student Unrest*, IEA Occasional Paper No. 26, 1969.

16. H. Johnson, 'The Economics of Student Protest', *New Society*, 7 Nov. 1968.
17. N. Saunders, *Alternative London* (published privately but available from W. H. Smith & Co. Ltd, 2nd edition, 1971).
18. M. Grant, *The Climax of Rome* (Weidenfeld & Nicolson, 1969), p. 150.
19. Ibid.

# 1 A RESTATEMENT OF ECONOMIC LIBERALISM

1. In *Two Concepts of Liberty*, reprinted with related essays and a new Introduction in *Four Essays on Liberty* (Oxford Paperbacks, 1969).
2. Hayek, *The Constitution of Liberty*.
3. Ibid., p. 41.
4. J. W. N. Watkins, 'Philosophy' in A. Seldon (ed.), *Agenda for a Free Society* (Hutchinson, 1961).
5. M. Friedman, *Capitalism and Freedom* (University of Chicago Press, 1962).
6. B. Barry, *Political Argument* (Routledge & Kegan Paul, 1965), pp. 38, 66, 94.
7. F. Machlup, 'Liberalism and the Choice of Freedoms' in Streissler (ed.), *Roads to Freedom* (Routledge & Kegan Paul, 1969).
8. J. W. N. Watkins, *Agenda for a Free Society*.
9. Hayek, *The Constitution of Liberty*, p. 16.
10. *Utilitarianism* (Everyman 1948 edition), p. 6.
11. E. J. Mishan, *Welfare Economics: An Assessment* (North-Holland Publishing Co., 1969), Chapters I and III.
12. E. J. Mishan, *Cost Benefit Analysis* (Allen & Unwin, 1971), Chapter 45.
13. E. J. Mishan, *Welfare Economics*, pp. 29, 85.
14. J. Meade, *The Theory of Indicative Planning* (Manchester University Press, 1970).
15. Some comments can be found on British experience with indicative planning in my own *Steering the Economy*, 3rd Penguin edition, 1971, especially Chapters 4, 7 and 8.
16. Hayek, *Studies in Philosophy, Politics and Economics*, Chapter 17.
17. For a good account of these complications, see I. M. D. Little, *A Critique of Welfare Economics*, 2nd edition (Oxford, 1956).
18. This argument is developed in my book *The Price of Economic Freedom* (Macmillan, 1970), which also contains a bibliography citing some of the empirical studies.
19. Cited in Brittan, *The Price of Economic Freedom*, pp. 51–2.
20. On all this, see Mishan, *Cost-Benefit Analysis*.
21. Machlup, *Roads to Freedom*.
22. For elaboration of these points, see Mishan, *Cost-Benefit Analysis*, especially Chapters 18 and 19.
23. R. W. S. Pryke, *Public Enterprise in Practice* (MacGibbon and Kee, 1971).
24. G. and P. Polanyi, 'The Efficiency of Nationalised Industries' in the *Moorgate and Wall St. Review*, Spring 1972.
25. Patrick Hutber, 'Letter Box Lunacy' (*Sunday Telegraph*, 7 November 1971).
26. C. Foster, *Public Enterprise* (Fabian Research Series 300, 1972).
27. H. L. A. Hart, *The Concept of Law* (Oxford, 1961), Chapter VII.

28. J. W. N. Watkins in *Agenda for a Free Society*.
29. I have derived this suggestion from Professor John Rawls's essays 'Justice as Fairness' and 'Distributive Justice', reprinted respectively in Laslett & Runciman (eds) *Philosophy, Politics and Society*, 2nd series (Blackwell, 1962) and 3rd series (Blackwell, 1967). A full statement of Rawls's position is to be found in his book *A Theory of Justice* (Oxford, 1972). This appeared after my own manuscript was completed. The expression 'derived from' has been used because, while the conception of disinterestedness used in the text arose as a result of reading Rawls, this does not imply an acceptance of his complete system – or conversely that he would necessarily approve of my own. See also the note at the bottom of p. 134 in the main text.
30. Hayek, *The Constitution of Liberty*, p. 153.
31. Ibid., p. 158.
32. Essay XIV in *Essays: Moral, Political and Literary* (Oxford, 1963).
33. It is expounded further in my book *Steering the Economy* (Penguin, 1971), Chapters 10 and 11.
34. F. A. Hayek, *Road to Serfdom* (Routledge & Kegan Paul, 1944, reissued 1971).
35. Hayek, *The Constitution of Liberty*, pp. 88 *et seq.*
36. D. Jay, *Socialism and the New Society* (Longmans, 1962).
37. F. A. Hayek, *Kinds of Rationalism* in 'Studies in Philosophy, Politics and Economics' (Routledge & Kegan Paul, 1967).
38. A. Downs, *The Economic Theory of Democracy* (Harper & Row, 1957).
39. Schumpeter, *Capitalism, Socialism and Democracy*, p. 261.
40. See Gordon Tullock, 'Public Decisions as Public Goods', *Journal of Political Economy*, February 1972.
41. These phrases were coined by Professor Paul Samuelson in *Problems of the American Economy* (University of Athlone Press, 1962).
42. E. J. Mishan, *The Costs of Economic Growth* (Penguin, 1969).
43. 'A Case for a Select Committee on Economic Affairs', by P. Jay and S. Brittan, *Second Report from the Select Committee on Procedure*, House of Commons 123, 1969–70, Appendix 2.
44. D. Jay, *Socialism in the New Society*, p. 9.
45. A. B. Atkinson, 'On the Measurement of Inequality', *Journal of Economic Theory*, No. 2, 1970.
46. Hayek, *The Constitution of Liberty*, pp. 125–6.
47. The earlier discussion on p. 94 is relevant here. The relevant references are given in Note 29 above.
48. Friedman, *Capitalism and Freedom*, p. 4.
49. Lord Robbins, *Politics and Economics* (Macmillan, 1963), p. 85.
50. J. M. Keynes, *General Theory*, reprinted 1936 edition, p. 374.
51. See National Income Blue Books and J. R. Hicks, *The Social Framework*, 4th edition (Oxford, 1971).
52. J. Tobin, 'On Limiting the Domain of Inequality', *The Journal of Law and Economics*, October 1970.
53. This point is well brought out in H. B. Acton, *The Morals of Markets* (Longman, 1971), pp. 51–5.
54. Plato, *The Republic*, trans.: Cornford (Oxford, 1941), pp. 161–4.
55. B. Russell, *History of Western Philosophy* (Allen & Unwin, 1946), p. 125.
56. For reflections on this phenomenon, see P. T. Bauer, *Dissent on Development*

(Weidenfeld & Nicolson, 1972), and H. G. Johnson (ed.), *Economic Nationalism in Old and New States* (Allen & Unwin, 1968).

57. R. Mundell, *Man and Economy* (McGraw-Hill, 1968).
58. Ibid., p. 9.
59. B. Barry, *Sociologists, Economists and Democracy* (Collier-Macmillan, 1970).
60. K. R. Minogue, *The Liberal Mind* (Methuen, 1963), p. 28.
61. Ibid., pp. 170–1, and p. 30.
62. Cted by Charles Schultze in *The Politics and Economics of Public Spending* (Brookings, 1968).
63. Prof. A. K. Sen is surely right in the discussion he inaugurated in the *Journal of Political Economy* in 1970 that liberalism may conflict with Pareto optimality, unless one or the other is defined in a specially restrictive way.

# 2 JOBS, PRICES AND TRADE UNIONS

1. The reference is, of course, to the Lipsey–Parkin article first published in the May 1970 issue of *Economica* and further defended by Parkin in the November 1970 issue. The reference has been deliberately relegated to a footnote, as the elaboration of models which turn out false is part of the process of scientific advance; the strictures are on the initially uncritical acceptance of it by so many, and on the channelling of so much of subsequent technical discussion into the statistical methods employed instead of into the model's degree of predictive success.
2. J. Wood, *How Much Unemployment?* (Institute of Economic Affairs, 1972).
3. Damodar Gujarati, 'The Behaviour of Unemployment and Unfilled Vacancies: Great Britain, 1958–71', *The Economic Journal* March 1972.
4. One of the best expositions of the consequences of such a breakdown is to be found in Keynes's early *Tract of Monetary Reform*, 1923, reissued by Macmillan in 1971.
5. This metaphor is taken from a compilation of Hayek's writings entitled *A Tiger by the Tail*, published by the IEA in 1972.
6. I have given a summary of this controversy in *Steering the Economy* (Penguin, 1971), pp. 156 *et seq.*
7. The expression 'economics of Keynes' is used to describe the interpretation put upon the doctrines held by the real life Keynes in the 1930s by Prof. Axel Leijonhufvud, as contrasted both with the national income models used in post-war economic forecasting and the 'neoclassical-Keynesian' synthesis appearing in many academic texts. Leijonhufvud's ideas can be found in *On Keynesian Economics and the Economics of Keynes* (Oxford, 1968). A briefer exposition will be found in his *Keynes and the Classics* (Institute of Economic Affairs, 1969); but the shorter work may be puzzling without the longer version by its side.
8. John Nelson-Jones, *The Wages of Fear* (Bow Publications, 1971).
9. Mackay *et al.*, *Labour Markets under Different Employment Conditions* (Allen & Unwin, 1971).
10. A notable restatement is *Labour and Inflation*, Fabian Tract No. 403.
11. W. Beckerman, *The Labour Government's Economic Record* (Duckworth, 1972).

12. A good survey of the most prevalent ideas for incomes intervention can be found in an article 'Incomes Policy and Inflation' by Frank Blackaby in the November 1972 issue of the *National Institute Review*.
13. J. Meade, *Wages and Prices in a Mixed Economy* (Institute of Economic Affairs, 1971).
14. See for instance Michael Grant, *The Climax of Rome* (Weidenfeld & Nicolson, 1968).
15. A good example is the article 'Why an Incomes Policy Would not Work' by David Metcalf and Ray Richardson, *The Financial Times*, 3 February 1971.
16. Lord Balogh, *Labour and Inflation*.

## 3  THE ECONOMICS OF THE ALTERNATIVE SOCIETY

1. T. S. Eliot, *The Idea of a Christian Society* (Faber, 1939), p. 62.
2. See for instance *A Social Democratic Britain*, Fabian Tract 404, 1971.
3. Lindbeck, *The Political Economy of the New Left*, p. 89.
4. See Note 17 to Prologue, above.
5. K. Marx, *Critique of the Gotha Programme*, 1875.
6. Carter, *Wealth*, p. 75.
7. *Policy for Poverty*, Institute of Economic Affairs.

## POSTSCRIPT TO 1987–8 EDITION

1. For a good exposition, see John Gray, *Liberalism* (Open University Press, 1986).
2. Explained on pp. 49–50 and 59–61 above, and discussed further on p. 230 below.
3. For a good example, see Irving Kristol, *Reflections of a Neo-Conservative* (Basic Books, 1983).
4. *Report of the Committee on Financing the BBC* (HMSO, 1986).
5. For a book based on the series, see D. Graham and P. Clarke, *The New Enlightenment* (Channel Four, 1986).
6. Matthew Hoffman, 'My Own Enlightenment' (*New Statesman*, 14 November 1986).
7. Albert Weale, *Political Theory and Social Policy* (Macmillan, 1983) p. 44.
8. Derek Parfit, *Reasons and Persons* (Oxford, 1984).
9. Ibid., p. 451.
10. A. K. Sen, *Collective Choice and Social Welfare* (Oliver & Boyd, 1970). For my own interpretation see *The Economic Consequences of Democracy* (Temple Smith, 1977) Chapter 2.
11. For a more extended discussion of utilitarianism see S. Brittan, *The Role and Limits of Government* (Temple Smith, 1983; Wildwood House, 1987) Chapter 2.
12. Robert Nozick, *Anarchy, State and Utopia* (Basic Books, 1974).

13. John Rawls, *A Theory of Justice* (Oxford, 1972).
14. Readers are also referred to the volumes of critical studies– Jeffrey Paul (ed.) *Reading Nozick* (Blackwell, 1982) and Norman Daniels (ed.) *Reading Rawls* (Blackwell, 1975). The citations from other writers on Rawls and Nozick can be found in these volumes unless otherwise stated.
15. Nozick, *Anarchy, State and Utopia*, pp. 149–50.
16. *Leviticus*, Chapter 25. The system is described in Brian Griffiths, *Morality and the Market Place* (Hodder & Stoughton, 1982) Chapter 3.
17. Jeffrey Paul (ed.), *Reading Nozick*, p. 5.
18. Ibid., p. 13.
19. See Albert Weale, *Political Theory and Social Policy* esp. pp. 97–8. See also R. M. Hare in *Reading Rawls* and Anthony Flew in E. Butler and M. Pirie (eds) *Hayek* (Adam Smith Institute, 1986).
20. I. Berlin, 'Two Concepts of Liberty', reprinted in *Four Essays on Liberty* (Oxford, 1969).
21. A. Weale, *Political Theory*, p. 42.
22. N. Frohlich, J. A. Oppenheimer and C. L. Eavey, 'Laboratory Results on Rawls's Distributive Justice', *British Journal of Political Science*, vol. 7, part 1, January 1987.
23. J. M. Buchanan, *The Limits of Liberty* (Chicago, 1975).
24. 'The Economic Burden of the State', *Oxford Review of Economic Policy* (Summer, 1986).
25. 'Markets, Liberty and the State', *New Statesman*, (2 January 1987).
26. Israel Kirzner, *Perception, Opportunity and Profit* (Chicago, 1979).
27. 'On the First Principles of Morality', Essay IV in *Essays, Moral Political and Literary*, 1777 (modern edition, Liberty Classics, Indianapolis, 1985).
28. For a more extended explanation along these lines, see S. Brittan, *Two Cheers for Self Interest* (Institute of Economic Affairs, 1985). See also Chapter 2, 'Two Cheers for Utilitarianism', in Brittan, *The Role and Limits of Government*.
29. Peter Jay, 'What is News?' in *The Crisis for Western Political Economy* (André Deutsch, 1985).
30. For a discussion of the pros and cons of corporate responsibility, see William J. Baumol, 'Business and Responsibility and Economic Behaviour', in E. S. Phelps (ed.), *Altruism and Economic Theory* (Sage, New York, 1975).
31. Arthur Scargill, *New Left Review*, July–August 1975, cited in N. Hagger, *Scargill the Stalinist* (Oak Tree, 1985).
32. TUC Rally, Bradford, reported in *The Daily Telegraph*, (13 April 1986).
33. First Presidential address, reported in *The Guardian* (6 June 1982).
34. 'Standard Reporter Attacked', Colin Adamson, *Evening Standard* (7 June 1984).
35. J. Benda, *The Treason of the Intellectuals* (English edition) (Republished W. W. Norton & Co., New York, 1969).
36. Benda, pp. 115–16.
37. For a standard account, see Denis Mack Smith, *Mussolini* (Granada, 1983).
38. 'Workers Flee Intimidation', *The Times* (15 December 1986).
39. *New Statesman* (5 December 1986).
40. Two of my earlier critiques of much simple-minded left-right dichotomies are to be found in *Left or Right – The Bogus Dilemma* (Secker & Warburg,

1968), and Chapter 13 of the first edition of the present book (not reprinted in this edition).

41. Interview with Matthew Parris, *Weekend World*, LWT (21 December 1986).
42. William S. Maddox and Stuart A. Lillie, *Beyond Liberal and Conservative*, (Cato Institute, Washington DC, 1984). I have substituted the clumsy label Left-Progressive, as the most suitable European term to go in place of 'Liberal', which means different things on the two sides of the Atlantic. I have also drawn in the text on related material in David Boaz: 'Yuppies and the Future of American Politics', *Cato Policy Report* (November–December 1984, Washington DC, USA).
43. Brittan, *The Role and Limits of Government*, pp. 44–7.
44. USA, Japan, Germany, UK, France, Italy, Canada.
45. *OECD Economic Outlook* (Paris, December 1986, Table R. 7).
46. See M. S. Levitt (ed.) *New Priorities in Public Spending* (Gower, 1987) Chapter 2.
47. Brittan, *Economic Consequences*, pp. 138–41.
48. J. Kay, C. Mayer and D. Thompson (eds) *Privatisation and Regulation* (Oxford, 1986). Readers should not be put off by the sour and carping tone of the editorial introduction. For a critical, but less hostile, analysis, see Cento Veljanovski, *Selling the State* (Weidenfeld, 1987).
49. See Richard Pryke in *Privatisation and Deregulation*.
50. Robert Alton, *Privatising the Post* (Centre for Policy Studies, 1987).
51. D. Henderson, *Innocence and Design* (the 1985 Reith Lectures) (Basil Blackwell, 1986).
52. Peter Vinter, leter to *The Times* (2 July 1981).
53. Henderson, *Innocence and Design*, p. 37.
54. Ibid., p. 85.
55. S. Brittan, *Economic Consequences*, pp. 170–2 and Martin Ricketts, *Lets into Leases* (Centre for Policy Studies, 1986).
56. Adam Raphael, 'The Luck of Lieutenant Thatcher', *The Observer* (28 December 1986).
57. C. M. Morris and I. Preston, 'Inequality, Poverty and the Redistribution of Income' (*Bulletin of Economic Research*, 1986). There is an excellent summary in J. Kay and C. M. Morris *Fiscal Studies* (November 1986).
58. Corporatism is discussed briefly in Chapter 1, (pp. 120–1), and more systematically in Brittan, *Economic Consequences*, Chapter 13. See also 'The State and the Private Sector' by G. White in M. S. Levitt (ed.) *New Priorities in Public Spending* (Gower, 1987).
59. A detailed discussion of the Thatcher Government's macroeconomic management and its relation to what had gone before can be found in Brittan, *Role and Limits*, Chapter 11.
60. J. Bruce-Gardyne, *Mrs Thatcher's First Administration* (Macmillan, 1985).
61. See S. Brittan, *How to End the Monetarist Controversy* (Institute of Economic Affairs, second edition, 1982).
62. For example, James Meade, *Wage Fixing* (Allen & Unwin 1982. This is volume one of his Stagflation study.)
63. R. Layard, *How to Beat Unemployment* (Oxford 1986). Layard's Centre for Labour Economics at the LSE has published a stream of papers covering different approaches to the problem.
64. *Economic Survey of United States* (OECD, Paris, November 1986).

65. Ibid., pp. 67–8.
66. H. G. Grubel and J. Bonnici, *Why is Canada's Unemployment Rate so High?* (Fraser Institute, Vancouver, 1986).
67. Ibid., p. 67.
68. See, for instance, Layard, *How To Beat Unemployment.*
69. For a good explanation of these points see the article by Patrick Minford in *Quarterly Economic Bulletin* (Liverpool Research Group in Macroeconomics, December 1986).
70. Martin Weitzman, *The Share Economy* (Harvard, 1984).
71. James Meade; *Different Forms of Remuneration and Participation* (Public Policy Centre, 1986); and *Alternative Systems of Business Organisation* (Allen & Unwin, 1986).
72. See, for instance, A. R. Prest and N. Barr, *Public Finance in Theory and Practice* (Weidenfeld, 1985) pp. 380–85.
73. The proposal is similar to John Williamson, *Options for improving the International Co-ordination of Economic Policy* (International Law Institute, Georgetown University, 1987). But my subsequent development departs from Williamson's proposals.
74. For an assessment by a variety of authors, see 'Thatcherism: An Assessment' (*Financial Times Publications*, 1987).
75. *Survey of Share Ownership* (Stock Exchange, 1987).
76. K. Bradley and A. Gelb, *Share Ownership for Employees* (Public Policy Centre, 1986).
77. *Report of the Committee on the Financing of the BBC* (HMSO, 1986).
78. *Homeworking in Britain* (Dept of Employment Gazette, February 1987).
79. *British Business* (Department of Trade and Industry, 17 October 1986).

# APPENDIX: MORALITY AND FOREIGN POLICY (1957)

1. George F. Kennan, *The Realities of American Foreign Policy* (Oxford, 1954) p. 47.

# Index